PERSPECTIVES

ON

MASS

COMMUNICATIONS

Warren K. Agee
University of Georgia

Phillip H. Ault
South Bend Tribune

Edwin Emery
University of Minnesota

HARPER & ROW, PUBLISHERS, New York
Cambridge, Philadelphia, San Francisco,
London, Mexico City, São Paulo, Sydney

1817

Sponsoring Editor: Phillip Leininger
Project Editor: Jo-Ann Goldfarb
Designer: T. R. Funderburk/Robert Bull
Production Manager: Marion Palen
Photo Researcher: Mira Schachne
Compositor: Lexigraphics Inc.
Printer and Binder: Halliday Lithograph Corporation

ILLUSTRATION CREDITS

Page 7: New York Herald Tribune; p. 15: Wide World; p. 16: Wilbur Schramm; p. 18: Contact, 1980; p. 46: Granger; p. 49: Bettmann Archive; p. 52: Granger; p. 64: Wisconsin Historical Society; p. 67: Edwin Emery; p. 69: Raymond B. Nixon; p. 71: Emporia Gazette, Emporia, Kansas; p. 73: Chicago Tribune; p. 79: Ebony Magazine; p. 81: UPI; p. 98: © 1981 Jefferson Communications, Inc., Reston, Virginia, reprinted by permission; p. 101: Los Angeles Times; p. 103: Washington Post; p. 105: New York Times; p. 107: Christopher Springmann; p. 118: Wide World; p. 120: UPI; p. 127: © 1981 G. B. Trudeau, reprinted by permission of Universal Press Syndicate; p. 153: NBC; p. 159: Photo Trends; p. 163: ABC; p. 165: CBS; p. 168: NBC; p. 169: Photo Trends; p. 176: Wide World; p. 180: Photo Trends; p. 188: Wide World; p. 193: Simon, Photo Trends; p. 197: NBC; p. 199: UPI; p. 233: © 1938 Life; p. 251: Foote, Cone & Belding; p. 271: The Advertising Council; p. 279: Wide World; p. 281: General Motors Corp.; p. 284: South Carolina Department of Youth Services; p. 320: © 1963 New York Herald Tribune; p. 332: © 1980 The Register and Tribune Syndicate, Inc., reprinted by permission; p. 342 (top left): School of Journalism, University of Wisconsin; p. 342 (top right, bottom left): School of Journalism, University of Missouri; p. 342 (bottom right): School of Journalism, University of Minnesota; p. 357: © 1979 The Quill and the Society of Professional Journalists, reprinted by permission; p. 389: WGBH Educational Foundation, PBS; p. 429: Fabian Bachrach; p. 441: Edwin Emery; p. 451: ABC News.

Perspectives on Mass Communications

Library of Congress Cataloging in Publication Data
Main entry under title:

Perspectives on mass communications.

1. Mass media—Addresses, essays, lectures.   I. Agee, Warren Kendall.   II. Ault, Phillip H., 1914-
III. Emery, Edwin.
P91.25.P38   302.2'3   81-20017
ISBN 0-06-040174-5   AACR2

ECTIVES
ON
MASS
COMMUNICATIONS

CONTENTS

PREFACE

With arm outstretched and brush held vertically in hand, eyes squinting, a painter sights toward the empty canvas. The artist is visualizing perspective in the picture about to come into being on the easel, perceiving depth in the objects to appear and their relationship to each other. Without that awareness, the painting would be chaotic. The goal of *Perspectives on Mass Communications* can be likened in a sense to that gesture. This book is designed to help students in introductory classes develop a perception of depth in the complex world of mass communications and a better comprehension of the relationship between the media and contemporary society.

We offer here more than a hundred selections, with accompanying editorial comment, as supplementary reading material for students making their first academic exploration of mass communications. We believe the range of content and flexibility makes the book attractive for adoption by users of all introductory textbooks. It is, naturally, especially well coordinated with the seventh edition of *Introduction to Mass Communications* by the same authors, Agee, Ault, and Emery (Harper & Row). The book can also stand independently as a multifaceted survey of the media.

Many readers are wondering as they peer into the world of the media, is this a place where I would like to make a career? With that in mind, we include biographical sketches of men and women who have won prominence in the media, past and present. As the student observes their individual successes, while simultaneously gaining knowledge of the context in which they were achieved—the problems, ethical questions, history, techniques, and pleasures of media work—perhaps he or she will find an answer to that question.

In part this is a "how to" book, showing realistically how the media operate. Also, it is a "Why is it done that way?" book, because it explains the historical, philosophical, and technical reasons for media practices, with specific examples.

The world these readings illuminate is always in flux. While fundamental purposes and standards remain constant, methods and objectives of mass communications change to suit the shifting currents of society, a society the media interpret and shape. The enormous developments in the machinery of mass communication and the buffeting to which practitioners in the field are subjected by often-conflicting pressures become apparent to readers.

Perspectives on Mass Communications is divided into six parts, along lines conforming in general with the patterns of most introductory mass communications textbooks.

Part One, The Role of Mass Communications, establishes a foundation. Using selections from such eminent specialists as Walter Lippmann, Harold D. Lasswell, and Wilbur Schramm, this section introduces the reader to the intellectual basis of communication—in Lippmann's words, "The World Outside and the Pictures in Our Heads"—and to inquiries into the nature and function of communication in society. The student discovers new terminology: *gatekeeping*, for example, which refers to the informational controls that are built into our mass media systems. Readers are led to consider the impact of the mass media in political campaigns and the influence of poll taking. There is a profile of George Gallup, best known of the pollsters.

We turn in Part Two to an examination of the print media. The first section discusses the historic press freedoms. This is followed by readings on the *Growth of the Print Media*, then come sections on *Newspapers in Action*, *Press Associations and Syndicates*, *The Role of Magazines*, and *A Book Is Born*.

All selections delineating the growth of press freedoms are from original documents, so the student feels the writer's or speaker's style and fervor undiluted. In the renowned John Peter Zenger trial, for example, our reading is an excerpt from the closing argument to the jury in Zenger's defense by Andrew Hamilton in his fulsome eighteenth-century eloquence. Reading his words 250 years after they were uttered, who is not moved by them?

> The Question before the Court and you Gentlemen of the Jury, is not of small nor private Concern, it is not the Cause of the poor Printer, nor of *New York* alone, which you are now trying: No! It may in it's consequence, affect every Freeman that lives under a British Government on the main of *America*. It is the best Cause. It is the Cause of Liberty.

In the *Newspapers in Action* section of Part Two, the focus shifts to the contemporary. Contrasting traditional journalism and the personalized "new journalism" approach, Ward Just dissects two articles about Senator Edward M. Kennedy. Students find an example of professional newspaper editing in an article by Phil Currie on how editors should plan for disaster, to be ready for the unexpected. Illustrating the broad choice of careers in newspaper work are a sketch of New York *Times* columnist James Reston, operating at the inner core of government power in Washington, and a look at David and Cathy Mitchell, the husband-and-wife California team who published the weekly Point Reyes *Light* so successfully that they won a Pulitzer Prize.

Part Three approaches the area of electronic and film media much as Part Two does the print media. First, there is a section on *The Growth of Radio, Television, and Film*, recalling such pioneers as David Sarnoff, Lowell Thomas, and H.V. Kaltenborn, as well as Edward R. Murrow, Walter Cronkite, Chet Huntley and other greats. Subsequent readings in Part Three deal with radio, recording, television, and photographic communication and film.

Greater emphasis occurs here on personalities, because in these fields the voice, appearance, and manner of individual performers is what helps bring success. The shifts in social standards during the last four decades become obvious in these Part Three readings. What a contrast there is between the ludicrous (in our eyes) network censorship to which Jack Benny's comedy programs were subjected—when the word *virgin* was forbidden to be mentioned on radio under any circumstances—and the rock world of the Bee Gees! Evident, too, is the emergence of women as television and radio newscasters, with Barbara Walters joining Dan Rather, Charles Kuralt, and John Chancellor in biographical reviews.

As we watch Norman Lear apply his master's touch to an episode of "All in the Family" and learn the results of "60 Minutes" crusades, we get a sense of television as it is today. But what about the future? Clearly, dramatic changes in programming and transmission are beginning to occur. An article by Peter W. Bernstein on "Television's Expanding World" explores the ways in which the medium may soon have an even stronger influence on our lives.

The techniques of mass communication are used not only to inform and entertain, but also to persuade. Part Four, The Persuasive Arts, deals with the closely related fields of advertising and public relations. We are exposed to advertising messages innumerable times a day. More than half the daily newspaper's content is advertising; sometimes it seems as though the same is true of radio and television, although of course it is not. The readings in this section concern the intricate structure of advertising motivation, psychology, graphics, and mechanics. Included are biographical sketches of Albert D. Lasker and Fairfax M. Cone, who pioneered many of the techniques.

In advertising, the basic purpose is to sell the product or service. Public relations seeks to build an image; it accomplishes this not so much by buying space and time in the media, as advertising does, but by building goodwill. Among other functions, it supplies the media with information showing the PR practitioner's company or client in the best light possible, and it creates events and seeks opportunities that will impress the public with the client's good intentions and commendable goals.

Our readings show two aspects of corporate public relations: how companies react to a disaster such as the Three Mile Island nuclear crisis, and how Paul Garrett established a PR philosophy for the General Motors Corporation. Other selections describe a social agency shaping a public relations program and promotional "hype" building up a celebrity. The attractive prospects of a public relations career for women are discussed, too.

Part Five, Research and Education, introduces the student to work being done in communication theory and the processes and effects of mass communication. The authors include Wilbur Schramm, Elihu Katz, Maxwell McCombs and Donald Shaw, John P. Robinson and Guido Stempel. Readings report the findings of these scholars in such areas as uses and gratification theory, agenda-setting, news diffusion, and content analysis. Putting research techniques to specific use, Drs. Jerome L. and Dorothy G. Singer examine the impact of television on children. The Singers cite both television's negative effects, relating increased aggressiveness in children to excessive watching of action-adventure shows, and its positive potential for development when they see programs that stimulate the imagination and impart knowledge.

Part Six covers criticisms and challenges. The media are under scrutiny and frequent attack by the public in general and by pressure groups in particular. Charges of many sorts are leveled at them: excessive power, arrogance, twisting the news, sensationalism, inaccuracy, shallowness and timidity, serving special interests, failing to give minorities a full voice, and more. Some of these accusations refer essentially to a single medium, while others are aimed broadly at all forms of mass communication. To provide cohesion, we have concentrated material of a critical nature in Part Six. Having studied in earlier parts the historical background, personalities, and operating methods of the media, students are now in position to discuss more effectively the criticisms and challenges the media face.

Part Six is divided into four sections. *The Media, the Courts, and the Public* includes an examination of how the media function under the First Amendment. In *The Media and Social Issues*, the manner in which publications, radio, and television meet their responsibility of serving the public is scrutinized by provocative and knowledgeable critics. *Who Owns the Media?* explains the controversial trend toward group ownership of newspapers and the growing power of conglomerate corporations whose ownership, cutting across traditional media lines, includes indiscriminately newspapers, TV and radio stations, magazines, book publishers, and film production companies, along with nonmedia interests. Also, there is an illuminating report on what the electronic revolution is doing, and may do in the future, to the press. Closing Part Six is a section on *International Media Roles*. In this day of instantaneous satellite transmission around the globe, national boundary lines in diffusion of information are partially obliterated. The emerging Third World countries demand a larger role in the creation and control of news. The readings include selections from Tom Wicker, Jules Feiffer, Anthony Smith, David Shaw, Benjamin DeMott, Louis Banks, Charles D. Ferris, Henry Grunwald, John B. Oakes, and Norman Isaacs.

We appreciate the assistance of our professional colleagues and others in assembling the material in this book from a multiplicity of sources. We wish to thank the staff at Harper & Row for their counsel, planning, and editorial guidance. We also especially thank the authors and publishers who have granted permission for the reprinting of the readings that follow. We hope that they will give students a better grasp of a field that is fascinating in its complexity and a little frightening in the influence it exercises over the lives and minds of all of us.

WARREN K. AGEE
PHILLIP H. AULT
EDWIN EMERY

PERSPECTIVES
ON
MASS
COMMUNICATIONS

Part One

THE ROLE OF MASS COMMUNICATIONS

T he communication revolution that stemmed from the industrial revolution in modern Western society had a major impact on social change and social progress. Mass communications, utilizing the technological advances of science and industry, developed to sophisticated levels in the print and electronic media. To understand properly the functions and activities of the mass media, it is necessary to explore the more general social role of communication.

Most scholars agree that by any basic definition communication involves the process of sharing information. Wilbur Schramm defines communication very broadly, indeed, as a sharing of information by one or more people in any human experience. While in this book we shall focus on mass communications and the mass media, we open with selections dealing with the development of communication theories that form the intellectual framework for the study of mass communications.

Walter Lippmann had a long career as a magazine editor, newspaper editor, and political columnist. The "public philosophy" he espoused in his columns made him a leading national authority. But Lippmann had another great impact, that upon the world of scholarship. His book *Public Opinion* broke new ground for political scientists when it appeared in 1922, and it also serves as a starting point for communication research. One phrase Lippmann used in his first chapter made the communication process come alive: "the pictures in our heads."

The thinking of the first generation of communications students was substantially influenced by Harold D. Lasswell, a professor of law at Yale University. His 1948 definition of the act of communication set the tone for communication research: "Who, says what, in which channel, to whom, with what effect?" He also defined the structure and function of communication in society, including the "surveillance" function. Lasswell's famed saying was later refined by David K. Berlo, who developed a model of the process of communication. His model includes the communication source, the encoder, the message, the channel, the decoder, and the communication receiver. Major areas of communication research—systems analysis, content analysis, media analysis, audience analysis, effect analysis—stem from the definitions in Berlo's model.

Wilbur Schramm, the leading interpreter of mass communications theory and research since the early 1950s, offers a definition of communication, which is followed by various statements defining mass communications, journalism and news. Schramm's career is discussed here, as is that of George Gallup, the pioneer in public opinion polling who also contributed heavily to readership studies techniques and to marketing research.

The Gallup Poll and similar operations predicting the outcome of elections and reporting the state of the public mind on important issues became standard features of the mass media. Inevitably they sharpened interest in the effects the media might have in changing voters' minds and in influencing public thought. L. John Martin, professor of journalism and mass communication at the University of Maryland, addresses himself to that problem in an article that also serves as a review of trends in communication research since the Lasswell era.

Lasswell's definition, called the "hypodermic model" of the communication process, implies that communication is something someone does to someone else. For a decade, communication researchers seeking to maximize the effectiveness of the process varied the formula in laboratory settings, altering the types of communicators, the kinds of messages, the media or channels used, and the audiences. By 1960 this preoccupation with analysis of effects had reached a dead end. It was clear, particularly in studies of voting choices, that a "hypodermic" message had very little effect.

When researchers reversed the model, and it was the audience, rather than the communicator, who decided on the messages that were received, their findings became much more consistent. This "uses-and-gratification," or "information-seeking," theory distinguishes between the informational and persuasive roles of communication. The mass media generally are unsuccessful in persuading and changing opinions, but they are clearly successful in informing. For most people the mass media are their sole sources of information on many topics. As Martin points out, this is the underlying principle of the agenda-setting model used to study the effects of mass communications. Researchers have found that the mass media not only tell people what to think about, but also establish the relative importance of the issues they choose to discuss. Newspapers have a format advantage over television in agenda setting. Studies utilizing the uses-and-gratifications model have shown modest but sometimes (in close elections) crucial effects of the mass media on voting choices.

Gatekeeper studies have been a part of communication research since 1950, when one study reported on the selection or rejection of news stories by a news editor. Three University of Minnesota professors of sociology and mass communication—Donohue, Tichenor, and Olien—enlarge on this concept in their article discussing mass media systems and information control. They point out that historically there have been constant efforts to control mass communication. He who controls knowledge can exercise social power; thus, in an authoritarian society control of the mass media through social systems is axiomatic. The authors discuss the social subsystems found in the mass media and the ways in which the organization of these systems may function to play down news rather than illuminate it.

A contributing editor of *Harper's,* Earl Shorris, harpoons what he regards as excessive use of the public opinion polling technique, which creates what he calls a "market democracy" in "a world according to Gallup." He provides an aggressive counter-view of communication research, charging that "Market democracy, initiated by public opinion polls, embraced by political manipulators, and used to its own advantage by the press, has replaced the deliberative machine of the American government." He provides a thoughtful comparison of the intricate nature of social decisions made by a diverse citizenry and the simpler choices of a product marketeer who needs only to know who and how many will buy. Public opinion polls, he complains, sometimes run on the latter pattern, even though they involve social decisions concerning political issues and candidates.

The selections that follow illuminate the role of communication theory. In Part Five of this book, devoted to research and education, other readings give examples of research in information seeking, agenda setting, content analysis, and other communication areas.

Section 1

BASIC MEANINGS: LAYING THE GROUNDWORK

It is essential, but not easy, to define the fundamental terms of communication. Here Walter Lippmann, Harold Lasswell, and Wilbur Schramm contribute thought-provoking definitions of "communication." Following them other members of the profession explain "mass communication," "journalism," and "news." From these meanings the whole field grows.

THE WORLD OUTSIDE AND THE PICTURES IN OUR HEADS

Walter Lippmann

With great ease, clarity, and brevity, these three paragraphs look at the distinctions between public affairs and each individual's intensely private views and responses, the filtering and interpreting of all this public information to create one's own personal understanding, which yet remains a part of "public opinion."

The world that we have to deal with politically is out of reach, out of sight, out of mind. It has to be explored, reported, and imagined. Man is no Aristotelian god contemplating all existence at one glance. He is the creature of an evolution who can just about span a sufficient portion of reality to manage his survival, and snatch what on the scales of time are but a few moments of insight and happiness. Yet this same creature has invented ways of seeing what no naked eye could see, of hearing what no ear could hear, of weighing immense masses and infinitesimal ones, of counting and separating more items than he can individually remember. He is learning to see with his mind vast portions of the world that he could never see, touch, smell, hear, or remember. Gradually he makes for himself a trustworthy picture inside his head of the world beyond his reach.

Those features of the world outside which have to do with the behavior of other human beings, insofar as that behavior crosses ours, is dependent upon us, or is interesting to us, we call roughly public affairs. The pictures inside the heads of these human beings, the pictures of themselves, of others, of their needs, purposes, and relationships, are their public opinions. Those pictures which are acted upon by groups of people, or by individuals acting in the name of groups, are Public Opinion with capital letters. And so in the chapters which follow we shall inquire first into some of the reasons why the picture inside so often misleads men in their dealings with the world outside. Under this heading we shall consider first the chief factors which limit their access to the facts. They are the artificial censorships, the limitations of social contact,

SOURCE: From Walter Lippmann, *Public Opinion* (New York: Macmillan, 1950). Copyright 1922, renewed 1950 by Walter Lippmann. Reprinted with permission of Macmillan Publishing Co., Inc.

Walter Lippmann

the comparatively meager time available in each day for paying attention to public affairs, the distortion arising because events have to be compressed into very short messages, the difficulty of making a small vocabulary express a complicated world, and finally the fear of facing those facts which would seem to threaten the established routine of men's lives.

The analysis then turns from these more or less external limitations to the question of how this trickle of messages from the outside is affected by the stored-up images, the preconceptions and prejudices which interpret, fill them out, and in their turn powerfully direct the play of our attention and our vision itself. From this it proceeds to examine how in the individual person the limited messages from outside, formed into a pattern of stereotypes, are identified with his own interests as he feels and conceives them. In the succeeding sections it examines how opinions are crystallized into what is called public opinion, how a national will, a group mind, a social purpose, or whatever you choose to call it, is formed.

THE STRUCTURE AND FUNCTION OF COMMUNICATION IN SOCIETY

Harold D. Lasswell

This fundamental description serves as a flexible but inclusive definition of communication. It has the great usefulness of listing simple elements that are basic to even the most complex situations.

The Act of Communication

A convenient way to describe an act of communication is to answer the following questions:

- Who
- Says What
- In Which Channel
- To Whom
- With What Effect?

The scientific study of the process of communication tends to concentrate upon one or another of these questions. Scholars who study the "who," the communicator, look into the factors that initiate and guide the act of communication. We call this subdivision of the field of research *control analysis*. Specialists who focus upon the "says what" engage in *content analysis*. Those who look primarily at the radio, press, film, and other channels of communication are doing *media analysis*. When the principal concern is with the persons reached by the media, we speak of *audience analysis*. If the question is the impact upon audiences, the problem is *effect analysis*.

Whether such distinctions are useful depends entirely upon the degree of refinement which is regarded as appropriate to a given scientific and managerial objective. Often it is simpler to combine audience and effect analysis, for instance, than to keep them apart. On the other hand, we may want to concentrate on the analysis of content, and for this purpose subdivide the field into the study of purport and style, the first referring to the message, and the second to the arrangement of the elements of which the message is composed.

SOURCE: From *The Communication of Ideas*, edited by Lyman Bryson (New York: Institute for Religious and Social Studies, 1948). Copyright 1948 by Institute for Religious and Social Studies.

Structure and Function

Enticing as it is to work out these categories in more detail, the present discussion has a different scope. We are less interested in dividing up the act of communication than in viewing the act as a whole in relation to the entire social process. Any process can be examined in two frames of reference, namely, structure and function; and our analysis of communication will deal with the specializations that carry on certain functions, of which the following may be clearly distinguished: (1) the surveillance of the environment; (2) the correlation of the parts of society in responding to the environment; (3) the transmission of the social heritage from one generation to the next.

THE NATURE OF COMMUNICATION
BETWEEN HUMANS
Wilbur Schramm

As the preceding definition of communication was practical—dealing with the elements of the act of communication—this one is intellectual. It looks at the absorption of information, the end result, rather than at the means or theories of transmittal.

Today we might define communication simply by saying that it is the sharing of an orientation toward a set of informational signs.

Information, in this sense, we must define very broadly. Obviously it is not limited to news or "facts" or what is taught in the classroom or contained in reference books. It is any content that reduces uncertainty or the number of alternative possibilities in a situation. It may include emotions. It may include facts or opinion or guidance or persuasion. It does not have to be in words, or even explicitly stated: the latent meanings, "the silent language," are important information. It does not have to be precisely identical in both sender and receiver—we doubt that it ever is, and we are unlikely to be able to measure that correspondence very completely anyway. The ancient idea of transferring a box of facts from one mind to another is no longer a very satisfactory way of thinking about human communication. It is more helpful to think of one or

---

SOURCE: From Wilbur Schramm, "The Nature of Communication between Humans," in *The Process and Effects of Mass Communication*, rev. ed., edited by Wilbur Schramm and Donald F. Roberts (Urbana, Illinois: University of Illinois Press, 1971). Copyright 1971 by the Board of Trustees, University of Illinois.

more people or other entities coming to a given piece of information, each with his own needs and intentions, each comprehending and using the information in his own way.

OTHER TERMS: MEANINGS AND FUNCTIONS

MASS COMMUNICATION

Mass communication is a process. And although modern technology in the form of the mass media is essential to the process, the presence of these technical instruments should not be mistaken for the process itself. Mass communication, as identified by Wright (1959), is distinguished by the following characteristics:

1. It is directed toward relatively large, heterogeneous, and anonymous audiences.
2. Messages are transmitted publicly, often timed to reach most audience members simultaneously, and are transient in character.
3. The communicator tends to be, or to operate within, a complex organization that may involve great expense.

—Reed H. Blake and Edwin O. Haroldsen, *A Taxonomy of Concepts in Communication* (New York: Hastings House, 1975). The Wright quotation is taken from Charles R. Wright, *Mass Communication* (New York: Random House, 1959).

Mass communications (with the *s*), as distinguished from the *process* of mass communication (without the *s*), refers to the multitude of messages that are transmitted, most often through the mass media, to a relatively large audience. The singular and plural forms of the term often are used interchangeably. The plural form frequently is used as a synonym for the *mass media*—the most common channels of mass communication.

—Warren K. Agee, Phillip H. Ault, and Edwin Emery, *Introduction to Mass Communications*, seventh edition (New York: Harper & Row, 1982).

JOURNALISM

Journalism is the occupation in which news is reported and interpretation and opinion based on the news are given. The aim of journalism is to serve the public and not a private interest. In its broadest usage, journalism encompasses all areas of mass communications. The Society of Professional Journalists, Sigma Delta Chi, in its annual *Directory*, defines journalism as including the following:

The direction of the editorial policy of, the editing of, the preparation of news and editorial content of newspapers, magazines, press or syndicate services, professional or business publications, radio and television, and the teaching of journalism so defined.

The newspaper must be founded upon human nature. It must correspond to the wants of the people. It must furnish that sort of information which the people demand, or else it never can be successful. The first thing which an editor must look for is news. If the newspaper has not the news, it may have everything else, yet it will be comparatively unsuccessful; and by news I mean everything that occurs, everything which is of human interest, and which is of sufficient importance to arrest and absorb the attention of the public or of any considerable part of it. There is a great disposition in some quarters to say that the newspapers ought to limit the amount of news that they print; that certain kinds of news ought not to be published. I do not know how that is. I am not prepared to maintain any abstract proposition in that line; but I have always felt that whatever the Divine Providence permitted to occur I was not too proud to report.

—Charles A. Dana, *The Art of Newspaper Making* (New York: D. Appleton, 1895).

NEWS

News is *information people urgently need* in getting their bearings in a rapidly changing world. Where the situation is ambiguous, or there are alternatives, or a decision has to be made, any new information that might affect the outcome is news. News is information that is important to someone. News is *perishable*. Once an event or situation is understood and the tension it has aroused eases, the accepted information becomes history. It is still interesting, but it no longer is pressing, no longer news.

—Tamotsu Shibutani, *Improvised News: A Sociological Study of Rumor* (Indianapolis, Indiana: Bobbs-Merrill, 1966).

. . . No matter how capable the reporter becomes in procuring information and in writing, if he does not learn to classify information; if he does not learn how to sift out and search for those things which are of value from the viewpoint of news, then he will lack what most editors say is a reporter's chief qualification. News, in its broadest sense, is that which is of interest to the readers—the public. . . .

A news story may not be of interest to every reader, but its importance or value is proportionate to the number of readers in whom it incites interest and to the degree of that interest. An analysis of a vast majority of all news stories published possibly will show that the fact such stories are of general interest and hence constitute news, is due chiefly to at least one of these elements:

1. The prominence of persons or places concerned.
2. The proximity of the event to the place of publication.

3. The unusualness of the event.
4. The magnitude of the event.
5. The human interest involved.
6. Timeliness.

—Walter Williams and Frank L. Martin, *The Practice of Journalism* (Columbia, Mo.: Missouri Book Co., 1922).

Joseph Pulitzer, publisher of the St. Louis *Post-Dispatch* and the New York *World*, instructed his staff to look for stories that were "original, distinctive, dramatic, romantic, thrilling, unique, curious, quaint, humorous, odd and apt-to-be-talked-about."

Turner Catledge, former longtime managing editor of the New York *Times*, said news is "anything you can find out today that you didn't know before."

From an unidentified source: "News is anything a good city editor says it is."

Stanley Walker, onetime great city editor of the New York *Herald Tribune*, said news "is more unpredictable than the winds. Sometimes it is the repetition with new characters of tales as old as the pyramids, and again it may be almost outside the common experience."

Section 2

PIONEERS AND TODAY'S LEADERS

George Gallup and his poll contributed the practical basis of much of communication research, as explained here. Wilbur Schramm, presented next, laid the theoretical groundwork. The work of both is evident in the three substantial articles following: L. John Martin theorizes on mass media in political campaigns, George Donohue and his associates examine the control of input into the mass media, and Earl Shorris bitingly criticizes government by poll.

TWO PUBLIC OPINION LEADERS: GEORGE GALLUP AND WILBUR SCHRAMM

Edwin Emery

Have you ever been questioned by an interviewer for the Gallup Poll? This is the question skeptics ask when they reject scientific public opinion measurement. To defend George Gallup's systematic analysis of mass media, one may use Wilbur Schramm's literate explanations of communication research.

GEORGE H. GALLUP

The Gallup Poll has become a familiar American—and, indeed, world—institution through which the science of public opinion measurement is identified in the public mind. George H. Gallup was a pioneer not only in opinion polling, but also in the development of reader-interest measurement techniques for the print media and for use in marketing.

While he was a young instructor in journalism at the University of Iowa, Gallup devised a method for calculating the amount of attention by readers to various items in a newspaper through interviews with selected persons representing various classes among the audience. Using this application of random sampling principles, he did reader-interest studies for the Des Moines newspapers and national periodicals.

Through patient refining of his sampling techniques, Gallup broke new ground and worked out a system for determining the opinions of a total group from interviews with a small number of persons. In 1935 he left teaching and launched his American Institute of Public Opinion in Princeton, New Jersey.

Fate smiled on Gallup. Before 1936 the highly respected *Literary Digest* had been successfully predicting the outcome of presidential elections by making telephone calls. That year the *Digest's* straw poll predicted that Republican candidate Alf Landon would defeat President Franklin D. Roosevelt. Gallup came up with a prediction giving Roosevelt 54 percent of the vote. Even so, he was 6.5 percent short of measuring the avalanche of New Deal votes that buried Landon 531 electoral votes to 8 and swept the *Digest* into oblivion.

SOURCE: This article was written expressly for this book.

George H. Gallup, Sr., with his son, George, Jr.

Gallup came to grief in 1948, along with rival pollsters and other political experts, when he failed to predict President Harry Truman's upset victory over Republican Thomas E. Dewey. Assuming that Dewey was certain of victory, Gallup measured only small samples during the summer and fall, adding them together cumulatively. He thus missed the sharp swing to Truman late in the campaign. The lesson was learned, and since 1952 the Gallup Poll has been off an average of only 1.2 percent in national election predictions, under the continued guidance of Gallup and his son. In 1980 widespread voter indecision and discontent led to difficulties in predicting voter turnout and a miscall of several percentage points on the margin of Ronald Reagan's victory.

Actually, election predictions are not George Gallup's most important contribution. The *Gallup Opinion Index* gives access to the results of hundreds of poll questions on political and social issues of national importance. And guiding the marketing of products is undoubtedly more rewarding financially.

WILBUR SCHRAMM

Wilbur Schramm has for 30 years ranked as the leading interpreter of mass communication theory and research methods, reaching

Wilbur Schramm

audiences at all levels of academic sophistication through some 22 books and 100 articles and papers.

A gifted writer, Schramm turned out humorous fiction for the *Saturday Evening Post* while he was a young member of the University of Iowa journalism staff, then headed by media historian Frank Luther Mott. From Iowa he joined the University of Illinois Journalism faculty headed by media law authority Fred Siebert. Schramm soon plunged into the newly opened field of communication research and became first director of Illinois' Institute of Communication Research, which had famed Charles Osgood as a member. His 1949 reader, *Mass Communications*, and pioneering 1954 *Process and Effects of Mass Communication* made him an established scholar.

In 1955 Schramm joined forces with still another leading media researcher, Chilton R. Bush of Stanford University, and became professor of international communication and director of Stanford's Institute for Communication Research, which quickly became the center for doctoral study in the field. Schramm also teamed with Daniel Lerner in international communication, editing from East–West Communication Institute seminar proceedings two volumes of basic readings, *Communication and Change in the Developing Countries* (1967) and *Communication and Change in the Last Ten Years—and the Next* (1976). In between times Schramm wrote his highly readable text, *Men, Messages, and Media: A Look at Human Communication* (1973, revised 1981), and co-authored *Responsibility in Mass Communication* with William L. Rivers (1969).

Continuing to move westward, Schramm left Stanford after 18 years to join the East–West Communication Institute in Hawaii. He held forth there from 1973 to 1975 as director and continued thereafter as a distinguished scholar. One year he was visiting professor, as first holder of a research chair at the Chinese University of Hong Kong. He then returned to the beaches and palm trees of Honolulu, still turning out provocative scholarly essays with one hand and patient basic explanations of communication principles with the other.

RECENT THEORY
ON MASS MEDIA POTENTIAL
IN POLITICAL CAMPAIGNS
L. John Martin

In this review of communication theory trends since Lasswell, the thesis is developed that the mass media play an agenda-setting role in politics and thus influence election campaigns.

"He's the media candidate," Senator Henry M. Jackson is reported to have said of Governor Jimmy Carter a few days before the Pennsylvania primary, the results of which caused the senator to withdraw from the 1976 presidential race.

> It [the press] feeds on itself. They decide he's got something unique. It has nothing to do with concrete, specific programs. They find him fascinating. The press can't nail him down on anything. They try, but they don't seem able to do it. . . . The press keeps facing a situation it can't quite solve."[1]

The power of the pen and of the press is conventional wisdom that goes back hundreds of years. Rosencrantz in *Hamlet* says that

---

SOURCE: From *The Annals* 427 (September 1976): 125–133. Copyright 1976 The American Academy of Political and Social Science.

A moment in the 1980 Carter–Reagan presidential campaign debate

"many wearing rapiers are afraid of goose-quills." But when this purported axiom was subjected to scientific investigation, doubts began to be expressed about its accuracy. Frank Luther Mott, the journalism historian, determined that, in the 35 presidential election campaigns from 1796 to 1940, the American press gave its majority support to the winning candidate 18 times and to the losing candidate 17 times.[2] Chance could not have played a more even-handed role.

Hypodermic Theories

Yet no one to the present day believes that the press is powerless. In fact, the power of the press is implicit in the idea of harnessing the mass media to perform important social, economic, military, and political tasks—a thought that occurred to the U.S. government in World War II, when it had to train a huge citizen army in a hurry. The Army's Education and Information Division needed to know which of the various available communication techniques were most effective in isolation, in sequence, and in combination. To answer these questions, an experimental section was organized under Yale psychologist Carl I. Hovland within the research branch of the division to study, among other things, the differential effects and effectiveness of the mass media.

Hovland and his staff conducted their empirical research in the context of a paradigm suggested by political scientist Harold D. Lasswell to describe the communication process: "Who says what to whom with what effect?" The studies dealt with the persuasiveness of the different media, but were later continued by the same group of psychologists at Yale University to include the effectiveness of various types of messages and communicators. The Yale Communication Research Program, as it was designated, had for its underpinnings Lasswell's "hypodermic model" of the communication process which, at least implicitly, suggests that communication is something someone does to someone else. The only question in this approach is, how does one vary the types of communicator (who) or the kinds of messages (what) or audiences (whom) to maximize the effectiveness of the process (what effect)? And that is ·what these communication researchers addressed themselves to for another 15 years or so.

The conclusion that many of them arrived at was that, all other things being equal, the more personal a medium the more efficiently persuasive it is. Thus, face-to-face communication is more effective than television, which is more effective than film, radio, and print—in that order.

But quite apart from the fact that this was not always the outcome of their research, all other things are seldom equal except in the laboratory. The difference between people in their natural habitats and people in a laboratory experiment was recognized by Hovland himself, who more than anyone was responsible for mass communication experiments in the laboratory. The reason, he said, you can prove so much more in the laboratory than in a survey of people in a real-life situation is that in the latter case people who have exposed themselves to a message did so voluntarily and many of them were on the persuader's side to begin with. In an experiment, opinion change is often measured minutes after the exposure, when the impact is greatest. Experiments are frequently carried out in classrooms where student-subjects are more receptive to the messages, which in any case are selected for their likelihood to show change.[3]

Gerhart D. Wiebe, a research psychologist for CBS and later dean of the School of Public Communication at Boston University, developed deductively a rationale for the greater effectiveness of more personal media; then he tested his theory empirically. He pointed out that the reason television is more vivid, more suggestive of "immediate reality" than radio, which in turn is more real than print, is that radio is one symbol system removed from reality (the spoken word), while print is two symbol systems—two levels of abstraction—removed. This is because the printed word is a symbol for the spoken word, which in turn is a symbol for reality. He said that television is experienced in an intimate frame of reference, while newspaper accounts are perceived in a distant frame of reference.[4] What led to the undoing of Senator Joseph R. McCarthy, in Wiebe's opinion, was that he was brought into an intimate frame of reference through the televising of the Army-McCarthy hearings. Wiebe contrasted this to the war in Indochina which, in 1954, was still being experienced in a distant frame of reference. Vietnam had not yet been brought into every American's living room by massive television coverage.

Then, in 1960, Joseph T. Klapper reviewed the research findings (mainly of the previous two decades) and came to the conclusion that "mass communication *ordinarily* does not serve as a necessary and sufficient cause of audience effects, but rather functions among and through a nexus of mediating factors and influences."[5] This was not a new idea. It had been noted by Hovland himself in a 1954 article referring to Mott's 1944 study and to a 1926 study by George A. Lundberg. Hovland had to admit that "press support of presidential candidates seems to bear no relationship to their success at the polls."[6] It was just that the hope had lingered that somehow a researcher might hit on the right formula—one that would guarantee a gambler's chance to those who are willing to invest their money in mass media time and space to cajole their fellow human beings into taking a desired line of action. But the best that Klapper could offer was the statement that "the efficacy of mass communication in creating opinion . . . can be gauged only in reference to issues on which, at the time of exposure, people are *known to have no opinion at all.*"[7]

Information-Seeking Theories

What put researchers on a new track was a series of consistency theories developed in the 1950s, especially Leon Festinger's cognitive dissonance theory. Simply put, these theories stated that people like their beliefs and judgments about things to be consistent with one another. To reduce the dissonance created by inconsistencies, people expose themselves to facts, events, and judgments through communication or selectively shut out such communication to avoid dissonance. They might even selectively perceive, or misperceive, and selectively retain information to the same end.

Consistency theories switched the Lasswellian paradigm around. No longer were communication specialists concerned about who says what to whom, since this is immaterial if the "whom" in the paradigm is unable or unwilling to receive the message. The question was, who needs to receive what messages from whom? The emphasis was on the seeking and avoiding of information rather than on the transmission of instruction or urging of opinion change. Furthermore, a distinction began to be made between informational communication and persuasive communication. The mass media had been weighed in the balance and found clearly wanting in persuasiveness—at least in the short run. People don't do things or change their attitudes or even opinions simply because they are asked to or told to by an individual, directly or through the mass media.

The change in perspective on the communication process also led to a rethinking of the findings of the relative effectiveness of the different mass media. Pollster Elmo Roper had for years been asking people questions about the medium they consider most informative and the one they believe to be the most credible. He found television to be the medium more than half the audience would want to keep if they had to give up all other media. Television also was the most credible medium in the Roper poll. Over the years, television has consistently been rated the major source of information about national candidates by 60 to 65 percent of the public, with newspapers being rated first by only a fourth to a third of the public. For information about state candidates, television has a much narrower edge over newspapers, while on local candidates, newspapers are considered a better source than television by more people. Friends and relatives are an important source of information only on local candidates (the major source for around one in five). Radio and magazines are rated a major source of information about political candidates—national, state, or local—by fewer than 10 percent of the population.[8]

In the light of information-seeking theories, communication specialist Alex S. Edelstein studied audiences in both the United States and Yugoslavia and concluded that sources of information were evaluated not in terms of their trustworthiness or credibility but in terms of their content, breadth of perception, and availability. Television provided the greatest breadth of perception, and if seeing was important to the audience, television was the preferred medium. Newspapers provided the greatest breadth of content and the most time to think, while radio was the most available medium.[9] Clearly, this view is based on a "uses and gratifications" theory rather than a hypodermic theory—the user of information being the one who determines what medium to use. He also makes the judgment about its believability, depending on whether it gratifies his needs. It is not the communicator who manipulates his medium or his message and its environment to create a desired effect.

Agenda-Setting Function

One bothersome problem with an audience-initiated and controlled communication model is that it appears to leave the man with a message—a political candidate, for instance—in an impotent, applicant position. His target will attend to his message only if it does not upset the target's existing beliefs and judgments. In other words, the politician would tend to be preaching to the already converted; and, in fact, one of the rules of thumb of persuasive communication (such as political campaigning and propaganda) is that "The people you may want most in your audience are often least likely to be there."[10] This follows logically from the selective exposure hypothesis mentioned above and supports consistency theories.

While this rule is not difficult to rationalize, it leaves one dissatisfied. Don't tell us, we feel like saying, that the mass media have absolutely no power beyond merely agreeing with their audience—since, after all, people by this rule expose themselves only to those parts of the press with which they already agree. Intuitively—since each of us can think of occasions when the mass media have influenced us or when we think we were influenced—we tend to reject this conclusion.[11] And it is here that communication theorists have recently come up with a new explanatory proposition—they don't yet call it a theory. The proposition involves once and for all separating persuasive from informational communication. The underlying assumption is that gaining new knowledge has little to do with how that knowledge will be used. It might result in an interpretation that is favorable to the thrust of the message or one that is unfavorable.

The text is taken from political scientist Bernard C. Cohen, who pointed out that "the press may not be successful much of the time in telling people what to think, but it is stunningly successful in telling its readers what to think about."[12] Picking up this theme, two communication specialists, Maxwell E. McCombs and Donald L. Shaw, in a landmark study in 1972 showed that undecided voters in the 1968 presidential election tended to give the same priorities to issues in the campaign as were given to the issues by the news media.[13] They concluded that the reason for this was that the press sets the agenda for its audiences. It provides the facts, for the most part, that make up the cognitive world of each individual. This agenda-setting power of the press is directive rather than reactive. The press does not merely reflect developments which also influence the general public in the same way. The press actually picks certain issues to play up at times that do not necessarily parallel the significance of those events.

G. Ray Funkhouser showed that this is so by doing a content analysis of three weekly newsmagazines for the 1960s. The number of articles on such issues as the Vietnam War, race relations, student unrest, and inflation peaked in years when the events themselves were not at their highest point of importance or activity. What is especially noteworthy and supportive of the agenda-setting role of the press is that the peaks in news coverage coincided with peaks in the proportion of people who picked these issues as the "most important problem facing America" in Gallup Polls. On the other hand, they were not the issues that people felt the government should devote most of its attention to. Funkhouser concluded that "the average person takes the media's word for what the 'issues' are, whether or not he personally has any involvement or interest in them."[14] And, one might add, he rates them as important whether or not they have the salience in reality that the press gives them.

All this agrees very well with what information-seeking theorists had been saying for some time and with what those basing their research on the agenda-setting paradigm are now saying. The mass media tend to inform rather than to change attitudes. The conclusions drawn from the information derived from the media may direct attitudes one way or another, and it is only when nothing is competing from one's own past experience that media experience becomes real and their values are adopted as one's own. This, however, happens very infrequently in our multimedia society.

Theoretically, of course, it could happen to people who do not expose themselves to many media or who do not take an interest in political issues. Their political experience would be limited and they would be inclined to accept a line proposed by the media. But the likelihood of their exposure to an issue raised by the media would be equally limited. Philip E. Converse of the Survey Research Center at the University of Michigan has found that, on most issues, only about 20 percent of the public can be termed an "issue public" that has a genuine opinion based on knowledge. While only about 10 percent of the public will answer "don't know" to an opinion question, for another 70 percent of the population, response sequences over time are totally random.[15]

Need for Orientation

Non-attendance to any side of a political issue discussed in the media is a far more important deterrent to media impact than the previously feared factor of selective exposure. That is, people generally expose themselves only to those views with which they already agree and avoid information that challenges their opinions. Social psychologists Jonathan L. Freedman and David O. Sears, in a paper that upset this neat, intuitive theory, concluded after reviewing most of the literature on the subject that there is no firm evidence that people prefer to be exposed to supportive information or to information that will reduce their unease at being bombarded by contradictory facts and opinions.[16] They did add, however, that "people are disproportionately exposed to supportive information, but for reasons other than its supportiveness."[17]

Agenda-setting by the media, however, may apparently occur without direct exposure to the media. If a person can name any issue, event, or candidate at all, the chances are pretty good that he learned about it through the mass media or through someone who was exposed to the mass media, since few of us are direct witnesses to the news of the day.

Does this mean that the media also determine the relative importance of issues? That is exactly what agenda-setting studies have shown they do. Through the sheer frequency with which a story is told, length of the story, headline size, and positioning, the media suggest to the general public how important an event, issue, or candidate is. "Salience of an item is one of the key attributes acquired from the mass media," according to McCombs and Shaw.[18] Not only is this true of media impact on the public, but the news agencies have a similar impact on newspaper wire editors, as several studies both in the United States and abroad have shown.[19] The editor tends to use more of a story, news category, or issue on which he receives more items and longer items from the wire services.

To what extent does this also determine the side people will take on an issue? Probably very little, although as McCombs and Shaw point out, "issues sometimes clearly work to the advantage of one political party or candidate."[20] All it takes is for the press to play up the issue. But coupled with the emphasis given it by the press, the issue must also find a responsive chord in the audience. Each of us has a need to relate to his environment, and if a given issue satisfies that need or stimulates it, we would turn to the mass media (or to our friends who are primed by the mass media) for orientation.[21] The theory is that the "need for orientation" leads to media use, which leads to agenda-setting by the mass media. But the theory says nothing about the side people will take on the issue. In fact, several studies have indicated that people will expose themselves to information that they need and that is relevant to them, regardless of whether the information conforms to their view of the issue or not. At the same time, they will avoid irrelevant information. This is in keeping with the refutation by Freedman and Sears of the selective exposure theory.

Applying these principles to political campaigns, if a voter finds a need for orientation to a particular issue, he will listen to all candidates, regardless of political party. This emerged in the McCombs and Shaw landmark study of the 1968 presidential election. Even though the three presidential contenders that year placed very different emphases on the issues of the day, voters seemed to expose themselves to all three candidates. The researchers found that their respondents' issue agendas (or priorities) agreed less with the agendas of their preferred candidate than they did with a composite agenda based on the priorities of all three candidates. [22]

Importance of TV

What of the differential effects of the mass media? Do communication specialists still believe that it is futile to talk of one medium being more efficient and effective than another? Given that it is the voter rather than the communicator who decides which medium will be attended to, researchers have found that certain things can be said about differences in mass media effects. Campaign consultant Walter DeVries found in the 1970 Michigan gubernatorial race that different types of television programs (such as newscasts, documentaries, editorials) were rated higher as important factors in influencing voting decisions than any other medium. Of 36 factors that play a role in political campaigning, 12 were rated 5.0 or better on an 11-point scale as influencing voting decisions. Significantly, the only one of these over which the candidate himself had any control was "contacts with candidates"—that is, personal campaigning. None of the purchasable types of advertising—for example, television or newspaper ads, political mailings, or telephone campaigns—was rated higher than 4.9. [23]

McCombs, however, has found that television, unlike newspapers, does not have an agenda-setting effect across time. Furthermore, when different agendas are set by newspapers and television stations, newspaper priorities have a higher correlation with voter agendas. [24] Others have shown that if agendas are studied in terms of issues, subissues, and specifics (such as individuals involved or solutions proposed), television tends to set the overall issue agendas but not the agenda of details. Even among TV-oriented respondents—that is, those who said television was their major source of news—newspapers tended to set their agendas on subissues and specifics. [25]

In the face of the great emphasis that is placed by political candidates and their campaign managers on television appearances, and in view of the fact that the candidates who spend the most on television advertising appear to win, it may be rash to downgrade television. Yet there is growing evidence that, although large proportions of voters are exposed to the airing of political campaign messages on television, it is the newspapers that tend to determine the salience of issues. Conceivably, newspaper editors and reporters are themselves influenced in their judgment by the volume of television exposure. Furthermore, voting is a short-term activity that requires no long-term attitudinal build-up, much as we would like to think of the vote as a considered judgment on the part of the electorate. Television may have a powerful short-term effect, ideally suited to the quick action requirements in politics. It may, therefore, be a useful medium to use immediately before an election. But for long-range effects, newspapers are still the most instrumental in determining saliences.

One additional theoretical note on mass media potential has emerged from a study of senatorial news coverage. Words appear to be more fruitful than deeds in putting a senator in the public eye. Activity and seniority do not seem to produce high media visibility for senators, according to a study by David Weaver and Cleveland Wilhoit. Being vocal or active in the Senate by introducing most bills, serving on most committees, participating in most roll-call votes is less effective than seeking out reporters with press releases and news conferences. Hence, the senators from the largest states with the largest staffs receive the most publicity in the press.[26]

Notes

1. Quoted in the *Washington Post*, 29 April 1976, p. 11A.
2. Frank Luther Mott, "Newspapers in Presidential Campaigns." *Public Opinion Quarterly*, vol. 8 (Fall 1944), p. 362. There were no campaigns in President Washington's two elections in 1789 and 1793, Jefferson's 1804 election, and Monroe's 1820 election.
3. Carl I. Hovland, "Reconciling Conflicting Results Derived from Experimental and Survey Studies of Attitude Change." *American Psychologist*, vol. 14 (1959), pp. 8–17.
4. Gerhart D. Wiebe, "A New Dimension in Journalism," *Journalism Quarterly*, vol. 31 (Fall 1954), pp. 411–20.
5. Joseph T. Klapper, *The Effects of Mass Communication* (Glencoe, Ill.: The Free Press, 1960), p. 8. Emphasis in original.
6. Quoted in ibid., p. 54.
7. Ibid., p. 55. Emphasis in original.
8. Burns W. Roper, *An Extended View of Public Attitudes toward Television and Other Mass Media, 1959–1971.* (New York: Television Information Office, 1971), pp. 8–9.
9. Alex S. Edelstein, "Media Credibility and the Believability of Watergate," *News Research Bulletin no. 1* (Washington, D.C.: American Newspaper Publishers Association, 1974), p. 5.
10. Marvin Karlins and Herbert I. Abelson, *Persuasion.* (New York: Springer Publishing Co., 1970), 2nd ed., p. 84.
11. The question, of course, is were we really influenced or were we merely delighted to find some "facts" or views expressed in the press that happened to agree with our own prior views?
12. Bernard C. Cohen. *The Press and Foreign Policy* (Princeton: Princeton University Press, 1963), p. 13.

13. Maxwell E. McCombs and Donald L. Shaw, "The Agenda-Setting Function of Mass Media," *Public Opinion Quarterly*, vol. 36 (Summer 1972), pp. 176–87.
14. G. Ray Funkhouser, "Trends in Media Coverage of the Issues of the '60s," *Journalism Quarterly* vol. 50 (Autumn 1973), pp. 533–38.
15. Philip E. Converse, "New Dimensions of Meaning for Cross-Section Sample Surveys in Politics," *International Social Science Journal*, vol. 16 (1964), pp. 25–26.
16. Jonathan L. Freedman and David O. Sears, "Selective Exposure," *Advances in Experimental Social Psychology*, vol. 2 (1965), pp. 58–97.
17. Ibid., p. 90.
18. Maxwell E. McCombs and Donald L. Shaw, "A Progress Report on Agenda-Setting Research." Paper presented at the Association for Education in Journalism Convention at San Diego, 18–21 August 1974, p. 30.
19. L. John Martin, *Analysis of Newspaper Coverage of the U.S. in the Near East, North Africa and South Asia* (Washington, D.C.: U.S. Information Agency Research Report R-2-76, 1976).
20. McCombs and Shaw, "A Progress Report," p. 40.
21. See Maxwell McCombs and David Weaver, "Voter's Need for Orientation and Use of Mass Communication." Paper presented at the International Communication Association Convention in Montreal, Canada, 25–28 April 1973.
22. Maxwell McCombs, "Agenda-Setting Research: A Bibliographic Essay," prepared for *Political Communication Review* (February 1976) ms. p. 2.
23. Walter DeVries, "Taking the Voter's Pulse," in Ray Hiebert et al., *The Political Image Merchants: Strategies in the New Politics* (Washington, D.C.: Acropolis Books, 1971), pp. 62–81.
24. McCombs, "Agenda-Setting Research," pp. 6–7.
25. Marc Benton and P. Jean Frazier, "The Agenda-Setting Function of the Mass Media at Three Levels of 'Information Holding,' " Paper presented at the Association for Education in Journalism Convention in Ottawa, Canada, August 1975.
26. David H. Weaver and G. Cleveland Wilhoit, "Agenda-Setting for the Media-Determinants of Senatorial News Coverage." Paper presented at the International Communication, Association Convention in Chicago, 23–26 April 1975.

GATEKEEPING:
MASS MEDIA SYSTEMS
AND INFORMATION CONTROLS

George A. Donohue, Phillip J. Tichenor, and Clarice N. Olien

The mass media serve as social subsystems whose primary concerns include the control of information. The authors in this portion of their article establish their thesis, discussing gatekeeping and the effects of distribution controls.

When man devised the first rudimentary form of mass communication centuries ago, he immediately developed ways of controlling it. Printer, king, teacher and merchant were almost equally inventive in contriving ways to bring information under control. Their diligence arose from man's historic recognition of a fundamental social principle: knowledge is basic to social power, and immense potential for developing power over other human lives rests with those who man the gates in the communication flow (Bagdikian, 1971; Galbraith, 1967; McDermott, 1969; Park, 1940).

Crises of confrontation between media agencies and government recently and historically should not obscure the fact that both have, as a prime function, the control of information. The main issue is over which organization exerts what control, how, and for what reason (Donohue et al., 1971; Revel, 1971). While knowledge control is as old as mankind, it has become a more prominent feature of modern civilization as more and more human activity becomes directed toward production and accumulation of knowledge (Galbraith, 1967; Harrington, 1967; Boulding, 1964). Mass media today may be seen as part (and only part) of a growing "knowledge industry" which accounts for more than a fourth of the gross national product (Machlup, 1962; Kerr, 1963). Indeed, the very essence of a nation's security and power among nations is dependent upon its structure for generating and utilizing increments of knowledge (Galbraith, 1967).

All large social organizations depend to some extent on information use and control, but now there are vast agencies and firms, in addition to the traditional mass media, whose prime missions center around knowledge development and control. Data processing

---

SOURCE: From *Current Perspectives in Mass Communication Research*, Sage Annual Reviews of Communication Research, vol. 1, edited by F. G. Kline and P. J. Tichenor, pp. 41–47. Copyright 1972. Reprinted by permission of the publisher, Sage Publications, Inc.

agencies, quasi-public research agencies, and information retrieval firms represent growing specialization and recognition of the role of knowledge in the total system. Present-day specialists at input and output levels are integrated into a configuration of organized intelligence which is often beyond the comprehension or concern of any one person, but which is vital for the decision-making processes which each person serves in the system (Galbraith, 1967; McDermott, 1969).

Knowledge today is organized to a high degree at all levels of society, and mass media represent one form of this refinement. The way in which mass media knowledge enters into social decision-making may not be the same as the way knowledge is used for executive decisions in industry, but the general principle of knowledge control in the service of other social needs is as applicable to mass communication as to any other level of human discourse. If mass communication is in actuality control of information and knowledge, then, in light of the way decisions are made in a modern, pluralistic society, the study of the gatekeepers who execute control decisions in the knowledge flow is especially urgent.

Gatekeeping As Information Control

Processes of "gatekeeping" in mass communication may be viewed within a framework of a total social system, made up of a series of subsystems whose primary concerns include the control of information in the interest of gaining other social ends (DeFleur, 1966). Questions for mass communication research in this area include *how* such controls are exercised, *where* in the process they occur, and what the *consequences* of these controls are for the overall social system as well as for the interdependent subsystems (Donohue et al., 1971). Mass media make up subsystems that cut across the source and audience subsystems and perform certain functions for both of these other subsystems and for the social system as a whole (Westley and MacLean, 1957; Parsons, 1967; Katz and Kahn, 1966).

"Gatekeeping," then, includes various forms of information or knowledge control. This is a more inclusive definition of the process than may have been intended by others. When White (1950) first applied the term to a wire service editor, he was using it in the specific sense of selecting or rejecting certain messages. That is, the flow of wire messages available to the medium was, for White, roughly analogous to the "flow" of food and other goods potentially available to housewives which Lewin (1951) had been studying when he introduced the "gatekeeper" term into social science literature. But while White was studying one aspect of information control, it is clear that far more than simple rejection or acceptance may be involved in message transmission through channel systems. "Information control," therefore, may be a more inclusive and appropriate term. For this discussion, "gatekeeping" in mass media is viewed as including all forms of information control that may arise in decisions about message encoding, such as selection, shaping, display, timing, withholding, or repetition of entire messages or message components. "Censorship" in this view is a special case of information control.

There is no assumption here that social control is the only function served by mass communication; rather, the assumption is that all communication processes have a control function within them, either manifest or latent.

Mass Media As Social Subsystems

Growing complexity of modern society has been accompanied by a tendency for communication systems to shift from a consensus approach to more of a conflict model of organization. However, social differentiation is not a uniform process, as Spencer (1898) pointed out when he drew the analogy between biological and social systems. Social differentiation has different effects on different social subsystems and, in the case of mass media, on different parts of a particular subsystem. Along with growth of media systems today, we have sharper differences in the functions which the media serve, and in the segments of the total system for which different media are relevant.

With differing media subsystems and differing functions, considerable conflict and social tension may develop. Social conflict, however, does not necessarily indicate a state of total disorder; conflict and tension, and their management, are fundamental aspects of modern pluralistic social organization (Coser, 1956). In today's pluralistic society, mass media are more likely to accommodate conflict in the interest of controlling it so as to perform certain functions (Olien et al., 1968). To a considerable extent, then, mass media are agencies for conflict management. Conflict control may include the *generation* of conflict situations as well as the direct dissipation of tension. The operations in this conflict management are complex and not always easily accommodated by media actors. Social and organizational strains which media agencies and personnel have in dealing with social conflict have, therefore, provided the focal point for much of the systematic research on "gatekeeper" phenomena which has been done in the past two decades.

In the context of a systems model, mass communication of political, technological, and cultural knowledge is controlled largely in the interest of system maintenance. However, the system (or subsystem) being maintained may vary in different situations. It may be the media subsystem itself. It may be the source subsystem with which the media have systemic relations or it may be the larger social system as a whole. "Maintenance" does not necessarily mean perpetuating the status quo, although that may occur. In the perspective being used here, maintenance refers to sustaining of a system and whatever dynamic processes which it may encompass. Maintenance functions may be fulfilled in at least two different, but overlapping ways.

Two Maintenance Processes   One process serving the maintenance function is *feedback control*, which is defined as the way in which system adjustments are made in response to information about system performance. Feedback takes many forms; a well-known type is feedback within a media system (as through a readership survey). In a more inclusive sense, however, media subsystems themselves may provide a feedback, or regulatory, function for other subsystems or for the total social system. In social philosophy, the feedback-control function is expressed in the conception of the "fourth estate" or "watchdog" role of the press (Hocking, 1947; Hachten, 1963; Rucker, 1968) and this role has been seen as especially crucial in a pluralistic but highly interdependent society. Mass media apply corrective pressures to subsystems that may be out of functional balance in relation to others. In this perspective "muckraking" was not a wayward act of newspapers sensationalizing for sensation's sake. While muckraking *may* have contributed to the sale of newspapers, it also had, quite clearly, a maintenance function for the total social system. Lippmann (1961), for example, viewed the muckrakers as applying certain public standards to the conduct of people in government and other high public office. Both the "surveillance" and "correlational" functions identified by Lasswell (see Schramm, 1960) may be seen as referring to feedback-control processes in system terms. Rachel Carson's *Silent Spring* and the reporting of it in mass media served a feedback function for the total social system. The *Selling of the Pentagon* and the *Pentagon Papers* issues are contemporary examples of the mass media serving a feedback-control function between different social subsystems—in this case, between executive government and one set of interest groups on the one hand and legislative branches and other interest groups on the other. In both cases, both the media and the executive government systems were dealing with information control, and the basic conflict was over whose efforts to control would prevail.

A second process is *distribution control* which may also serve the total system maintenance function without a complete feedback process occurring. Some mass communication is purely distributive, in either a positive or a negative sense. System maintenance may result from either withholding knowledge or selectively distributing it. Media in some communities may serve a maintenance function by avoiding or restructuring certain tension-laden information (Olien et al., 1968). In other communities, maintenance may be served by reporting tension-filled messages on some topics at length. Advertising in all forms may be viewed as contributing to market control or management, so that demand for products can be controlled and predicted (Galbraith, 1967). This principle is most clear in institutional advertising.

Timing of distribution may be a key aspect of control. Holding up release of information until a crucial act has taken place is well known, both in national security cases and in everyday community news management. Some distribution is primarily utilitarian for other subsystems, such as dissemination of certain kinds of information about medicine, household problems, and industry. The vast efforts of public relations and public information offices in public and private agencies reflect the widespread attention given to distributional aspects of information control for system maintenance.

Types of Knowledge The special concern here is with communication of knowledge, whether it is in the political, scientific, or cultural realm. Knowledge can be thought of as fitting in one of two broad control categories, "knowledge of" and "knowledge about." When a message transmits "knowledge of" a topic, it is creating familiarity and acquaintance with that topic or events associated with it. The recipient gains awareness in a general way, but little more. When a message transmits "knowledge about" a topic or issue, it provides increments of formal and analytic knowledge, or what might approach understanding in depth. These two categories reflect a continuum and relative characteristics rather than discrete types (Park, 1940). In general, most mass-communicated information about public affairs tends to fall toward the "knowledge of" end of the continuum and therefore has special control properties. In the small community, for example, confining public affairs reporting to "knowledge of" (or what some editors refer to as "sticking to the facts") is a standard device for maintaining awareness without delving into the controversial aspects of the issues, which reporting in depth would entail.

Information and Social Stresses Information control is not the exclusive property of any single social subsystem. Feedback may be functional at one system or subsystem level but dysfunctional for maintenance of another subsystem, leading to some major social stresses. It may be functional for a governmental (or scientific) agency to withhold information and "not rock the boat," whereas such information may be seen by media people as essential for "the public right to know." The latter is an everyday way of saying that if information is widely diffused, it may arouse certain pressures for regulation or change on some social groups or segment. Such observers as Cater (1964) find reporters frequently disagreeing with politicians who think news which is good for their agency is also good for the country as a whole.

Modern media systems exist at least partly for control of conflict, but not necessarily for its elimination; modern society assumes a certain level of conflict as subsystems interact (Coser, 1956). This principle may be recognized widely in the political realm. Yet it also applies to other social sectors, such as science, culture, the arts, and education, even though there may be strong pressures within each sector to maintain a consensus orientation. This pressure for consensus is especially strong in science (Hagstrom, 1965), but it exists to some degree in all subsystems.

References

Bagdikian, B. H. 1971. *The Information Machines.* New York: Harper & Row.
Boulding, K. 1964. *The Meaning of the Twentieth Century.* New York: Harper & Row.
Cater, D. 1964. *The Fourth Branch of Government.* New York: Random House.
Coser, L. A. 1956. *The Functions of Social Conflict.* New York: Free Press.
DeFleur, M. L. 1966. *Theories of Mass Communication.* New York: McKay.
Donohue, G. A.; Tichenor, P. J.; and Olien, C. N. 1971. "Mass Media Functions, Knowledge, and Social Control." Paper presented to the Association for Education in Journalism.
Galbraith, J. K. 1967. *The New Industrial State.* New York: Houghton Mifflin.
Hachten, W. A. 1963. "The Press As Reporter and Critic of Government." *Journalism Quarterly* 40:12−18.
Hagstrom, W. O. 1965. *The Scientific Community.* New York: Basic Books.
Harrington, M. 1967. "The Social-Industrial Complex." *Harper's*, November, pp. 55−60.
Hocking. W. 1947. *Freedom of the Press.* Chicago: University of Chicago Press.
Katz, D.; and Kahn, R. L. 1966. *The Social Psychology of Organizations.* New York: John Wiley.
Kerr, C. 1963. *The Uses of the University.* Cambridge, Mass.: Harvard University Press.

Lasswell, H. D. 1960. "The Structure and Function of Communication in Society." In *Mass Communications*, edited by W. Schramm. Urbana: University of Illinois Press.

Lewin, K. 1951. *Field Theory in Social Science*. New York: Harper & Row.

Lippmann, W. 1961. *Drift and Mastery*. Englewood Cliffs, N.J.: Prentice-Hall.

McDermott, J. 1969. "Knowledge Is Power." *The Nation*, April 14, pp. 458–60.

Machlup, F. 1962. *The Production and Distribution of Knowledge in the United States*. Princeton, N.J.: Princeton University Press.

Olien, C. N.; Donohue, G. A.; and Tichenor, P. J. 1968. "The Community Editor's Power and the Reporting of Conflict." *Journalism Quarterly*, 45:243–52.

Park, R. E. 1940. "News as a Form of Knowledge." *American Journal of Sociology* 45:669–86.

Parsons, T. 1967. "A Paradigm for the Analysis of Social Systems and Change." In *System, Change and Conflict*, N. S. Demerath and R. A. Peterson. New York: Free Press.

Revel, J. F. 1971. "Without Marx or Jesus." Review in *Saturday Review*, July 24, 14–31.

Rucker, B. 1968. *The First Freedom*. Carbondale: Southern Illinois University Press.

Spencer, H. 1898. *The Principles of Sociology*. Volume 1. New York: D. Appleton.

Westley, B. H; and MacLean, M. S., Jr. 1957. "A Conceptual Model for Communications Research," *Journalism Quarterly* 34: 31–38.

White, D. M. 1950. "The Gatekeeper: A Case Study in the Selection of News," *Journalism Quarterly* 27:383–90.

MARKET DEMOCRACY
Earl Shorris

A contributing editor of *Harper's* provides a counter-view of the social values of public opinion research. Pollsters can market a candidate much like a product, he contends, with deplorable results.

According to reports in the press, the rough, ill-fit mosaic of American political opinion has smoothed and flowed into clear distinctions, so that the most casual observer can now know the will of the people at any time on any subject. We need no longer wait for elections nor endure the irritating slowness of political debate: the

---

public-opinion polls daily announce the general will. Political romanticism has arrived in America.

The disputatious, disagreeable nature of Americans has not changed; the Madisonian view of democratic government as the balancing machine of a large and diverse nation remains the popular ideal; yet the slow-moving and reasoning democracy of the Constitution has in fact become as quick and passionate as the market for cheap music or bathroom tissue. Market democracy, initiated by public-opinion polls, embraced by political manipulators, and used to its own advantage by the press, has replaced the deliberative machine of American government. Political thought has been reduced to the simplicity of the market, the diversity of voices that enabled the constitutional democracy to function for two hundred years has been simplified to the "yea" and "nay" that can be understood by the electrical binary mind of the pollster.

Romanticism, born of the view of man as the market, predicated on the buy/no-buy decision, as fierce as holy war, has eliminated the sound of the individual voice. The interests of the poor, of those who do not conform, of the ethnic and racial minorities, the religious objectors, the tiny redoubts of conscience have been disenfranchised. No one counts, only everyone counts.

Public-opinion polls of themselves could not have worked such a change in American politics. When opinion polls were introduced into politics, Churchill scoffed at them. Harry Truman simply overcame them. For public-opinion polls to pervert the Constitution required the complicity of the press, that institution which even the aristocratic de Tocqueville thought able to restrain the tyranny of the majority in America. The press saw two advantages in the polls: news could be manufactured on demand, either for the expense of a few thousand dollars or for the publicity given to the pollster; but more seductively, the polls gave the press something it had long coveted, the power of the source. With the public-opinion poll as a tool, the press could not only manufacture news on demand, it could control the content of the news by choosing the subject of the poll. If one considers a public-opinion poll a simulacrum of an election, control of the polls seems to give the press control of the process of democracy. For the sake of the illusion of power the press has inflated the importance of the polls to such degree that the political nature of the nation may be permanently changed and the ability of government to exercise its constitutional function permanently damaged.

The validity of public-opinion polls, that is, their relation to reality, has little relation to their effect on government. We are told the numbers of those polled and the margin of error. Walter Cronkite reports the results through his most solemn phlegm, the New York *Times* draws pie charts to enhance our perception. We are convinced. Harris and Gallup are part of the American vocabulary.

That public-opinion polling runs counter to the Madisonian notion of diversity, which is at the core of the American machine of government, can be seen in the genesis and the nature of the polls. The Gallup Poll of Princeton, New Jersey, originated not in the shadow of the Institute for Advanced Study, where Einstein spent his last years, but in a New York advertising agency, where it was used for marketing studies. And while marketing and American government are both democratic processes, they are entirely different forms of democracy. Marketing lacks the complexity and the subtlety of politics: buyers of washday detergents are not differentiated by their views on foreign policy, abortion, transfer payments, et cetera, and Duz really didn't do everything; it did not, for example, govern a nation of 200 million people.

The single-mindedness of marketing fits perfectly with the capabilities of public-opinion polling, which perforce divides the nation into clear factions: those who will and those who won't buy the product. The marketer wishes only for the largest possible number of buyers, and he cares not a damn for the lot of the nonbuyers. His work is analogous to that kind of raw democracy Aristotle called mob rule; and his primary tool, the marketing survey or public-opinion poll, delivers exactly what is needed for the accomplishment of his work.

The inductive method used in public-opinion polling poses no problem for the marketer. He wishes to simplify the market, to divine from the small sample something akin to a general will about his product. Since he has no use for diversity, the tools for discerning it have not been included in his information-gathering system. Practicality drives him, his technique is utterly utilitarian; a method that produced more information than he needed would be wasteful.

Change concerns the marketer more than any other factor. He constantly adjusts his strategies and his products to meet the demands of the public. He sees the market as dynamic: population increases, income increases, styles change, products become outmoded, new products replace them. In the eyes of the marketer, stability means a shrinking share, failure, the eventual destruction of his business. His survey methods are therefore quick and inexpensive. He does not risk leadership; he responds, he panders to whatever his polls tell him is the general will about his product, and the faster he can respond the more successful a mass marketer he will be.

Yet another and perhaps more decisive link exists between marketing and many public-opinion polls. Marketing studies often serve as hosts for public-opinion polls. Questions about public issues are added on at the beginning or the end of a market survey paid for by one of the pollster's business clients. The same methods of sampling, questioning, and tabulating are used for both surveys. Single-mindedness, haste, the creation of factions, the broad, seemingly passionate shifts of feeling associated with romanticism are inevitable.

Time distinguishes between passion and reason. The marketer hurries his survey, because he cares about passion, impulse. Shoppers, unless they are mad, do not spend time in contemplation of the relative merits of paper towels and dishcloths. The marketer, does not wish to know the responses of lunatics, he cares about normal people, so his surveys are designed to measure normal, impulsive responses. On the other hand, one must be either impassioned or mad to decide in a matter of moments, without prior notice, to answer by telephone to the most serious political questions of the time.

In elections, the candidates debate the issues, they publish campaign literature, platforms, policies, people speak to each other in debate over whom they prefer to elect. Reason and justice have their chance. The immediate responses of aggression, self-defense, selfishness, and greed may be mitigated by argument and contemplation.

Opinion polls demean the people by misrepresenting their capacity for goodness and then telling them in the press that their selfishness is the voice of the majority. Instinctual behavior becomes normative. The voices of diversity are conflated, made into vast factions, and cast with daily regularity at the machine of government. The mob, mute but for the violence of its "yea" or "nay," speaks directly to the Executive, to the Constitution itself, eliminating the tempering qualities of time and representative government. Passions rule, the quadrennial rhythm of government becomes diurnal.

Through a process of self-aggrandizement, engineered with the complicity of the press and abetted by the timidity of the elected members of the government, the polls have arrogated to themselves the power of plebiscites or referenda. Not only do they deal daily with questions of economic policy, foreign relations, and other activities generally reserved for the Executive branch, they deal with such constitutional questions as equal rights, freedom of expression, capital punishment, and due process. To Madison the work of the pollsters would have seemed anarchic: "As every appeal to the people would carry an implication of some defect in the government, frequent appeals would, in great measure, deprive the government of that veneration which time bestows on everything, and without which perhaps the wisest and freest governments would not possess the requisite stability. The danger of disturbing the public tranquility by interesting too strongly the public passions, is a . . . serious objection against a frequent reference of constitutional questions to the decision of the whole society." And it should be noted that Madison was not concerned here only with "altering" the Constitution; he feared frequent appeals to the society as a whole as a means of "enforcing" the Constitution.

Underlying the machinery of government codified in the Constitution is the desire to permit rationality rather than romanticism to rule. For all the dissension over federalism, duration of office, and so on, not a man at the Constitutional Convention would have disagreed with Madison's belief that "the reason, alone, of the public . . . ought to control and regulate the government. The passions ought to be controlled and regulated by the government."

To Madison the first danger of the conflation of diversity into passionate factions was that a government of free men would pass over into tyranny. He had no more taste for raw democracy than did Plato or Aristotle; the name of Rousseau and the romantic notion of government would always be anathema to him. But the less dramatic result of a nation without diversity and stability, those vital parts of the machine of reasonable government, would come in the meekness of government, in what Hamilton called "an unqualified complaisance to every sudden breeze of passion." Those symptoms are already manifest in American government: Nixon could not sustain his price-control programs, Ford was almost completely paralyzed during his brief term, and Carter, the first President to awaken every morning of his term to "the prospect of annihilation," cannot govern at all.

Part Two
THE PRINT MEDIA

F rom the ancient days of Egyptian hieroglyphics chiseled on stone tablets, the written word has been the tool for recording human history and thought. The development of printing with movable type by Johannes Gutenberg in the mid-1400s broadened the impact of writing a thousand fold, bringing knowledge out of the cloister and into the hands of the people.

Marvelous as this spread of information was to humankind's well-being, the autocratic rulers of nations saw printing as a weapon that could threaten their power by disseminating protests against their rule. They sought to control the printed word by controlling those who wrote and printed it. Words that could be interpreted as disrespectful or antagonistic to government were declared illegal and suppressed. The licensing of printers was one effective method of government control—to retain his license, the printer could print only material approved by the rulers. This constituted prior restraint, a fundamental form of censorship.

Part Two opens with excerpts from famous papers and reprints of trials that trace the emergence of free expression in print, beginning with John Milton's rousing statement in his *Areopagitica* published in 1644, "Give me the liberty to know, to utter, and to argue freely according to conscience, above all liberties." Concepts of the right to criticize government and public men flowered in the American colonies. A legal milestone in the prolonged battle for freedom to print the truth was the acquittal by a jury of John Peter Zenger, a printer in New York, when he was put on trial in 1735 for seditious libel because he printed material critical of the royal government. In this section are key excerpts from the closing address to the jury by Andrew Hamilton, Zenger's attorney.

Freedom of the press became a bedrock principle of American law when it was included in the First Amendment to the Constitution of the United States. From that day to this, those who find the amendment interfering with their personal ambitions and blocking their plans have tried to restrict its application. An unending fight is necessary to see that its intent is not eroded in practice.

In 1981 The United States observed the fiftieth anniversary of the handing down by the Supreme Court of its decission in the case of *Near* v. *Minnesota*. This has become known as the landmark decision on prior restraint, and the bedrock case ensuring the press the protection of the First Amendment. In the half century since 1931 the courts have looked to Chief Justice Charles Evans Hughes' decision in *Near* for guidance on First Amendment challenges, notably during the Pentagon Papers crisis of 1971. Highlights of the *Near* v. *Minnesota* decision are presented here.

With this philosophical and legal base laid, the remaining selections in Part Two examine the development and present functioning of the print media in the United States. In colonial days, the weekly newspaper was the primary vehicle for spreading printed news and opinion. At the end of the eighteenth century daily newspapers emerged, as populations of Eastern seaboard cities grew sufficiently to make their publication economical. Books and magazines examined news and ideas at greater length, and entertained their readers with fiction that sometimes portrayed social trends and national moods more penetratingly than did the news stories of the day. Press associations came into being to supply newspapers with stories from other cities, and syndicates arose to provide entertainment, fact, and opinion features.

Many newspapers and magazines that have helped to shape American thought reflect the strong personalities of those who edit, publish, and write for them. Size of circulation isn't essential: often the words of the editor are more powerful than the vehicle in which they appear; William Allen White achieved national fame while writing in a newspaper with a circulation of only two thousand in a remote Kansas prairie town. Biographical sketches of White and other men and women who have won distinction in the newspaper, magazine, and book fields are included in this part. The purpose of these sketches is two-fold: to emphasize the enormous amount of individual effort behind the printed products we hold in our hands, and to provide a look at those who provide that effort.

The persons whose careers are described cannot be called typical; their special skills have raised them far above the ordinary level. Yet other individuals of marked achievement might just as readily have been chosen. These are but a sample for young aspirants of what individuals can achieve in media careers.

While attention usually is focused on the metropolitan dailies, thousands of weekly newspapers form a vigorous share of the publishing scene, reporting in detail the everyday affairs of life in their limited areas of circulation. Occasionally one achieves national attention.

The weekly Point Reyes, California *Light,* a splendid example, surprised the newspaper world in 1979 by winning the Pulitzer Prize for Public Service. A young husband and wife team, David and Catherine Mitchell, were honored over the massive staffs of the big city dailies for more than eighty articles and editorials they published about Synanon, the controversial drug rehabilitation center six miles north of Point Reyes, which was involved in allegations of terrorism. Included here is an article examining how the Mitchells operated their newspaper, written a short time before their Pulitzer award was announced.

Diversity within the print media is immense. While editors like the Mitchells worked within the small perimeter of a weekly newspaper, other journalists report stories of global significance from the White House or fly around the country with presidential candidates; still others make critical editorial decisions on the publication of stories, organize their staffs to cover disasters, or, like Garry B. Trudeau drawing "Doonesbury," work individually in quiet corners to produce material that will be seen in newspapers and magazines or published in book form. The pages that follow offer glimpses of these practitioners and decision-makers, whose efforts flourish under the protection of the press freedoms won so strenuously by their predecessors.

Section 3

HISTORIC
PRESS
FREEDOMS

The statements in this section are landmarks in
development of the free press principle, by
Milton in the mid-seventeenth century, from the
Zenger trial and the Bill of Rights in the
eighteenth century, by early leaders of the
American Republic, and by Chief Justice Charles
Evans Hughes in the twentieth century.

SELECTIONS
FROM *AREOPAGITICA*
John Milton

In 1644 the English poet was threatened with prosection for unlicensed printing after he published a pamphlet in which he advocated freedom of divorce. In response he wrote in his eloquent essay, quoted in part here: "Let her and falsehood grapple; who ever knew truth put to the worse, in a free and open encounter?"

. . . Truth indeed came once into the world with her divine master, and was a perfect shape most glorious to look on: but when he ascended, and his apostles after him were laid asleep, then straight arose a wicked race of deceivers, who as that story goes of the Egyptian Typhon with his conspirators, how they dealt with the good Osiris, took the virgin Truth, hewed her lovely form into a thousand pieces, and scattered them to the four winds. From that time ever since, the sad friends of Truth, such as dare appear, imitating the careful search that Isis made for the mangled body of Osiris, went up and down gathering up limb by limb still as they could find them. We have not yet found them all, Lords and Commons, nor ever shall do, till her Master's second coming; he shall bring together every joint and member, and shall mold them into an immortal feature of loveliness and perfection. Suffer not these licensing prohibitions to stand at every place of opportunity forbidding and disturbing them that continue seeking, that continue to do our obsequies to the torn body of our martyred saint. . . .

Methinks I see in my mind a noble and puissant nation rousing herself like a strong man after sleep, and shaking her invincible locks: Methinks I see her as an eagle mewing her mighty youth, and kindling her undazzled eyes at the full midday beam; purging and unscaling her long abused sight at the foundation itself of heavenly radiance, while the whole noise of timorous and flocking birds, with those also that love the twilight, flutter about, amazed at what she means, and in their envious gabble would prognosticate a year of sects and schisms.

What should ye do then, should ye suppress all this flowery crop of knowledge and new light sprung up and yet springing daily in

SOURCE: From *English Prose Writings of John Milton*, edited by Henry Morley (London: George Routledge and Sons, 1889), pp. 341–49.

this city, should ye set an oligarchy of twenty ingrossers over it, to bring a famine upon our minds again, when we shall know nothing but what is measured to us by their bushel? Believe it, Lords and Commons, they who counsel ye to such a suppressing, do as good as bid ye suppress yourselves; and I will soon show how. If it be desired to know the immediate cause of all this free writing and free speaking, there can not be assigned a truer than your own mild, and free, and human government: it is the liberty, Lords and Commons, which your own valorous and happy counsels have purchased us, liberty which is the nurse of all great wits; this is that which hath rarified and enlightened our spirits like the influence of heaven; this is that which hath enfranchised, enlarged and lifted up our apprehensions degrees above themselves. Ye can not make us now less capable, less knowing, less eagerly pursuing of the truth, unless ye first make yourselves, that made us so, less the lovers, less the founders of our true liberty. We can grow ignorant again, brutish, formal, and slavish, as ye found us; but ye then must first become that which ye can not be, oppressive, arbitrary, and tyrannous, as they were from whom ye have freed us. That our hearts are now more capacious, our thoughts more erected to the search and expectation of great and exact things, is the issue of your own virtue propagated in us; ye can not suppress that unless ye reinforce an abrogated and merciless law, that fathers may despatch at will their own children. And who shall then stick closest to ye, and excite others? not he who takes up arms for cote and conduct, and his four nobles of Danegelt. Although I dispraise not the defense of just immunities, yet love my peace better, if that were all. Give me the liberty to know, to utter, and to argue freely according to conscience, above all liberties.

What would be best advised then, if it be found so hurtful and so unequal to suppress opinions for the newness, or the unsuitableness to a customary acceptance, will not be my task to say; I only shall repeat what I have learned from one of your own honorable number, a right noble and pious lord, who had he not sacrificed his life and fortunes to the church and commonwealth, we had not now missed and bewailed a worthy and undoubted patron of this argument. Ye know him I am sure; yet I for honor's sake, and may it be eternal to him, shall name him, the Lord Brook. He writing of episcopacy, and by the way treating of sects and schisms, left ye his vote, or rather now the last words of his dying charge, which I know will ever be of dear and honored regard with ye, so full of meekness and breathing charity, that next to his last testament, who bequeathed love and peace to his disciples, I can not call to mind where I have read or heard words more mild and peaceful. He there

John Milton

exhorts us to hear with patience and humility those, however they be miscalled, that desire to live purely, in such a use of God's ordinances, as the best guidance of their conscience gives them, and to tolerate them, though in some disconformity to ourselves. The book itself will tell us more at large being published to the world, and dedicated to the Parliament by him who both for his life and for his death deserves, that what advice he left be not laid by without perusal.

And now the time in special is, by privilege to write and speak what may help to the further discussion of matters in agitation. The temple of Janus with his two controversial faces might now not unsignificantly be set open. And though all the winds of doctrine were let loose to play upon the earth, so truth be in the field, we do injuriously by licensing and prohibiting to misdoubt her strength. Let her and falsehood grapple; who ever knew truth put to the worse, in a free and open encounter? Her confuting is the best and surest suppressing. He who hears what praying there is for light and clearer knowledge to be sent down among us, would think of other matters to be constituted beyond the discipline of Geneva, framed and fabricated already to our hands. Yet when the new light which we beg for shines in upon us, there be who envy, and oppose, if it come not first in at their casements. What a collusion is this, whenas we are exhorted by the wise man to use diligence, *to seek for wisdom as for hidden treasures early and late*, that another order shall enjoin us to know nothing but by statute. When a man hath been laboring the hardest labor in the deep mines of knowledge, hath furnished out his findings in all their equipage, drawn forth his reasons as it were a battle ranged, scattered and defeated all objections in his way, calls out his adversary into the plain, offers him the advantage of wind and sun, if he please; only that he may try the matter by dint and argument, for his opponents then to skulk, to lay ambushments, to keep a narrow bridge of licensing where the challenger should pass, though it be valor enough in soldiership, is but weakness and cowardice in the wars of truth. For who knows not that truth is strong next to the Almighty; she needs no policies, no stratagems, no licensings to make her victorious, those are the shifts and the defenses that error uses against her power: give her but room, and do not bind her when she sleeps, for then she speaks not true, as the old Proteus did, who spake oracles only when he was caught and bound, but then rather she turns herself into all shapes, except her own, and perhaps tunes her voice according to the time, as *Micaiah* did before Ahab, until she be adjured into her own likeness. Yet is it not impossible that she may have more shapes than one. What else is all that rank of things indifferent, wherein truth may be on this side, or on the other, without being unlike herself? What but a vain shadow else is the abolition of those *ordinances, that handwriting nailed to the cross*, what great purchase is this Christian liberty which *Paul* so often boasts of? His doctrine is, that he who eats or eats not, regards a day, or regards it not, may do either to the Lord. How many other things might be tolerated in peace, and left to conscience, had we but charity, and were it not the chief stronghold of our hypocrisy to be ever judging one another . . .

THE JOHN PETER ZENGER TRIAL

Excerpts from Andrew Hamilton's Address to the Jury

Hamilton, a prominent, elderly Philadelphia attorney, agreed to defend Zenger in 1735 after many New York attorneys had refused to take the case. Moved by Hamilton's plea, the jury bravely found Zenger not guilty of seditious libel, a verdict enshrining printer Zenger and his New York *Weekly Journal*.

Gentlemen; The Danger is great, in Proportion to the Mischief that may happen, through our too great Credulity. A proper Confidence in a Court, is commendable; but as the verdict (what ever it is) will be yours, you ought to refer no Part of your Duty to the Discretion of other Persons. If you should be of the Opinion, that there is no Falshood in Mr. *Zenger's* Papers, you will, nay (pardon me for the Expression) you ought to say so; because you don't know whether others (I mean the Court) may be of that Opinion. It is your Right to do so, and there is much depending upon your Resolution, as well as upon your Integrity.

The loss of liberty to a generous Mind, is worse than Death; and yet we know there have been those in all Ages, who for the sake of Preferment, or some imaginary Honour, have freely lent a helping Hand, to oppress, nay to destroy their Country. This brings to my Mind that saying of the immortal *Brutus*, when he look'd upon the Creatures of *Caesar*, who were very great Men, but by no Means good Men. "You Romans *said* Brutus, *if yet I may call you so, consider what you are doing; remember that you are assisting Caesar to forge those very chains, which one day he will make your selves wear.*" This is what every Man (that values Freedom) ought to consider: He should act by Judgment and not by Affection or Self-Interest; for, where those prevail, No Ties of either Country or Kindred are regarded; as upon the other Hand, the Man, who loves his Country, prefers it's Liberty to all other Considerations, well knowing that without Liberty, Life is a Misery. . . .

Power may justly be compar'd to a great River, while kept within it's due Bounds, is both Beautiful and Useful; but when it overflows it's Banks, it is then too impetuous to be stemm'd, it bears down all

---

SOURCE: Text of trial printed by Zenger's shop in 1736, as reprinted in *Interpretations of Journalism*, edited by Frank Luther Mott and Ralph D. Casey (New York: F. S. Crofts & Co., 1937).

Artist's conception of the Zenger trial courtroom scene

before it, and brings Destruction and Desolation wherever it comes. If then this is the Nature of Power, let us at least do our Duty, and like wise Men (who value Freedom) use our utmost Care to support Liberty, the only Bulwark against lawless Power, which in all Ages has sacrificed to it's wild Lust and boundless Ambition, the Blood of the best Men that ever liv'd.

I hope to be pardon'd Sir for my Zeal upon this Occasion; it is an old and wise Caution. *That when our Neighbours House is on Fire, we ought to take Care of our own.* For tho' Blessed be God, I live in a Government where Liberty is well understood, and freely enjoy'd: yet Experience has shewn us all (I'm sure it has to me) that a bad Precedent in one Government, is soon set up for an Authority in another; and therefore I cannot but think it mine, and every Honest Man's Duty, that (while we pay all due Obedience to Men in Authority) we ought at the same Time to be upon our Guard against Power, wherever we apprehend that it may affect ourselves or our Fellow-Subjects.

I am truly very unequal to such an undertaking on many Accounts. And you see I labour under the Weight of many Years, and am born down with great Infirmities of Body; yet Old and Weak as I am, I should think it my Duty if required, to go to the utmost Part of the Land, where my Service cou'd be of any Use in assisting to quench the Flame of Prosecutions upon Informations, set on Foot by the Government, to deprive a People of the Right of Remonstrating (and complaining too), of the arbitrary Attempts of Men in Power.

Men who injure and oppress the People under their Administration
provoke them to cry out and complain; and then make that very
Complaint the Foundation for new Oppressions and Prosecutions. I
wish I could say there were no Instances of this Kind. But to
conclude; the Question before the Court and you Gentlemen of the
Jury, is not of small nor private Concern, it is not the Cause of the
poor Printer, nor of *New-York* alone, which you are now trying: No!
It may in it's Consequence, affect every Freeman that lives under a
British Government on the main of *America*. It is the best Cause. It is
the Cause of Liberty; and I make no Doubt but your upright
Conduct, this Day, will not only entitle you to the Love and Esteem of
your Fellow-Citizens; but every Man who prefers Freedom to a Life
of slavery will bless and honour You, as Men who have baffled the
Attempt of Tyranny; and by an impartial and uncorrupt Verdict,
have laid a noble Foundation for securing to ourselves, our Posterity
and our Neighbours, That, to which Nature and the Laws of our
Country have given us a Right,—the Liberty—both of exposing and
opposing arbitrary Power (in these Parts of the World, at least) by
speaking and writing Truth.

THE CONSTITUTIONAL FOUNDATION

Here are printed not only the First Amendment, but also the Fourth and
Sixth Amendments, because they too are considered by courts that are
called upon to determine the rights and freedoms of the American press.

The First Amendment to the United States Constitution

Congress shall make no law respecting an establishment of religion, or prohibiting the free exercise thereof; or abridging the
freedom of speech, or of the press; or the right of the people
peaceably to assemble, and to petition the Government for a
redress of grievances.

The Fourth Amendment

The right of the people to be secure in their persons, houses, papers,
and effects, against unreasonable searches and seizures, shall not
be violated, and no Warrants shall issue, but upon probable cause,

---

SOURCE: The First, Fourth, and Sixth Amendments to the United States Constitution.

supported by Oath or affirmation, and particularly describing the place to be searched, and the persons or things to be seized.

The Sixth Amendment
In all criminal prosecutions, the accused shall enjoy the right to a speedy and public trial, by an impartial jury of the State and district wherein the crime shall have been committed, which district shall have been previously ascertained by law, and to be informed of the nature and cause of the accusation; to be confronted with the witnesses against him; to have compulsory process for obtaining witnesses in his favor, and to have the Assistance of Counsel for his defense.

THE IMPORTANCE
OF PRESS FREEDOM
Thomas Jefferson
This selection and the next are by two renowned early American leaders, Thomas Jefferson and Alexander Hamilton, who were political opponents in the first years of this Republic. Jefferson was considered the spokesman of the liberals, Hamilton the champion of the conservatives. But they agreed on major elements of press freedom. Jefferson was continually and viciously attacked by the free press he here unhesitatingly defends.

From a Letter to Edward Carrington, Paris, January 16, 1787
. . . The people are the only censors of their governors; and even their errors will tend to keep these to the true principles of their institution. To punish these errors too severely would be to suppress the only safe-guard of the public of the public liberty. The way to prevent these irregular interpositions of the people is to give them full information of their affairs thro' the channel of the public papers, & to contrive that those papers should penetrate the whole mass of the people. The basis of our governments being the opinion of the people, the first object should be to keep that right; and were it left to me to decide whether we should have a government without newspapers or newspapers without a government, I should not hesitate to prefer the latter. But I should mean that every man should

SOURCE: From *The Writings of Thomas Jefferson*, edited by Julian P. Boyd (Princeton, N.J.: Princeton University Press, 1952), XII, 48–49; and edited by Paul Leicester Ford (New York: G. P. Putnam's Sons, 1892–1899), VIII, 346–47.

Thomas Jefferson

receive those papers & be capable of reading them. I am convinced that those societies (as the Indians) which live without government enjoy in their general mass an infinitely greater degree of happiness than those who live under the European governments. Among the former, public opinion is in the place of law, & restrains morals as powerfully as laws ever did anywhere. Among the latter, under pretence of governing they have divided their nations into two classes, wolves & sheep. I do not exaggerate. This is a true picture of Europe. Cherish therefore the spirit of our people, and keep alive their attention. Do not be too severe upon their errors, but reclaim them by enlightening them.

From the Second Inaugural Address, Washington, March 4, 1804
During this course of administration, and in order to disturb it, the artillery of the press has been levelled against us, charged with whatsoever its licentiousness could devise or dare. These abuses of an institution so important to freedom and science are deeply to be

regretted, inasmuch as they tend to lessen its usefulness, and to sap its safety; they might, indeed, have been corrected by the wholesome punishments reserved and provided by the laws of the several States against falsehood and defamation; but public duties more urgent press on the time for public servants, and the offenders have therefore been left to find their punishment in the public indignation.

Nor was it uninteresting to the world, that an experiment should be fairly and fully made, whether freedom of discussion, unaided by power, is not sufficient for the propagation and protection of truth—whether a government, conducting itself in the true spirit of its constitution, with zeal and purity, and doing no act which it would be unwilling the whole world should witness, can be written down by falsehood and defamation. The experiment has been tried; you have witnessed the scene; our fellow citizens have looked on, cool and collected; they saw the latent source from which these outrages proceeded; they gathered around their public functionaries, and when the constitution called them to the decision by suffrage, they pronounced their verdict, honorable to those who had served them, and consolatory to the friend of man, who believes he may be intrusted with his own affairs.

No inference is here intended, that the laws, provided by the State against false and defamatory publications, should not be enforced; he who has time, renders a service to public morals and public tranquillity, in reforming these abuses by the salutary coercions of the law; but the experiment is noted, to prove that, since truth and reason have maintained their ground against false opinions in league with false facts, the press, confined to truth, needs no other legal restraint; the public judgment will correct false reasonings and opinions, on a full hearing of all parties; and no other definite line can be drawn between the inestimable liberty of the press and its demoralizing licentiousness. If there be still improperties which this rule would not restrain, its supplement must be sought in the censorship of public opinion.

THE RIGHT
TO CRITICIZE PUBLIC MEN

Alexander Hamilton

In 1804 Hamilton served as defense attorney for Harry Croswell, who had been indicted for a libel on Thomas Jefferson, then President of the United States. This is an excerpt from Hamilton's argument before the Supreme Court of the State of New York.

. . . After these preliminary observations, and before I advance to the full discussion of this question, it may be necessary for the safety and accuracy of investigation, a little to define what this liberty of the press is, for which we contend, and which the present doctrines of those opposed to us, are, in our opinions, calculated to destroy.

The liberty of the press consists, in my idea, in publishing the truth, from good motives and for justifiable ends, though it reflect on government, on magistrates, or individuals. If it be not allowed, it excludes the privilege of canvassing men, and our rulers. It is in vain to say, you may canvass measures. This is impossible without the right of looking to men. To say that measures can be discussed, and that there shall be no bearing on those who are the authors of those measures, cannot be done. The very end and reason of discussion would be destroyed. Of what consequence to show its object? Why is it to be thus demonstrated, if not to show, too, who is the author? It is essential to say, not only that the measure is bad and deleterious, but to hold up to the people who is the author, that, in this our free and elective government, he may be removed from the seat of power. If this be not to be done, then in vain will the voice of the people be raised against the inroads of tyranny. For, let a party but get into power, they may go on from step to step, and, in spite of canvassing their measures, fix themselves firmly in their seats, especially as they are never to be reproached for what they have done. This abstract mode, in practice can never be carried into effect. But, . . . if the power be allowed, the liberty, for which I contend, will operate as a salutary check. In speaking thus for the freedom of the press, I do not say there ought to be an unbridled license; or that the characters of men who are good, will naturally tend eternally to support themselves. I do not stand here to say that no shackles are to be laid on this license.

SOURCE: *People* v. *Croswell* (1804), as reprinted in *Freedom of the Press from Zenger to Jefferson*, edited by Leonard W. Levy (Indianapolis, Indiana: Bobbs–Merrill, 1966).

I consider this spirit of abuse and calumny as the pest of society. I know the best of men are not exempt from the attacks of slander. Though it pleased God to bless us with the first of characters, and though it has pleased God to take him from us, and this band of calumniators, I say, that falsehood eternally repeated would have affected even his name. Drops of water, in long and continued succession, will wear out adamant. This, therefore, cannot be endured. It would be to put the best and the worst on the same level. . . .

Some observations have, however, been made in opposition to these principles. It is said, that as no man rises at once high into office, every opportunity of canvassing his qualities and qualifications is afforded, without recourse to the press; that his first election ought to stamp the seal of merit on his name. This, however, is to forget how often the hypocrite goes from stage to stage of public fame, under false array, and how often, when men attain the last object of their wishes, they change from that which they seemed to be; that men, the most zealous reverers of the people's rights, have, when placed on the highest seat of power, become their most deadly oppressors. It becomes, therefore, necessary to observe the actual conduct of those who are thus raised up. . . .

NEAR v. MINNESOTA: LANDMARK DECISION ON PRIOR RESTRAINT
Chief Justice Charles Evans Hughes

The Minnesota "gag-law" of 1925, permitting suppression of malicious and scandalous publications, was used by state courts to close J. M. Near's controversial *Saturday Press*. The United States Supreme Court in its 1931 5−4 decision for the first time applied the freedom of the press guarantees of the First Amendment against the states through the due process clause of the Fourteenth Amendment. Chief Justice Hughes ruled the Minnesota law unconstitutional because it permitted prior restraint upon publication, setting the tone for later twentieth century decisions. Excerpts of the ruling follow.

. . . If we cut through mere details of procedure, the operation and effect of the statute in substance is that public authorities may bring the owner or publisher of a newspaper or periodical before a judge

---

SOURCE: *Near v. Minnesota ex rel. Olson,* 283 U.S. 697 (1931).

upon a charge of conducting a business of publishing scandalous and defamatory matter—in particular that the matter consists of charges against public officers of official dereliction—and unless the owner or publisher is able and disposed to bring competent evidence to satisfy the judge that the charges are true and are published with good motives and for justifiable ends, his newspaper or periodical is suppressed and further publication is made punishable as a contempt. This is of the essence of censorship.

The question is whether a statute authorizing such proceedings in restraint of publication is consistent with the conception of the liberty of the press as historically conceived and guaranteed. In determining the extent of the constitutional protection, it has been generally, if not universally, considered that it is the chief purpose of the guaranty to prevent previous restraints upon publication. The struggle in England, directed against the legislative power of the licenser, resulted in renunciation of the censorship of the press. The liberty deemed to be established was thus described by Blackstone: "The liberty of the press is indeed essential to the nature of a free state; but this consists in laying no *previous* restraints upon publications, and not in freedom from censure for criminal matter when published. Every freeman has an undoubted right to lay what sentiments he pleases before the public; to forbid this, is to destroy the freedom of the press; but if he publishes what is improper, mischievous or illegal, he must take the consequence of his own temerity." (4 Bl. Com. 151, 152; see Story on the Constitution, secs. 1884, 1889.) The distinction was early pointed out between the extent of the freedom with respect to censorship under our constitutional system and that enjoyed in England. Here, as Madison said, "the great and essential rights of the people are secured against legislative as well as against executive ambition. They are secured, not by laws paramount to prerogative, but by constitutions paramount to laws. This security of the freedom of the press requires that it should be exempt not only from previous restraint by the Executive, as in Great Britain, but from legislative restraint also." (Report on the Virginia Resolutions, Madison's Works, vol. IV, p. 543.) This Court said, in *Patterson* v. *Colorado* (205 U.S. 454, 462): "In the first place, the main purpose of such constitutional provisions is 'to prevent all such *previous restraints* upon publications as had been practiced by other governments,' and they do not prevent the subsequent punishment of such as may be deemed contrary to the public welfare. (*Commonwealth* v. *Blanding*, 3 Pick. 304, 313, 314; *Respublica* v. *Oswald*, 1 Dallas, 319, 325.) The preliminary freedom extends as well to the false as to the true; the subsequent punishment may extend as well to the true as to the false. This was the law of criminal libel apart from statute in most cases, if not in all. (*Commonwealth* v. *Blanding, ubi sup.;* 4 Bl. Com. 150.)" . . .

The objection has also been made that the principle as to immunity from previous restraint is stated too broadly, if every such restraint is deemed to be prohibited. That is undoubtedly true; the protection even as to previous restraint is not absolutely unlimited. But the limitation has been recognized only in exceptional cases. "When a nation is at war many things that might be said in time of peace are such a hindrance to its effort that their utterance will not be endured so long as men fight and that no Court could regard them as protected by any constitutional right." (*Schenck* v. *United States,* 249 U.S. 47, 52.) No one would question but that a government might prevent actual obstruction to its recruiting service or the publication of the sailing dates of transports or the number and location of troops. On similar grounds, the primary requirements of decency may be enforced against obscene publications. The security of the community life may be protected against incitements to acts of violence and the overthrow by force of orderly government. The constitutional guaranty of free speech does not "protect a man from an injunction against uttering words that may have all the effect of force." (*Gompers* v. *Buck Stove & Range Co.,* 221 U.S. 418, 439. *Schenck* v. *United States, supra.*) These limitations are not applicable here. Nor are we now concerned with questions as to the extent of authority to prevent publications in order to protect private rights according to the principles governing the exercise of the jurisdiction of courts of equity.

The exceptional nature of its limitations places in a strong light the general conception that liberty of the press, historically considered and taken up by the Federal Constitution, has meant, principally although not exclusively, immunity from previous restraints or censorship. The conception of the liberty of the press in this country had broadened with the exigencies of the colonial period and with the efforts to secure freedom from oppressive administration. That liberty was especially cherished for the immunity it afforded from previous restraint of the publication of censure of public officers and charges of official misconduct. . . .

The fact that for approximately one hundred and fifty years there has been almost an entire absence of attempts to impose previous restraints upon publications relating to the malfeasance of public officers is significant of the deep-seated conviction that such restraints would violate constitutional right. Public officers, whose character and conduct remain open to debate and free discussion in the press, find their remedies for false accusations in actions under libel laws providing for redress and punishment, and not in proceedings to restrain the publication of newspapers and periodicals. The general principle that the constitutional guaranty of the liberty of the press gives immunity from previous restraints has been approved in many decisions under the provisions of state constitutions. . . .

The statute in question cannot be justified by reason of the fact that the publisher is permitted to show, before injunction issues, that the matter published is true and is published with good motives and for justifiable ends. If such a statute, authorizing suppression and injunction on such a basis, is constitutionally valid, it would be equally permissible for the legislature to provide that at any time the publisher of any newspaper could be brought before a court, or even an administrative officer (as the constitutional protection may not be regarded as resting on mere procedural details) and required to produce proof of the truth of his publication, or of what he intended to publish, and of his motives, or stand enjoined. If this can be done, the legislature may provide machinery for determining in the complete exercise of its discretion what are justifiable ends and restrain publication accordingly. And it would be but a step to a complete system of censorship. The recognition of authority to impose previous restraint upon publication in order to protect the community against the circulation of charges of misconduct, and especially of official misconduct, necessarily would carry with it the admission of the authority of the censor against which the constitutional barrier was erected. The preliminary freedom, by virtue of the very reason for its existence, does not depend, as this Court has said, on proof of truth. (*Patterson* v. *Colorado, supra.*) . . .

For these reasons we hold the statute, so far as it authorized the proceedings in this action under clause (b) of section one, to be an infringement of the liberty of the press guaranteed by the Fourteenth Amendment. We should add that this decision rests upon the operation and effect of the statute, without regard to the question of the truth of the charges contained in the particular periodical. The fact that the public officers named in this case, and those associated with the charges of official dereliction, may be deemed to be impeccable, cannot affect the conclusion that the statute imposes an unconstitutional restraint upon publication.

Judgment reversed.

Section 4

GROWTH
OF THE PRINT
MEDIA

This section opens with statements about the roles of newspapers by Robert E. Park, Samuel Bowles, and Benjamin Franklin. Next the careers of several historically significant newspaper men and women are presented. Then the special roles of two unique national newspapers, the *Christian Science Monitor* and *Wall Street Journal*, are examined. The concluding articles look at the pioneering achievements in the magazine field of John H. Johnson, publisher of *Ebony*, and Gloria Steinem, editor of *Ms*.

THE NATURAL HISTORY
OF THE NEWSPAPER

Robert E. Park

This 1925 statement by a famed sociologist has become a basic definition
of the social growth and social roles of the newspaper. What he said about
the press, the only important medium of that time, has its parallels
in the roles of today's broadcast media.

The newspaper has a history; but it has, likewise, a natural history.
The press, as it exists, is not, as our moralists sometimes seem to
assume, the willful product of any little group of living men. On the
contrary, it is the outcome of a historic process in which many
individuals participated without foreseeing what the ultimate product of their labors was to be.

The newspaper, like the modern city, is not wholly a rational
product. No one sought to make it just what it is. In spite of all the
efforts of individual men and generations of men to control it and to
make it something after their own heart, it has continued to grow
and change in its own incalculable ways.

The type of newspaper that exists is the type that has survived
under the conditions of modern life. The men who may be said to
have made the modern newspaper—James Gordon Bennett,
Charles A. Dana, Joseph Pulitzer, and William Randolph Hearst—
are the men who discovered the kind of paper that men and women
would read and had the courage to publish it.

The natural history of the press is the history of the surviving
species. It is an account of the conditions under which the existing
newspaper has grown up and taken form.

A newspaper is not merely printed. It is circulated and read.
Otherwise it is not a newspaper. The struggle for existence, in the
case of the newspaper, has been a struggle for circulation. The
newspaper that is not read ceases to be an influence in the
community. The power of the press may be roughly measured by
the number of people who read it.

The growth of great cities has enormously increased the size of
the reading public. Reading, which was a luxury in the country, has
become a necessity in the city. In the urban environment literacy is

SOURCE: From Robert E. Park, Ernest W. Burgess, and Roderick D. McKenzie, *The
City* (Chicago: University of Chicago Press, 1925), Chapter IV. Copyright 1925 by
the University of Chicago Press. Reprinted by permission.

almost as much a necessity as speech itself. That is one reason there are so many foreign-language newspapers.

Mark Villchur, editor of the *Russkoye Slovo*, New York City, asked his readers how many of them had read newspapers in the old country. He found that out of 312 correspondents only 16 had regularly read newspapers in Russia; ten others from time to time read newspapers in the Volast, the village administration center, and twelve were subscribers to weekly magazines. In America all of them were subscribers or readers of Russian newspapers.

This is interesting because the immigrant has had, first and last, a profound influence on the character of our native newspapers. How to bring the immigrant and his descendants into the circle of newspaper readers has been one of the problems of modern journalism.

The immigrant who has, perhaps, acquired the newspaper habit from reading a foreign-language newspaper is eventually attracted to the native American newspapers. They are for him a window looking out into the larger world outside the narrow circle of the immigrant community in which he has been compelled to live. The newspapers have discovered that even men who can perhaps read no more than the headlines in the daily press will buy a Sunday paper to look at the pictures.

It is said that the most successful of the Hearst papers, the New York *Evening Journal*, gains a new body of subscribers every six years. Apparently it gets its readers mainly from immigrants. They graduate into Mr. Hearst's papers from the foreign-language press, and when the sensationalism of these papers begins to pall, they acquire a taste for some soberer journals. At any rate, Mr. Hearst has been a great Americanizer.

In their efforts to make the newspaper readable to the least-instructed reader, to find in the daily news material that would thrill the crudest intelligence, publishers have made one important discovery. They have found that the difference between the high-brow and the low-brow, which once seemed so profound, is largely a difference in vocabularies. In short, if the press can make itself intelligible to the common man, it will have even less difficulty in being understood by the intellectual. The character of present-day newspapers has been profoundly influenced by this fact.

THE BRILLIANT MISSION
OF THE NEWSPAPER
Samuel Bowles

This leading nineteenth-century editor made a prophetic statement
reflecting his intense personal devotion to his nationally known small
Massachusetts daily and to the entire press.

The increase of facilities for the transmission of news brought in a
new era. The railroad car, the steamboat, and the magnetic
telegraph, have made neighborhood among widely dissevered
States, and the Eastern Continent is but a few days' journey
away.—These active and almost miraculous agencies have brought
the whole civilized world in contact. . . .

The appetite for news is one of those appetites that grows by what
it feeds on. . . . The mind accustomed to the gossip of nations,
cannot content itself with the gossip of families.

The tendency of this new state of things has, as yet, hardly
claimed a moment's consideration from the moralist and the
philosopher. Nations and individuals now stand immediately responsible to the world's opinion; and the world, interesting itself in
the grand events transpiring in its various parts, and among its
various parties, has become, and is still becoming, liberalized in
feeling, and, being called away from its exclusive home-field, has
forgotten, in its universal interests, the petty interests, feuds, gossips
and strifes of families and neighborhoods. The wonderful extension
of the field of vision; this compression of the human race into one
great family, must tend to identify its interests, sympathies and
motives.

The brilliant mission of the newspaper is not yet, and perhaps
may never be, perfectly understood. It is, and is to be, the high
priest of History, the vitalizer of Society, the world's great informer,
the earth's high censor, the medium of public thought and opinion,
and the circulating life blood of the whole human mind. It is the
great enemy of tyrants, and the right arm of liberty, and is destined,
more than any other agency, to melt and mould the jarring and
contending nations of the world into that one great brotherhood
which, through long centuries, has been the ideal of the Christian
and the philanthropist. Its mission has just commenced. A few years
more, and a great thought uttered within sight of the Atlantic, will
rise with the morrow's sun and shine upon millions of minds by the

---

SOURCE: From the Springfield *Republican*, Editorial, January 4, 1851.

side of the Pacific. The murmur of Asia's multitudes will be heard at
our doors; and laden with the fruit of all human thought and action,
the newspaper will be in every abode, the daily nourishment of
every mind.

AN APOLOGY
FOR PRINTERS
Benjamin Franklin

The most famed colonial printer and editor speaks up for all, and does so
with the pungent humor for which he is known. His defense of the freedom
of opinion is made more telling by his wittiness.

Being frequently censur'd and condemn'd by different Persons for
printing things which they say ought not to be printed, I have
sometimes thought it might be necessary to make a standing
Apology for my self, and publish it once a Year, to be read upon all
Occasions of that Nature. Much Business has hitherto hindered the
execution of this Design; but having very lately given extraordinary
Offence by printing an Advertisement with a certain N. B. at the End
of it, I find an Apology more particularly requisite at this Juncture,
tho' it happens when I have not yet Leisure to write such a Thing
in the proper Form, and can only in a loose manner throw
those Considerations together which should have been the Substance of it.

I request all who are angry with me on the Account of printing
things they don't like, calmly to consider these following Particulars.

1. That the Opinions of Men are almost as various as their Faces;
an Observation general enough to become a common Proverb, *So
many Men so many Minds.*

2. That the Business of Printing has chiefly to do with Mens
Opinions; most things that are printed tending to promote some, or
oppose others.

3. That hence arises the peculiar Unhappiness of that Business,
which other Callings are no way liable to; they who follow Printing
being scarce able to do any thing in their way of getting a Living,
which shall not probably give Offence to some, and perhaps to
many; whereas the Smith, the Shoemaker, the Carpenter, or the
Man of any other Trade, may work indifferently for People of all
Persuasions, without offending any of them: and the Merchant may

---

SOURCE: From the *Pennsylvania Gazette*, June 10, 1731.

The Pennſylvania GAZETTE.

Containing the freſheſt Ad- *vices Foreign and Domeſtick.*

PHILADELPHIA.

On Friday laſt the Governor ſent down to the Houſe of Repreſentatives the following MESSAGE, *in Anſwer to their* ADDRESS *of the 5th Inſtant.*

His Honour the Governor in Council to the Gentlemen of the Aſſembly.

GENTLEMEN,

YOUR dutiful Expreſſions of his Majeſty, your Gratitude for the many Bleſſings you enjoy under his Government, and the juſt Senſe you entertain of my Concern for the Safety of the Province, notwithſtanding our Difference of Opinion in other Matters, render your Addreſs very acceptable to me. I ſhould have thought my ſelf happy not to have been laid under a Neceſſity, by the Poſture of Affairs in *Europe*, of preſſing a Matter ſo diſagreeable to the Religious Sentiments of many of the Inhabitants of this Province ; but as I think my ſelf indiſpenſibly obliged by the Duty I owe to his Majeſty, in Diſcharge of the Truſt repoſed in me by your honourable Proprietors, and from a diſintereſted Regard for the Lives and Fortunes of the People under my Government, to warn you of the impending Danger, I hope you likewiſe, will have patience with me, and continue to entertain the ſame charitable Sentiments of my Intentions.

In my Speech to you at your firſt Meeting, I conſidered you as the Repreſentatives of the whole Body of the People, as a part of the Legiſlature, and as Proteſtants, and as ſuch I deſired you to turn your Thoughts upon the defenceleſs State of the Province, and to put yourſelves into ſuch a Condition, as becomes loyal Subjects to his Majeſty, and Lovers of your Religion and Liberties. As it did not become me to diſtinguiſh the particular Religious Perſuaſion of every Member of your Houſe, I could ſpeak of your Religion no otherwiſe, than in Contradiſtinction to the bloody Religion of *France* and *Spain* : But now, from what you yourſelves have declared, I muſt lament the unhappy Circumſtances of a Country, populous indeed, extenſive in its Trade, bleſſed with many natural Advantages, and capable of defending itſelf, but from a religious Principle of its Repreſentatives againſt bearing of Arms, ſubject to become the Prey of the firſt Invader, and more particularly of its powerful Neighbours, who are known to be well armed, regular in their Diſcipline, inured to Fatigue, and from thence capable of making long Marches, in Alliance with many Nations of *Indians*, and of a boundleſs Ambition.

Far be it from me to attempt the leaſt Invaſion on your Charter, or your Laws for Liberty of Conſcience, or to engage any Aſſembly in Meaſures that may introduce Perſecution for Conſcience-ſake. I have always been a profeſs'd Advocate for Liberty, both Civil and Religious, as the only rational Foundation of Society, and I truſt that no Station of Life will ever alter my Sentiments. Religion, where its Principles are not deſtructive to civil Society, is to be judged of by H I M only who is the Searcher of all Hearts, and I think it is as unreaſonable to perſecute Men for their Religious Opinions as for their Faces : But as the World is now circumſtanced, no Purity of Heart, no Set of religious Principles will protect us from an Enemy. Were we even to content ourſelves with Cottages, and the ſpontaneous Productions of Nature, they would rob us of of the very Soil : But where Treaſure is, they will be eager and watchful to break in and Spoil us of it. You yourſelves have ſeen the Neceſſity of acting in civil Affairs as Jurymen and Judges, to convict and condemn ſuch little Rogues to Death as break into your Houſes, and of acting in other Offices, where Force muſt neceſſarily be uſed for the Preſervation of the publick Peace : And are the Fruits of your Labour, and the Labour of your Forefathers reſerved only to be given up all at once to his Majeſty's Enemies, and the Enemies of your Religion and Liberties ? The Freeholders of the Province have choſen you for their Repreſentatives, and many of the principal Inhabitants have publickly petitioned you, that ſome Meaſures may be taken for the Defence of the Country : Where then will be the Inconſiſtency or Partiality of complying with what I have recommended and they have deſired ? Whatever Expence it ſhall be attended with, they will with Reaſon expect you ſhall bear your Proportion of it, as was done here in the Sum granted to Queen *Anne* for reducing *Canada*, and as has always been done by Men of the ſame Religious Perſuaſions in *Britain* for carrying on a War againſt the publick Enemy ; but none of them I believe are ſo unreaſonable as to expect, that ſuch as are principled againſt bearing Arms ſhall be compelled to act, or be puniſhed for not acting, againſt their Conſciences. Thus I am inſtructed by your Proprietors, in a manner moſt affectionate to you, to guard you from, and this is perfectly agreeable to my own Inclinations.

A Mind employed as mine has been about the Defence of the Province, has long ſince made it ſelf acquainted with

An issue of Benjamin Franklin's *Pennsylvania Gazette* and the famed colonial cartoon, "Join, or Die"

buy and sell with Jews, Turks, Hereticks and Infidels of all sorts, and get Money by every one of them, without giving Offence to the most orthodox, of any sort; or suffering the least Censure or Ill-will on the Account from any Man whatever.

4. That it is as unreasonable in any one Man or Set of Men to expect to be pleas'd with every thing that is printed, as to think that nobody ought to be pleas'd but themselves.

5. Printers are educated in the Belief, that when Men differ in Opinion, both Sides ought equally to have the Advantage of being heard by the Publick; and that when Truth and Error have fair Play, the former is always an overmatch for the latter: Hence they chearfully (sic.) serve all contending Writers that pay them well, without regarding on which side they are of the Question in Dispute.

6. Being thus continually employ'd in serving both Parties, Printers naturally acquire a vast Unconcernedness as to the right or wrong Opinions contain'd in what they print; regarding it only as the Matter of their daily labour: They print things full of Spleen and Animosity, with the utmost Calmness and Indifference, and without the least Ill-will to the Persons reflected on; who nevertheless unjustly think the Printer as much their Enemy as the Author, and join both together in their Resentment.

7. That it is unreasonable to imagine Printers approve of every thing they print, and to censure them on any particular thing accordingly; since in the way of their Business they print such great variety of things opposite and contradictory. It is likewise as unreasonable what some assert, "That Printers ought not to print any Thing but what they approve;" since if all of that Business should make such a Resolution, and abide by it, and End would thereby be put to Free Writing, and the World would afterwards have nothing to read but what happen'd to be the Opinions of Printers.

8. That if all Printers were determin'd not to print anything till they were sure it would offend no body, there would be very little printed.

9. That if they sometimes print vicious or silly things not worth reading, it may not be because they approve such things themselves, but because the People are so viciously and corruptly educated that good things are not encouraged. I have known a very numerous Impression of Robin Hood's Songs go off in this Province at 2s. per Book, in less than a Twelvemonth; when a small Quantity of David's Psalms (an excellent Version) have lain upon my Hands above twice the Time.

10. That notwithstanding what might be urg'd in behalf of a Man's being allow'd to do in the Way of his Business whatever he is paid for, Yet Printers do continually discourage the Printing of great

Numbers of bad things, and stifle them in the Birth. I my self have constantly refused to print any thing that might countenance Vice, or promote Immorality; tho' by complying in such Cases with the corrupt Taste of the Majority I might have got much Money. I have also always refus'd to print such things as might do real Injury to any Person, how much soever I have been solicited and tempted with Offers of Great Pay; and how much soever I have by refusing got the Ill-will of those who would have employ'd me. I have hitherto fallen under the Resentment of large Bodies of Men, for refusing absolutely to print any of their Party or Personal Reflections. In this Manner I have made my self many Enemies, and the constant Fatigue of denying is almost insupportable. But the Publick being unacquainted with all this, whenever the poor Printer happens either through Ignorance or much Persuasion, to do any thing that is generally thought worthy of Blame, he meets with no more Friend-ship or Favour on the above Account, than if there were no Merit in't at all. Thus, as Waller says,

> Poets lose half the Praise they would have got
> Were it but known what they discreetly blot;

Yet are censur'd for every bad Line found in their Works with the utmost Severity.

HISTORIC EDITORS
Edwin Emery, Warren K. Agee, and Phillip H. Ault
Threads of continuity in newspaper progress are found in the personalities of exceptionally able journalists. The editors of this book present here four dynamic nineteenth- and twentieth-century American editors.

MARGARET FULLER

Margaret Fuller was 30 years old in 1840 when she asserted leadership over a group of New England transcendentalists and Boston literary figures who were organizing to publish *The Dial*. When she died in a shipwreck ten years later, she had won her place as a literary figure, newspaperwoman, and feminist voice.

She became the first editor of *The Dial* through persistence, intellectual leadership, and ability to charm the participants in the drawing-room literary conversations of the transcendentalists.

SOURCE: This article was written expressly for this book.

Margaret Fuller

Competition was keen in Margaret Fuller's circle; when she yielded the editorship it was to Ralph Waldo Emerson, who gained it with some assistance from George Ripley. *The Dial* appeared only 16 times, yet it remains of great significance, for it included some of the most famous figures of American literature and journalism as contributors and editors.

By the time she left *The Dial,* Fuller was closely associated with another famous American journalist, Horace Greeley of the New York *Tribune,* who hobnobbed with the writers from Brook Farm and Boston. Fuller lived for a time in Greeley's home and from 1844 to 1846 she was a *Tribune* staff member. Her column of comment from Washington in this period earned her a place among early women journalists.

There was a strong streak of personal independence in Fuller, however, and she chose to go to Italy in 1846. One of her commissions was to write commentaries for the *Tribune.* But primarily she was engaged in her own writing for book publication.

In Italy Fuller fell in love, had a child, and was married. Accounts vary as to the sequence of events, but her choices were in the full twentieth-century ideal of feminist liberation. The great European revolutions of 1848 were in full swing and Italy was a seedbed of liberal political thought and revolutionary action. It was undoubtedly an exciting, heady life, but by 1850 Fuller was ready to return home and take part in the women's rights movement.

But off the New Jersey shore the ship bearing her home sank with Margaret Fuller, her child, her husband, and her manuscripts. Biographers have since struggled with the problem of her personal philosophy and her true place in American letters, unanswerable questions without the lost manuscripts that would show her development in those extraordinary European years. Nevertheless, she won a clear place in American letters and journalism with *The Dial* and her work for the *Tribune*.

HENRY W. GRADY

Henry W. Grady, a brilliant reporter and managing editor of the Atlanta *Constitution*, achieved even greater fame as an orator-statesman whose speeches about the New South in the 1880s helped destroy the lingering animosities of the Civil War and to reestablish cordial social and economic relations between the North and South.

Grady was born in Athens, Georgia, graduated from the University of Georgia, and then attended the University of Virginia for two years, mainly to enhance his debating skills. The sparkling style and humor of two news letters sent to the *Constitution* from Virginia earned him a further assignment, followed by employment as associate editor of the Rome, Georgia *Courier*.

In 1872 Grady bought a one-third interest in the Atlanta *Herald*. Although the paper was acclaimed as the liveliest and newsiest in the city, after four years it fell victim to the financial depression of 1873.

Grady got a job in 1876 as a Georgia reporter on space rates payments for the New York *Herald*. As a resourceful newsgatherer and a rapid, able writer, Grady won renown in covering the Florida canvassing board's deliberations late that year, when the Hayes-Tilden presidential election depended on the outcome, and in later obtaining the confessions of two men whose fraudulent manipulations had helped put Hayes in the White House.

The ebullient and genial young reporter made friends with the approximately 500 persons, both North and South, whom he interviewed. One was the president of the Louisville & Nashville Railroad, whose revelation to Grady of the railroad's pending expan-

Henry W. Grady

sion to Atlanta and thence to the coast won the reporter another scoop.

When the railroad president and Grady visited Cyrus W. Field, the millionaire merchant and promoter of the first trans-Atlantic cable, Field was so impressed with Grady that he loaned him $20,000 with which to buy a one-quarter interest in the *Constitution*. A wise investment in L. &. N. stock enabled Grady to repay the loan within two years.

As managing editor of the *Constitution* from 1880 to 1889, Grady built an extensive network of correspondents, developed special news departments, such as sports and society, and infused the staff with much of his own fire and enthusiasm. When a devastating earthquake struck Charleston, South Carolina, in August, 1886, Grady outsped other outside reporters to the scene and his accurate, colorful stories won wide attention.

Four months later, as the first Southerner invited to address the New England Society of New York, Grady delivered a stirring oration on "The New South" that found a place in history books and crystallized the concept of industrial advancement as a basis for the salvation of the South and reconciliation with the North. He concluded the address with a question:

Now, what answer has New England to this message? Will she permit the prejudice of war to remain in the hearts of the conquerors, when it has died in the hearts of the conquered? Will she transmit this prejudice to the next generation, that in their hearts which never felt the generous ardor of conflict it may perpetuate itself? Will she withhold, save in strained courtesy, the hand which straight from his soldier's heart Grant offered to Lee at Appomatox? Will she make the vision of a restored and happy people, which gathered above the couch of your dying captain, filling his heart with grace; touching his lips with praise, and glorifying his path to the grave—will she make this vision on which the last sigh of his expiring soul breathed a benediction, a cheat and delusion? If she does, the South, never abject in asking for comradeship, must accept with dignity its refusal; but if she does not refuse to accept in frankness and sincerity this message of good will and friendship, then will the prophecy of Webster, delivered in this very society forty years ago amid tremendous applause, become true, be verified in its fullest sense, when he said: "Standing hand to hand and clasping hands, we should remain united as we have been for sixty years, citizens of the same country, members of the same government, united, all united now and united forever."

Grady's death of typhus pneumonia at the age of 39 cut short his career when he had become the accepted prophet of the New South. A monument bearing his bust stands in downtown Atlanta, and his name is honored in the city's Henry W. Grady Hospital and the Henry W. Grady School of Journalism and Mass Communication at the University of Georgia, a particularly fitting memorial.

WILLIAM ALLEN WHITE

William Allen White was one of the most influential editors on the American scene during the first four decades of this century. He achieved eminence not on a metropolitan newspaper, as one would expect, but as editor of a small daily paper in Kansas. When he first won national attention with his views published in the Emporia *Gazette*, the paper had a circulation of only 2000 copies.

White came from the rural newspaper background common in the late nineteenth and early twentieth centuries. Cities were small, yet many of them had at least two newspapers struggling to survive where there was barely enough advertising and circulation revenue to support one.

William Allen White

White, the son of a doctor-storekeeper, was born in Emporia February 10, 1868. He first worked on his hometown country weekly at the age of twelve, as a printer's apprentice. He put himself through college with money earned as a printer and reporter. After graduation he became a reporter in Kansas City. By saving and borrowing, he scraped together $3000 in 1895 and purchased the Emporia *Gazette*, whose circulation was a mere 500. He was then 27 years old. The *Gazette* was his operating base for the rest of his life.

The extremely energetic White struggled to make the *Gazette* grow and worked nights and weekends at freelance writing. Earnings from his published short fiction and magazine articles helped to meet the newspaper's payroll.

The appearance of his name in national magazines also brought him professional attention. In those days, newspapers extensively reprinted, with proper credit, editorials and commentary their editors clipped from other papers they received as exchanges. White's writings were widely reprinted around Kansas. An especially fervent editorial of his, "What's the Matter With Kansas?," was circulated in this manner during the 1896 election. Republican Party leaders saw it and reproduced it for national distribution.

At that time newspaper editors were far more openly involved in party politics, thus it was not unusual that White became active among Kansas Republicans, advocating a liberal line that angered old-line conservatives. Through politics and writing, he became acquainted with national figures, developing close personal ties with President Theodore Roosevelt.

White represented the liberal Republican point of view throughout his career. Through wide travel and frequent talks with leaders in politics, he acquired a more international outlook than many other newspaper editors held in the years between the two World Wars. During the period before Pearl Harbor, when the United States was being drawn reluctantly out of its traditional isolationism, he was chairman of the Committee to Defend America by Aiding the Allies, an influential organization angrily condemned by isolationists.

White died late in World War II. He was active and effective at his editorial craft almost until the end.

ROBERT R. McCORMICK

For four decades Robert R. McCormick was the driving force building what he called the "World's Greatest Newspaper," the Chicago *Tribune*, undeniably one of the most controversial, as well as one of the most influential, American dailies.

McCormick was a grandson of *Tribune* founder Joseph Medill. He became publisher in 1914 when his brother Medill was elected senator from Illinois. Joseph Medill Patterson, a cousin, founded the New York *Daily News* in 1919 and another cousin, Eleanor Medill Patterson, bought the Washington *Times-Herald*. McCormick eventually took control of both of these papers, too.

But it was the *Tribune*, operating in what McCormick called "Chicagoland," that was his love. McCormick, known as "The Colonel" (a title won in World War I), presided in the Tribune Tower on Michigan Avenue and at his thousand-acre farm and estate named Cantigny for the major French battle in which he participated. McCormick was a student of military history and he looked at international affairs from that viewpoint. He was an ultraconservative isolationist who exhibited a deep distrust of foreigners, especially Englishmen, New York financiers, Eastern Establishment intellectuals and educators.

During the New Deal years, the *Tribune's* news and editorial

Robert R. McCormick

columns were devoted to attacks on President Franklin Roosevelt and almost all his domestic and international policies. Washington correspondents in 1936 voted the *Tribune* runner-up to the Hearst newspapers as "least fair and reliable." In 1948 an erroneous election result banner headline, "DEWEY DEFEATS TRUMAN," focused national attention on the *Tribune's* unprofessional conduct.

The Colonel never wavered, calling his editorial page "the hair on our chest." But after his death in 1955 and the passing of his key associates from positions of control, the *Tribune* found new direction. During the 1970s it moderated its editorial policies, drew better lines between news and opinion areas, returned to the vigorous local coverage that had been a *Tribune* hallmark, and won three Pulitzer Prizes for investigative reporting. In 1977 the "World's Greatest Newspaper" slogan disappeared as the *Tribune* settled down to a contest with Chicago's other surviving daily, the *Sun-Times*, for supremacy in Chicagoland.

A CONSERVATIVE APPLAUDS
THE *MONITOR*
John K. Andrews, Jr.

The *Christian Science Monitor* enjoys a national audience and the respect
of serious-minded readers who appreciate its international reporting in
depth and its lively coverage of national issues. While the paper is liberal in
tone, it here wins a conservative's plaudits.

You call yourself a conservative. Fine. You know what you believe
about man, his communities, and their government. You know what
candidates you like in the next election and where you stand on the
issues. But tell me this, my friend: What does your conservatism
have to say about journalism and the mass media?

Yes, you subscribe to the right journals, you belong to Accuracy
in Media, you've read Efron, Herschensohn, and Kevin Phillips. You
see exactly what the *Times* and Cronkite and the rest are trying to do
to this country and you'll be damned if you're going to let them do it.
Fine again; I'm with you. But do we realize just how largely all of our
activity and concern is confined to the question of access—control,
command—in an existing news industry under existing ground
rules? How much it takes for granted the more basic question of
process which underlies the whole system?

The news and information web of a democratic society is its
nervous system. Poison that system, drug it, drive it to excess—and
free institutions will sicken. A true conservatism, then, enjoins us to
the urgent work of conserving (in some cases restoring) fundamental
values of ends and means in the journalism of our time—a work
far deeper than the superficial Agnew skirmishes over news
balance and viewpoint that have preoccupied the Right for most of
a decade now.

What *kind* of print publications, what *kind* of electronic news
dissemination, will best equip the millions for citizenship under
ordered freedom, for decision-making in a mass democracy? What
image of man should the news industry hold? What should be its
operative definitions of truth, relevance, progress, justice, and so
on—not simply the definitions held to by individual players in the
game, but those built into the structure itself? And—once the
answers to such meta-issues begin to emerge—how can we perform
the Augean task of conserving and restoring our media without

violating exactly those values of diversity, liberty, noncoercion, and open markets (in ideas and in commerce) that we honor most?

One gentle but potent weapon available to anyone with a printing press (the citadel of broadcasting can be stormed later) is the contagiousness of success. This weapon is already being wielded in some quarters where many conservatives might not think to look, so my nomination for the most effective combatant of all may surprise you: it's the Boston-based *Christian Science Monitor.* As I see it, the *Monitor's* crisp, penetrating, dignified, yet lively coverage of events and trends presents not only a clear picture of the present day, but a prophetic glimpse ahead to what increasing numbers of America's news organs must become if we are to fashion the sort of future conservatives hope for. You and I may not agree with the paper on religion, and it may not agree with us on politics—yet we could find no firmer ally in our shared commitment to the profoundest kind of media reform.

Its offbeat name notwithstanding, the tabloid *Monitor* is a bona-fide hard-news daily newspaper. The paper's national coverage is strong. Its Washington bureau chief is Godfrey "Budge" Sperling, whose breakfast briefings have become one of the capital's most prestigious newsmaking forums. Garnish is provided by fifty-year man Richard Strout, a fine reporter, for all his liberal passion. Energetic bureaus are maintained in other major U.S. cities, and the *Monitor* tries to post its real stars to the London, Paris, Bonn, Moscow, and Tokyo offices. Keen observers report from Asia, Africa, the Midwest, and Latin America. Departments such as economics, education, the natural sciences, home and family, entertainment, literature, and the arts are covered more thoughtfully and conservatively, though in less mechanical detail, by the *Monitor's* specialists than by any metropolitan daily in my acquaintance.

The *Monitor's* op-ed articles offer a wide cross-section of writers, staff and guests, ranging from centrist to a bit on either side. The paper's own editorials, at their best, achieve a tough-minded idealism that is very constructive indeed. Compassion, political independence, courage, and the long view are *Monitor* trademarks. But that is *Monitor* editorials at their best. There *is* a fly in the ointment: not infrequently, blandness, a slightly preachy tone, and the cheery chirp of Polyanna manage to creep in as well. This can give *Monitor* pronouncements a shifting ideological coloration that is rather like Hubert Humphrey on some days, 21-karat Goldwater on others.

In one sense, perhaps, the *Monitor* is a cousin to some of the specialized kinds of journalism that have been profiled in these pages from time to time in M. J. Sobran's "The Printed Word": the news magazines, the journals of opinion, and the activist intellectual magazines like *Commentary* and *Commonweal* which serve major religious groups. But in another sense, the *Monitor* is one of a kind. Openly committed to a mission of spiritually leavening human thought—or, as founder Mary Baker Eddy put it, "to spread[ing] undivided the Science that operates unspent"—the paper seems to be more than holding its own in a society and an age that are deeply suspicious of such missions. It is operated as the direct arm of an unorthodox and sometimes prickly Christian church—yet it limits explicit religious articles to one brief inside-page piece per issue, and plays other news and comment straight, with no theological or sectarian propagandizing. It perennially ranks in or near newspapermen's own listing of the top-ten U.S. dailies, and wields an influence in the American Establishment out of all proportion to the size of its parent organization.

The *Monitor* has attained a respectably large international readership (current circulation is about 172,000 daily in North America, 16,000 for the weekly overseas edition), cutting clean across denominational lines. In recent years the paper has built a worldwide syndicate—some 177 other papers buy its material; a *Monitor* radio syndicate, established a year ago, numbers over 120 stations in the United States.

Have conservatives examined the consequence of today's all but unquestioned idea that "news" equals raw sensory reports of individual occurrences worldwide, and that "being informed" equals being passively bathed in wave after ceaseless wave of such reports throughout one's life?

The sociology of knowledge in our culture has become inseparable from an all-pervading *pathology* of the media—an unholy mixture of mesmeric voyeurism, subliminal suggestion, instant gratification, Faustian power-lust, cynical manipulation, bite-size factoids, and sheer tribal myths.

The significance of the *Monitor* here—not singlehanded, certainly, but as the pioneer of a new method—is in its potential for cutting clean to the bone, through news sociology and pathology alike, with an altogether fresh *epistemology* that is best known in our time under the denominational name of Christian Science.

The radical apostolic witness which the *Christian Science Monitor* bears by its works in the very midst of the pagan spectacle of modern mass communications is my reason for predicting that the paper will become an increasingly formidable regenerative force in journalism and the society at large.

THE WALL STREET JOURNAL

Warren K. Agee

The largest circulating newspaper in the United States avoids pictures and comics, uses old-fashioned headlines, and otherwise defies journalistic conventional wisdom, except for the basic injunction to offer well-written, important news.

There is no newspaper like *The Wall Street Journal*. Formerly a financial daily of limited scope, it has now broadened its editorial content and its advertising base, capitalized on technological and marketing innovations, and moved into the international field.

In appearance, as in content, virtually no paper resembles the *Journal*. On the assumption that photographs and large headlines simply waste space for its type of reader, the newspaper instead offers lucidly written summaries of national and world news and of developments in business and finance, along with comprehensive stories about a variety of subjects, expanded coverage of leisure and the arts, editorials with a conservative viewpoint, and market reports. With a readership high in educational, business, and professional achievements or ambitions, the *Journal* has a "class audience" that is also a "mass audience" buying almost two million copies each day Monday through Friday. This gives it the largest circulation of any American newspaper.

In 1882 two New England newspapermen, Charles Henry Dow and Edward D. Jones, established the financial news service on which *The Wall Street Journal* was founded in 1889. Charles W. Barron owned the company from 1902 until his death in 1928, and today his heirs own 60 percent of the shares.

The *Journal's* circulation surged to 500,000 during 18 years of leadership under publishing genius Bernard "Barney" Kilgore. Since Kilgore's death in 1967, former newsmen have continued to dominate the management. William F. Kerby, former Washington correspondent and managing editor, was board chairman until his retirement in 1978. At that time the additional role of chairman of the board was assumed by Warren Phillips, who had been a foreign correspondent and managing editor before becoming president in 1972 and chief executive officer in 1975.

Phillips, who was born in 1926, is generally regarded as chief

SOURCE: This article was written expressly for this book.

architect of Dow Jones & Company's diversification program. The conglomerate today owns, among other enterprises, a group of small-town dailies, a book company, a general consumer magazine, newsprint mills, a weekly business magazine and *The Asian Wall Street Journal* published in Hong Kong, a computerized news-retrieval service, and international economic wire services sold in 40 countries, as well as the *Journal* and *Barron's Financial Weekly*, a tabloid newspaper.

The Wall Street Journal was the first newspaper published with the aid of a space satellite. To speed delivery, the *Journal* daily transmits its pages via satellite to a national network of printing plants. From these plants facsimile editions are delivered by mail and an expanding private delivery system that was developed in the interests both of speed and of reducing the postal bill, which during the 1970s increased from under $6 million to more than $38 million.

News from the *Journal*, *Barron's*, and the Dow Jones News Services is provided via news-retrieval computers to more than 8500 subscriber terminals, making the company the world's largest provider of news-demand services to offices and homes.

MAGAZINE INNOVATORS
Edwin Emery and Warren K. Agee

Among our current magazines, *Ebony* excels both in photojournalism and in serving black audiences, while *Ms.* is famed as a voice of the women's movement. Their creators are depicted here as truly innovative editors.

JOHN H. JOHNSON AND *EBONY*

As publisher of one of the country's leading magazines, *Ebony*, John H. Johnson has achieved a national prominence rivaled among black journalists only by that of his fellow Chicagoan, John H. Sengstacke of the *Daily Defender*, who was the first of his race to sit on the board of the American Society of Newspaper Editors.

Johnson Publishing Company produces not only *Ebony*, by far the leader in photojournalism in the United States since the collapse of *Life* and *Look*, but also *Jet* and *Black World*. *Jet* is a news magazine; *Black World* was patterned on the *Reader's Digest*.

Johnson attended the University of Chicago, then in 1942 with

SOURCE: This article was written expressly for this book.

John H. Johnson

$500 borrowed from his widowed mother, he launched his digest magazine. It sold, and in 1945 he was able to start *Ebony*, a monthly imitation of *Life*, as a magazine for middle-class blacks. It sold, too, and in the mid-1970s reached a circulation of 1.3 million copies 70 percent home-delivered.

In response to the growth of black militancy in the 1960s, *Ebony* became more concerned with black problems and added extensive essays to its pictures and cartoons. It survived where *Life* failed because it was a prime medium for advertising focused on a black audience, whereas *Life* had only a general audience like that reached by television.

Jet, a pocket-sized and breezy news weekly, became the second-ranking magazine for a black audience. Johnson's efforts to provide an outlet for black authors in *Black World* constituted an unprofitable area of his publishing empire, but his concern for this concept of responsible publishing enhanced his standing in the black community and in the entire world of publishing.

GLORIA STEINEM AND *MS.*

Gloria Steinem, a passionate and glamorous leader of the women's liberation movement, has risen to national prominence since 1970 as editor of *Ms.* magazine and also as a celebrity in her own right. This granddaughter of an Ohio suffragette is considered by many to be today's principal creative spirit in the movement, which began with the publication of Betty Friedan's *The Feminine Mystique* a decade earlier.

Steinem was born in Toledo, Ohio, in 1936. She was only 12 years old when her parents separated. Life in Toledo became so grim that at the age of 15 she moved to Washington to live with an older sister. After graduation from Smith College magna cum laude, she undertook graduate study in Delhi and Calcutta, India. It was India that radicalized her: "America is an enormous cupcake in the middle of millions of starving people," she says. She returned to America, became a free-lance writer for numerous magazines, and wrote for the NBC-TV show, "That Was the Week That Was."

For a month Steinem posed as a bunny at the New York Playboy Club in order to write for *Show Magazine* a scathing two-part series that undermined the sexism of Hugh Hefner. The force of that report inspired publisher Clay Felker to ask Steinem to write a column, "City Politic," for *New York* magazine.

Always an activist, Steinem has worked for John F. Kennedy, Eugene McCarthy, George McGovern, and others of similar political persuasion. Her strong belief in the justice and necessity of the demand for equal rights for women led her to active participation in the feminist movement. This activism is expressed and affirmed by her editorship of *Ms.*

Ms. magazine rose quickly to national attention after Felker inserted its debut issue in *New York*. Steinem, a better editor than a writer, brought to *Ms.* the best female writers of the day. By 1980 the magazine had more than a half-million paid subscribers and a reported readership of more than 2.5 million people.

Steinem and her associates plan to keep *Ms.* in the vanguard of the women's right movement. "In the seventies, we made discoveries," she says. "Now we need the structural changes to make the symbolic changes reality. The two biggest issues in the eighties will be reproductive freedom and economic equality for women."

Women who work at home as housewives ought to get paid for it, Steinem believes. "Feminism makes love and family relationships possible for the first time because there's a chance for a real partnership," she asserts.

Gloria Steinem

Writer Tom Wolfe says the media want activists who are accessible, quotable, and attractive. Gloria Steinem fills that bill, although she dislikes being regarded as a sex symbol. She hopes that, partly through the influence of the magazine she edits, women will achieve status in American life equal to the contributions they make.

Section 5

NEWSPAPERS IN ACTION

Selections in this section discuss contemporary newspaper work. Coverage of public figures, advance planning for disasters, and new printing techniques are examined. So are the careers of Katherine Graham, James B. Reston, and Otis Chandler. The pleasures of weekly newspapering, as seen at the Pulitzer Prize—winning Point Reyes *Light,* are scrutinized.

NEWSPAPER DAYS:
THE TEDDY KENNEDY WATCH
AND PRIVATE LIVES, PUBLIC PRINT
Ward Just

Just wrote in *The Atlantic* about the differing techniques by which newspapers cover Senator Edward M. Kennedy and his family. Then, after reflection, in the following issue he added further thoughts on reporting about public figures. This selection includes portions of both articles.

The Teddy Kennedy Watch

This is a piece mostly about writers and reporters, but it will have to begin with Chappaquiddick. I would be obliged if you would continue reading for a moment, as I have no intention of rehashing the event, just of noting that as we go to press the tenth anniversary is here, and it is a singular event in our politics. The other recent anniversaries, the various assassinations, Nixon's resignation, and the fall of Saigon, were intensely public and visible. Chappaquiddick happened in the dark and remains unexplained—not just the why, which in any event is open to question, but the veriest details. There are but two uncontestable facts. An Oldsmobile sedan went off Dyke bridge. A young woman, Mary Jo Kopechne, drowned. On everything else—time, circumstances, occupants of the car—there is only a man's word.

I suspect it will be a newspaper anniversary for the rest of my lifetime, owing to the identity of the survivor. Ted Kennedy presents a special challenge to a journalist. There is no one remotely like him in American public life, variously prince and lowlife, son of a Croesus, brother to one murdered President and another murdered President-presumptive, the most popular politician in America, and a man obliged to live forever with the possibility—an actuary would say probability—of his own violent death. A flawed man, examples of every flaw litter the public record, and that is precisely the challenge. The material is too rich, too lurid, too vivid, and so abundant. So it is Kennedy's character, "the inner man," that fascinates journalists, and it's only unfortunate that a man's character is the quality least accessible to writers obliged to live by the

SOURCE: From *The Atlantic*, September 1979, pp. 64–67, and October 1979, pp. 53–54. Copyright © 1979, by The Atlantic Monthly Company. Reprinted with permission.

facts. This is a life that belongs in a novel by Tolstoy or a play by Shakespeare.

It is always interesting when major newspapers gear up for Kennedy anniversaries, and in June both the Boston *Globe* and the New York *Times* undertook to solve, if not the mystery of Chappaquiddick, at least the mystery—or "mystique" as the *Times* had it—of Ted Kennedy. For obvious reasons the *Globe* has a special relationship with Kennedy, and its coverage of the event a decade ago was plentiful even by Massachusetts standards: it forced the moonwalk to a position below the fold on page one. (Students of excess will recall that the moonwalk was Nixon's Greatest Day Since the Creation.) In the years since, the *Globe* has been pertinacious in its reporting of Kennedy's public career and private life. The *Globe's* anniversary piece was by the paper's associate editor, Robert Healy, and appeared in the Sunday *New England* magazine. The New York *Times* assigned a freelance writer, Anne Taylor Fleming. At the risk of being obvious, I would point out that these are important pieces, not least because they are carefully read in the trade. No editor wants to be thought soft on Kennedy, particularly in a piece pegged to the Chappaquiddick anniversary. The piece must be immediate and fresh, and it is obviously a subject on which an editor deploys heavy artillery.

It is helpful to know that Healy is an experienced political reporter and an old friend of Kennedy's. I use "old friend" in the newspaper sense, meaning that he has personally witnessed all the public occasions—announcements of candidacy, election night vigils, and the rest, which in Ted Kennedy's career is a melancholy inventory—as well as off-hours sport. Newspapermen have these relationships and they are complicated; true friendship requires a loyalty and discretion that no reporter can ever fully give. I have no doubt (but no evidence, either) that Healy has fifty Kennedy stories that will never see print and that any one of them would make a one-day headline in his newspaper or the lead item in a gossip column. These would be details, an unguarded remark, an escapade here or there. But they would be verified details: names, places, dates, exact quotes, and no blind sources.

For a combination of reasons—friendship, protecting the source, an unwillingness to use personal observation in the public print—I suspect that Healy has held back. No surprises. In my own newspaper days, I did; every newspaperman I have ever known has (though I left the business ten years ago, and ethics do change). Of course, there's a paradox: Healy's piece is heavy with authenticity, and is by no means soft.

Anne Taylor Fleming is something else, a reputable journalist with no particular qualifications to examine a senator of the United States. I think most readers would find Fleming's the more interesting of the two pieces. She's a very good stylist with excellent instincts and an apparent knack for persuading the men and women around Kennedy to talk. She's sympathetic to the subject but has put herself at a distance from the material. It's an attractive distance and guarantees, in skillful hands, authenticity. It's the sort of authenticity that tugs at a reader and causes his head to nod in agreement: *Yes, that's fascinating. That must be the way it is.* It's personal journalism of an alluring kind, objective in the sense that the facts march in a single direction and there is no hint—nor reason to suspect—that some facts are suppressed in favor of other facts. All facts and impressions are marshaled and sent in search of the objective. Fleming's lead discloses the method: "This is a story about Edward M. Kennedy. It is a story about his family, mainly about the men in that family and the men who came to spend their lives with them, who came to envy them their brotherhood, who came to want the love they had for each other, a love they expressed shyly, as men seem to, as Irish men particularly seem to, in banter and bravado, their fierce tenderness camouflaged in semigenial competition." That's a model lyrical lead, the turn coming in the clause "as men seem to." With those four words Fleming introduces herself into the piece and never leaves it thereafter. She's necessary to it, her tone of voice a personal guide through Kennedy country. I think it is the most intriguing profile of Kennedy and the family and the retainers that I have read anywhere.

Therefore, I must be speaking as a newspaperman when I confess that I prefer Healy and believe his the better piece.

He writes woodenly, as newspapermen seem to, sometimes. The lead "Senator Edward Kennedy walked down the steps of the American Airlines 727 at the Salt Lake City airport and was surrounded by local and network television crews and press. His aides carried declassified minutes of the 1953–1962 Atomic Energy Commission meetings that revealed government arrogance and deception on the order of the Nixon tapes." That's the reporter's method, a careful setting of circumstance followed by the blunt assessment. It's arguable that it doesn't matter that the airplane was a 727, or that it's irrelevant that the event occurred in Salt Lake City. Neither fact has resonance (in the sense that a DC-10 or the city of Dallas would have resonance). As facts they are neither symbolic of anything nor especially interesting. They are merely true.

This is an examination of method as opposed to content, but it's necessary to characterize the two articles beyond their leads. Healy's is analytical as opposed to judgmental. It is thorough and specific almost to an extreme: I counted fifty-five names, not including the family (about twice as many as in part one of Fleming's piece). Healy hurries through a description of Joan Kennedy and her life with the Senator to end with the simple statement that she had a drinking problem and still does. That is a plain fact unbuttressed by quotation and stripped of emotion. There is no authority for the statement other than Healy. But in this context, Healy is quite enough. Healy seems to me to be interested in the Senator in the present tense, "Kennedy Now"—in military terminology, a description of the order of battle and an appreciation of the strategy and tactics of the coming campaign.

Fleming's piece came in two parts on successive Sundays, the first focusing on Kennedy's behavior from childhood to the Senate, his relationship with his brothers, and his position now as head of the family, and the second on his private life since Chappaquiddick and the personal considerations ruling his decision to run or not to run for the presidency. It's difficult to characterize Fleming without extensive quotation because, like prewar American fiction, her piece follows a single narrative line. It is the one she promises in the lead. She is writing a *story*, with characters and a plot and events that are connected each to the others and given a specific gravity. There is a sense of predestination in Fleming's piece, of one episode flowing inevitably from another; the novel that comes to mind is *The Great Gatsby*, without the holocaust at the conclusion. Perhaps it is enough to refer to the end of part one of Fleming's piece. She is discussing Mary Jo Kopechne, quoting an unnamed friend of Kennedy's. What must have bothered Kennedy, Fleming quotes the friend saying, was that Mary Jo never liked him and thought him a playboy. It was Bobby she worked for and Bobby she worshipped. "So," Fleming ends, speaking in her own voice now, the "so" signaling the epiphany to come, "what he [Kennedy] had done, in his mourning for Bobby, he had done to one of Bobby's girls."

A poignant turn of the screw, I suppose.

Ernest Hemingway believed that successful fiction should leave a reader feeling more than he understands. That's an excellent formula—for fiction. But I think it has become a characteristic of modern journalism (so much of which borrows from fictional techniques, specifically those pioneered by Dr. Hemingway, who also observed that the secret of writing is to know what to omit) and I think it is disastrous. It is especially disastrous when it happens in newspapers, even newspapers' magazines. The newspaper environment is very special; it exists to accommodate news, and the secret is knowing what to put in, not what to leave out. My own prejudice: Always beware a beautifully written newspaper story unless it is a description of surfaces, something visible, usually physical—a witness sweating, a soldier dying, the whirl of the floor at a political convention. Wonderfully rendered interiors are evidence to me that the writer is reaching; the prose is employed to polish the facts and connect them, usually to link cause to effect and back again.

I trust Healy, and I seem to trust him precisely because the facts do not resonate. One way or another, a resonant fact is usually an ironic fact. Irony is the modern reporter's weapon of choice, but in these days it's a weapon without sights. That's one of the lessons of the helter-skelter world we live in. As Joan Didion has so brilliantly disclosed, there is no narrative line to events; or no narrative line you can believe or ought to believe. It's satisfying that all the machinery is visible in Healy's piece. Awkward facts, inconvenient facts, startling facts, useless facts, facts that are boring, silly, and important—each assigned a weight, but not too much weight. His writing neither conceals nor enhances the material. The reporter's prose is a windowpane permitting the reader to see the assembled facts. When a sentence begins "But . . .," it does not mean that the glass is suddenly cloudy or skewed. It means only that the facts themselves are in doubt or that there are several facts pointing in different directions. It is not a speculative "But" but a cautionary "But." It is also true that a reporter of Healy's energy and ability always has too many facts, and a reporter with facts is like a general with battalions: If you have them, you use them. Elegance, or "economy of means," is not a characteristic of journalism any more than it is of war.

I was halfway through the Fleming before I realized that I'd read nothing new. There were fresh quotes and fresh descriptions and original connections, but the data itself was unchanged. What I was reading was familiar stuff arranged in a novel pattern. Order was imposed on the chaos of a life and the particularity of a family, and while I personally found Fleming's order persuasive and intelligent, it was still a kind of literary order. It was the kind of literary order evident in the clause following the one that introduces the author: ". . . as Irish men particularly seem to."

This is the arrangement a modern journalist, as opposed to an old-fashioned reporter, imposes on the material, particularly when the material is as inherently mysterious (I imagine a nuclear physicist would say unstable) as a life, and especially Ted Kennedy's life. In the manner of the spiritualist, the modern journalist seeks to codify and make explicable that which is, at its essence, unknowable. He is writing, after all, about real people, not fictional creations. The newspaperman, with his abrupt transitions and gruff verbs, imposes no order at all beyond what he knows to be verifiable. In Kennedy's case, of course, that is quite a lot. Much is on the record and much can be inferred from the record. But it's no surprise that Healy devotes the majority of his piece to a discussion of the public career, issues embraced, choices accepted or refused. His past? His psyche? Ted Kennedy is both the product of his past and the author of it, and where that line is drawn God alone knows. All the rest is bull.

My hunch—I have not talked to Healy, or to Fleming—is that Healy, very much a man of the newspaper métier, is at ease with disorder and mystery and is something of a fatalist as well. It is senseless and impertinent to attempt to arrange the past from the evidence of the present if you were not there to witness it; it is as impertinent as being too damned certain about a person's motives. There is no reliable pattern discernible from a life until that life ends—except of course the pattern formed by the public record. Byron left his love letters, a politician leaves his clip file. My hunch, further, is that Fleming would disagree. Like a novelist, she would argue that if you thought about the matter intelligently, you could draw intelligent conclusions, arranging the past, locating the present, and speculating about the future—and if you were intelligent enough, and did your reporting thoroughly and wisely, you could capture the Kennedys no less fully than William Faulkner captured the Sartorises.

Now I'm reaching. But it seems to me implicit in the method. As much as I admire the spit and polish, the sheer readability, of Fleming's work, it remains uncomfortably close to fiction or to a television docudrama. The matter is not easily resolved because it is a question not of loaded dice or inaccurate facts but of writing that evokes too much. Fleming's piece, like others of the genre, seems to me intended to disclose not fresh facts but a fresh interpretation of the known facts, much of it based on unnamed informants. It's an attempt to locate the subject as a man, simultaneously father, son, husband, uncle, and politician, to "figure him out" on the evidence of his childhood and adolescence and young manhood, his reaction to horror, and his behavior in his most intimate relationships. His work on the Senate Judiciary Committee is less important than his connection with his brothers, and who is to say that this is untrue? It's only that the one is knowable and the other a little less knowable. But Kennedy as Kennedy is naturally more interesting and therefore more alluring; in my opinion, too alluring. Fleming's lead, seductive as it is, reaches, and the reach exceeds the grasp. For Edward M. Kennedy, substitute Sylvester Stallone. Read it again, making that clause read: ". . . as Italian men particularly seem to." Or Ingmar Bergman, Chou En-lai, or Humphrey Bogart, and Scandinavian men, veterans of the Long March, or drinking companions. . . .

Private Lives, Public Print

On the sound theory that there is no last word on anything, I have been reflecting on last month's piece ("The Teddy Kennedy Watch"), and it has occurred to me that it would be worthwhile to go a bit deeper into the question of private lives in the public print. The truth is, I have second thoughts—or, anyway, additional thoughts. I made the point that with living persons, such reportorial excursions were bound to end in rumor, half-truth, innuendo, and, ultimately, myth. Those would be the results of the more serious attempts of journalism to deal with spectacular or sensational lives, depending as they do on secondary, often unnamed, sources and the stylistic requirement to produce a seamless narrative. No retreat from that opinion, but a recent issue of *Rolling Stone* has complicated the matter.

The cover subject in this issue is the new phenom of the music biz, Rickie Lee Jones, twenty-four. At the time of this writing her album is number five on the charts, owing largely to the strength of a song called "Chuck E.'s in Love." Rickie Lee Jones makes Ted Kennedy look like Fred Waring. No part of her lurid private life is spared, meaning brushes with the law, the sauce, numerous redheaded strangers, and (in her words) "every kind of drug you can do." This is a young woman on the run, and I found her an extraordinary and courageous character, as I found the piece humane and large-minded.

> Near the bottom of La Cienega, Rickie Lee and I make a pit stop in a tiny roadside greasy spoon whose clientele is so unsavory that the joint features its own resident rent-a-cop. Rickie Lee, dressed to kill or maim in a skin-tight, black nylon stretch suit and spike heels, enters with relish, and she creates a minor stir among the night stalkers clustered around the grill when she leans over the counter to place her order.
>
> "I love places like this," she whispers. "Anything can happen in them, and usually does. I like taking *any* kind of a risk. I've done every kind of drug you can do. . . ."

In detailing the life of the jazz singer (the quotes come from the subject, her mother, and her friend, the singer Tom Waits), reporter Timothy White also manages to describe a particular world, a world certainly not confined to the music business but somehow typical of it. It's obvious that in the milieu of modern musicians a lawless, sensual, or outrageous life is not a professional liability; far from it. Rickie Lee Jones is not running for the presidency. But at the same time she is aware of the problems that come with instant celebrity and the invasion of her privacy, and in the beginning seems wary of *Rolling Stone* and its inquiring reporter. She wants to control the interview and in the end seems to have decided that the French solution is preferable to the English: No need to invade, I'll not resist. The result is heavyweight journalism about a chaotic, scattered, painful life—the life related to the music, the music related to the life, all of it of a piece. The narrative is not arbitrary or in any way literary; it flows from the facts; I mean, the reporter's direct observation. No filtration devices, and no imaginative leaps. White's account is not sentimental, prurient, soft, or speculative. In the language of a newspaper editor I know, it is just one hell of a damn fine reporting job.

It's true, no doubt, that editors and readers expect a different sort of life and personality of senators than of jazz musicians. If they didn't, the late Charlie Mingus would even now be chairman of the Senate Finance Committee. Exhibits A & B, Wayne Hays and Wilbur Mills. Teams of reporters were unleashed on the two congressmen. The Washington *Post* covered Hays as if he and his typist were a separate, and virulent, branch of government. Keyhole journalism at its least convincing, but sensational because it played against a presumption of rectitude. It occurs to me that in Washington, even the most blameless, upright, Presbyterian life—who? the attorney general? Cyrus Vance?—is seen through a veil. The politician, for very good reason, won't let the reporters inside. Therefore, in the absence of direct observation, the modern reporter plumbs the psyche, "character," "conscience," "inner man," whatever, most of it on the authority of unnamed informants. And, in the instance of the recent spate of pieces on Ted Kennedy, we are left adrift in a Jungian sea.

The point about *Rolling Stone's* profile of Rickie Lee Jones is this: the lady lives. She lives on the page the way a great fictional character does, and what's interesting to me is that White manages this without resorting to any fictional tricks or armchair psychiatry. He employs the oldest, most shopworn techniques in the reporter's trade: a precise setting of scene, vivid personal description, and a marvelous ear for spoken language.

I learned more that I could believe about the music business and one singer in that single issue of *Rolling Stone* than I learn about politics and politicians in a month of *Time* or a year of *Newsweek*, and not only because the material was sensational, but because it was directly observed.

DEALING WITH DISASTER:
HOW EDITORS PLAN

Phil Currie

As Director, News Staff Development, for the Gannett Co., Inc., Currie wrote this article for *The Gannetteer*, which circulates primarily among staff members of the Gannett newspapers.

A series of explosions and fires recently ripped through a chemical-recycling plant near Camden, N.J. Describing his newspaper's coverage, Metro Editor Lyford M. Moore of the *Courier-Post* later wrote:

"The *Courier* first got word of the explosion when the police radio blurted: 'Get everybody out of here. This place is a disaster area.' Within minutes, we had a reporter and photographer en route to the scene, another pair en route to a burn center and still another team to the hospital closest to the blast."

That's the way it works.

When everyone else is getting out, newspeople are getting in, and getting in within minutes at that.

Instant reaction is important when disaster strikes. And planned reaction is extremely important in any disaster—whether it's a flood, a blackout, an explosion, a blizzard, a massive fire, a police emergency or an airplane crash.

What's the state of planning at your newspaper?

Is the city desk ready to act in all emergencies?

Do reporters know what to expect?

Are they primed on what to do in a variety of emergencies?

Every emergency will have its unique qualities, but many will have a certain amount of predictability. That's where planning comes in—a means of anticipating the worst and knowing how you will deal with it.

For openers, have at the city desk, the photo desk and each key editor's home, the following:

(1) Home telephone numbers of each staffer.

(2) A map showing where each staffer lives, so that you might tap the one closest to the disaster if needed. (That list also can include such special information as which reporters or photographers have

SOURCE: From *The Gannetteer*, March 1978. Copyright 1978 by The Gannett Co., Inc. Reprinted by permission.

CB radios in their cars and which might have four-wheel-drive vehicles in case of snowstorms.)

(3) A list of editors in the order they should be called in an emergency, with home phone numbers.

(4) A list of other department heads who might be called in emergencies because their areas (advertising, production, circulation) may be affected. The list should include home phone numbers. And, for your own good, don't forget the publisher.

Newspapers should have a typed-out set of disaster plans for various contingencies. Key editors and the photo chief should have the plans at home as well as at the office. Keep them in a looseleaf notebook so they can be changed periodically as needed.

Disaster-plan books could include the following:

Action to be taken in case of an airplane crash, an explosion, a massive fire, a sizable public disturbance, weather emergencies (hurricanes, tornados, blizzards, typhoons, floods, mudslides, depending on your location), blackouts.

For each emergency, the book should include the names and phone numbers of key sources. For example, the blizzard plan would have not only police and fire numbers and contacts but also the names and numbers of key people in the department of public works, the utilities, the Red Cross, Civil Defense, the National Guard, etc. And airline and airport numbers (private, if available). Addresses are desirable, too, in case the telephones are out.

Most plans should list hospital numbers, hospital spokesmen and information on the hospitals' own emergency procedures if disaster strikes.

Usually one hospital is designated as the first receiver of patients if an airline crash occurs, for example. Likewise, airports have their own disaster plans; those, too, should be in your planbook. It also helps to know police and fire radio code numbers.

A word of caution: These lists have a way of getting outdated. Update them once a year, at least.

Also, involve pertinent reporters in the initial planning and distribute the basic game plans to them. Include in the plans a list of appropriate definitions. (For example, indicate the difference between a travelers' advisory, a snow emergency and a state of emergency. Readers will want to know.)

Your means of attacking the story obviously will depend on the kind of emergency you are dealing with, but some general guidelines can be followed. In a fast-breaking emergency:

(1) Get an assessment of the problem as quickly as possible. Calls to police and fire dispatchers will give you a starting point. Make a

call to the ambulance company, too, if that is a separate operation. Calls to people in the affected area (airport, neighborhood, community) will give you more.

(2) Quickly get to the scene a reporter and a photographer. Make sure they have essential equipment (walkie-talkies, if you have them; flashlights; gas masks; whatever). Have them get a fast sizeup then get back to an editor by telephone quickly so that further deployment can take place as needed. Someone will have to go to the appropriate hospital, no doubt.

(3) Determine whether it would pay to have one editor on the scene. In an air crash, an explosion and some floods it might. That editor can make on-the-spot decisions on coverage.

(4) Get someone to the control center, whatever it is. That may be police headquarters in a disturbance, or the power company in a blackout, or the department of public works in a snowstorm. The control point is where basic, accurate, official information can be gathered—and it's where the action is, to be captured in a story later.

(5) Monitor police radios but *do not* write what you hear without confirmation.

(6) If the disaster calls for it, hire a plane and get air photos. They easily may be the most dramatic shots you have.

(7) Have reporters interview witnesses on early arrival at the scene. They may be hard to find later. If some people can't talk long, have reporters at least get their names and where they can be reached later. Reporters should make notations quickly of what they see, as well, so words describing the disaster are on paper for later use.

(8) Reporters should check with the desk frequently to report what they have found and to receive new instructions. Even if nothing spectacular has happened, periodic checks are important so editors can plan from their end. This is especially true in such far-reaching disasters as floods. When checking in, reporters should leave phone numbers where they can be reached.

(9) Look for heroes; most disasters have them. Also look for the miraculous-escape stories; often there is one.

Blizzards, floods and other similar news emergencies may bring a different set of problems, although most of the approaches already mentioned apply to some extent.

But obviously in a natural disaster one difficulty may be not having a staff to deploy.

If you have warning that a bad storm is coming, it's wise to keep some staffers in a hotel or motel near the office so they'll be within walking distance to work if the disaster hits. Be sure to tell them what time to get to work—it's bound to be earlier than usual because you'll have fewer people and more to do.

For those stuck at home if, say, a blizzard hits, special transportation is needed.

Some papers have emergency plans whereby staffers are picked up in four-wheel-drive vehicles. Even snowmobiles can be useful, if you know where to get them in a blizzard.

Reporters without transportation also can make telephone calls in most cases and should be assigned stories that can be picked up by phone. They can dictate the finished story or, if the editor prefers, call in notes for the main story before deadline.

Remember in such emergencies to use ALL departments of the newsroom. A sportswriter can be assigned to the city desk for the storm's duration; a Lifestyle-section feature writer can be switched rapidly. The same goes for editors, who may have to be reporters again for a time.

Prolonged storms require broadened coverage. For example, people will be stranded on highways, in motels, at truck stops, at airports or bus terminals. All points are worth checking for the overall story and for great individual sidebars.

And the "How Did It Happen?" and "How Long Is It Going To Keep Happening?" stories are essential.

It's wise, in emergencies, to have at least one editor coordinating the disaster coverage and one or two reporters writing the main story. One editor should look at all copy to avoid duplication and to avoid major holes. So should the writer of the main story.

And for a sidebar, someone in the office should check the history on such disasters: When was the last time it happened, and where, and how bad was it?

While people are covering the disaster, editors and others in the shop must plan what to do with the information the newspeople gather.

The first question to answer quickly is: Should the press be stopped or an edition held for the first information on the disaster? That's the decision for the top editor or, in his or her absence, a predetermined substitute (usually the assistant managing editor, the news editor or the city editor).

After you tell the pressroom to stop or hold, notify circulation— and let the promotion department know you've got a possible big story.

If you are not on edition, be sure the various departments are notified of the pending big story. In bad storms, press starts may have to be moved up, so close coordination with production and circulation becomes essential.

Think about the space needed for copy and photos. If the paper is still on edition, there may be ways to shift ads for a later edition to open more room for coverage.

If you are planning a run later that day or the next, you should determine whether space should be increased, with additional pages added for photo and word coverage. If the paper goes up, let promotion know you will have "extra" coverage of the disaster.

Get the graphics people working on maps to show where the disaster struck, or what the scene is like (say, at an airplane crash), or whatever is appropriate. Have reporters at the scene make a rough sketch to be copied by an artist. (If you have a large-enough department, send an artist to the scene to do the sketch himself.)

Editors should determine the most logical ways to divide the stories. In an air disaster, that division might be stories on what happened, who the victims are, who survived, interviews with witnesses, and so on.

Focusing on how you will tackle the overall story will help determine what to assign and how to plan the paper.

If you are covering storms, lists may be appropriate. And make sure the how and why angles are covered; in second-day stories especially, make certain they receive prominent play.

In a disaster, advise all reporters to keep notes on whatever area they are covering. As soon as possible, have someone write a comprehensive "What They Were Doing and What Happened" overall story. (Usually, this would come not in the first paper you put out after the disaster but the second. If you are dealing with blizzards or tornados, the story may come a week later. But in the end, it always is fascinating.)

In all cases, think about tomorrow's paper, too, and how to plan for it.

All stories you write will serve the readers by informing them. But some stories can be of special help to them in a disaster, and wise editors will provide those stories.

First, the basics. Readers need to know quickly certain facts about the disaster. A nutshell report on the front page is an easy way to give them the information.

In a blizzard, for example, the "nutshell" might tell how much snow has fallen, how strong the winds are, how soon the snow and winds are expected to stop, whether the roads are closed, whether the airport and other transportation centers are closed, and what to expect next. Any emergency "messages" on health or other essential items that need to be conveyed to the community could be included briefly with a reference to the detailed stories.

Next, make sure that readers can find in the paper information that will help them cope with the crisis.

In a blizzard again, that might be a list of grocery stores open despite the storm; it might be telephone numbers to call for various emergencies; it might include a list of fuel-oil dealers who can make it to homes in emergencies; it might say what to do if people are without electricity.

In a flood, you might warn readers to boil water or let them know what other precautions to take. Often your county extension service will be the best source of such advice.

Next, consider a column of "Information for Stranded People" telling when the airport is to open, or when the roads will be cleared, or which roads—if any—are open at the time of publication. Consider conditions outside the immediate area for air travelers.

Remember the readers if the newspaper has special problems. If a blackout delays a press start, explain on the front page why the papers are late. If the blizzard slows some deliveries or makes others impossible immediately, tell readers so that when their papers finally arrive, they will know you were thinking of them.

If a storm forces early publication, explain why the late stocks might be missing or some other feature might be left out. If you shift pages to get in additional disaster news, let readers know if their favorite column is in an unusual location. In short, tell readers what you are doing (or what is happening) to their paper.

Finally, consider ongoing reader-help features.

When a tornado struck Fremont, Ohio, last year, the *News-Messenger* established a "Storm Report" column. Readers could call questions to a specific number or write the paper. The *News-Messenger* answered the questions in the column.

"The column will run as long as there are enough inquiries to justify it," the *News-Messenger* told its readers.

That's the kind of service that makes even a disaster more bearable for readers.

BIG CITY DAILIES PRESSED
TO ADOPT OFFSET PRINTING
A. Kent MacDougall

The technological revolution in newspaper production that replaced
metal with film in the printing process is described here in terms of the huge
offset presses used to print major dailies.

Three years ago *The Wall Street Journal* bought a $3 million Goss
Metro-Offset printing press capable of turning out one-thousand
48-page *Journals* a minute—and put it into storage.

Failing to utilize such an expensive piece of equipment may strike
the casual observer as peculiar business management. But if *The
Wall Street Journal* had held off ordering the press until its decision
last year to build a new plant outside Chicago to house it, the press
wouldn't have been delivered in time for the plant's scheduled
opening next January.

This is because Rockwell International Corp., which used to
deliver Goss presses in a year or so, has such a backlog of unfilled
orders that it is telling prospective customers they must wait two to
three years for delivery.

The order backlog may be satisfying to Rockwell International,
which builds most of the printing presses purchased by large
American newspapers, but it is posing problems for the
expansion-minded papers like *The Wall Street Journal*. And it has
prompted Japanese and West German press manufacturers to enter
the U.S. market. One Japanese company already has sold eight
presses for relatively quick delivery to U.S. papers.

The surge in demand for big offset presses is a recent phenomenon. During the 1960s and early 1970s, while weeklies and small-
and medium-sized dailies converted from conventional letterpress
to offset printing, most big-city dailies held back. Not only did they
have heavy investments in letterpresses, but they found serious
technological drawbacks in offset that have only recently been
largely overcome.

The big papers have paid for their delay. The sharper, cleaner
look and color capability that offset has given weeklies and small
dailies have made black-and-white metropolitan dailies produced
by letterpress often look drab, even dirty, by comparison.

SOURCE: From the Los Angeles, *Times*, January 21, 1979. Copyright, 1979, Los
Angeles Times. Reprinted by permission.

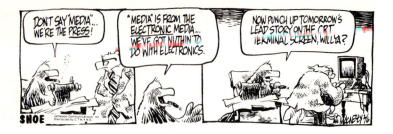

"Major metropolitan newspapers didn't used to have to worry much about printing quality," says John Morton, newspaper stock analyst for the brokerage firm of John Muir & Co. "But now they are competing against better-looking suburban weeklies and dailies, as well as against magazines and color television, and they are having to pay more attention to appearance."

Another reason for the move to offset is that many big papers need additional press capacity to accommodate proliferating suburban and life-style sections and burgeoning advertising volume.

The first big-city paper to convert from letterpress to offset was the St. Louis *Post-Dispatch*, which phased in offset between 1968 and 1972. Since then many others have followed suit.

Offset's early acceptance was due largely to its compatibility with fast, flexible, labor-saving methods of setting type and composing pages on paper and on film rather than in molten metal, as was traditional with letterpress. Offset also lent itself to the preparation of printing plates by photographic means rather than by casting them in metal.

Whereas a letterpress prints directly from printing plates onto a continuous roll, or web, of paper, an offset press prints indirectly. It has a rubber roller that picks up inked images from the printing plates and then transfers, or offsets, them onto the paper. The plates themselves never touch the paper. The soft rubber roller leaves a clearer and cleaner impression on the paper than do letterpress' hard metal or plastic plates.

Since offset became practical for large dailies, letterpress orders have just about dried up. The last major metropolitan daily to make a sizable investment in letterpresses was the Detroit *News*, which opened a $42 million suburban letterpress plant in 1973.

Production experts generally agree that offset presses whether foreign or American have largely overcome the technological drawbacks that once made them unsuitable for the high-speed, sustained runs required by the metropolitan dailies. Offset press speeds have been increased to 60,000 or more copies per hour. Making offset printing plates requires less time than it used to and the plates last longer. Offset inks are more competitively priced. And wastage of newsprint, the low-grade paper used by newspapers, has declined significantly, though it typically remains somewhat higher than with letterpress.

Offset presses used to waste about twice as much newsprint as letterpress. But better electronic controls over inking and improved press crew practices have reduced web breaks and other causes of newsprint waste.

Web breaks occur when the continuous roll of paper passing through the press tears, forcing stoppage of the press while the paper is rethreaded. Web breaks continue to be a problem, partly because newsprint has become thinner and weaker.

The American Newspaper Publishers Association says that newsprint began deteriorating in quality even before producers cut its weight 6 per cent in 1973 to conserve wood, meet increased demand and help profits. The thinner newsprint of today not only is more web-break prone, the ANPA says, but also is less opaque, increasing show-through and advertiser demands for rebates and reruns. The show-through problem is generally more acute with letterpress papers than with offset ones.

Newsprint producers concede some quality deterioration but note that they have had to run their newsprint-making machines faster and to keep older machines in service longer in order to keep up with rising consumption. They also point out the difficulty of making a single grade of newsprint that is optimum for several types of printing methods.

One printing method that requires good newsprint to work well entails the modification of letterpresses to accept offset printing plates. A number of papers have modified their letterpresses in this way to take advantage of the compatibility of offset-plate preparation with labor-saving photocomposition and also to postpone a major investment in offset. Printing experts say that retrofitting letterpresses to accept offset plates improves printing quality, but not to offset standards.

LEADERS OF THREE
GREAT NEWSPAPERS

Phillip H. Ault and Warren K. Agee

Otis Chandler, Katharine Graham, and James B. Reston are leading personalities of the top-ranked United Shates dailies: the Los Angeles *Times*, the Washington *Post*, and the New York *Times*.

OTIS CHANDLER

During the past quarter century the Los Angeles *Times* has become one of the nation's largest and best newspapers, after many years as a lucrative and politically influential regional publication, but one whose political and commercial attitudes warped its news coverage. Most of this noteworthy improvement occurred after Otis Chandler succeeded his father as publisher of the *Times* in 1960.

The newspaper for eight decades was privately owned by the Chandler family and a few other stockholders and concerned itself primarily with Southern California. Although it rode the crest of the area's enormous population growth to impressive financial success, its news and coverage of the nation and the world was poor, its coverage of cultural affairs weak.

Otis Chandler, a rugged, heavy-muscled man who was a champion shot putter at Stanford University, served an apprenticeship in all departments of the *Times* under his father Norman. In 1959 Norman set the Times Mirror Company on a new course of diversification and expansion outside its home area. In order to concentrate on these corporate goals, in 1960 he turned over responsibility as publisher of the *Times* to his son. Otis was the fourth generation of Chandlers to fill that position.

Under the command of Otis, and the editorship of Nick Williams and his successor William Thomas, the *Times* during the 1960s expanded its news and editorial department enormously. Coverage of the arts was enlarged. A syndicate alliance was created with the Washington *Post*. The Washington staff was strengthened, a corps of able foreign correspondents added, and national reporters assigned. Today the newspaper lists nineteen foreign news bureaus and eleven national offices. The result is a newspaper with a national outlook and power rather than the one it was, tinged with provincialism.

Norman Chandler's concentration on corporate growth for the parent Times Mirror Company also brought notable success. The

---

SOURCE: This article was written expressly for this book.

Otis Chandler

company became publicly owned, with its shares traded on major exchanges. By the time of Norman Chandler's death in 1973, the Times Mirror Company had acquired book publishing firms, magazines, other newspapers, and interests in cable television and other diversified fields.

That growth continued under the corporate chairmanship of Franklin D. Murphy, former chancellor of the University of California at Los Angeles. Otis served as vice-chairman of the Times Mirror Company as well as publisher of the *Times* until 1980, when he turned over the publisher's position to Tom Johnson. Otis in turn succeeded Murphy as Times Mirror chairman upon his retirement.

The company owns the Dallas *Times Herald*, the Denver *Post*, and *Newsday* on Long Island, all major metropolitan area dailies; the venerable Hartford, Connecticut *Courant*, and three community daily newspapers, the Stamford *Advocate* and Greenwich *Time* in Connecticut and the *Orange Coast Daily Pilot* in California. It also owns *Sporting News*. From the profits it made as a local newspaper company and by aggressive management, the Times Mirror Company has become a national conglomerate.

KATHARINE GRAHAM

Katharine Graham, widely regarded as the most powerful woman in America, assumed charge of the Washington Post Company in 1963. During the intervening years she and her team of executives have converted the *Post* from a slackly organized family business into a solidly successful, publicly held corporation ranking on *Fortune* magazine's list of the 500 largest United States companies.

Along the way Graham ordered the publication of the Pentagon Papers in direct support of the New York *Times* and equally direct defiance of the federal government, fought a three-year battle with the Nixon administration, and broke a bitter pressmen's union strike, this last act, in the opinion of the *Post's* management, saving the paper from years of labor struggle.

Graham was born in New York City in 1917, the fourth of five children of Eugene Meyer, a banker, and Agnes Ernst Meyer, an author and philanthropist. Her father bought the *Post* for $825,000 at a bankruptcy auction in 1933. After earning a B.A. degree from the University of Chicago in 1938, Graham worked a year as a reporter for the San Francisco *News*, then joined the editorial staff of the *Post* and worked in the Sunday, circulation, and editorial departments until 1945.

She married Philip Graham in 1940, thereafter devoting most of her time to raising her four children. Her husband succeeded Meyer as publisher in 1946, and three years later Meyer turned over the paper's voting stock to the Grahams. During the next 14 years the Grahams bought out the rival Washington *Times-Herald*, acquired two television stations, purchased the controlling stock in *Newsweek* magazine, and turned the *Post* into the largest-circulation newspaper in Washington.

Despite this success, Philip Graham's manic-depressive illness resulted in his death by suicide in 1963. When Katharine Graham then assumed control of the *Post*, she expressed her philosophy as publisher by quoting part of a 1935 statement by her father:

> The newspaper's duty is to the readers and to the public at large, and not to the private interests of the owner. In the pursuit of truth, the newspaper shall be prepared to make sacrifice of its material fortunes, if such cause be necessary for the public good. The newspaper shall not be the ally of any special interest, but shall be fair and free and wholesome in its outlook on public affairs and public men.

Graham took those precepts seriously and, in the process, greatly increased the *Post's* national and worldwide prestige. Publication of

Katharine Graham

the Pentagon Papers so rankled the Nixon administration that she was barred from the White House for three years. With the paper's reputation at stake, she strongly supported managing editor Ben Bradlee and reporters Bob Woodward and Carl Bernstein in the Watergate disclosures, for which the *Post* won a Pulitzer Prize.

In January, 1979, Graham relinquished the position of publisher to her son, Donald Graham. She continued, however, as board chairman and chief executive officer of the company's vast holdings, which include, in addition to the *Post* and *Newsweek*, newspapers in two other cities, four television stations, a newsprint company, and shared ownership of a national news service (with the Los Angeles *Times*) and the *International Herald Tribune.*

Graham's civic, business, and professional organizational activities, including membership on the board of the Associated Press, culminated in 1980 in her election as president of the American Newspaper Publishers Association. This honor bestowed by her peers acknowledges her position of eminence in her profession.

JAMES B. RESTON

No reporter has walked so authoritatively through the corridors of high governmental power in the United States in recent years as James B. Reston of the New York *Times*. He is a premier example of how a newspaper writer can develop news sources and make those contacts yield exclusive stories, often of major national and international significance.

"Scotty" Reston's career (his nickname comes from the fact that he was born in Scotland) is a classic success story that young reporters dream for themselves.

At the age of eleven his parents brought Reston to the United States from Clydebank, Scotland, where he was born November 3, 1909. After graduating from the University of Illinois in 1932, in the midst of the Depression, he wrote about sports for the Springfield, Ohio *Daily News*. He spent part of 1934 as publicity director for the Cincinnati Reds baseball team, a far cry from his later intimate access to the White House. Later that same year he joined the Associated Press, which sent him to London in 1937; there, in 1939, he switched to the New York *Times*.

His dispatches to the *Times* reported vividly on the German aerial blitz of the British capital in the early days of World War II. When he returned to the United States and joined the *Times'* Washington bureau in 1941, the book he wrote about the war, *Prelude to Victory*, brought him national attention.

From then on, his advance in the hierarchy of the *Times* was smooth and steady. He won distinction as Washington bureau chief of the newspaper and in turn became a columnist, associate editor, executive editor, vice-president, and a member of the board of directors.

Those who watched Reston work in his younger years as a Washington reporter marveled at his skill in coaxing information from upper-echelon political and diplomatic officials and in getting them to give him newsworthy documents. One of his first spectacular exclusives was publication of the full position papers of the allied powers during the Dumbarton Oaks conference in 1944, when the outline of the postwar peace was being formulated. Another was the first interview by an American correspondent with Soviet Premier Aleksei Kosygin.

Spry and self-assured, with an easy smile and a bounce to his walk, Reston was admired by younger members of the staff for the quick access he had to the highest news sources. He won the respect of his sources for his accuracy and reliability, and that of his readers for the clarity and logic with which he explained complex situations

James B. Reston

in an informal style more graceful than much other *Times* writing of that period.

He was able to talk intimately with national and world leaders because they realized that through him their views would be reported prominently in the New York *Times*. They also knew that his stories and columns would be fairly balanced, without the cynicism often evident in Washington among politicians and reporters.

Reston won two Pulitzer Prizes for his reporting, in 1945 and 1957, and has received many other forms of professional and academic recognition. He remains an active and leading newspaperman, a dominant presence in his field.

POINT REYES
SEES THE *LIGHT*
Daniel C. Carson

A husband-and-wife team built a foundation of community support for their weekly that enabled them later to courageously combat the Synanon terror regime in their Marin County neighborhood and win a 1979 Pulitzer Prize. In 1981 they put the *Light* up for sale so they could work in other areas of journalism.

The bearded young man swerved and stopped the fluorescent-orange VW bug in front of the grocery store. He hopped out, pulled a stack of newspapers from the back seat of the convertible, and hurriedly stepped inside the store.

"How's it going?" asked a short, balding man behind the counter as the taller man placed the newspapers in a rack.

"Pretty good," said the publisher of the Point Reyes *Light*.

Small-time journalist? No. Small town journalist? Yes, Dave Mitchell has decided to ignore the disdain of his big-city colleagues and practice what he preaches.

What he preaches is the merit of independent, small town newspapering.

When he and his wife Cathy, both 33, took over the struggling Thursday weekly two years ago, the new owners informed their readers, "Our love is community journalism, chronicling an area's history as it happens. For us, that is far more interesting than political advocacy."

Dave Mitchell professed to be surprised that so many journalism job-seekers—particularly journalism grads—look upon a job on a rural weekly only as a last resort. Sounding not unlike a Bible-thumping minister, he sang the psalms of reporting in the sticks.

"Here is where the news really happens. It doesn't happen back in Washington," he said.

"Let's say you're watching Roger Mudd on the evening news interviewing some senator who's a swing vote on a law meaning rivers all over the country are going to be cleaner. You think, 'God, how I'd love to do that.'

"The bill gets passed. Where it really starts to take on significance is when some rancher out here one day discovers he's going to lose

SOURCE: From *feed/back*, Fall 1977, pp. 28–31. Copyright 1977 by Journalism Department, San Francisco State University. Reprinted by permission.

David and Cathy Mitchell and their Pulitzer Prize—winning newspaper

his farm if he doesn't comply with the new regulations. All of a sudden, the whole character of an area is changing overnight. A whole ranching industry is being wiped out.

"There's an interesting story if there ever was one. These are the stories that deal in people. Politics becomes stale very quickly."

For those not inspired by the glory of Mitchell's unfurled journalistic banner, he offered a more practical argument.

"When you're working on the Washington *Post*, or the San Francisco *Chronicle*, I'll bet you a hundred dollars you're not the reporter who goes out to interview Vice President Walter Mondale when he visits. When you're in a small town, you are the guy that does it."

While he has not covered Walter Mondale, Mitchell has interviewed the governor, senators, representatives, and dozens of other government officials.

The territory covered by the Point Reyes *Light* doesn't include your average cow towns. Bolinas, Inverness, Point Reyes Station, Stinson Beach—once places for Italian-Swiss immigrant dairymen to pick up supplies and congregate on Saturday nights—now are dominated by a rather different group of inhabitants. The *Light's* first and only full-time reporter, Keith Ervin, called them "the hip community."

The influx of writers, medium-income IBM executive dropouts and near-broke street people into West Marin [County] began in January, 1971, when the *Arizona Standard*, an oil tanker, collided with another tanker in the tule fog of the Golden Gate. The ship's slimy, black cargo drifted into the Marin headlands, fouling its fabulous wildlife. Ecology groups organized expeditions to the headlands to save the birds. The oily mess receded, but many a liberal ecologist stayed, or vowed to return.

Return they did. In five years, it is estimated, the population of West Marin doubled to 15,000.

The impact of that growth has left some difficult problems, indeed, for the communities dotting the West Marin coast. The sudden numbers of would-be ecologists moving into 10-by-10 shacks have, ironically, polluted the oyster beds of Bolinas Lagoon with their failing septic systems. Land values have skyrocketed, raising county property taxes and economically squeezing all but a rich elite living off trust funds and endowments. The overnight introduction of a self-contained community with a radical viewpoint has led to sharp clashes with the once-dominant farmers, retired persons and other long-time residents.

Because there is no local government in West Marin other than a few utilities districts, the battle is carried out in county supervisor meetings in San Rafael on the other side of the peninsula, in Washington bureaucracies, and, sometimes, in the streets.

"Considering the number of people in the area, we have a disproportionate amount of arson going on up here," noted Dave Mitchell. "Schools have often gotten torched. New developments, also. And just a year ago, the new Bank of America right down the street from the *Light* office was burned down. There's an undercurrent of violence here."

The continuing clash of lifestyles provides the No. 1 source of news for the *Light*, as well as its most difficult problem: How can a small paper survive in a region with such a diverse readership?

Yet the Point Reyes *Light* has survived, and has improved its financial and community standing. The reason seems to be the paper's owners, who have had the common sense not to alienate any segment of West Marin. While that has not meant editorial timidity, in many ways Dave and Cathy Mitchell are at home among their strongest critics.

Cathy Mitchell was born in Charleston, W. Va., and grew up in Tennessee and Florida. Temporarily a refugee from Small Town America, she studied journalism at Florida State University in Tallahassee and completed a master's in communications at Stanford in 1967, where she and Dave met.

Dave Mitchell, a native of San Francisco raised in Berkeley, completed both a bachelor's in English and a master's degree in communications at Stanford. He and she adamantly opposed the Vietnam War, and Dave lined up a teaching job after graduation to avoid the draft.

So began their eight-year odyssey through the journalistic backwoods of the United States. Sometime between jobs in Leesburg, Fla., and Fayette, Iowa, they were wed. Along the way, they gave up teaching and started writing.

Dave got a taste of chain newspapering when he worked as city hall reporter for the Council Bluffs *Daily Nonpareil* (Iowa), owned by the conservative Thomson group. "I knew I wanted out after three months," Mitchell recalled.

The couple went west, first to the Sonora *Daily Union-Democrat*, then, 2½ years later, to the weekly Sebastopol *Times*—Dave as the editor. With Cathy as feature editor, and a cooperative publisher giving the Mitchells editorial freedom, the *Times* won several awards for news and feature coverage. When the publication changed hands in March, 1975, though, the Mitchells were suddenly out of a job.

After a frustrating, four-month job search, Dave Mitchell placed an ad in *Editor & Publisher*, highlighting his small town newspaper background. He was contacted by Michael F. Gahagan, the owner of a foundering weekly located in Point Reyes Station. Gahagan offered to hire Mitchell as general manager if he could keep the tabloid afloat. Mitchell took one look at the books and told Gahagan the paper couldn't afford to pay him a salary.

In July, 1975, Gahagan and his wife sold the business and the equipment to the Mitchells for an undisclosed sum. "A good price" were the only words used by Mitchell to describe the transaction.

The equity from the Mitchells' recently sold home and an inheritance provided the needed capital. The *Light* offices were not included in the price; the one-story building is rented.

The new owners began publishing in August, 1975. The changes began with their first issue.

A historic but erratic 1910 Gauss printing press—several tons of cast iron framework, brass fittings, and stainless steel rollers—was sold for $1. The new owner bore the several-thousand-dollar cost of removing it.

The switch to taking copy to an outside offset printer freed the *Light's* publishers. Dave took off the ink-stained printer's cap worn by Gahagan and concentrated on editing and reporting and writing. Cathy took a job teaching journalism at Santa Rosa Junior College and acted as *Light* business manager.

The switch also freed the paper's format. A new logo was designed, more and better-quality pictures complemented news features, and a readable body type and down-style headlines were adopted. The 20-cent tabloid continued to average 16 pages.

The imprint of the new publishers was more than aesthetic, however. The focus of news coverage was different.

Said Dave Mitchell, "The paper, before we bought it, had pretty much become the mouthpiece of the college-educated hip clique in their early 30s that was dominating Inverness affairs. The result was that people not in that group found the paper uninteresting. And circulation in Stinson Beach and Bolinas just about dropped off to nothing."

To correct the problem, he said, "We went after the broader community." In addition to easing off Inverness coverage, that meant dropping the poetry section in the paper and adding stringers for sports and community news.

The changes "caused a terrific amount of resentment," said Dave Mitchell, but not nearly so much as their maverick editorial line.

Taking a liberal rather than radical position on the ecology issue, Dave and Cathy Mitchell backed installation of a sewer system in the area to the ire of several environmental groups concerned such a move might unleash "runaway growth." His was not a popular stand. Sewers were later voted down 3−1.

More recently, the *Light* chided no-growth advocates:

"Much of the environmental consciousness of Marin County seems an attempt to keep the 'riff-raff' out. We too have supported limits on residential growth—but in candid moments must admit such limits can have the secondary effect of reserving an area for the rich. . . .

"Even more worrisome is the increasing tendency to equate style with environment. Marin County residents, especially West Marin residents, dress tweedy, hip or western, depending on occupation. And woe be any applicant who shows up at a permit hearing in white shoes and a seersucker suit."

Some strongly approve of the paper's style and content.

An aide to Supervisor Gary Giacomini, who represents West Marin, commented, "The *Light* is viewed as a good, reliable source of information." He added, "They've had some nice things to say about Gary."

Dave Puch, responsible for public information for Point Reyes National Seashore, said, "Considering that the publisher is covering news from the community's point of view in an area where the single largest land owner is the federal government, we have been treated fairly."

Others are critical of the *Light*.

"It's too bad the economics of small town journalism don't allow them to do a little more background research," said Paul Kayfetz, president of the Bolinas Public Utilities District board of directors. Kayfetz has found himself in frequent disagreement with *Light* editorials and news stories.

In particular, he said, they don't always double-check with sources on stories. "But they don't slant their news coverage to agree with editorial policy," he added.

Elizabeth Whitney was assistant editor of the paper when the Mitchells took control. Dissatisfied with its new direction, she quit and started a biweekly feature tabloid called the *Tomales Bay Times* with her friends that published one year and stopped in May.

"He didn't want to take risks," said Whitney, 35, of Dave Mitchell. "He doesn't want to be controversial. A paper should do more than write about what happens. It should be a community leader, it should deal with the issues."

While the *Tomales Bay Times* published, she and the Mitchells were bitter opponents. Feelings ran deep when the Mitchells accused the *Times* publisher of "sabotage" by asking merchants to withdraw their advertising from the Point Reyes *Light*. She denied the charge. No lawsuit was ever filed.

"I feel he and Cathy came equipped with a formula," criticized Whitney. "Cover zucchini and beer contests—small town stuff. I think the paper should be more sophisticated and more relevant to the talent and interests here."

She added sharply, "They're certainly very careful to keep the business interests happy."

Dave Mitchell took issue with Whitney's charge that he tailors editorial content to business specifications. He is aware of the problem small town papers face when they cover news about clients, though.

"Just this week one of our better advertisers had been vandalized and he told me he didn't want it in the paper. It's always an awkward thing to handle, no matter how firm your principles are, because you don't want to alienate the guy," said Mitchell.

What does he do in such situations? "My way out of this dilemma is to make the guy feel sorry for me. As long as I've been here, I've been able to do that every time."

Nevertheless, the paper will push for more advertising "just so we're not vulnerable to leverage from any one story," he said.

Despite the criticism and the 50–60-hours-a-week work schedule and the uncertain future of a small town paper, the Mitchells seem to like what they've got going in Point Reyes Station: control of an editorial product from start to finish.

Moreover, the changes in the paper have apparently paid off with new readers and advertisers. Said Dave Mitchell, "We weren't making a profit for the first six months. For the first year as a whole we still had a loss. Now we're comfortably in the black."

One-third of the press run is sold on newsstands stocked by Mitchell himself in his weekly jaunt down the coast in the VW. Circulation has moved up from 1750 in 1974 to 2400 now.

Small town life has intrinsic benefits, too.

"Where else," said Dave Mitchell as he relaxed in an office lined with typewriters, comfortable furniture and a Regency police scanner, "can you look out your window and watch deer grazing on the hill?"

Section 6

PRESS ASSOCIATIONS AND SYNDICATES

Between them, the Associated Press and United
Press International provide news to virtually
every American newspaper, radio and TV
station, and to media in many foreign countries.
Here are discussed two men who had principal
roles in building these services, Kent Cooper of
AP and Roy Howard of UP (now UPI); star
Washington reporters Walter Mears of AP and
Merriman Smith and Helen Thomas of UPI; and
the two news bureaus in operation. Examples of
feature syndicate work are shown by Garry
Trudeau and his immensely popular comic strip,
"Doonesbury," and Russell Baker, the humor
columnist whose home paper is the
New York *Times.*

TWO HISTORIC FIGURES

Edwin Emery and Phillip H. Ault

These biographies of Kent Cooper and Roy W. Howard serve to highlight the histories of the AP and the UPI, the two American entries among the international news agencies.

KENT COOPER: BUILDER OF AP

The name of Kent Cooper is fundamental in the history of the Associated Press, oldest United States press association and one of the five major international news agencies. As general manager of the AP from 1925 to 1948, Cooper shaped both its policies and its staff to agree with his own concepts.

Cooper started reporting, at only 14, for his local Indiana paper. When his college career was ended by the death of his father, Cooper joined the staff of the Indianapolis *Press*. From there he went to the Scripps-McRae News Service, becoming Indianapolis bureau chief for that press association, which was to evolve into the United Press, AP's major rival. There Cooper developed the idea of the "pony service," through which out-of-the-way newspapers received their news by abbreviated telephone calls rather than by more expensive telegraph or teletype.

In 1910 Cooper took his ideas of press association service to Melville Stone, general manager of the Associated Press. Stone made the young Hoosier traffic chief of the AP. He became an assistant general manager in 1920 in an administrative shuffle that made Frederick Roy Martin general manager when Stone retired in 1921. At Martin's retirement in 1925, Cooper was ready to take over the Associated Press. Through his subsequent career he demonstrated his strong administrative qualities, but he never was what the craft calls a "newspaperman's newspaperman."

Cooper's business qualities were needed in the rapidly changing years after World War I. More bureaus had to be opened, and staffs had to be expanded. Automatic newsprinters, called teletypes, had come into service after 1913. State news services, permitting exchange of regional news on wires subsidiary to the main AP trunk wires, were expanded. The AP started a news photograph service in 1927. In the most progressive move of the Cooper era, the board of

SOURCE: This article was written expressly for this book.

directors approved the AP Wirephoto system in 1935 after a sharp battle between picture-minded publishers and their more conservative colleagues.

Cooper was conservative in his approaches, and it was 1940 before the AP joined its rivals in selling news to radio stations. The AP World Service was not formally established until 1946, even though restrictive agreements Stone had made with foreign news services not to sell AP news abroad had been ended in 1934. Cooper wrote a book, *Barriers Down*, about the matter. When managing editors of AP dailies formed the Associated Press Managing Editors Association in 1931, Cooper frowned on its members' criticizing the AP's news coverage and writing style. They did so anyway, and after 1947 they issued annual reports by their Continuing Study Committee.

Two brilliant AP news executives left the press association before Cooper's retirement. One was Byron Price, director of the Office of Censorship during World War II, and the other was Paul Miller, who became chief executive of the Gannett newspapers. Still, a capable successor, Frank J. Starzel, a more traditional newsman, carried on Cooper's work after 1948. Cooper's story of it all is told in his 1959 autobiography, fittingly entitled *Kent Cooper and the Associated Press*.

ROY W. HOWARD: CHALLENGER WITH GALL

Roy W. Howard, whose name is perpetuated in the Scripps-Howard Newspapers, was among the most aggressive, successful, and colorful newspaper leaders during the first half of this century. He was a founder of the United Press (now United Press International) and built the Scripps-Howard chain, led by the New York *World-Telegram*, into a major force in journalism. Yet it was Howard's misfortune that when many old-timers mentioned him, it was as the man who filed the false Armistice story from France in 1918, erroneously reporting the end of World War I. His dispatch touched off jubilant celebrations across the United States, followed by denunciations when the news proved to be not true.

The word for Howard was "dapper." A short man, bright-eyed, with what one contemporary called "gall written all over his face," Howard dressed meticulously, wore spats, and carried a light walking stick. To look older, as a young man he grew a neat mustache that remained a characteristic of his appearance.

Howard was born in Gano, Ohio, on January 1, 1883, graduated from high school in Indianapolis in 1902, and became a reporter on the Indianapolis *News*. During the next five years he was a sports writer and general reporter in St. Louis and Cincinnati, and in 1907 was news manager in New York for Publishers Press news service. On June 19 that year, Howard and two other men established the United Press with the financial backing of Edward Wyllis Scripps, who wanted a competitor for the Associated Press to serve his and other newspapers. Howard was then only twenty-four, just five years out of high school.

Howard's rise was spectacular. A hard and clever worker, both as a reporter and editor and as a salesman, he built the United Press operations on a shoestring in the days when press association stories were transmitted from city to city by Morse code at thirty words a minute. After the early years as general manager, he became president of United Press in 1912.

In 1921 his role broadened tremendously. Leaving the UP presidency, he became board chairman of that organization, as well as chairman of the NEA feature service and chairman of the Scripps-McRae Newspapers, soon renamed the Scripps-Howard Newspapers. After the chain purchased the New York *Telegram* and then the *World*, creating the New York *World-Telegram*, he was editor of that paper while supervising the chain operations. Under his direction, the Scripps-Howard papers at times showed marked liberal editorial positions on some matters, while being conservative on other issues.

When all the facts about Roy Howard's false Armistice story came to light, he was shown to be the innocent victim of circumstances. Anxious to be close to the war action, Howard was in France, at Brest, on November 7, 1918. German forces were in retreat. Admiral Henry B. Wilson, the U.S. Navy commander at Brest, told Howard he had just received official word from Paris that the Armistice had been signed. He said Howard was free to cable the news to New York, which Howard did immediately. Two hours later the admiral received notice from Paris that the Armistice report was "unconfirmable." Howard quickly cabled this development to New York, but the cable message was delayed and the damage was done. This was one time, he said later, when in his constant fight for "scoops" he got a story that was too exclusive.

Howard died in 1964 after a career that was diverse both in scope and influence.

WALTER MEARS: AP MAN AT WORK

Timothy Crouse

Crouse fastened the phrase "The Boys on the Bus" to the press corps following a political candidate, emphasizing their dependence on pace-setting peers. Walter Mears later became AP's White House correspondent.

In 1972, the Dean of the political wire-service reporters was Walter Mears of the AP, a youngish man with sharp pale green eyes who smoked cigarillos and had a nervous habit of picking his teeth with a matchbook cover. With his clean-cut brown hair and his conservative sports clothes he could pass for a successful golf pro, or maybe a baseball player. He started his career with the AP in 1955 covering auto accidents in Boston, and he worked his way up the hard way, by getting his stories in fast and his facts straight every time. He didn't go in for the New Journalism. "The problem with a lot of the new guys is they don't get the formula stuff drilled into them," he told me as he scanned the morning paper in Miami Beach. "I'm an old fart. If you don't learn how to write an eight-car fatal on Route 128, you're gonna be in big trouble."

About ten years ago, Mears' house in Washington burned down. His wife and children died in the fire. As therapy, Mears began to put in slavish eighteen-hour days for the AP. In a job where sheer industry counts above all else, Mears worked harder than any other two reporters, and he got to the top.

"At what he does, Mears is the best in the goddam world," said a colleague who writes very non-AP features. "He can get out a coherent story with the right point on top in a minute and thirty seconds, left-handed. It's like a parlor trick, but that's what he wants to do and he does it. In the end, Walter Mears can only be tested on one thing, and that is whether he has the right lead. He almost always does. He watches some goddam event for a half hour and he understands the most important thing that happened—that happened in public, I mean. He's just like a TV camera, he doesn't see things any special way. But he's probably one of the most influential political reporters in the world, just because his stuff reaches more people than anyone else's."

Mears' way with a lead made him a leader of the pack. Covering the second California debate between McGovern and Humphrey on May 30, Mears worked with about thirty other reporters in a large,

SOURCE: From Timothy Crouse, *The Boys on the Bus* (New York: Random House, 1973), pp. 20–22. Copyright © 1972, 1973 by Timothy Crouse. Reprinted by permission of Random House, Inc.

Walter Mears (left) and AP colleagues interview a President

warehouse-like press room that NBC had furnished with tables, typewriters, paper and phones. The debate was broadcast live from an adjacent studio, where most of the press watched it. For the reporters who didn't have to file immediately, it was something of a social event. But Mears sat tensely in the front of the press room, puffing at a Tiparillo and staring up at a gigantic monitor like a man waiting for a horse race to begin. As soon as the program started, he began typing like a madman, "taking transcript" in shorthand form and inserting descriptive phrases every four or five lines: HUMPHREY STARTED IN A LOW KEY, or McGOV LOOKS A BIT STRAINED.

The entire room was erupting with clattering typewriters, but Mears stood out as the resident dervish. His cigar slowed him down, so he threw it away. It was hot, but he had no time to take off his blue jacket. After the first three minutes, he turned to the phone at his elbow and called the AP bureau in L.A. "He's phoning in a lead based on the first statements so they can send out a bulletin," explained Carl Leubsdorf, the No. 2 AP man, who was sitting behind Mears and taking back-up notes. After a minute on the phone Mears went back to typing and didn't stop for a solid hour. At the end of the debate he jumped up, picked up the phone, looked hard at Leubsdorf, and mumbled, "How can they stop? They didn't come to a lead yet."

Two other reporters, one from New York, another from Chicago, headed toward Mears shouting, "Lead? Lead?" Marty Nolan came at him from another direction. "Walter, Walter, what's our lead?" he said. [Nolan was the Boston *Globe* correspondent.]

Mears was wildly scanning his transcript. "I did a Wallace lead the first time," he said. (McGovern and Humphrey had agreed near the start of the show that neither of them would accept George Wallace as a Vice President.) "I'll have to do it again." There were solid, technical reasons for Mears' computer-speed decision to go with the Wallace lead: it meant he could get both Humphrey and McGovern into the first paragraph, both stating a position that they hadn't flatly declared before then. But nobody asked for explanations.

"Yeah," said Nolan, turning back to his Royal. "Wallace. I guess that's it."

Meanwhile, in an adjacent building, The New York *Times* team had been working around a long oak desk in an NBC conference room. The *Times* had an editor from the Washington Bureau, Robert Phelps, and three rotating reporters watching the debate in the conference room and writing the story; a secretary phoned it in from an office down the hall. The *Times* team filed a lead saying that Humphrey had apologized for having called McGovern a "fool" earlier in the campaign. Soon after they filed the story, an editor phoned from New York. The AP had gone with a Wallace lead, he said. Why hadn't they?

Marty Nolan eventually decided against the Wallace lead, but NBC and CBS went with it on their news shows. So did many of the men in the room. They wanted to avoid "call-backs"—phone calls from their editors asking them why they had deviated from the AP or UPI. If the editors were going to run a story that differed from the story in the nation's 1700 other newspapers, they wanted a good reason for it. Most reporters dreaded call-backs. Thus the pack followed the wire-service men whenever possible. Nobody made a secret of running with the wires; it was an accepted practice.

MERRIMAN SMITH AND HELEN THOMAS: UPI AT THE WHITE HOUSE
Edwin Emery

"Thank you, Mr. President!" was the closing line for Merriman Smith at White House news conferences during the many years he was senior correspondent in service. Helen Thomas matches his prestigious role for UPI as she crisply questions the President.

SOURCE: This article was written expressly for this book.

Helen Thomas at the White House

For years the abrasive but immensely successful dean of the White House correspondents was Merriman Smith. When he died in 1970 his place as chief of the United Press International team was taken by a seasoned political writer, Helen Thomas, who shot to prominence as the first woman head of the White House Correspondents Association and a renowned Washington personality.

Smith had covered the White House for 30 years, reporting on the presidents and their policies from Franklin Roosevelt to Richard Nixon. Thomas began with John Kennedy and during 20 years has put queries to six presidents, in particular handling the turbulent Watergate era for UPI. Together Smith and Thomas have given that worldwide news agency an aura of excellence in White House coverage, featuring hard-hitting, authoritative personalities.

Thank You, Mr. President was the title of Smith's first book, an account of his early years covering the White House in the Franklin Roosevelt years. Smith was at Hot Springs, Georgia, in 1945 as one of the news pool reporters who received the first word that Roosevelt had died. Eighteen years later, he was sitting in the news pool car following President John F. Kennedy through the streets of Dallas when shots rang out. The instinctively ready-for-action Smith had taken the front seat by the telephone. He dictated a running story to the UPI Dallas bureau, crouching low in the speeding car while his Associated Press competitor in the rear beat him over the head with an umbrella. UPI's first Pulitzer Prize went to Smith that day.

Legendary for his highly disciplined reportorial skills, his instinctive reactions to impending political sensations, and his hard-nosed assessments of White House policies and occupants, Smith eventually slipped in effectiveness, a victim first of alcohol and then of cynicism. But it was still difficult for Helen Thomas to take his place at banquet tables across the country as an interpreter of Washington news and predictor of things to come. She did it nicely, adding off-the-record sessions with gossipy material about the White House families and staff members that kept listeners entranced at meetings of editors, journalism students, and even reporters.

In 1975 Thomas published *Dateline: White House* in which she recounted her impressions of the Kennedy, Johnson, Nixon, and Ford eras. She was winning one honor after another as "the first woman to . . .," an accolade she found it hard to smile for. Marriage to an associate in the White House press corps gave her another momentary spotlight. But the spotlight she likes best is the one of putting to the President a hard-to-answer question on a crucial topic.

"We are not loved," she says, "and if we want to be loved, we should not be in this business. But they are Presidents, and if they don't want to be watched, they should not be Presidents."

THE EDITORS' SCHEDULE

The press associations open each daily cycle on their circuits with a schedule telling editors what major stories to expect, how long they are, whether fresh material may develop on them later, and if pictures are available. This one by UPI is typical.

PM newsked 6–10
Good morning. The UPI report for Tuesday afternoon newspapers will include:

Blacks Pelt Carter Limo
(CARTER) Miami — President Carter's visit to Miami is marred by a group of unruly blacks who booed and pelted his limousine with a beer bottle and wads of paper. 550. May be led. Pictures.

SOURCE: From United Press International teletype, June 10, 1980.

Deep Rift in OPEC

(OPEC) Algiers, Algeria — OPEC hawks and moderates in deep split over pricing, and six more months of price confusion on world oil market looms. 500. May be led.

Miracle Cures in Moscow

(HEALER) Moscow — A former waitress who claims she can perform miracle cures is rumored to number Soviet President Leonid Brezhnev among her clientele in a tale reminiscent of the mad monk Rasputin and the czar's family. 300. May be led.

Gold-Plated Wages in Washington

(SENATE) Washington — Those silver-tongued orators in the Senate are paying their best assistants gold-plated wages. 450. Will stand.

National

(POTTS) Atlanta — Convicted killer Jack Potts, who decided on the eve of his execution to appeal his death sentence, goes to court today—he's changed his mind again and wants to die. 450. May be led. File photo.

The Economy

(ECONOMY) Updated — The sale of new single-family homes hits new depths, and it appears the price of oil to heat those homes and commute back and forth from them will reach new heights. 500. Should stand.

Health

(EYE) Washington — A government advisory council says more research is needed before it can endorse surgery to correct nearsightedness, a common vision disorder. 400. Will stand.

Foreign

(AFGHAN) New Delhi, India — Soviet tanks and bombers lay waste to villages around Kabul in an attempt to thwart a rebel offensive, but hundreds of insurgents sneak into the capital. 500. May be led.

(QUAKE) Mexicali, Mexico — A little girl was crushed to death, 100 people were injured and hundreds fled crumbling adobe homes during a powerful earthquake that rumbled through Baja California. 500. May be led. Picture.

(IRAN) Tehran, Iran — President Abolhassan Bani-Sadr warns hard-liners against holding a trial of the 53 American hostages. 400. May be led.

PRESS ASSOCIATIONS AT THE SCENE: AP AND UPI TELL HOW IT'S DONE

Both the AP and UPI publish newsletters sent to news editors and their own bureaus. In the examples reprinted here, AP relates the organizational details of tornado coverage, while UPI reports on the difficulties of news work in Central America. Both reflect the flavor of press association life.

Members, Staff Move on Tornado Story (from the *AP Log*)

The Associated Press combined membership cooperation and quick staff action in Iowa and New York when killer tornadoes slashed through the north-central Iowa towns of Algona and Manson June 28.

First word of the disaster came from amateur radio operators.

"If it hadn't been for hams, there wouldn't have been any information from those areas," a tired Bob Christensen said as he reviewed the early hours of the disaster coverage.

Christensen, 37, is general manager of member broadcast station KHBT-FM in Humboldt, Iowa. He has been an amateur radio operator for 25 years. With the call letters WOZPM, Christensen is a central part of a ham network reserved for just such emergencies.

Christensen provided the early information when he contacted the AP bureau in Des Moines and kept an open line for about three hours to relay details from radio operators on the scene.

News editor Don Beman returned to the bureau and organized the staff early in the evening when the seriousness of the situation became apparent.

At the General Desk in New York, Ellen Nimmons worked from copy sent on the highspeed collection wire and telephoned information.

Staffer Kiley Armstrong, a national AP award-winning broadcast writer, was in the office working on a special story. She took over the broadcast desk, pumping out National Weather Service warnings and the latest news copy. That freed temporary staffer Jule Lutz to gather information.

Night supervisor Val Corley reached State Senator Berl Priebe of Algona by telephone at his home, providing the only substantial quotes from the scene for many hours. Iowa members had ten leads before the AM cycle closed.

Meanwhile, plans were made to abandon the Des Moines bureau as tornadoes headed for the city, stopping just on the edge of the city and veering to the south before striking the metropolitan area.

SOURCES: From The *AP Log*, July 9, 1979; and the *UPI Reporter*, March 27, 1980.

The staffers were prepared to go to below-the-ground levels of the building in which the bureau is located.

In Omaha and Kansas City, staffers and technicians stood by in case they had to step in to file wires and handle incoming calls from the tornado area.

After the storm cells cleared the Des Moines area and it had become apparent where the damage was heaviest, Beman sent staff writer Brian Friedman to Algona. He also sent staff writer Michael Holmes and stringer photographer Bill Daniels to Manson.

Photo arrangements for Algona were made through one member newspaper, the Mason City *Globe-Gazette*, and one non-member paper, the Spencer *Reporter*, after the photographer for that paper called and offered his services.

Iowa photo editor Bob Jarboe was on vacation but he called the bureau to offer his services. He became the pool photographer traveling with state officials the next morning to survey the damage.

Christensen was busy, too, on the air at his station, filling in on an announcer's day off.

Friedman stayed on the story through Sunday, reporting from both Algona and Manson on Saturday and writing of the special memorial church services on Sunday.

AP obtained exclusive pictures of the funnel cloud as it struck Algona. John Cullen, a photographer for the Algona Publishing Company, took the dramatic pictures, which moved to AP members early Saturday morning and which showed in papers across the country, with the company's copyright credit.

Algona publisher Denny Waller made his building available to Friedman and AP photographer Jim Mone from Minneapolis. Mone printed Cullen's pictures for AP and shot a color project for weekend editions.

Also helping during the coverage was broadcast member KLGA in Algona, where news director Randy Renshaw cut short a vacation to air an all-night newscast to keep information flowing in the town. KLGA is normally a daytime only station.

Covering the Violence of Central America (from the *UPI Reporter*)

Central America is an increasingly important story for the United States but covering it is becoming ever more dangerous.

Since ABC-TV reporter Bill Stewart was shot to death in cold blood in Nicaragua last year, American correspondents have become acutely conscious that a U.S. passport is no guarantee against violence—intended or arbitrary—death threats, deportation or harassment. Local nationals face sanctions such as licensing, pressures, and dismissal. In one case at least, a reporter was tortured.

Juan Tamayo, UPI's Mexico City-based news editor for the area, reports that 90 per cent of foreign reporters now wear bulletproof vests in San Salvador when covering leftist marches likely to be ambushed by right-wing snipers.

"They're uncomfortable, but I even thought of wearing mine to bed after the hotel chambermaid showed me a bullet hole in the mattress," said Tamayo on a recent visit to a violence-prone city.

Tamayo's name and that of almost every other foreign reporter who has covered the Salvadoran story appeared on "death lists" of journalists marked for killing by San Salvador rightists.

Just who gives the orders is sometimes a mystery.

UPI's resident correspondent in San Salvador, Demetrio Olaciregui, was seized by plainclothes gunmen March 13, bundled into a car and deposited over the border in Honduras. Protests brought an apology—but not an explanation—from Defense Minister Jose Guillermo Garcia, and Olaciregui, a Panamanian, was readmitted March 20. Four days later he was told he'd been declared persona non grata.

Attempts to sort out Olaciregui's status were complicated when San Salvador erupted into violence following the long-feared assassination of Archbishop Oscar Romero.

Earlier a non-Salvadoran journalist fled the country after men armed with machine guns waited outside his house and gave him a slit-throat gesture every time he appeared.

In separate incidents, two reporters were seized by gunmen who argued among themselves whether or not to kill their captives. Both survived but one, a Mexican, was put on the next plane out of town.

Much of the harassment seems to be the work of right-wing security men acting without the direct knowledge of the ruling junta but taking advantage of its inability to stop repression.

In Panama, the government lifted the radio licenses of four commentators who criticized the government. One of them, an avowed leftist, was beaten by national guardsmen last December when he tried to lead a march protesting the arrival of the Shah of Iran. Two UPI photo stringers were fired by their pro-government newspapers in the mistaken belief they helped UPI obtain and transmit a picture of the beating.

Reporters in Guatemala are under constant threat from both left- and right-wing extremists who view almost every story as propaganda for the other side. The atmosphere is worsening, but violence is not new. It was in Guatemala a few years ago that UPI stringer Raul Gonzalez was kidnapped by right-wingers, tortured, and shot in the stomach.

Jose Napoleon Duarte, a member of the El Salvador junta,

summed up the situation in much of Central America when he told
the Inter American Press Association at a meeting in Costa Rica,
March 20, that because of the climate of violence "It is impossible to
give any kind of guarantees" for the safety of reporters.

—Gerard Loughran, Foreign Editor.

SYNDICATED GENIUS: GARRY TRUDEAU
Phillip H. Ault
"Doonesbury" captured a nation's imagination through its satirical
approach to politics, cultural fads, and social foibles. Nearly everybody still
recalls how Trudeau made Joanie Caucus an honest woman in 1981, even
as he satirized conventional marriage rites.

Although hardly a comic strip in the traditional sense, "Doonesbury" is a phenomenon of the comic strip world. Garry B. Trudeau
uses the strip format as a vehicle for his comments on contemporary
political and social foibles so cleverly that some newspapers publish
"Doonesbury" on the editorial page rather than on the comic page.

The Pulitzer judges recognized Trudeau's unique achievement in
1975 by awarding him the Pulitzer Prize for Editorial Cartooning. He
is the only comic strip artist so honored.

In a medium where the intellectual demand usually is minimal,
Trudeau makes his readers think. He assumes their knowledge of
the day's news. Without such awareness, his ironic thrusts at
prominent newsmakers may pass unrecognized. His satire generally is gentle, usually subtle, but occasionally he draws cries of pain
from his victims, no matter how much they deserve the treatment.

"Doonesbury" is peopled by familiar characters who keep reap-
pearing, including Michael J. Doonesbury; Zonker, whose obsession
is to have the perfect suntan; the utterly amoral Uncle Duke; Joanie
Caucus, whose life in the Washington bureaucracy opens doors for
the satire of government; Rick Redfern, her live-in political reporter
friend; and Zeke Brenner, the unscrupulous caretaker. To these are
added such occasional figures as the Secretary of Symbolism, a
device for debunking the public relations postures of President
Reagan and Governor Edmund G. Brown Jr. of California.

Trudeau, who himself shuns publicity, was born in New York in
1948, and graduated from the Yale University School of Art and
Architecture. His strip first appeared in the Yale student newspaper,

---

SOURCE: This article was written expressly for this book.

DOONESBURY by Garry Trudeau

where it was seen by James F. Andrews of the little known Universal Press Syndicate. Better-established syndicates refused to take on "Doonesbury" because of its unorthodox style and its mocking allusions to prominent personalities that keep libel lawyers alert. UPS began syndication of "Doonesbury" in 1970. The strip was soon a smashing success, especially among young adult readers who chuckled at its anti-establishment tone.

Yale subsequently gave an honorary degree to this slim, dark-haired, heavy-eyebrowed alumnus whose gift for satire is revealed in his writing as well as in his strip. For example, Trudeau once wrote in *Rolling Stone* a tongue-in-cheek interview with his own imaginary rock star, Jimmy Thudpucker, during which he satirized rock music, the Nixon administration, federal funding, Margaret Trudeau, and Mick Jagger, all in a few hundred words.

That is the same stuff of which the "Doonesbury" strip is made. In the strip it is packaged with spidery artwork that frequently violates the cliches of the form by having nearly expressionless faces and a minimum of physical action, yet occasionally there are panels of unexpected visual fantasy. It is a unique and highly individual contribution to journalism.

THE GOOD HUMOR MAN: RUSSELL BAKER
From *Time*
Russell Baker writes 750 words three times a week for the New York *Times* and 475 other papers buying his syndicated column. His light humor, sometimes carrying a social message, won a Pulitzer Prize for commentary in 1979. *Time* offers this portrait of a "good humor man."

SOURCE: From *Time*, June 4, 1979, p. 48. Reprinted by permission from Time, The Weekly Newsmagazine; Copyright Time Inc. 1979.

A man is getting ready for bed. He takes off his shoes, then his socks. He looks idly at his feet. Hmmm. They are feetlike, ordinary. They do not look interesting, but they look tired, and it is time to wedge them down between the sheets to the bed's own foot, where they will wiggle a bit and then fall dormant. The man lifts his feet into bed, but as he does, he feels the tingle of a half-formed thought. Oddly, it is about umbrellas. Something about umbrellas getting mixed up in restaurants. It is not the dazzling sort of thought that stings the thinker into wakefulness, and the man does not follow it to its conclusion, if there were any. Soon he is asleep.

Next day the man goes to his office, hangs up his coat and sits at a typewriter. Time passes. No typing occurs. The man's natural optimism wilts. He is vacant of ideas, except for one that grows progressively more attractive: this, finally, is the day for throwing himself out of the office window.

But, hark! A thought! It concerns, let's see, umbrellas and—what's this—feet. Of course. The logical connection is clear. The man's face takes on a look of confidence, and he begins to type. "The world is as follows," he writes. Nice, crisp beginning, no fooling around. He continues, "Upon removing his shoes at bedtime, P. B. Sykes observes that the feet inside his socks are not his feet, but quite obviously someone else's feet. His wife, noting an unusual expression on his face, inquires if something is wrong. 'No,' says Sykes, quickly dousing the light."

The man, who is tall, high-shouldered and middle-aged, and who seems sober, gets up from the typewriter and paces about the room. Time passes again, this time into the end zone. Is the writer faltering? No! He finds the thread, and hurriedly types; "Next morning he finds the strange feet still there. 'How's everything, P. B.?' a dozen people ask him before lunch. To each, Sykes replied, 'Fine.' He telephones a doctor. A receptionist says the next available appointment is three months distant. Sykes says he has an emergency. 'What seems to be the trouble?' asks the woman. Sykes cannot tell her the truth, for he is certain she is incapable of believing that feet can be switched like umbrellas traded in a restaurant mix-up, and will think him mad and dispatch him to psychiatry."

By now the man is typing at great speed. Sykes never does find his own feet, but at a party one day he confides his loss to an editor, who signs him to a three-book contract. The surrogate feet become television celebrities, Robert Redford and Dustin Hoffman star in the movie version of Sykes' life, and he goes off to make a television commercial for corn plasters. There he meets Alexander Solzhenitsyn, another celebrity, who is making a commercial for Russian dressing in spray cans. The man's typescript concludes: "That is what the world is like."

It is 6 P.M., and once again the office window has been cheated of its prey. A few hours earlier P. B. Sykes and his strange feet did not exist. Now they do, brought into being by a process as astonishing and mysterious as the sprouting of legs on tadpoles. In Sykes' case, it happened five years ago. It still happens, three times a week, inside the wondrous mind of Russell Wayne Baker, 53.

For the past 17 years, Baker has written "Observer," a 750-word humor column that appears in the New York *Times* and 475 newspapers that subscribe to the *Times* News Service. This year Baker won the Pulitzer Prize, journalism's highest award, for commentary. It was the first time a writer who is considered basically a humorist received the commentary award since it was established as a separate Pulitzer in 1970.

His column walks the high wire between light humor and substantive comment, a balancing act so punishingly difficult that in the entire country there are not a dozen men and women who can be said to have the hang of the thing. Of these good humor men and women, Baker is consistently the most literate. What impresses Pulitzer judges and other journalists about Baker's high-wire heroics is not simply the talent they require, though the requirement is very high, but Baker's extraordinary range. Humor is his usual vehicle, but he can also write with a haunting strain of melancholy, with delight or, as in his 1974 meditation on inflation-pinched old people shopping timidly at the supermarket, with shame and outrage: "Staring at 90-cent peanut butter. Taking down an orange, looking for its price, putting it back . . . Old people at the supermarket are being crushed and nobody is even screaming."

The humanitarian element of New Deal liberalism—the sense that society's unfortunate people ought to have some help—is very much a part of Baker's makeup. He tends to be thoroughly cynical about Big Business and nearly as disenchanted with Big Government and Big Labor. But his scope is vast. The ten columns for which he won the Pulitzer deal with tax reform, the ever shorter life span of trends, inflation, the difference between serious and solemn, loneliness, fear, dying, a boyhood summer, Norman Rockwell and the death of the *New Times* magazine.

Baker's other great gift is his consistency. Each year he finds the endurance to be sharp and fresh and surprising nearly 150 times. The gross wordage he turns out over a year would amount to a fair-size novel.

Section 7

THE ROLE OF MAGAZINES

The editor of every magazine tries to give the publication a distinctive character that will appeal to the audience it is intended to reach. The next two articles examine how one magazine, *Esquire,* approached the problem, and how free-lance writers can sell articles by shaping them to fit an editor's needs.

WHAT EVERY MAN NEEDS TO KNOW . . . HISTORY REPEATS ITSELF AT *ESQUIRE*

Harold Hayes

Harold Hayes was editor of *Esquire* from 1963 to 1973, an era during which the magazine published America's top writers. Here he depicts the power struggle preceding his editorship, and mourns the fall of *Esquire* since then to a nonliterary level.

> Society is changing its definition of manhood at too rapid a rate, leaving the man in the middle.
>
> Esquire understands this.
>
> And it intends to help with the problem, in an important meaningful way.
>
> Because in the midst of all this unsettling change, a man is still expected to know what wrench to use, what to wear for each occasion, what wine to order, how to make important decisions about his life, how to entertain a woman, where to vacation, and how to buy a stereo system that sounds like a concert hall. . . .
>
> —From "Why We Bought *Esquire*," a full-page ad in the Business Day supplement of the New York *Times*.

"We grew up on *Esquire*," say its new young owners, Phillip Moffitt, age 32, and H. Christopher Whittle, age 31, in their ad. So did I. When I was nine, my father, a Baptist minister, wouldn't let it in the house and I sneaked looks at it next door. When *they* were nine, I went to work there. This was about eight months before Ralph Ginzburg and Clay Felker were hired. Ginzburg came over from *Look*, where he had acquired some expertise in newsstand promotion. Felker came from *Life*, where it was rumored he had run into trouble by scrambling the identifying captions on pictures of Notre Dame football players, some of whom lacked their front teeth.

Ginzburg wore tweed suits, bow ties and cordovan shoes. He kept an army canteen filled with water on his desk at all times. He had a forced loud laugh which in the absence of other office sounds was disagreeable. Felker was a smoother number but hot-tempered and blunt. None of us liked the other two very much but this was mainly, it is now clear, because the editor's job was open, and each of us wanted it badly.

Esquire always has been in trouble of some kind—and it was in trouble when we arrived, this time from the embarrassing success of

---

SOURCE: From *The New Republic*, May 26, 1979. Copyright 1979 by Harold Hayes. Reprinted by permission.

a fleshier version of itself. Where the postmaster general and the cardinal had failed, Hefner's *Playboy* had forced *Esquire* to reposition itself in the ad markets by cleaning up. *Esquire* was now to be a *"leisure"* magazine. Nevertheless, and despite the efforts of founder Arnold Gingrich, who had returned three years earlier to help save it, the rate of decline held steady. We three were the infusion, red hot corpuscles sent to rescue the body *chic*. Soon driven witless by the competition imposed upon us, each of us strove to find more operating principles that would assure the magazine's survival and thereby rid him forever of the other two. Safely but lamely—I wasn't sure what would work but I wasn't about to say so—I argued for ideas: let ideas shape the content. Ginzburg favored the shot-to-the-kidney cover line ("Careless Love Can Kill You"). Felker argued for service: "The future of all magazines," he said often, fervently and with total conviction, "is *service.*"

Magazines of service are so plentiful today, and so successful, that the world has bloated beyond recognition. In the past year's awards, the American Society of Magazine Editors included as a category "service to the individual." The finalists consisted of a comprehensive guide on hi-fi equipment, a survey of organic food, an article on the salutary effect of laughter on the immunological system, a series on garden vegetables, and a home-study course for nurses in the treatment of diabetics. Only the word "service" held the contenders in the same stadium.

Service—a service magazine, a service magazine feature—is supposed to leave the reader in an improved position, brighter, wiser, better informed on how to chart his way across the troubled seas of life—e.g., which wrench to use. God knows where the inspiration first came from. Horace Greeley? Social Darwinism? For most editors it is the *intent* that is confusing: service to whom? Ralph Nader's periodic reporting on consumer rip-offs is service. So was Woodward's and Bernstein's reporting on Nixon. An article on selecting wrenches might serve your occasional wrench shopper, but to help him in the choice is not inherently the editor's job, or necessarily part of the editor's required skills. Indeed there is not an editor I know now, or ever have known, who could help me find the right wrench or even knew where to find it for himself.

As the declared intentions of Moffitt and Whittle leave little doubt about their interpretation of the words, it is worth noting that the *Esquire* of the late 1950s would seem in retrospect to be exactly what they have in mind. As imposed from above, the service "budget" called for eight pages of men's wear, four of travel, two of liquor, and an expandable "Talking Shop" section. "But that's just for *starters!*" as the promotion director used to say at regular luncheons for prospective advertisers. "Special sections! Boats in February, hi-fi in February *and* November, business in March, golf in April, cars in June, Pacific travel in August, back-to-school in September. . . ." *Esquire* was a portable flea market. Then and for several years thereafter, it should also be noted, *Esquire* continued to go to hell in a bucket.

Sometimes, although rarely, the decline of a magazine can be arrested. *Cosmopolitan* (who can remember that it once published excellent fiction?) is a living example, delivered from insolvency by the inspired perception of Helen Gurley Brown that a woman without a man is a dollar looking for a pocket. So striking was her success—so logical to the front office—it is difficult now to argue that there is any other solution. Service is the logic of the ledger. Ledger logic orders the convening of readers by the editors to shop the wares advertised by manufacturers. Since most magazines arise today from such a premise, and since the magazine business is booming again (up 11 percent in revenues for March 1979 over March 1978), ledger logic prevails even when it brings disaster.

But in fact, *Esquire* magazine was saved in the 1960s by its constituency of writers. In our best moments those of us who worked there clung to the faith that a writer's consciousness, in whatever direction it is beamed, is the only thing truly interesting about a magazine. "But what's your game plan?" magazine brokers and market strategists always ask. "What's your market?" The answer now seems even odder than it did then: just divvy up the space you have among the best writers you can find and give them interesting things to write about. There were gewgaws and gimcrackery, too, some humor and fun stuff, even service. But the base line of *Esquire* in the 1960s was that it was a writer's magazine. And what riches we had! We brought back old ones (Dorothy Parker, John Steinbeck, Dwight Macdonald), enticed contemporary ones (Vidal, Styron, Richardson, Baldwin, Mailer) and found some new ones (Talese, Wolfe, Wakefield, Wills, Sack, Herr). Nobody enjoyed reading it more than we did. And by God, by 1967 the money was rolling in.

Ginzburg left *Esquire* in 1958; Felker in 1962. Time and separation eroded the ire each of us had nursed toward the other two, turned it, as time will sometimes do, into hard-burned respect. Each convinced at our first meeting the other two should be locked away (an accommodation eventually to be visited upon Ginzburg by the Supreme Court for worse reasons than ours), we didn't pause at parting to say good-bye. But I later called Ralph's wife, while he was in jail, to see if he would write us a circulation promotion; and much later, Felker and I tried without success to get together a political weekly to cover the unfolding Watergate trials.

Both men advanced according to their talents. In one of his recent promotion ads, Ginzburg says he has made his million. I believe him. The founder and publisher of *Eros*, *Avant Garde*, *Moneysworth* and others, he has raised the conventions of circulation promotion to Einsteinian levels of curved space. The *Times* reported recently that he now sells off the names of his subscribers to other publications, to be used for *their* subscription promotions, for more money than he makes from his own magazines.

As for Felker, he has won two, lost two—founded his own New York company and lost it to Rupert Murdoch several years ago, and bought the old *Esquire* in 1977 to lose it last month to Moffitt and Whittle. "In the end," he told *Time* magazine, summing up, "I will do something in journalism. I am a journalist." I believe him, too. The service Felker had in mind from the first was not the service offered by, say, *Vogue*, which is that of a catalogue. His had a journalistic edge to it. The objective was to produce features that would move the reader uptown, to the high rent district where smart people belong. The trick in achieving this was not to dump a lot of expensive garbage into the pages, but to show the reader how much better things were where he was not.

The obsessions of an editor, as with Brown's empathy for frustrated singles, soon define a magazine's personality. Felker is obsessed with power and style. Power and style are not evoked by back-lit photographs of merchandise; they are a state of mind. And they are highly susceptible to desire. You deal with them *journalistically*, as you would with politics or any other important institutions.

In the 1960s, with his new magazine *New York*, and later with *New West*, Felker was free to do his stuff. From the psyche of Pat Nixon to the "Best Bet" in suede shoe tongues, Felker offered his services, drawing about him the most intensely acquisitive readers from the two most impatiently ambitious upwardly-mobile communities in the country, New York City and Los Angeles. Power joined to style forms trends, and Felker was good at this, too. Tom Wolfe's "Radical Chic" and "The Me Decade," while implicitly mocking the magazine carrying them, ran in *New York*. The first issue of *Ms.* was "piggy-backed" inside *New York*, offering his out-front readers a unique preview of what has since become yet another service phenomenon.

In the toughest quarters of town, where ledger logic ruled, Felker's service was soon to be a quantum leap beyond conventional service. Helen Gurley Brown was Tiffany lamps and white wine with the fish; Felker was Hi-Tech, and take-overs with the brandy. Felker's readers didn't want just another new object to replace the one wearing out; they wanted to chuck it all and take a place in *New York* magazine's state of mind. This was quite an accomplishment. And by God, the money poured in there, too.

Soon enough, hardly a major city in the country was without its own version of *New York*. All that was needed for *Los Angeles* magazine to take off was for Felker to announce his intention to buy it. The fever spread to newspapers. All those readers out there, needing help with their lifestyles, were simply being ignored—a forgotten multitude. Help arrived by the carload of newsprint, and special sections flourished—Home, Leisure, Lifestyle, Food, Health, etc. Already enjoying a virtual monopoly in most towns, newspaper publishers had suddenly discovered gushers in their own backyard. All you had to do was put together a special section on "Living"— five or six food articles, a few recipes, household hints—and what supermarket could afford to stay out?

Felker's state of mind led straight to the land of plenty. Although he was duly recognized as the visionary—Murdoch buying him out should be evidence enough, but the editor of the New York *Times* said so, too—Felker doubtless would see this too-quick consolidation of his principles as the vulgarization of an ideal. Nevertheless, more than anyone else, Clay Felker is responsible. It is doubtful that any magazine concept, including Luce's news magazine and picture journalism, has so profoundly affected American journalism, however deleterious in the long run it may prove to be. The man is indeed a journalist.

But is he to blame? Not really. No more than the mechanic who makes a better wrench is liable for a drunken plumber. Service journalism is a tool. Its consequences depend on how you use it. Instructional help for nurses in the treatment of diabetics is an important service. (It won the ASME category.) Cooking recipes for housewives are helpful and harmless. Who would begrudge the sale of advertising space to support the publication offering these things?

The worst that can happen is that a publication sells off its credibility to its advertisers. Not as bad, but bad enough, is the erosion of intent into mindless irrelevancy, e.g., The Daily Wrench Guide to Shoppingmart Town, State of Mind, USA. A danger invisible to the reader, but surely the most insidious, is the loss of editorial space available for anything else—for writers, for example, who have interesting things to say. As we discovered in the late 1950s, *Esquire* had become more a marketplace than a magazine.

Clay Felker struggled honorably to preserve the better qualities of the *Esquire* magazine he published against an alien market climate he had himself helped to form. "The future of magazines is service"—he was right the first time, and *Esquire* just isn't much of a service magazine, and never was. Felker seemed finally to realize this during the year and a half he owned it. He threw out the satin sheet and rubber suit advertising, and the cut rate circulation, trimmed it down and worked hard at making it interesting. There was service—"The Right Stuff," as he called his gift section—but not too much, and not at the expense of editorial content. Finding the right writers to make things interesting takes time, however; and after a reported loss to his backers of five million dollars, Felker's time ran out. How cruel for him—for all of us who treasure it—to read in the newly expanded business service section of the New York *Times* the advertisement purchased by Moffitt and Whittle telling us why they bought it.

HOW TO READ AN EDITOR'S MIND AND MANUSCRIPTS
Myrtle Nord
A former teacher of article writing in Colorado practices her precepts currently as a freelance writer. Myrtle Nord's advice is concise, humorous and simple: Give editors what they want. She also had the foresight to retain the copyright for this article. . . .

An editor told me once that he didn't know what he wanted in an article until he saw it. I didn't believe him. After I looked over several issues of his magazine, I could have told him what he wanted. He wanted six anecdotes and two quotes in every thousand words, with the remainder running fifty percent facts, explanations, or information and the rest divided into opinions of the writer, both pro and con.

I sold him every article I sent him.

You don't have to meet editors face to face to discover what they want; you only have to meet their writing needs—and this you can determine by *really studying* their editorial columns. I have done this with a number of smaller markets over the years, and while my checks are sometimes modest in size, so is the number of rejections I've been receiving since I discovered my blue-pencil system.

Modern Woodman pays only $35 per article, for instance, but after I studied their freelance contributions, I picked off $70 from one submission of two articles, a thing that isn't supposed to be done—first time out. And I'm not a woodman. After studying one issue of *Woman's Circle Homeworker*, I've been counting my $50 checks as regularly as I have a suitable idea and get the manuscript to them. Historical markets have definite patterns, depending on their read-

---

ership. After studying *True Frontier* I submitted a 1,000-word article. They wrote back asking for 500 words more! I expected $50, but I got $80.

Picking Out Ingredients

I came upon my method after reading some advice from Lenore Hershey, editor of *Ladies' Home Journal*. "Read the magazine," she said. "And that means page by page, piece by piece, cover to cover, and then when you know it exactly, go it one better. Research."

She couldn't say more clearly what a writer must do—not just to write for the *Ladies' Home Journal,* but to write for any magazine in the hope of selling it. So how to "go an editor one better"? Blue pencil her magazine! You'll find there is almost a standard formula followed in every department in every magazine.

Get out your blue pencil. Get out a red one, a green one, and a black one, too. You may need six or more in different colors. You can analyze published articles as well as an editor can analyze unpublished ones.

There are many "ingredients" that go into making an article. You may not be able, on first try, to pick them all out, but with diligence you can. You'll have to read and re-read the same articles in the same magazine several times, but if you are serious about studying a magazine, never read one without your pencils at the ready. You are out to discover what the editor wants and you're out to go her one better.

You and Me, Babe

Start by looking for quotes, and anecdotes. Circle each quote in, say, black, and each anecdote in red. Notice how long they are. Go back now and re-read. Underline all the expository facts, information and explanations in, for instance, green. Underline the positive ideas and the negative ideas in different colors, or mark them in such a distinctive way that you can recognize them at a glance. Negative ideas and phrases are those that contain words like "can't," "don't," "never," "not," "none," etc. with an unfavorable connotation, while positive ones are more unequivocal. Both positive and negative concepts are often contained in the same sentence or paragraph.

Check the viewpoint. Does the editor want the writer to speak directly to the reader as "you"? And how often is "you" used? In what person does he like his articles written? First person? Then how often is "I," "me," or "my" used? "He," "she," "them," or "they?" How soon into the piece does he want a specific statement of what the article is about? Underline and star!

Kiwanis Magazine editor David B. Williams reports, "Writers should understand that editors really mean what they say when they state their needs in terms of length, topic and style." If you study the magazine you want to write for in this way, a pattern will emerge, style will become clear, and you will suddenly know how to write for it. At a glance you can see how many facts you are going to need, how many quotes you must have, and how many anecdotes. Not only that, you will know approximately where each one will best be placed in the article you want to write for that magazine.

Reading an Editor's Mind

Every facet of a complete article will be there before your eyes. Begin by analyzing one- or two-page articles. Then move your powers of analysis—and your colored pencils—to the full-length features. You will soon see the blueprint that every article has, and the editor's preferences—which every magazine has. Doing all this will not guarantee the sale of your article, but it will provide a graphic display of what the editor wants in an article, and how he prefers to have it constructed.

While few editors will confess to looking for "formula-written" pieces for their pages, the fact is that most magazines go for the same *type* of writing over and over again. Once you break a few articles down to their basic elements, you are studying the very framework of an article to be constructed for that market. Thus, when an editor says, "Study our slant," or "Study the magazine to see what we do and how we do it," she is actually asking you to become familiar with her publication's flavor, tone and mood—and to know all of her preferences before you submit.

After you've studied the market using my method, your writing will be simplified. If a particular editor wants four quotes and two anecdotes per thousand words, give them to her. That's what I did. In *Writer's Market*, the editor of the *The Saturday Evening Post* says, "Send us a great article and we'll buy it." He doesn't point out the quantity of facts he requires, or how many quotes he wants—or where they come from. Maybe he doesn't really know. But you can discover his subconscious prerequisites if you will study his magazine and use a blue pencil on it. He expects you to know your business.

When the first draft of your own article is finished, pencil it in the same way. Again, at a glance you can see if you have followed the format, conformed to the requirements, captured the flavor, tone, mood, and written with the right slant. You may have to do this for two or three articles from each magazine you want to write for, and you will have to do it whenever there is a change in editors or a change in magazine policy.

This is my second article submission to *Writer's Digest*, and my second acceptance. You now know how I did it. (Don't tell WD's editor, but he likes a minimum of four anecdotes, several successful sales, a "you"—as in "you can do it"—voice for how-to articles, and a fresh approach to solving old writing problems.) If you learn to "study" your market by this method and have material suitable for your chosen magazine, you too can write the way the editor prefers—the first time. Don't submit manuscripts that don't fit the format. Editors are deluged with them. Go them one better. Give them what they want.

Section 8

A BOOK IS BORN

A warm personal relationship often develops
between the author of a book and the publishing
house editor who handles the author's
manuscript. They work together for months. An
editor can help an author improve a manuscript
by suggestions and criticisms. While few editors
face tasks as difficult as Maxwell Perkins did in
preparing Thomas Wolfe's *Look Homeward,
Angel,* the following selection shows how editing
of book manuscripts is done.

A LITTLE HONEST HELP
A. Scott Berg

"I need a little honest help," wrote young Thomas Wolfe in a note
accompanying 1114 pages of book manuscript containing 330,000 words.
Scribners editor Maxwell Perkins obliged, helping Wolfe shape it into *Look
Homeward, Angel.*

As autumn 1928 arrived, a vivacious Frenchwoman named
Madeleine Boyd, wife of literary critic Ernest Boyd and the New York
agent for many European authors, came with an armful of manu-
scripts to see Maxwell Perkins. In the course of their meeting she
spoke of an extraordinary novel of great length written by a huge
North Carolinian named Thomas Wolfe. Then she went on to talk
about other books. When Perkins brought her back to Wolfe's *O
Lost*, she seemed hesitant. "Why don't you bring it in here,
Madeleine?" he said, pressing further. She finally consented upon
Perkins's promise that he would read every word of it. . . . .

"The first time I heard of Thomas Wolfe," Max wrote two decades
later in an unfinished article, "I had a sense of foreboding. I who
loved the man say this. Every good thing that comes is accompanied by trouble."

When *O Lost* reached Perkins, he had a lot of other work on his
hands. This new manuscript of hundreds upon hundreds of pages
was easy to ignore in favor of the dozens of smaller proposals and
first drafts of books that crossed his desk every week. But accompanying the manuscript was a moving note for the publisher's
reader in which the author explained a few of the elements of his
work. It said, in part:

> This book, in my estimate is from 250,000 to 380,000 words long. A book of
> this length from an unknown writer no doubt is rashly experimental, and
> shows his ignorance of the mechanics of publishing. That is true. This is
> my first book. . . .
>
> But I believe it would be unfair to assume that because this is a very long
> book it is too long a book. . . . The book may be lacking in plot but it is not
> lacking in plan. The plan is rigid and densely woven. . . . It does not
> seem to me that the book is overwritten. Whatever comes out of it must

SOURCE: From A. Scott Berg, *Max Perkins: Editor of Genius* (New York: Dutton,
1978), pp. 128–35. Copyright © 1978 by A. Scott Berg. Reprinted by permission of
the publisher, E. P. Dutton.

come out block by block and not sentence by sentence. Generally I do
not believe the writing to be wordy, prolix or redundant.

I have never called this book a novel. To me it is a book such as all men
may have in them. It is a book made out of my life, and it represents my
vision of life to my twentieth year.

I have written all this, not to propitiate you . . . but to entreat you, if you
spend the many hours necessary for a careful reading, to spend a little
more time in giving me an opinion. If it is not publishable, could it be
made so? . . . I need a little honest help. If you are interested enough to
finish the book, won't you give it to me?

Max took up the pages and was at once enthralled by the
opening, in which the hero's father, W. O. Gant, as a young boy,
watched a procession of ragged Confederate troops. Then followed
100 pages about W. O.'s life, long before the birth of his son Eugene,
the actual protagonist of the story. "All this was what Wolfe had
heard," Max later recalled, "and had no actual association with
which to reconcile it, and it was inferior to the first episode, and in
fact to all the rest of the book." . . .

When Max had finally lived up to his end of the bargain he had
struck with Madeleine Boyd, he had not a shadow of a doubt about
the value of the book. But he did recognize major stumbling blocks
that could keep it from getting into print. He knew, for example, that
so intense a work would be resented by a good many people at
Scribners, for it was "very strong meat." The book would also
require considerable "reorganization" and a great deal of cutting.
Max realized he should not even try to get Scribners committed to it
before determining what the author was like and how difficult it
would be to get him to revise. But he was determined to see the book
published. Remembering his battles to publish Fitzgerald and
Hemingway, he was sorry for a moment that he was not a publisher
on his own. . . .

Perkins returned to work from his New Year's holiday on Wednesday, January 2, filled with trepidation at meeting the creator of
the manuscript that covered his desk. Max had been forewarned of
Wolfe's unusual appearance, but he was nonetheless startled by the
massiveness of the six-foot six-inch, black-haired man leaning
against the jamb, filling his doorway. Years later Max recalled,
"When I looked up and saw his wild hair and bright countenance,
although he was so altogether different physically, I thought of
Shelley. He was fair, but his hair was wild and his face was bright
and his head disproportionately small." . . .

Perkins talked about a scene early in the manuscript between the
hero's father—the stonecutter W. O. Gant—and the madam of the
local brothel, in which she was purchasing a tombstone for one of

her girls. In his eagerness Wolfe blurted, "I know you can't print that! I'll take that out at once, Mr. Perkins."

"Take it out?" Perkins exclaimed. "It's one of the greatest short stories I have ever read!"

Max proceeded to discuss different parts of the book from a stack of notes he had made, suggestions for revisions and rearrangements of scenes. Wolfe reeled off whole paragraphs he was willing to excise immediately. At each one, it seemed, Perkins interrupted him to say, "No—you must let that stay word for word—that scene's simply magnificent." Wolfe's eyes grew moist. "I was so moved and touched to think that someone at length had thought enough of my work to sweat over it in this way that I almost wept."

Out of an instinctive tendency to postpone what was difficult, not out of cunning, as Wolfe might have suspected, Perkins left the hardest point for the last. O Lost lacked any real form, and the only way he could see to provide that structure was by selective cutting. Specifically, Perkins thought that despite the wonderful first chapter about the hero's father as a boy, the book should begin with the father already grown in Altamont, the fictional name of Wolfe's hometown, thus framing the story within the experience and the memory of the boy Eugene. Wolfe was not yet willing, during this first editorial session, to agree to so radical a cut as the first 100 pages. But he was not put off by the suggestion. In fact, he had never been so light of heart. "It was the first time, so far as I can remember," Wolfe recorded later, "that anyone had concretely suggested to me that anything I had written was worth as much as fifteen cents."

A few days later Perkins and Wolfe met again. Tom brought notes along indicating how he proposed to set to work in shaping his novel. He agreed to deliver 100 pages of corrected manuscript every week. . . .

On January 8, 1929, Perkins wrote Wolfe that Charles Scribner's Sons had formally accepted O Lost for publication. . . .

O Lost was a portrait of a writer in his youth, living within the mountains that encircled Asheville, North Carolina. Even before it had been edited, publishing gossip had bloated the book's length into titanic proportions. People who had seen the manuscript swore it stood several feet off the ground. In fact, it was 1,114 pages of onionskin, contained some 330,000 words, and stood five inches high. Wolfe himself realized a book that size was probably unreadable and certainly unwieldy. And so in one of his writing journals, he drafted a proposal for condensation: "First to cut out of every page every word that is not essential to the meaning of the writing. If I can find even 10 words in every page this wd. = 10,000 or more in entire mss." By the middle of January he had begun.

"When they accepted my book," Wolfe wrote his friend George W. McCoy of the Asheville *Citizen*, "the publishers told me to get busy with my little hatchet and carve off some 100,000 words." Perkins gave Wolfe some general suggestions for keeping his hero in sharp focus and let him go off alone to cut. The author put in long hours and returned a few weeks later, pleased with his new version of *O Lost*. Perkins was enthusiastic as ever about the poetic quality of the writing, but was not satisfied: For all Wolfe's work, the book was only eight pages shorter. He had made many of the deletions Perkins had suggested, but the new transitions he wrote to connect the severed portions of the narrative had swollen into thousands of words. . . .

Once, sometimes twice a week, without appointment, Wolfe went to Scribners, carrying 100-page sections. If he did not appear, Perkins wrote Wolfe or simply called him up to find out why.

By spring Tom and Perkins were working every day on the revision of the book. "We are cutting out big chunks," Tom wrote his sister, Mabel Wolfe Wheaton, "and my heart bleeds to see it go, but it's die dog or eat the hatchet. Although we both hate to take so much out, we will have a shorter book and one easier to read when we finish. So, although we are losing some good stuff, we are gaining unity. This man Perkins is a fine fellow and perhaps the best publishing editor in America. I have great confidence in him and I usually yield to his judgment."

In time, rumors about the editing of *O Lost* were exaggerated as much as those about the size of the original manuscript; Perkins's evaluation of his efforts on it diminished proportionately. Ultimately he characterized his work as "a matter of reorganization." Whole chunks of the narrative were, in fact, lifted and replaced elsewhere in the book. In truth, however, the most dramatic labor done on the novel was in cutting. Ninety thousand words—enough to fill a large book—were eliminated. . . .

To create cohesion among the stories and lives which crisscross-ed within *O Lost*'s hundreds of pages, Max recommended that the whole saga be "unfolded through the memories and senses of the boy, Eugene." The first and largest cut, then, was the typescript's introductory 1,377 lines. Tom finally agreed with Perkins's criticism that when he had tried to go back into the life of his father before he arrived in Asheville, events not drawn directly from Wolfe's own experience, "the reality and the poignance were diminished." So Gant's history before he arrived in Altamont was reduced to three pages and his remembrance of the Civil War to twenty-three words: "How this boy stood by the roadside near his mother's farm, and saw the dusty Rebels march past on their way to Gettysburg." . . .

Getting through to the end of the story, however, was more

difficult. After a point Perkins had to search not for whole pages to be excised but often merely single phrases. His criterion throughout was his conviction that the interaction between Eugene and his family was the book's absolute center and that any sequences leading the reader away from this central theme had to be removed. . . .

Deletions were as difficult for Perkins to suggest as they were for Wolfe to execute. Still, he pointed out several characters he felt did not warrant as much attention as Wolfe had given them. "I remember the horror with which I realized . . . that all these people were almost completely real, that the book was literally autobiographical," Max said almost twenty years later to another of his authors, James Jones. "But Mr. Perkins, you don't understand," Tom would appeal every time Max sentenced a character to the chopping block. "I think these people are 'great' people and that they should be told about." . . .

Perkins and Wolfe made real progress with O Lost that April. They continued to meet whenever a section was done, and they believed the manuscript would soon be short enough for one volume. Max proposed new revisions, and Wolfe retreated to his apartment either to make further repairs or to begin new parts. With the last of Perkins's suggestions came a confession: his disapproval of the title. Neither he nor any of his colleagues especially liked O Lost. Tom came up with many others and finally brought in a list. Max and John Hall Wheelock were each drawn to a three-word phrase from Milton's Lycidas, the one title Wolfe had also secretly thought the best—Look Homeward, Angel.

Part Three

THE ELECTRONIC AND FILM MEDIA

"What hath God wrought?"

With those words, transmitted between Washington and Baltimore in 1844 by dots and dashes over a telegraph line developed by Samuel F. B. Morse, the age of communication with electricity began. It was the forerunner of the electronic age, which began when Lee De Forest invented the vacuum tube in 1907 and made radio transmission possible.

In the meantime, Cyrus W. Field had laboriously laid a telegraph cable on the bottom of the Atlantic Ocean, the beginning of intercontinental communication by electrical means, in 1868; Alexander Graham Bell had invented the telephone a decade later; and Guglielmo Marconi had perfected wireless telegraphy in 1895.

The wireless was quickly put to work saving lives at sea, notably in 1898 and 1909, but most dramatically in 1912, when the "unsinkable" luxury liner *Titanic* struck an iceberg on her maiden voyage to the United States. The story of how a 21-year-old Russian immigrant, David Sarnoff, remained at his telegraph key for 72 hours, as New York City's only contact with the desperate search for survivors, is told here in an excerpt from Lloyd Morris's book, *Not So Long Ago*. Morris also relates the prophetic 1916 proposal by Sarnoff, later the prime developer and leader of the Radio Corporation of America, for the construction of a "radio music box."

The motion picture got its start when Thomas A. Edison invented the Kinetoscope in 1889. He combined his Kinetoscope with his phonograph recording, and the first synchronized sound films were shown in Paris as early as 1902, when silent movie theaters became popular. D. W. Griffith, whose pioneering achievements are described early in this Part, developed story-telling techniques for the movies. Lee De Forest's vacuum tube provided the amplification for the first "talking motion picture," starring Al Jolson, in 1927.

With entertainment the prime ingredient, radio caught on quickly during the 1920s. During the Depression and pre–World War II years millions listened each week to such entertainers as Amos 'n' Andy, Eddie Cantor, Fred Allen, Jack Benny, and Fibber McGee and Molly. Milt Josefberg provides humorous examples of censorship difficulties encountered by "The Jack Benny Show," and an entertaining history of the "Fibber McGee and Molly" show is taken from Jim Harmon's book, *The Great Radio Comedians*. When newspaper columnist Walter Winchell turned to broadcasting in 1929, his gossipy accounts of the lives of Broadway and Hollywood celebrities, voiced in the staccato bursts of a telegraph key and accompanied by those sounds, provided another brand of entertainment.

With the economic picture grim and war imminent, news commentators came into their own. CBS correspondents took the lead: In sonorous tones H. V. Kaltenborn reported the Spanish civil war and World War II; Edward R. Murrow provided equally graphic reports, including ones of the fire bombing of London; Eric Sevareid established himself as a distinguished correspondent; Elmer Davis won huge success even before he was appointed director of the Office of War Information; and Lowell Thomas offered relief from the serious war reports with his light, human-interest approach to the news.

During the decades after the war, television became a major broadcast medium and nightly network news programs achieved increasingly high ratings. Among the anchormen whose voices and faces became familiar in homes throughout the land are NBC's Chet Huntley and David Brinkley and CBS's Walter Cronkite.

Television loomed on the horizon as early as 1923, when the first electronic television tube, the iconoscope, was patented by Vladimir Zworykin, who headed a group of more than 40 engineers at the RCA laboratories, giving the public of the United States its first view of television in operation at the World's Fair in New York City in 1939. In 1948, after extensive further development, television emerged as a mass medium.

With television commanding attention in the evening, radio increasingly emphasized news programs in the early morning and late afternoon and also became an arm of the music recording industry. Car radio became popular, and transistor sets provided portability. Frequency modulation (FM) broadcasting achieved increasing popularity. Young listeners began to carry AM—FM—audiocassette sets with them everywhere, and their addiction to "rock 'n' roll," "disco," and country-western music is chronicled in Frank Trippett's article, "Portable Music for One and All." Pop recording stars became the rage. One of the most popular groups was the Bee Gees, whose story is told in an excerpt from a *Rolling Stone* article by Timothy White.

Television, of course, changed American life dramatically, and several facets of its programming are explored in the selections that follow. A passage from Geoffrey Cowan's book, *See No Evil,* reveals the creative process at work in the planning of an episode from Norman Lear's "All in the Family." Television news is looked at first through the biographies of John Chancellor, Barbara Walters, Dan Rather, and Charles Kuralt. An article from *TV Guide* analyzes the crusading tactics of the top-rated CBS program, "60 Minutes." How to keep documentaries on the air in the face of ratings wars, industry backbiting, and changing viewer tastes is discussed in "Are Those Powerful Documentaries Gone Forever?". Additional insights into the world of television news are found in the articles "It Could Be Watergate or a Spelling Bee" and "Local-News Blues." A brief look at the program "Three's Company" poses the question: Does television imitate life or does life imitate television? What's ahead in television's expanding world of videotapes, videodiscs, video games, cable systems, pay-TV networks, subscription over-the-air television, and satellite transmission is explored in a *Fortune* article by Peter W. Bernstein.

Two Frenchmen are credited with the earliest developments in photography. Joseph Nicéphone Nièpce produced the first negative images in 1823, and Louis Jacques Mandé Daguerre developed the daguerreotype in 1839. The invention in 1851 of a collodion wet plate process by Frederick Scott Archer, an English sculptor, enabled Mathew Brady to take his celebrated photographs of the Civil War. The Eastman Kodak Company, headed by George Eastman, introduced a transparent film on a flexible support in 1889. The invention of the famous Speed Graphic press camera in 1912 was followed in the 1920s with the first small candid cameras, the German Leica and Rolleiflex, and the age of the picture magazine and photojournalism dawned.

How *Life* magazine photographers overcame tremendous obstacles to take their most famous pictures is told in the article, "God the Photographer," from Dora Jane Hamblin's *That Was the Life.* The work of photojournalists is typified by the careers of Margaret Bourke-White and Gordon Parks, both *Life* photographers and writers.

The world of documentary cinematography is explored in an excerpt from Roy Paul Madsen's book, *The Impact of Film.* And in a selection from her book, *Reeling,* film critic Pauline Kael reveals how difficult it is for a film that is not a big media-related event to find an audience. She also explores the shifts in popular taste as she sees them revealed in films.

Section 9

THE GROWTH OF RADIO, TELEVISION, AND FILM

Development of these media as all-pervasive forms of entertainment and information delivery is due first to the skill of inventors and engineers, and second to the emergence of star performers whom the public enjoyed and admired. Selections in this section look at both aspects through biographical sketches of major contributors of both types.

DAVID SARNOFF, INDUSTRIAL PROPHET
Lloyd Morris

A son of poor immigrants, Sarnoff developed both the electrical
knowledge and the industrial vision to change radio from a transmitter of
dot-dash Morse code messages heard through earphones into a home
entertainment and information medium for the family. From his
imagination emerged the Radio Corporation of America.

On the last day of September, 1906, the chief engineer of the
Marconi Wireless Telegraph Company of America refused to hire a
telegraph operator, but offered the applicant a job as office boy at
five dollars and a half a week. The applicant accepted the job. His
name was David Sarnoff, and he was fifteen years old. Born in
Russia, he had been brought to the United States by his parents six
years earlier. As the eldest of five children, the death of his father
had forced him to become a wage-earner at the age of ten. He had
worked as a newsboy, then became a telegraph messenger. From
his meager earnings he had bought an instrument, taught himself
Morse code, and after six months had thought himself qualified for
an operator's job. At the Marconi Company he studied persistently,
and in 1908 was sent to the station at Nantucket to qualify as an
operator. Two years later, he was made manager of the station at
Sea Gate, New Jersey.

By this time, he had read every treatise on wireless telegraphy he
could procure, and was eager to take a course in electrical engineering at Pratt Institute in Brooklyn. When the John Wanamaker
stores made arrangements with the Marconi system to establish
experimental point-to-point stations in their New York and Philadelphia establishments, Sarnoff applied for assignment to the New
York store, and was transferred there. In April, 1912, he picked up a
terrifying message, "The S. S. *Titanic* ran into iceberg. Sinking fast."
The great liner, new queen of the seas, was on her maiden voyage,
westbound to New York. The S. S. *Carpathia*, receiving the same
message at sea, steamed through the fog toward the doomed liner.
Apprised of the tragedy, President William Howard Taft ordered off
the air all wireless stations except those engaged in rescue work.
Meanwhile Sarnoff sat at his instrument board for seventy-two hours

SOURCE: From Lloyd Morris, *Not So Long Ago* (New York: Random House, 1949),
pp. 431–34. Copyright 1949 by Lloyd Morris. Reprinted by permission of Random
House, Inc.

David Sarnoff

without relief, picking up the heart-breaking details of the disaster, maintaining New York's only contact with the desperate search for survivors. Seven hundred and six of those who had been on board—largely women and children in lifeboats, or clinging to driftwood—were saved; fifteen hundred and seventeen perished in midocean. That any lives were saved was due only to wireless, and the disaster profoundly impressed on the public the importance of radio service. A new law was passed by Congress, strengthening the existing requirements concerning equipment and operators on seagoing vessels. But out of the tragedy there had come a rumor that the work of rescue was impeded by the chit-chat communications of operators at sea. So Congress passed another law, requiring the licensing of operators and transmitting stations, including all amateurs.

By 1916, having risen through a series of promotions, Sarnoff was assistant traffic manager of the Marconi company. In that year he sent a memorandum to Edward J. Nally, the company's general manager, proposing an innovation which, at the time, must have seemed little short of fantastic. "I have in mind a plan of development which would make radio a household utility in the same sense as a piano or phonograph," he wrote. "The idea is to bring music into the house by wireless . . . For example, a radio telephone transmitter, having a range of say twenty-five to fifty miles can be installed at a fixed point where instrumental or vocal music or both are produced . . . The receiver can be designed in the form of a simple 'radio music box' and arranged for several different wave lengths, which could be changeable with the throwing of a single switch or pressing of a single button . . ." Painstakingly, and in detail, the twenty-five-year-old visionary went on to elaborate his project. The music box could be supplied with amplifying tubes and a loudspeaker, and a small loop antenna could be developed to go with it. Thus the music box could be placed on a table in the parlor or living room, the switch set, and the transmitted music be received. This device would do away with the headsets in current use. Within the radius specified, there would be hundreds of thousands of families, all capable of being served simultaneously by a single transmitter. In addition to music, lectures could be broadcast; events of national importance could be announced and instantly received; baseball scores could be transmitted through the air by the use of one set installed at the Polo Grounds. "This proposition," he argued, "would be especially interesting to farmers and others living in outlying districts removed from cities. By the purchase of a 'radio music box' they could enjoy concerts, lectures, music, recitals, etc. which may be going on in the nearest city within their radius."

By methods of mass production, Sarnoff suggested, his proposed "radio music box" could be sold to the public for about seventy-five dollars; he thought one million sets might be sold within three years. "Aside from the profit to be derived from this proposition," he pointed out, "the possibilities for advertising for the company are tremendous; for its name would ultimately be brought into the household and wireless would receive national and universal attention." In making this suggestion, Sarnoff was not proposing that revenue could be earned by the sale of advertising time on the air. His memorandum was based on the assumption that the Marconi company would continue to do its major business in the field of wireless telegraphic service. But he felt that broadcasting could be made a secondary, and highly profitable, activity. Lacking privacy of communication, radio telephony was unlikely to yield a large commercial traffic in the immediate future. Fessenden and De Forest had already discovered this, to their cost. But it was a fact that the chiefs of great communications services were not yet ready to acknowledge. Sarnoff, in his memorandum, was the first to suggest a means of making wireless telephony a profitable service.

But his project was actually a major prophecy. For it added, to the experiments in broadcasting previously made, one vital new element: the "radio music box." Sarnoff understood—as did nobody else at the time—that, so long as listening was confined to individuals each equipped with a headset, the radio audience would inevitably be limited to youthful fans. Not until listening could be made a group pastime, through an instrument like the phonograph playable in the family living room, would radio emerge from infancy. Only such an instrument would enable it to become a medium of mass communication, a social agency of incredible power, and a great independent industry.

This was the development prefigured by Sarnoff's memorandum. Foresight is not universally recognized and, like many another visionary, Sarnoff had to wait.

H. V. KALTENBORN, FIRST OF THE COMMENTATORS
Irving E. Fang
During the late 1930s, when the world was drifting toward World War II, Kaltenborn's broadcasts had an important, often exciting role in awakening Americans to the reality of what was happening. He combined news analysis and commentary for CBS.

Bullets and artillery shells whined overhead as the 58-year-old man picked his way carefully from the farmhouse to a nearby stack. It was an incongruous sight, for the man clearly was no farmer. On this summer's day he wore a dark business suit with a Phi Beta Kappa key strung across his ample stomach. Wire rim spectacles hugged his nose. A steel helmet covered his thinning hair. Across one arm the man held a coil of cable leading back to the house. As he walked to the haystack he played out the cable, at the end of which dangled a microphone.

Where are we? This is 1936. We are in a corner of France which by the accident of a sharp bend in a meandering little river jutted into Spain. The farm sat on a hillside, so when the man reached the haystack he was able to see the battle being waged on three sides of him, his view blocked only by a mortar wall which offered some protection from the bullets. The family living on the farm had evacuated it before the battle began. Inside the farmhouse now, an assistant of the 58-year-old man, a French radio engineer, had wired the other end of the cable to a telephone line, and this line led

SOURCE: From Irving E. Fang, *Those Radio Commentators!* (Ames: Iowa State University Press, 1977), pp. 17–32. Copyright © 1977 by The Iowa State University Press.

northeast to the city of Bayonne; from there the man's voice and the other sounds picked up by the microphone would be transmitted to Bordeaux to Paris to London to Rugby and from there by shortwave to New York and all of America.

The man, H. V. Kaltenborn, was the first radio commentator in the United States. He remained one of America's leading commentators for thirty years, "the dean of radio commentators." The broadcast he was trying to send would be the first in history of a battle in progress. If he could get through, it would be the first time that people sitting in the safety of their homes thousands of miles away, an ocean away from Europe's war, could hear a war actually happening. It took him 11 hours of trying before he succeeded in reporting the bloody battle for the city of Irun, the first decisive battle of the Spanish civil war. Its capture by the Rebels, supported by Hitler and Mussolini, gave an early hint of the long dark night about to descend upon Europe.

One problem after another beset Kaltenborn as he tried to reach CBS News in New York from his haystack. His transmission lines were shot up twice and had to be repaired under fire. Connections with Paris got fouled up. When everything else was ready, an engineer in Bordeaux who was supposed to relay the transmission to Paris decided to step out for an aperitif. Kaltenborn recalled: "When I finally got communications through to New York and told them I could give them a description of a battle in progress with the actual sounds of rifle and artillery fire, I received back this answer: 'Stand by. Too many commercial programs just now. Will call you later.'" New York eventually did give Kaltenborn the go-ahead. By this time it was 9 P.M., local time. Rifle and machine gun fire continued through the darkness, their sputter a counterpoint to Kaltenborn's calm and familiar voice for the next 15 minutes telling Americans listening in the United States in the afternoon about this battle. . . .

In Europe another crisis was bubbling up in 1938, this one hotter than the Anschluss or any of the other crises of the past few years. The *fuehrer* was demanding that Czechoslovakia cede the largely German-speaking Sudetenland. In effect, Czechoslovakia was asked to dismember itself. Understandably, the Czechs refused and bravely prepared for war. British Prime Minister Neville Chamberlain, anxious to keep peace at all costs, offered to go to Germany to negotiate the matter personally with Herr Hitler. From Edward R. Murrow and the staff of correspondents he had assembled in European capitals came frequent reports of moves in a diplomatic situation that threatened to send Europe into another multination war. These reports arriving at CBS in New York along with news from the wire services needed to be put in perspective for a network audience beginning to pay serious attention to events across the Atlantic. The news commentator selected to provide that perspective was H. V. Kaltenborn. For twenty days of the Munich crisis, he hardly left CBS Studio 9. He slept near the microphone on an old army cot which a custodian had dug up along with an old army blanket for cover. News director Paul White would wake him with wire service bulletins. "A flash, Hans," White would say, punching a special button that connected Studio 9 with all 115 stations of the CBS network, interrupting different regional feeds for different parts of the country. Kaltenborn made 102 broadcasts, certainly a record of sorts for twenty days. All were impromptu, as he intermingled the latest wire service news, reports from CBS correspondents, and speeches by European leaders with his seemingly bottomless fund of knowledge of European affairs. Sponsored programs were cancelled left and right to bring reports in from Europe and to give H. V. Kaltenborn the scope to interpret the news.

A lengthy program interruption for overseas correspondent pickups and a Kaltenborn analysis would be followed by an announcer saying something like: "We would like to express our appreciation again at this time to the makers of Oxydol, sponsors of 'The Goldbergs'; the makers of Ivory Soap, sponsors of 'Life Can Be Beautiful'; the makers of Chipso, sponsors of 'The Road of Life'; and the makers of Crisco, sponsors of 'This Day Is Ours.' "

A *Time* reporter peeked into Studio 9, then filed a report saying:

> As Hitler's Berlin speech was relayed through CBS's Studio 9 last week, a man who looks like a prosperous professor sat at a desk, listening through earphones. Before the hysterical roar at the end of the speech died away, he began to talk into a microphone with clipped, slightly pompous inflections, using facial expressions and gestures as if he were addressing a visible audience. Without pause Hans von Kaltenborn has translated and distilled a 73 minute speech, and for 15 minutes proceeded extempore to explain its significance and predict (correctly) its consequences. This incident and many another like it led even rival networks to pay tribute to "H. V." Kaltenborn last week. That he offered better comment on the crisis than anyone else was because he also offered a better combination of talents.

Clearly, here was a man suited to this time and place. It was Kaltenborn's finest hour. Portable radios were just coming on the market. Many were sold during that September 1938. People in offices and on city streets huddled around them to listen when Kaltenborn came on.

Kaltenborn later recalled the pressure he worked under:

> Every one of these talks was entirely unprepared, being an analysis of the news as it was occurring. The talks were made under a pressure I have not experienced in seventeen years of broadcasting. . . . Night and day through Studio Nine milled engineers and announcers. Even as I

talked I was under constant bombardment by fresh news dispatches carried to my desk from the ticker room. I read and digested them as I talked. Despite the crisis, the network still observed split-second timing, even of special programs. I had to watch the control-room engineer for my cues. Earphones clamped over my head as I broadcast brought me the voice of the speakers abroad whose words I followed with my commentary. At times, while I talked, my attention had to focus on four things at once in addition to the words I was speaking. Between talks there was still no time for rest. Four tickers just outside Studio Nine ground out cable dispatches on continuous sheets, hundreds of feet of them every hour, miles of them by the time the crisis was well advanced. Every word had to be reviewed in order to get the complete picture in my mind.

Fluent in both French and German, Kaltenborn could directly translate and immediately comment on the speeches of European leaders, interspersing observations of his personal interviews with Hitler, Mussolini, and other actors on the European stage.

Fascinated listeners also heard Kaltenborn tell correspondent Maurice Hindus in Czechoslovakia what was going on in the rest of the world, for Prague was largely dependent upon cable and telephone service routed through Berlin. During the Munich crisis, that service had totally failed. That Hindus could communicate at all was due to the foresight of Czech radio authorities who, figuring their country was next on the Nazi menu after Austria, built a transmitter powerful enough to beam a signal directly to North America. Without it, censorship in Berlin would almost have sealed Czechoslovakia off from direct communication with the outside world.

All in all, it was an exhausting performance for a 60-year-old man, even one who kept as fit as Kaltenborn. At one point he was so groggy because of broken sleep that when a prayer for peace was delivered by the Archbishop of Canterbury, he analyzed that, too.

PACE-SETTERS OF AIRWAVES AND FILM
Phillip H. Ault and Warren K. Agee
Eight additional contributors to the growth of radio, television, and film are presented here in readings highlighting their personal impacts on audiences and their roles in shaping professional excellence.

LOWELL THOMAS

Lowell Thomas was by far the most durable of all radio broadcasters. For nearly half a century he was a friendly voice reporting the

---

SOURCE: This article was written expressly for this book.

Lowell Thomas at the microphone

news with heavy emphasis on its human interest aspects. He first appeared on the air, sponsored by *Literary Digest,* on September 29, 1930, and was heard regularly on CBS until 1976, when he was 84. He remained active until his death in 1981.

Thomas was already an international personality when he turned to radio. He had toured the world, lecturing and showing films of his adventures in the Middle Eastern desert and beyond the Khyber Pass, and he had written several books.

He began his broadcasting simultaneously on NBC and CBS, the former in the East, the latter in the West, succeeding the colorful war correspondent Floyd Gibbons. At first Thomas was the only daily broadcaster on the air for any network. In those early days he obtained his news material by reading the New York evening newspapers. Although Thomas avoided editorial comment, his broadcasts had a personal tone because of the way he stressed human interest stories, injected comment about his world travels, and talked in a casual, colloquial style. His nightly sign-off, "So long until tomorrow," became a household phrase.

The Thomas broadcasts were so popular in the 1930s that one night when, as a publicity stunt, Western Union offered to let anyone in his audience send a telegram to him free, he was overwhelmed with 265,567 of them.

On April 6, 1892, Lowell Thomas was born the son of a doctor in Greenville, Ohio. He grew up in the mining camp at Cripple Creek, Colorado, attended the University of Northern Indiana at Valparaiso, then worked on a newspaper in the Colorado mining camps and later on the Chicago *Evening Journal*. At 24 he was head of the speech department of Princeton University. During World War I, he filmed war action in Europe and the Middle East and "discovered" the fascinating British desert warrior, Lawrence of Arabia.

A dapper man, slim and curly-haired, Thomas had a resonant voice that conveyed warmth, and the oratorical training to use it skillfully.

During the 1930s and 1940s, Thomas also was the voice of the Fox-Movietone newsreels, a demanding job in itself. Frequently, because his desire for travel was insatiable, he did his broadcasts from remote places around the world, especially from challenging ski slopes. He was still skiing in his eighties.

Neither pontifical nor flamboyant, Thomas held his audience for so many years because he treated the news in human terms, looking always for the revealing sidelight and the off-beat chuckle.

EDWARD R. MURROW

Before and after World War II network correspondents of the highest caliber exerted a profound influence over public affairs with their expert reporting and analysis of the events of that turbulent era. Accurate, informed reporting was the hallmark of the news team that Edward R. Murrow developed for CBS in Europe, beginning in 1937. It was Murrow who developed the first "World News Roundup," aired on March 13, 1938, and carrying the short-wave reports of both broadcasters and newspapermen: William L. Shirer in London, Edgar Ansel Mowrer in Paris, Pierre Huss in Berlin, Frank Gervasi in Rome, and Murrow in Vienna, which had just been occupied by German troops. Graphic accounts of daily developments continued throughout the war; it was radio journalism's finest hour. Eric Sevareid, a member of the CBS team, later observed:

Never, surely, in the history of human travail had so many owed so much to so few human voices. . . . Churchill speaking to the world. J. B. Priestley speaking to his own people. Ed Murrow speaking to America each night, the timbre of his powerful, steady voice reflecting the spirit of England and persuading millions of Americans that the cause was not lost even when it seemed beyond saving. . . .

Murrow was in London during its siege by German planes and mechanized fire bombs. Here is a portion of his report on September 22, 1940. It profoundly affected his American audience, which had grown accustomed to his opening line, "This is London . . .":

I'm standing again tonight on a rooftop looking out over London, feeling rather large and lonesome. In the course of the last fifteen or twenty minutes there's been considerable action up there, but at the moment there's an ominous silence hanging over London. But at the same time a silence that has a great deal of dignity. Just straightaway in front of me the searchlights are working. I can see one or two bursts of antiaircraft fire far in the distance. Just on the roof across the way I can see a man wearing a tin hat, a pair of powerful night glasses to his eyes, scanning the sky. Again, looking in the opposite direction, there is a building with two windows gone. Out of one window there waves something that looks like a white bed sheet, a window curtain swinging free in this night breeze. It looks as though it were being shaken by a ghost. There are a great many ghosts around these buildings in London. The searchlights straightaway, miles in front of me, are still scratching that sky. There's a three-quarter moon riding high. There was one burst of shellfire almost straight in the Little Dipper. . . .

Down below in the streets I can see just that red and green wink of the traffic lights; one lone taxicab moving slowly down the street. Not a sound to be heard. As I look out across the miles and miles of rooftops and chimney pots, some of those dirty-gray fronts of the buildings look almost snow-white in this moonlight here tonight. And the rooftop spotter across the way swings around, looks over in the direction of the searchlights, drops his glasses and just stands there. There are hundreds and hundreds of men like that standing on rooftops in London tonight watching for fire bombs, waiting to see what comes out of this steel-blue sky. The searchlights now reach up very, very faintly on three sides of me. There is a flash of a gun in the distance but too far away to be heard.*

After the war, Murrow conducted his own radio and television news programs. One of his most memorable "See It Now" broadcasts occurred on March 9, 1954, when Senator Joseph R. McCarthy of Wisconsin was conducting a congressional investigation into domestic Communism, using smear tactics that became known as "McCarthyism." Murrow ended his broadcast with these words:

*Quoted in Edward W. Bliss, Jr., *In Search of Light: The Broadcasts of Edward R. Murrow* (New York: Knopf, 1967), pp. 37–38.

. . . No one familiar with the history of this country can deny that congressional committees are useful. It is necessary to investigate before legislating. But the line between investigation and persecuting is a very fine one, and the junior senator from Wisconsin has stepped over it repeatedly. His primary achievement has been in confusing the public mind as between the internal and the external threat of Communism. We must not confuse dissent with disloyalty.

We must remember always that accusation is not proof and that conviction depends upon evidence and due process of law. We will not walk in fear, one of another. We will not be driven by fear into an age of unreason if we dig deep in our history and our doctrine and remember that we are not descended from fearful men, not from men who feared to write, to speak, to associate and to defend causes which were for the moment unpopular.

This is no time for men who oppose Senator McCarthy's methods to keep silent, or for those who approve. We can deny our heritage and our history, but we cannot escape responsibility for the result. As a nation we have come into our full inheritance at a tender age. We proclaim ourselves, as indeed we are, the defenders of freedom—what's left of it—but we cannot defend freedom abroad by deserting it at home. The actions of the junior senator from Wisconsin have caused alarm and dismay amongst our allies abroad and given considerable comfort to our enemies. And whose fault is that? Not really his; he didn't create this situation of fear, he merely exploited it and rather successfully. Cassius was right. "The fault, dear Brutus, is not in our stars but in ourselves."*

ELMER DAVIS

Elmer Davis was one of the most widely known and respected journalists of the first half of the twentieth century. He was born in Aurora, Indiana, in 1890, attended Franklin College, studied for three years as a Rhodes Scholar in England, spent fifteen highly profitable years as a novelist and free-lance writer, and reported news for the New York *Times* for ten years before joining the Columbia Broadcasting System.

For three years, on the eve of World War II and during its first six months, millions each evening heard his perceptive radio commentaries about world affairs, delivered in twangy Hoosier accents and tinged with dry humor and telling barbs. His clear-eyed reporting and his ability to cut through conflicting news reports to find the truth led President Franklin Roosevelt to appoint Davis as director of the Office of War Information in June, 1942.

Davis's job was exceptionally difficult because his office had to coordinate information from the military and numerous government agencies, wrestle for funds each year with a Congress suspicious that OWI would become Roosevelt's personal propaganda vehicle, and overcome opposition from a large segment of the press that

*Ibid., pp. 247–248.

Elmer Davis

publicly resented having to do business with an official "spokes-man."

The OWI news bureau had 250 regular employees, and 300 reporters and correspondents used its facilities. Davis established a Domestic Branch, which, according to the director, "did not with-hold news because we did not like it, nor delay it to produce a greater effect," and an Overseas Branch, which also told the truth to foreign peoples but with selective emphasis and timing. The OWI worked harmoniously and effectively with George Creel's Office of Censorship.

Of his office's domestic operations, Davis declared that, "It is the job of OWI not only to tell the American people how the war is going, but where it is going and where it came from—its nature and origins, how our government is conducting it, and what (besides national survival) our government hopes to get out of victory."

At war's end, Davis dissolved the office and received the plaudits of his countrymen, including high government and military officials and the press, and of the nation's allies. Even Davis's harshest critics gave the operation generally high marks, both for informing the American people about the progress of the war and for telling the world of America's aspirations, through the United Nations, for world peace. As a final act of service to his government, Davis wrote a thoughtful and brutally frank treatise on the handling of information in a democracy at war. After its declassification, the report was published as one of the Association for Education in Journalism's *Journalism Monographs* (No. 7, August, 1968), edited by Ronald T. Farrar.

For his work with CBS, and after the war with the American Broadcasting Company, Davis three times won the prestigious George Foster Peabody award for radio news reporting and information. He died in 1958. "He was called the Mount Everest of commentators," said the New York *Times*, "towering in serenity and grandeur over the foothill Cassandras of his time."

ERIC SEVAREID

A profoundly sensitive and thoughtful man, a keen observer and skilled writer and public affairs commentator, Eric Sevareid exerted a considerable influence over millions of CBS radio and television listeners in a broadcast career that spanned 40 years.

Sevareid was born in 1912 in Velva, North Dakota, the son of a bank employee with Norwegian roots. His family moved to Minneapolis, where he worked on his high school newspaper, and after graduation he was hired as a reporter by the Minneapolis *Journal*. His employer let him take night and afternoon classes at the University of Minnesota, where he majored in political science with a strong emphasis in journalism and worked on the campus daily. In his fascinating autobiography, *Not So Wild a Dream* (1946), Sevareid described his thoughts about journalism:

> A journalist is a jack-of-all-trades and master of none—except his own, which is being a jack-of-all. I had to know, not only how to write a sentence with a beginning and end, but something of history, government, economics, science, languages, and art in its various forms. I had at least to grasp the rudiments of these, to know what was known and established in these fields and what men still sought in them. For it is this which is at the core of "news" and its understanding.

Sevareid covered World War II in Europe as a member of Edward R. Murrow's remarkable staff, then became one of CBS's most distinguished correspondents and commentators. His profundity and wit may be enjoyed most fully in his book, *Small Sounds in the Night* (1956). Similar published collections of his commentaries are *In One Ear* (1952) and *This is Eric Sevareid* (1964). All merit reading by those who would write or who enjoy good writing.

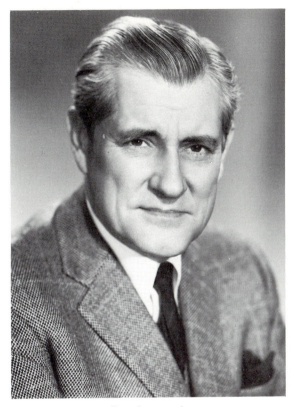

Eric Sevareid

In his final commentary on the "CBS Evening News with Walter Cronkite" program in 1977, Sevareid summed up his life's work and the rules he had followed:

By my time of life one has accumulated more allegiances and moral debts than the mind can remember or the heart contain. So I cannot enumerate my betters, my mentors and sustainers during so many years of trying to use, with sense, this communications instrument, as unperfected as the persons who use it. But they know that I know who they are.

Many are gone, including the man who invented me, Ed Murrow. Some died in the wars we were reporting. I have gone the normal span of a man's working life, rather abnormal in this calling, and it's a happy surprise.

We were like a young band of brothers in those early radio days with Murrow. If my affections are not easily given, neither are they easily withdrawn. I have remained through it all with CBS News, and if it is regarded as old-fashioned to feel loyalty to an organization, so be it.

Mine has been, here, an unelected, unlicensed, uncodified office and function. The rules are self-imposed. These were a few:

- Not to underestimate the intelligence of the audience and not to overestimate its information.
- To elucidate, when one can, more than to advocate.
- To remember always that the public is only people, and people only persons, no two alike.
- To retain the courage of one's doubts as well as one's convictions, in this world of dangerously passionate certainties.
- To comfort oneself, in times of error, with the knowledge that the saving grace of the press, print, or broadcast, is its self-correcting nature. And to remember that ignorant and biased reporting has its counterpart in ignorant and biased reading and listening. We do not speak into an intellectual or emotional void.

One's influence cannot be measured. History provides, for the journalist, no markers or milestones. But he is allowed to take his memories. And one can understand, as he looks back, the purpose of the effort and why it must be done.

A friend and teacher, the late Walter Lippmann, described the role of the professional reporter and observer of the news in this manner:

> We make it our business to find out what is going on, under the surface and beyond the horizon, to infer, to deduce, to imagine and to guess what is going on inside—and what this meant yesterday and what it could mean tomorrow. In this way we do what every sovereign citizen is supposed to do but has not the time or the interest to do it for himself. This is our job. It is no mean calling and we have a right to be proud of it and be glad that it is our work.

In the end, of course, it is not one's employers or colleagues that sustain one quite so much as the listening public when it be so minded. And I have found that it applies only one consistent test: not agreement with one on substance, but the perception of honesty and fair intent. There is, in the American people, a tough, undiminished instinct for what is fair. Rightly or wrongly, I have the feeling that I have passed the test. I shall wear this like a medal.

Millions have listened, intently or indifferently, in agreement and in powerful disagreement. Tens of thousands have written their thoughts to me. I will feel, always, that I stand in their midst.

This was Eric Sevareid in Washington. Thank you and goodby.

WALTER CRONKITE

For much of two decades, the 1960s and 1970s, the preeminent television newscaster in the United States was Walter Cronkite. His authoritative, neutral manner and deep-timbered voice projected an image of avuncular wisdom as he presided on the "CBS Evening News with Walter Cronkite," and at the CBS anchor desk during marathon broadcasts of space missions, national political conventions, and election returns. He frequently interviewed Presidents and world leaders. His somber, unruffled style created such an air of believability that public opinion polls list him among the most trusted persons in the country.

Cronkite served as a war correspondent for United Press in Europe during World War II, returned to the United States after the war, and entered radio. In 1950 he joined CBS News. As the network developed its television news programming during the 1950s, Cronkite was assigned to television and covered his first political convention in 1952. At that time Ed Murrow was the star of the CBS television news staff. Cronkite became the central figure on the CBS Evening News in 1962.

During the early and middle 1960s, NBC news with its anchor team of Chet Huntley and David Brinkley consistently led CBS in the ratings, but the Cronkite show took the lead in 1967 and retained it through the 1970s.

Cronkite prided himself that he was not merely a "pretty-boy news reader," a type he disdained. His own appearance on the screen was solidly traditional, with white cuffs and cuff links adding a touch of formality. As managing editor of the Evening News, as well as its anchor man, he had an important role in the selection of stories. Much of his success resulted from his diligent preparation for events he covered, so he could give them perspective and extemporize intelligently before ending, "And that's the way it is."

After retiring from his familiar role on the Evening News in 1981, Cronkite continued to appear on specials and documentaries for the network, launching his successful "Universe" show. His successor on the news show was Dan Rather, a Texan who achieved prominence while covering the White House and clashing on the air with President Nixon during the Watergate crisis. Rather brought a more aggressive, harder-hitting style to the program.

CHET HUNTLEY AND DAVID BRINKLEY

"Good night, David." "Good night, Chet." So went the sign-off on one of America's greatest television news programs, the "Huntley/Brinkley Report" for NBC News, which dominated the nightly ratings through much of the 1960s. Huntley read the news from New York, Brinkley added the Washington report and comment with a bit of eyebrow-lifting, and millions of Americans imitated their crisp signoff technique.

A somewhat desperate National Broadcasting Company put together the Huntley-Brinkley team for the 1956 political conventions to offer battle to the CBS News team, which was then dominant. It worked, and by 1964 CBS and Walter Cronkite had been driven into temporary eclipse by this unlikely teaming of personalities. Chet Huntley was a deep-voiced, craggy, somewhat conservative man, reflecting warmth and courage in his conventional approach to the news. David Brinkley was a cynically whimsical reporter, famed for

Chet Huntley and David Brinkley on 1968 election night

his dry wit, his expressive querying of conventional politics, and his editorial comments, which eventually became his sole stock in trade. Together they pleased a great audience of Americans in an association that lasted from 1956 to 1970, when Huntley retired.

While Brinkley had called for American withdrawal from Vietnam as early as 1967, particularly criticizing the air bombings, Huntley found the liberal movements and turmoil of the 1960s disturbing. He went home to his native Montana as operator of his $20-million Big Sky resort, which soon became the target of conservationists. When Huntley died of cancer in 1974, Brinkley told his nightly audience how often the pair had heard young persons say, "I grew up with you guys."

Brinkley found himself teamed with both John Chancellor and Frank McGee after Huntley's retirement, and he escaped into "David Brinkley's Journal," a nightly commentary. But NBC News again called on him in 1976 to help raise the audience ratings for the evening news as co-anchor with John Chancellor. It was another happy teaming of talents, and Walter Cronkite again had his hands full defending his turf. Brinkley had even more startling news stories to raise an eyebrow over, and he did it with the same dry-voiced approach Americans had come to admire. In the 1980s he continued his witty commentaries on his own program for ABC News.

D. W. GRIFFITH

David Wark Griffith is recognized as the most significant pioneer of the American motion picture industry because he did more than any other person to develop the techniques of storytelling with film.

After a childhood in Kentucky, where he was born in 1875, Griffith traveled as a minor actor. In 1908 he first performed in the movies for the Edison Company in New York. That same year he cautiously directed his first film, *The Adventures of Dollie*, for Biograph.

Motion pictures were in their crude infancy. Most films lasted about ten minutes and were primitive in story line, photography, and lighting. The performers were filmed full length, as though they were acting on a stage. Since there was no sound, they gestured and "mugged" extravagantly to make the viewer understand the story with the aid of captions.

Griffith quickly created devices giving the camera mobility. He

D. W. Griffith (middle), pioneer movie producer and director

developed the close-up and cross-cutting, the technique of quickly switching shots from one performer to another to show their actions as the story climax develops. He introduced backlighting, by use of reflectors, and numerous other aids to cinematic narration. Although he made his films without a script, he rehearsed his casts meticulously. Often he acted out the various roles to show performers what he wanted from them.

Most renowned of Griffith's pictures is *The Birth of a Nation*, released in 1915, a monumental depiction of the Civil War and the Reconstruction period. When it is shown at festivals today, the film seems jerky and stilted, because it has been chopped up during the intervening decades and usually is shown at a speed different from the original. When compared to other pictures of that era, however, *The Birth of a Nation* stands out as far ahead of its time. Among other famous Griffith films are *Intolerance*, *Way Down East*, and *Orphans of the Storm*.

Slender, quiet, usually good-humored, Griffith was a tremendously hard worker. Many early-day stars and directors learned their trade from him. His innovations were used so universally that some became clichés. During the 1920s his career declined and Hollywood passed him by. For sixteen years before his death in 1948 he was virtually inactive, living in a hotel room, quite forgotten, almost like a character in a contemporary film by a director steeped in Griffith technique.

Section 10

RADIO, THEN AND NOW

Contemporary radio differs enormously from the pretelevision days, when radio was the main home entertainment. This section recalls two famous network comedy shows and a controversial commentator from the past, then turns to radio as it is today.

JACK BENNY VERSUS THE CENSORS
Milt Josefberg

Jack Benny was an immensely popular comedian on network radio and, unlike some others, made a successful transition to television. For many years Josefberg was a script writer for Benny. Here he illustrates how intense network censorship was in the 1940s and 1950s.

. . . We had countless scrapes with the censors, and in these earlier, more innocent days the censors were stricter even though the material was far more bland. For instance, on rare occasions you were allowed to say "hell" on a dramatic show, but it was verboten in comedy. Also, under no conditions were you permitted to make a reference to a rival network. This once caused a complaint from Fred Allen which became a classic. Fred said, "NBC denies the existence of hell and CBS, though not necessarily in that order."

We also had some classic combats with the censors, and some of them were completely pointless. For instance, in one sketch where Jack was a college student, we used the device where Jack would act as the narrator, speaking through the filter mike, to set the scene, and then he and the other performers would do their dialogue on the regular microphones. At this point in the sketch Jack was describing his meeting with the campus queen. He said, "Then *she* came into the room. You could tell she was the campus queen because she was wearing seventeen fraternity pins. No sweater, just pins."

Now the actress who played the part of the campus queen was Veola Vonn, who . . . was built. To give you an idea of her build, if you walked into a room and Raquel Welch was standing next to Veola, you'd push Raquel aside and say, "Excuse me, sir, I want to talk to the girl." But in writing about her entrance for the college sketch, her figure didn't figure in our thoughts. We just thought it was a funny line: "She was wearing seventeen fraternity pins. No sweater, just pins."

Our censor must have worked hours with a tape measure because he came screaming into the studio saying that the joke was dirty. Seventeen small fraternity pins couldn't possibly cover all of

---

SOURCE: From Milt Josefberg, *The Jack Benny Show* (Westport, Conn.: Arlington House, 1977), pp. 175–79. Copyright © 1977 by Milt Josefberg. Reprinted by permission.

Miss Vonn's frontage. To appease the censor we offered to change the number to one hundred and seventeen fraternity pins, but it was still no go. He claimed that number of pins was still too few to cover the view. How he arrived at his final figure we'll never know, but he insisted that we say three hundred and fifty fraternity pins. We quickly acquiesced because we didn't feel it would affect the line in any way—but it did. It got the biggest, dirtiest laugh of the year, because the audience evidently figured that we said she was wearing three hundred and fifty fraternity pins because we wanted to show how big her bosom was, and only a girl with a build like that could carry all those pins.

Despite the fact that this was the era of radio and only a few thousand people ever saw Miss Vonn perform, compared to the many millions who heard her, her bust measurements caused another conflict with the censor.

We did many sketches on the Benny broadcasts, and most of them were our versions of famous movies, plays, and novels. On one occasion we decided to do a "Klondike" show, using the frozen North with its howling winds and freezing weather as the basis of our humor, and perform our version of Robert W. Service's famous poem, *The Shooting of Dan McGrew*. As in all sketches of this type, we had Jack do narration and then we went into dramatization. However, on this show Jack's narration was simply the recitation of the four-line stanzas of the poem, with each quatrain furthering our story line. We didn't tamper with Mr. Service's poem, and after the big shoot-out ending of the sketch, Jack recited the final lines:

Pitched on his head and pumped full of lead
Was dangerous Dan McGrew,
While the man from the creeks lay clutched
To the breast of the Lady that's known as Lou.

Now while this may not have been Shakespeare or even Rod McKuen, it has been a part of our literary folklore for over half a century, and we quoted the last line exactly as it was written. However, because Veola Vonn played "The Lady That's Known As Lou," we had to alter the final sentence to read, "clutched in the arms of the lady that's known as Lou."

Censors sometimes blue-penciled our scripts with good reason, but occasionally we couldn't figure out how their minds, if any, worked. On one show we were doing a Wild West sketch. The script called for the sound of a buffalo stampede, and one of the cast members was to yell, "Look out everybody—it's a buffalo stampede." We got our script back from the censor, where it was always sent immediately after being mimeographed to receive what was called "Official Continuity Acceptance," and the censor had attached a very interesting note. He called our attention to the earth-shaking fact that at that particular time, in that exact location in America, there were no buffaloes. There were only bison. Therefore, we would be misleading our millions of listeners if we were to say that it was a buffalo stampede. It's lucky for the censor who brought us this historic news that John Wayne wasn't our guest or the Duke might have put a bullet through his head.

We finally made this man feel that he had done his duty to all of those millions listening out in radio land when we said that we would keep the line, "It's a buffalo stampede," but that we would make our sound-effects men give us the sound of a bison stampede. He left, looking at us in a peculiar manner, but that's the way we did it.

Sometimes we'd put in stage directions that were only instructions for the performers. Once we hired an actress to play a prim old maid, and in her directions we had the words: "She speaks in the voice of a virgin prune." Now even though no one outside of our cast, which got a chuckle at this impossible voice description, would ever see or hear this line, the censor objected. The word "virgin" could never in any manner, shape, or form be used in a radio script. . . .

The last time I ever had a hassle with a censor involving Jack Benny was when he was a guest star on a "Here's Lucy" program for Lucille Ball's 1971 season. In the script which I wrote with Ray Singer, Jack has been reminiscing about the women in his life. Suddenly he looks at his wristwatch, realizes that it's very late, and tells Lucy that he and a friend of his have a date with two chicks.

As he said this, the doorbell rang, and Jack opened it, admitting George Burns who was making a surprise cameo appearance. Jack welcomed George, said that he'd be ready to leave in a minute, and asked what time they were supposed to pick up the girls. George told Jack he's already picked them up and called out, "Trixie, Ginger, come on in." Lucy reacted when Trixie and Ginger walked in, because they were two of the cutest eighty-year-old ladies our casting department could hire.

Their appearance and Lucy's reaction was good for a big laugh. Then one of these octogenarians said, "We're sorry we're late, Jack, but we had to stop and pick up the pill." Lucy, in wide-eyed surprise, asked, "The pill?" And George Burns answered, "Yes, the one that keeps us awake." Then George, Jack, and the two old ladies exited.

Believe it or not, we had censor trouble—and not just the usual phone call this time, but a personal visit from the head censor who claimed that our joke about "the pill" would corrupt every person past the age of puberty. Lucy said, "For heaven's sake, if anyone knows what purpose the pill serves, then just looking at the four of them"—and she pointed to Jack, George, and the two "girls"— "makes the viewer realize that not one of them is under seventy-five years old, and they don't need the pill." At which Burns said to Lucy, "I don't think you have to waste money on it either." We all were laughing at this—all of us, that is, except the censor.

At this point Jack resorted to the type of logic I've mentioned earlier. . . . "Look," he said to the censor, "if a viewer hears this dialogue and *knows* about the pill, then that person also knows we're way past the age when we need it, so we can't corrupt them. On the other hand, those who know nothing about the pill have seen or heard ads and commercials for 'No Doz' which is used to keep you awake, and it's funny that four people like us would go on a date and have to take a pill to keep us awake for the evening."

I don't know whether Jack's logic swayed the censor, or whether he was a bit in awe of the formidable three B's—Ball, Benny, and Burns—but he let us do it. The mere mention of "the pill" by the eighty-year-old lady got a worthwhile whoop from the audience, and George's blackout line got an even bigger laugh plus applause.

FIBBER McGEE AND MOLLY AT WISTFUL VISTA
Jim Harmon

The rattle, crash, and bang that resulted when Fibber McGee opened the door of his overloaded closet was one of radio's cherished gags. It happened every week at 79 Wistful Vista. Fibber and his wife Molly were favorites for a long time, corny yet endearing.

The most practiced liar in Radioland, Fibber McGee, would inevitably have for his best friend the most pompous windbag on the air, Throckmorton P. Gildersleeve. They were the foremost of many citizens on a street called Wistful Vista. (The name seems even more appropriate in retrospect than it did at the time.) Every Tuesday evening during the colder months of the thirties and forties these two cronies got together with a group of other colorful suburbanites. The hostess was the Fibber's wife, Molly. . . .

The scene was virtually always the McGees' living room into which dropped the same guests every week. . . . you could easily imagine you were listening to a comedy remote from the McGees' living room at 79 Wistful Vista.

SOURCE: From Jim Harmon, *The Great Radio Comedians* (New York: Doubleday, 1970) pp. 23–31. Copyright © 1970 by Jim Harmon. Reprinted by permission of Doubleday & Company, Inc.

Fibber McGee and Molly (Jim and Marion Jordan) at Wistful Vista

The setting, itself, was the typical American living room, and, in fact, you never had much occasion to go into the McGees' kitchen or dining room, certainly not the bedroom. The only other door ever opened besides the front door was the one to the hall closet. Behind it was hidden the accumulated memorabilia of most American families, opening on a million past mistakes—bladeless can openers, never-used skis, long-discarded mandolins. Out it all came in a shameless cascade—*BAM! POW! THUD! SMASH! KER-R-R-RASH! Tinkle, Ting!* It was an auditory pop-art experience. . . .

When the program first went on the air, Fibber was a compulsive daydreamer and liar, and his tall tales lacked charm. He was not someone to whom the audience could relate and the series had a limited potential. However his character began to mellow in less than a year and soon he was doing no more impractical dreaming than the rest of us—that is, still quite a lot. And like the rest of us, Fibber had someone to hold him down closer to reality—the little woman, Molly.

Molly was the practical one of the family . . . . Her Irish brogue was laced with Gaelic wit and she was capable of advising Fibber that his latest scheme was no more practical than a square egg; that it was as original as spreading butter on bread; that it stood to make them as much money as selling subscriptions to a censored edition of the *National Geographic*. But in spite of it all, Molly stood dutifully by and tried to help her husband through whatever nonsense he was up to that week.

In private life, Fibber McGee and Molly were actually a married couple, Jim and Marion Jordan. They had met shortly before World War I at a choir rehearsal at St. John's Church in Peoria, Illinois. . . . They married in 1918—not a good year for unruffled domestic bliss. After several attempts to enlist, Jim Jordan was called up on a draft quota and was sent to France. . . . When he got back, Jim and Marion spent the next several years going between mundane jobs and vaudeville appearances, while raising two small children. They got their first radio work singing commercials on WJBO in 1925. . . .

It was 1931 before they got together with Don Quinn, a one-time cartoonist turned radio script writer. Their first series together was called "Smackouts," about a talkative grocer who was always "smackout" of everything. It was a mixed success, but it drew the attention of John J. Lewis, an important advertising agency representative, and he helped the trio to get a network show. It was for this show that Don Quinn created the characters, Fibber McGee and Molly. Success in radio and in several Hollywood films soon followed. . . .

It was Don Quinn who molded the Jordans into the McGees with his masterful scripts. . . . all that was needed to start off one of their Tuesday night shows was the tiniest of premises. Fibber might be looking through the old photo album of all their dear old friends in Peoria—"There's Fred Lompac—we were together all through high school—never could stand him." Or Molly might be trying to get Fibber to gather up their forest of empty milk bottles and take them in for 2¢ on the bottle. Or on any number of occasions, they might be cleaning up the disaster left by opening that hall closet door.

Fibber: Gotta straighten out that closet one of these days, Molly. I don't see that electric cord anyplace . . . Oh, my gosh!
Molly: Now what?
Fibber: Look! My old mandolin—remember?
Molly: What are you getting so misty eyed about it now for? It falls out of the closet every time you open it.

Fibber. It always falls out of the closet but this is the first time the case has busted open. My gosh—my old mandolin.
(Plunks a tune.)
Needs a little tuning, I guess.

Molly: A little tuning! That's as melodious as a slate pencil!

Fibber: Remember how we used to go canoeing on the Illinois River and I used to serenade you . . . ?

Molly: I never knew whether you took up the mandolin because you loved music or hated paddling.

Fibber: And remember the time you dropped the paddle to applaud one of my songs and we had to paddle home with the mandolin?

Molly: I wasn't applauding. I was swatting mosquitoes.

Somehow, the McGees never managed to spend a quiet Tuesday evening at home alone. There was always a parade of guests dropping in . . . . One of their guests in later years was Doctor Gamble, a medico who was vastly more intelligent, if not always more clever, than McGee. Fibber would dazzle him with another of his trademarks: stupefying eliteration. . . .

The conflict between Doctor Gamble and McGee was allegedly good humored, although I've come within a whisker of being punched in the jaw for less. This rivalry was typical of that between McGee and a number of his guests, including not only Gamble (played by Arthur Q. Bryan) but Gale Gordon as Mayor LaTrivia, who was a well-meaning vote-solicitor but who McGee and even a mischievous Molly always tricked into some exasperating tongue twister. "Why, yes, Mrs. McGee, I suppose you would call the minister who sells gasoline in Peoria as a sideline a part-harm, petrol-packing possum—that is a part-time pistol-peddling parson—I MEAN, A POT-FARMED POSSUM-PINKING PAR-TRIDGE!!! Oooooh, *good day!*"

A more restrained rivalry was present between McGee and the Old Timer. Fibber would launch into a new joke he had heard about a man who had cut himself a toupée from his wife's mink stole and was promptly attacked on the street by a rabbit-hunting dog. "That's pretty good, Johnny," the Old Timer would wheeze, "but that ain't the way I heerd it. One feller sez to the other feller, he sez— 'Say, I see you sprouted a new head of hair over night.' The other feller replies 'Over night? I had to pay the store on this for six months!' ". . .

One of the supporting characters . . . was the snooty society matron from whom the McGees heard altogether too much. When McGee would make a spectacle out of himself with one of his lamebrain schemes, Mrs. Uppington was sure to appear on the scene. "But Mrs. McGee . . . we simply *cawnt* have your husband making a spectacle of himself . . . He is lowering the tone of the whole neighborhood!" Even tolerant Molly could lose her cool. "Don't give me that Vassar Vaseline, dearie! Next thing you'll get so exclusive you'll want our fire department to have an unlisted phone number!" Mrs. U. would then come back with something devastating like: "Well reahhhly, Mrs. McGee!" . . .

. . . Undoubtedly the most important supporting character ever on the show was the Great Gildersleeve, originally played by Harold Peary.

As with Doc Gamble and Mayor LaTrivia, Gildersleeve and McGee were constantly at each other's throats. The self-satisfied, lovably pompous fat Dutchman would naturally be in conflict with Fibber McGee who always tried to deflate every windbag—except himself. "Now, McGee," Gildy would rumble ominously when Fibber's insults finally began to work through his well-padded hide. They could even argue about crossing the street to mail a letter.

WALTER WINCHELL: GOSSIP ON THE AIR
Phillip H. Ault

Winchell graduated from the ranks of Broadway and movie gossip writers and broadcasters to a role as self-anointed expert on national politics and foreign affairs. His "hot tips" were accepted for a time by audiences hypnotized by his staccato delivery of entertainment patter.

Most raucous of the national radio commentators during the 1930s was Walter Winchell, a former vaudeville singer and dancer whose brashness, staccato style of speaking, and know-it-all manner attracted a gigantic following. Despite his crudity and frequent blunders that made knowledgeable editors and reporters cringe, he had enormous popular appeal.

Winchell came up from the tenements and streets of New York, where he was born April 7, 1897. At thirteen he quit school without finishing sixth grade.

Using the knowledge and acquaintances he acquired on the vaudeville circuits, Winchell began writing a Broadway gossip column for the tabloid New York *Evening Graphic*, whose loose journalistic standards helped to shape Winchell's own. In 1929 he switched the column to Hearst's morning tabloid, the *Daily Mirror*. There it ran for a remarkable thirty-four years, until 1963, written in part by assistants and publicity men.

Winchell's broadcasting career started in 1929, when he went on the air with the same type of Broadway and Hollywood gossip he put in his column. Breathlessly he opened each program with the

---

SOURCE: This article was written expressly for this book.

Walter Winchell

salutation, "Good evening, Mr. and Mrs. America and all the ships at sea! Let's go to press!" Then he plunged into a rapid-fire miscellany of show business items sprinkled with political opinions, international reports (for which he had no personal background), celebrity stories, and hot Washington news tips. His reports on a cafe society debutante's engagement and Adolf Hitler's latest war-like move in Europe were delivered with equal emphasis.

In his brassy style, Winchell coined words and phrases that gave his broadcasts zest and worked their way into the language. He reported a pregnancy as "infanticipating," called liquor "giggle water," recorded that a broken romance "went phfft," and said a divorced couple had been "Renovated" because the Nevada city was a place where many spouses went for quick divorces in those days.

He never hesitated to use his network broadcasts and his news-paper column to promote pet causes, pay off favors, and attack his enemies. His was a world of superpatriotism, of arbitrary opinions often based on false information, and of good guys and bad guys, without shades of gray. He had no intellectual depth and pretended to none. Yet his hold on his audience was so intense that he greatly aided the third-term election campaign of President Franklin D. Roosevelt in 1940. He was a close friend and volunteer publicity agent for J. Edgar Hoover, whose deeds as director of the Federal Bureau of Investigation he glorified on the air.

Winchell believed his own legend. He carried a gun, drove with a red light on his car, and held court nightly in the Stork Club, a New York night club whose fame he built up with his broadcasts. The Winchell style of commentary did not fare well on television, however, although he was the successful narrator of one crime series, "The Untouchables." He died in 1972.

PORTABLE MUSIC FOR ONE AND ALL
Frank Trippett in *Time*

Radio today is everywhere. The transistor enables manufacturers to produce sets in such small boxes that they can be carried in the pocket or hand as the listener walks or works. Trippett explores the social significance of this phenomenon in this *Time* essay.

They are everywhere, and always going full blast. They play nothing but frenzied music, day and night. They are inescapable. The innocent can get battered with jazz at the newsstand, rock at the bus stop and the diabolical thump-and-shriek of disco before and after. "Shake, shake/Shake your booty" blares forth from one of them, but not quite in time to drown out another one that is roaring out with "Ring my bell/Ring my bell, my bell/Ting-a-ling-a-ling." It is as though the Great God Muzak has berserked out of the dentist's office and run amuck with all his decibels exposed. Actually, the public tranquility is being regularly murdered by that handy modern convenience, the portable transistor radio. Its proliferation is nothing if not phenomenal.

So, evidently, is its addictiveness. Radio buffs have begun to cling to portables full time as though they were life-support systems. Thus meandering music has become commonplace in every metropolis and conspicuously so in the big ones such as Detroit, Boston, Chicago, Los Angeles and New York. While the portables are played ostensibly for private enjoyment, the music is freely shared with the world—but not always to applause. Indeed, many captive listeners consider the force-fed entertainment an assault. Whatever else it may be, the new wave of unavoidable music is pervasive—

SOURCE: From *Time*, July 23, 1979, p. 60. Reprinted by permission from Time, The Weekly Newsmagazine; Copyright Time Inc. 1979.

and the dial is rarely turned to bring in even the most important news.

The main legions of portable fans are mostly young and predominantly—but not always—black or Hispanic. They do not quite add up to a subculture, but they may represent the rise of a new species of radio fan. Their ears are tuned in constantly to what they call the box. Their boxes come in all sizes, with the biggest the size of suitcases and the best equipped with auxiliary tape decks. The fancy status symbols of the genre—Sanyos or Sonys or JVCs— cost up to $400, but for a mere $55 a box-toter can get a General Electric tape model that comes with a shoulder strap, a 5-in. heavy magnet speaker, an automatic program advance, a variable tone control, an eight-track cassette player and, of course, great promise: It is called Loudmouth II. To the new breed of listener, such equipment has already begun to seem a natural part of existence, inevitable. Says one of them, young messenger Anthony Edwards of Manhattan: "You got your box, they got their box, everybody into their own box. You got to keep the sound moving with you."

And do they ever keep it moving. They play their boxes at work, at leisure, alone, in crowds. In Chicago, they often gather on the street around somebody's car at night and party while working out their boxes in ensemble. Their boxes go with them to parks, in elevators, along beaches. On Fire Island, N.Y., a local ordinance against radio sounds on the shore drew forth about 1,000 box-lovers with their music blaring maximally in protest. Boxes go with them on bikes, in recreational skiffs, even on roller skates. In Manhattan's Central Park, the box phenomenon has linked up with the roller-skating craze to produce a bizarre form of discoing that not only defies description but seriously discourages it. Box-toters seem insatiable. Affectionate couples, a blaring box snuggled between them, have been observed moving their lips, presumably yelling sweet nothings at each other over 90 or so decibels of *their* song. Who needs it?

No, the appropriate question is, why? Or, better yet, why, why, why? Why take a portable everywhere? Why play it so loud? Why play it at all in crowded public places? Only the great, washed middle class offers that simple, singular answer; the cavalcade of music amounts to a continual bombardment by the surly troops of the underclass. But social scientists have indulged in more intricate thinking. The box brigade's music, some believe, would seem aggressive only to people unsympathetic to young, poor minority folks. Says Tufts University Sociologist Peter Dreier: "Music is played in public all the time, in shopping centers, record stores and dentists' offices. Nobody minds. But when poor kids do it, suddenly it's a problem."

Other analysts suspect that the music is simply a social comfort to the box-toter, a "security blanket," in the phrase of Sallie Churchill, a social work professor at the University of Michigan. Or a mode of claiming identity. "They're invisible people most of the time," says Sociology Professor Joseph Helfgot of Boston University. "Here is something large and loud that makes them suddenly visible." It may also be a method of walling off the real world. Says Theodore Goldberg, associate professor of social work at Wayne State University: "The kids can just forget when they turn on the music."

The box-toters themselves are not much given to self-analysis. They do not wonder about their practice but blandly accept it. Such is the force of fad and habit; they could not question their need for the music any more than they question their need for air. When coaxed to speak, they see the big carry-around sound as both a relief from loneliness and an aid to socializing. Clearly their constant music shuts them off from a world that has not lately said anything they would prefer to hear.

It is remarkable, in a way, that the world of the city manages so often to notice them, such is the jarring of racket that is the urban norm. After all, an inevitable clamor has tested the sanity of urbanites since the city was first invented. Caesar futilely decried Rome's noisiness, and the situation has got steadily worse ever since. The typical metropolis today suffers not only incessant horn bleats but the ingenious cacophony of screaming sirens, screeching tires, shattering jackhammers, clangorous garbage cans, raucous trucks and roaring buses, not to mention those interesting citizens who haunt all city streets shouting ominous sermons into the middle distance.

Given such ear-rattling circumstances, one might suppose that the addition of even frenetic music to the urban uproar would be greeted with widespread inattention. Still, the city dweller, though besieged by chronic noise among other civic abominations, is not indifferent to his plight. Certain noises, those of traffic, for instance, are inherent in city life; essential and irreducible, they must be borne. The music of the boxes is not in that category. So the spread of the box-toters is raising a public rumpus over a valid social issue—the public's right not to enjoy the private entertainment of an individual.

Irritation at force-fed music has alrady prompted a few police crackdowns to keep the radios silent on buses and trains, and has moved many municipalities to exercise existing antinoise laws to hold the volume down in other public spots. The backlash against the box-toters has been widely mild so far, but how their increasing numbers will fare in the face of increasing irritation is anybody's guess.

Finally, the more interesting question is how the constant listeners will lure through a prolonged addiction to the resonant emptiness of radio music. By shutting out the world so habitually, they seem almost to be seceding from it. Yet an invitation to them to come back in might as well be laid aside. Who would hear it?

FM BROADCASTING: WHAT IT IS
Sydney W. Head

Radio programs are heard either on amplitude modulation or frequency modulation—AM or FM. The audience for FM has grown spectacularly. Listeners know that FM music has greater fidelity, but few know why. This selection explains.

Frequency modulation broadcasting, usually referred to as *fm* in the United States and as *vhf* radio in Europe, occupies a block of frequencies in the very high frequency band. . . . In the United States 100 channels have been so designated, running from 88 to 108 MHz. With channel width set at 200 kHz, this band can accommodate 100 channels. The FCC numbered them 201 to 300, the first 20 being reserved exclusively for noncommercial educational (public broadcasting) use.

In the vhf region of the spectrum . . . . the propagation path is direct so that fm has no allocation problems arising from the different behaviors of ground waves and sky waves. An fm broadcast transmitter has a stable coverage pattern, its shape and size depending on power, height of transmitting antenna above the surroundings, and terrain formation. Maximum signal reach is approximately to the horizon. Another advantage of fm to the allocation planner is that the fm signal blanks out interference from other stations much more effectively than does the am signal. An fm signal must be only twice as strong as a competing signal to override it, whereas an am signal must be twenty times as strong.

From the listener's standpoint, however, a more important advantage of fm over am is its freedom from static. It can provide undistorted reception in areas where and at times when satisfactory am reception is impossible. A related advantage is fm's greater fidelity. Fm's high channel capacity enables the reproduction of sounds up to 15,000 cycles per second, a pitch so high that not everyone has sufficiently sharp ears to hear it. Nevertheless, such

---

high frequencies play an important role in high-fidelity sound reproduction. The characteristic quality of a sound comes not from its fundamental pitch—the pitch by which we identify it—but rather from *overtones*. Being multiples of a fundamental pitch, overtones reach higher into the sound frequency spectrum. Overtones supply the acoustic nuances implied by such sound terms as *timbre, color,* and *quality*.

Fm scores over am in still another way, with its greater dynamic range. This refers to the range in degrees of loudness between the faintest reproducible sound and the loudest. The human ear has an amazing capacity to adjust to extremes of loudness and softness without being overloaded, but sound reproducing systems have much less flexibility. Very faint sounds tend to become lost in the noise of the system itself, whereas very loud sounds tend to overload the system and cause distortion. Am broadcasting even sacrifices some of the dynamic range it could have by artificially compressing the signal in order to obtain maximum average power output.

Fm's 200-kHz channel has twenty times the capacity of an am channel. In addition to enabling a threefold increase in sound fidelity—from 5,000 to 15,000 cycles per second—these additional frequencies enable fm stations to multiplex a variety of auxiliary signals in the channel. Stereophonic sound, facsimile, subscription background music, reading for the blind, medical conferences, school bus programs, and potentially many other secondary services may be multiplexed on fm channels simultaneously with the normal, monophonic sound service.

Section 11

RECORDING

Musicians of the "pop" scene are a special class of mass communicators. Although their means is music, and their medium the recording, the successful ones are adept participants in all the media. Their unique cultural niche, and their reactions to it, are special phenomena of our age. Groups come and go, but their place and their response hardly change.

THE BEE GEES—EARTHY ANGELS
Timothy White

Rock music groups rise to almost instant fame through their recordings and sometimes vanish almost as quickly. The Bee Gees have had a more lasting success than most. In this extract from his article about them, White gives us a glimpse into the frenzied pop world of high-decibel sounds, flashing lights, drugs, adulation, and promotional "hype."

The Bee Gee trio of Robin, Barry, and Maurice Gibb is one of the wealthiest, most successful and certainly most pervasive musical forces in what group leader Barry solemnly calls "the pop wilderness."

The Bee Gees first attracted national attention in the late Sixties with their mordant, adenoidal hymns to mining disasters, hapless lovers, self-delusion and broken hearts. They have released more than thirty runaway hit singles, their output since 1975 consisting mostly of the buoyant, uptempo toe-tappers that helped spawn the billion-dollar disco industry.

Whether it be through the *Saturday Night Fever* or *Grease* soundtracks, their own albums or those of their beneficiaries, the Bee Gees' slick, bleating harmonies and rug-cutting rhythms have become an unignorable presence in our culture.

When they first emerged in England in the late Sixties, the then five-member group (with Australians Vince Melouney on lead guitar and Colin Peterson on drums) seemed more than a little bit precious. Toothy lead singer Robin warbled urgently in his drainpipe vibrato about some willowy girl who was "such a holiday," while the rest of the band, clad in quasi-Elizabethan garb, posed like footmen behind him.

Sibling strife in 1969 caused the group, now down to a foursome, to disintegrate. Amidst rumors of bitter battles, manic spending sprees, hard drinking and drug abuse, the estranged brothers released two undistinguished solo albums. A year and a half later the brothers reconciled, carrying on as a trio, and a subtle evolutionary process began. The lads started to loosen up, grow scruffy beards and trade their velvet morning coats for jeans and body shirts. Their album titles shifted from high-minded handles like

The Bee Gees in action

Trafalgar to the lighthearted *Life in a Tin Can*. And whereas Robin had previously been the frail, quavery focal point, now Barry assumed center stage with a more aggressive, flamboyant vocal tack.

"There's three of us and there's always been three of us, and since school days it was us three against the world," says Barry Gibb, 32, stretched out on a snowy white couch in his castlelike Miami Beach villa as he remembers the Gibbs' earliest days in Manchester, England. Born on the British Isle of Man, the boys shuttled back and forth between their first home and England as their bandleader father, Hugh, bounced from job to job. Music was as much a refuge as an avocation, and the brothers were singing together and performing publicly before they reached their teens.

From the start, the Bee Gees' sound has been compared—usually unfavorably—to the Beatles' early work, and it is only recently that the Gibbs feel comfortable enough to mention both groups in the same breath. But far more striking are the Bee Gees' deep, across-the-board insecurities and regrets, feelings they have been masking with cutup antics since their vaudeville days.

"We had to get to know each other again," a somber Barry says of the brothers' reconciliation. "We knew when we came back together that it would take us five or six years to become anything like what we were before we started on the drugs, and before we got fame and huge egos and all that. And six years is what it took. We had to become brothers again and forget those little things that aggravated us about each other. It was an awful lot to get rid of."

"It's nice to see Robin in the shape he's in now," he confides. "If you'd seen Rob six years ago you would have gotten a fright, and I've gotta say that about all of us. We got into pills—Dexedrine—and liquor too. The only thing that we never got involved with was LSD."

When it's mentioned that the Bee Gees should now feel vindicated and secure in their success, the leader of the band is incredulous.

"In this position," he argues, "we are constantly up against the wall with people saying, 'Please us!' It's an invisible thing, but you can feel the wall behind you, and you can hear the whole industry saying, 'Give us a surprise, we *expect* you to outdo yourselves.' "

"It always goes on that way," Barry nods to himself in exasperation, wringing out his sweaty palms. "I mean if *Spirits* is a monster—pray that it is—then once again we'll be up against the wall."

Now it's my turn to be incredulous. This seems like an unusually joyless attitude, especially considering that *Spirits Having Flown* has presently produced three hit singles and sold more than four million copies in the States alone.

"We spent ten months doing this new album," he explains. "You've gotta believe that a lot of times we cut a track, then said. 'No! No good!' A lot of tracks we cut a dozen times. We just did not want to go wrong with this album."

To understand the Bee Gees' brotherly chemistry, it's essential to observe them together on their own turf, Maurice making fun of his balding head and filling every moment of dead air with a quip, while Barry encourages him coyly; Robin all the while sitting off in a corner, appearing distracted but actually waiting for the precise moment to deliver a devastating barb.

Though the Gibbs have uniformly skittish gazes, each has a wholly distinctive spark in his eyes. Robin's are hard and self-absorbed; Barry's are open, inquiring and vulnerable; and Maurice's are kindly but pained, melancholy. As he hurries around his house, showing me his new outdoor Jacuzzi, his video projector, the specification sheets for the jet he's purchased, the photos of boats he covets and the brochures for the English manor house he is interested in buying, I get the eerie feeling that I am more comfortable as a brief visitor to his world than he is living in it.

For all the hard knocks, trials and disappointments they must endure, it's still a good time to be a Bee Gee. But there is much uncertainty ahead. Chief theorist/strategist Barry Gibb is acutely conscious of maintaining the Bee Gees' well-scurbbed "image" as he maps out future merchandising ventures with the sober, detached air of a Madison Avenue advertising executive.

"People have come up to us and said, 'Do you realize how much power you have now?' " Barry says. " 'You could change the world with some of the things you say.' And I say to them *(bitterly)*, 'Leave me alone.' "

"Power is fleeting; so is ego," he cautions. "When you start putting religion or whatever into it and tell the world how it can be saved, it just rubs against people. Politicians have no idea how to save the world, so why should pop stars?"

Section 12

TELEVISION

As this section opens, Norman Lear is applying the touch that has made him such a brilliant television producer. Our glimpse of him at work is accompanied by a sample television form sheet showing the mechanics involved in script preparation. On the news side a galaxy of network stars pass, followed by some less glamorous aspects of television news. Then entertainment presents itself. The section signs off with a survey of television's intriguing future.

NORMAN LEAR FIXES A SCRIPT

Geoffrey Cowan

Lear probably has done more than any other single participant to break down television's taboos and to stimulate the medium's willingness to handle delicate topics. The appearance of his "All in the Family" in 1971 was a milestone.

The most effective editor is a tasteful creator who insists on imposing his own standard of quality on a program. By asking questions and probing the meaning and point of the material, such an editor can actually improve and enrich a show which would otherwise have exploitive or tasteless moments. Using his "belly standard" as his guide, Norman Lear may well be the best editor in television. Some of his associates, in fact, contend that editing—that is, creating story ideas and inspiring others to implement them successfully—is Lear's greatest skill.

At 4:30 P.M. on Wednesday, January 18, 1978, Lear attended a run-through of "All in the Family." Although he had been involved some weeks earlier in a general discussion of the episode's theme, he had not read the script. The episode was scheduled for taping on Friday night.

The premise of the show was simple enough. It is midwinter. Edith and Gloria are away for the weekend, and Archie and Michael accidentally lock themselves in the storage room of Archie's new bar. During the run-through there were some amusing lines and there was some wonderful acting, but the core of the show seemed cheap and hollow. The implications of the two men getting drunk and spending the night together were played for all they were worth. The run-through ended with a policeman who, after walking in on Archie and Michael asleep together under a blanket, mildly accuses Archie of being gay.

After the run-through, an observer had a brief conversation with one of the writers, commenting that the segment was filled with sex and dirty jokes. The writer, who had not worked on the episode and evidently found it distasteful, agreed. "Once you start to write a series of sex jokes, it's hard to break away from them," he explained.

SOURCE: From Geoffrey Cowan, *See No Evil* (New York: Simon & Schuster, 1979), pp. 290–93. Copyright © 1979 by Geoffrey Cowan. Reprinted by permission of Simon & Schuster, a Division of Gulf & Western Corporation.

Norman Lear

At that moment Norman Lear got up and walked toward the center of the room. After a run-through the cast and key creative personnel all get together to discuss the show and how it can be improved. The discussion process is called "notes." If there are serious problems, the session can last for hours.

"Well, what do you think?" someone asked Lear.

"I don't know," he answered. "I can't relate to this episode at all. Maybe I shouldn't even be in on these notes." He was wearing a neck brace and he seemed to be in some pain.

"Come on, Norman," Rob Reiner said solicitously. "What are your concerns?"

"Well, this isn't anything like the show we talked about in my office. It's all sexual innuendo. It doesn't have any meaning. I thought that we were going to use this premise to reveal something about Mike and Archie." Lear pointed out that even the sex-related humor would be funnier against a backdrop of a poignant story.

Within a few minutes something extraordinary started to happen. A group of professional men and women were sitting in a circle trying to figure out how to make the show significant. Lear suggested that it should be a program about what these two men, who are so careful not to appear vulnerable or reveal themselves, discover when they are locked away alone. He proposed that the theme center on race prejudice, on the roots of Archie's hatred for Jews and blacks. Everyone participated. One person suggested that Archie's father was the source of his prejudice. Then someone said, "No, lots of people have racist fathers and don't become bigots themselves." A third person suggested that Michael could reveal that his father had been a bigot too.

The story began to emerge. Archie and Michael would be drinking Scotch, and as they drank they would become more honest with each other. Why did Archie, with a racist father, become a bigot when Michael, with his, didn't? Archie could explain that he had loved his father even though he was a tough, mean bastard, that your father was always right, because he had brought you into the world.

But why did Archie always call people names—like "Polack" (for the first time Michael would explain how that hurt his feelings) and "meathead"?

A black writer told a story from his youth. When he was in grade school a kid had lost one of his shoes. His family was too poor to buy another pair, so he came to school with one boot and one shoe. And kids started to tease him. They called him "shoebootie."

It was a perfect story. Everyone agreed that it should apply to Archie, to his experience while growing up in the Depression.

Within two hours the creative team had breathed poignancy and warmth into the episode. If they hadn't found the roots of race prejudice, they had at least found a way of peeling back a few layers of two men who are known and loved by most Americans.

As the story emerged, there was no policeman in the last scene. Archie, having revealed so much of himself to Michael and fogged over by the liquor, starts to fall asleep. And Michael pulls an old awning over Archie to keep him warm.

Two nights later the show was taped in front of a live audience. For only the third time in eight years they gave Carroll O'Connor and Rob Reiner a standing ovation.

It was the creative process at its best.

And it proved that quality doesn't hurt ratings. On Sunday, February 12, for the first time since the imposition of the Family Viewing Policy, "All in the Family," with that episode, was aired at 8:00 P.M. The all-important Nielsen ratings that week listed "All in the Family" as the fifth most popular show in America.

(Following on p. 195 is a page of a typical television form sheet showing script methods in a local station.)

TELEVISION FORM SHEET

NAME: (CLIENT, PRODUCER OR BOTH)
DATE: (DATE OF TELECAST(S)
TIME: (TELECAST TIME IF KNOWN)
(ANNCR OR TALENT: LIVE
   STUDIO OR ANNCR'S BOOTH)

VIDEO

THE VIDEO DESCRIPTION IS ALWAYS LISTED IN "CAPS" ON THIS SIDE.

SOME EXAMPLES ARE:

ROLL FILM (PRODUCT) (FILM #)

1. (DESCRIBE SCENE # AND EVERY SCENE THEREAFTER *IF* THE COPY IS TO SYNCHRONIZE WITH FILM SCENES. EACH NEW SCENE IS LISTED DIRECTLY OPPOSITE THE FIRST WORD OF THE PARAGRAPH WITH WHICH IT SHOULD BE RUN. LIST SCENES BY NUMBER.

ROLL FILM (PRODUCT) (FILM # SOF)

(SOF INDICATES THAT THE SOUND IS ON THE FILM SOUNDTRACK. IN SUCH CASES ALWAYS LIST THE SYMBOL "SOF" ON THE AUDIO SIDE OF THE PAGE ALSO.)

SL OR 35MM: (DESCRIBE SLIDE AND LIST ITS NUMBER)

EVERY SUCCEEDING SLIDE AFTER THE FIRST IN A SERIES IS LISTED AS:

TAKE SLIDE OR 35MM (SLIDE DESCRIPTION)

LIVE STUDIO: (DESCRIBE THE INTENDED SCENE OR SCENES IN PROPER SEQUENCE.) INDICATE A "TAKE" OR "DISS." THE FORMER INDICATES A DIRECT VIDEO TRANSITION; THE LATTER A SLOW VIDEO DISSOLVE FROM ONE SHOT TO ANOTHER.

SPECIFIC SHOTS MAY BE INDICATED ACCORDING TO COMPOSITION:
   WS: COVER SHOT, EST SHOT
   MS: MEDIUM SHOT
   CU: CLOSE-UP
   BCU: CLOSE-UP (BIG)
   ECU: EXTREME CLOSE-UP

CAMERA MOVEMENTS INCLUDE: DOLLY IN, TILT UP OR DOWN, TRUCK RIGHT OR LEFT.

Audio copy should begin at this point. It should be double-spaced. Underline for emphasis. Use lower case for audio script. Use CAPS and place in parenthesis any special instructions to talent or announcer. . . . (WITH SPIRIT LAUGH)

Music should be cued as follows:

MUSIC: IN AND UNDER ON CUE

MUSIC: IN

MUSIC: OUT

MUSIC: (THEME) UP ON CUE

Note that music (and sound) cues are underlined. When the audio portion of a commercial is on recording or electrical transcription . . . they should be indicated as follows:

START REC: (IDENTIFY RECORDING. PRODUCT ETC.)

START ET: (IDENTIFY ET AND CUT NUMBER. LIST PRODUCT)

Whenever REC or ET is used the script should be written out word for word. When SOF is used, the final sentence should be included.

For continued script

——MORE——

ANCHOR PERSONS WITH IMPACT
Warren K. Agee, Edwin Emery, and Phillip H. Ault
As the 1980s opened, four of the most effective television news
personalities were Chancellor, Walters, Rather, and Kuralt, discussed here
by the editors of this book.

JOHN CHANCELLOR

Television news anchor people should be articulate and smooth,
naturally extemporaneous, always at ease—but, above all, they
must be reporters first and news announcers second. Such a person
is John Chancellor, who succeeded the late Chet Huntley as anchor
for the "NBC Nightly News" in 1970 and served until 1982.

Everything that happened to the Chicago native (born in 1927)
from the time he was hired as a copyboy for the Chicago *Sun-Times*
after World War II prepared Chancellor for his career as one of
America's best-known newsmen. He reported briefly for the *Sun-
Times* before NBC News employed him in 1950. He edited and shot
film, reported for the old John Cameron Swayze "Camel News
Caravan" program, covered some of the first civil rights stories,
served as a correspondent in Vienna, London, Moscow, Brussels,
and Berlin, was host of the "Today" show, covered the White House,
and directed a television documentary starring his long-time associate, David Brinkley.

In 1966 President Lyndon Johnson persuaded Chancellor to serve
as director of the Voice of America. Two years later he returned to
NBC News, shortly moving to his evening anchor position. "Being an
anchor," says Chancellor, "involves much more than reading copy
(which in my case I mainly write myself) off a prompter. It means
writing and helping to produce special documentary programs; it
means doing special events, which can't be scripted; and it means
doing political conventions and election night programs, which are
the best fun of all."

Election night coverage, however, isn't all fun. Chancellor and
his counterparts on the other networks must spend days doing their
homework—learning everything possible about candidates, voting
trends, political machinations of every sort, and officeholders for
generations back. Sitting at the nerve center of a vast and highly
complex reporting organization, Chancellor can be at ease only by
drawing on his years of news experience reinforced by the facts and
figures he has virtually memorized.

From copyboy to reporter to TV jack-of-all-trades to VOA director

SOURCE: This article was written expressly for this book.

John Chancellor

to anchor, John Chancellor has packed a lifetime of experience into scarcely more than thirty years. His next step? "A return to reporting for the 'Nightly News,'" he declares. "I don't want to cover fires and hurricanes, but I do hope that I might be able to explain some things that are going on. I hope that someday I might try to answer some of those questions in a useful way."

BARBARA WALTERS

Barbara Jill Walters has been one of the most widely known persons in television journalism, one of the most highly paid, and certainly one of the most controversial—is she a newsperson, a show business entertainer, or both?

When she has a famous public figure on camera, Walters knows how to go after the news like a hunter going for the jugular vein. Audiences have watched her body tense, her eyes harden, as she leaned in with a line like "I know this is terribly personal, but—" or "If the Israelis agree, then you will agree?" And her quarry willingly bares the neck—Mamie Eisenhower told her about a drinking problem; Sadat said he would go to Camp David.

Until 1976 Walters was a part of a big NBC "show biz" program, the highly successful "Today" show that brought the morning news and a lot of entertainment. Walters, cool and dramatic with her make-up, developed her interviewing technique under time-free conditions. She could adjust her in-depth interviews to any reasonable length, or cut off unproductive ones.

Then front-page headlines announced that ABC had given Walters a five-year contract for $5 million, making her the highest paid news personality. She was to co-anchor the "ABC Evening News" with former CBS newsman Harry Reasoner, and also do special news interview shows. "It was the worst year of my professional and personal life," Walters later said about 1976. The viewing audience saw Harry and Barbara glare at each other, the program floundered, and news ratings did not jump (they did later when all ABC ratings improved).

A new ABC news division chief, Roone Arledge, kept Reasoner on the news program (he later returned to CBS) and gave Walters feature assignments. These soon became the kinds of interviews she had done for the "Today" show: "I wanted fewer nights on the air, more time to do in-depth interviews, interviews with juice in them."

Walters balanced her subjects: Jimmy and Rosalynn Carter, the former Shah and Empress of Iran, Bo and John Derek. "We have tried to mix the interviews so they would be both entertaining and informational," she says. To a certain extent Walters has been a victim of her own media publicity—no accomplishment could match the expectations. She has undoubtedly succeeded as often as any of her competitors.

DAN RATHER

When Dan Rather succeeded Walter Cronkite in 1981 as anchorman for the "CBS Evening News," after six years as a hard-nosed correspondent for the top-rated "60 Minutes," the event was the culmination of more than twenty years of television reporting that took the soft-spoken Texan to all parts of the world, into the Johnson and Nixon White Houses, and finally to the apex of network stardom.

Along the way Rather made countless friends, even among the competitors whom he beat out through sheer aggressiveness and tenacity. The son of a pipeline worker and a waitress, Rather grew up in Houston and worked his way through Sam Houston State Teachers College, where a dedicated journalism teacher virtually adopted him and drilled him on the fundamentals of newsgathering.

Dan Rather

After a part-time job with the Houston *Chronicle*, Rather worked for radio station KTRH before joining KHOU-TV, the CBS affiliate in Houston, in 1960. He caught the eye of CBS news officials during three days of arduous coverage of Hurricane Carla and was hired as a correspondent at $17,500 a year. During the next 13 years Rather covered civil rights violence in the South, the Kennedy assassination, Lyndon Johnson's White House, the India-Pakistan and the Vietnam wars, other overseas crises, and finally the Richard Nixon White House before wrangling a weekend anchor assignment as an added plum to his Washington duties.

Rather was punched in the stomach by one of Mayor Daley's security guards on the floor of the 1968 Democratic National Convention in Chicago and survived an attempt by President Nixon to humiliate him in public. In 1975 he joined Mike Wallace and Morley Safer as a correspondent for "60 Minutes."

In 1980 ABC, NBC, and CBS each offered the 48-year-old newsman $8 million spread over five years to become their evening-news

anchorman. After three months of (in his words) "joyous" deliberations and conferences, Rather chose to remain with CBS, thus
beating out Roger Mudd for that position and becoming, with
Cronkite, one of the two highest-paid broadcast journalists in the
country.

CHARLES KURALT

Most stories on network news shows report global tensions, violence, politics, natural disasters, scandals, and tragedies. There
isn't much fun in the news. Realizing this, program producers seek
change-of-pace material to brighten their newscasts and provide
perspective by reminding viewers that not everything in life is grim.
That is where Charles Kuralt comes in.

Kuralt's "On the Road" features for CBS made him the best known
purveyor of "soft" news on television. For 13 years he roamed the
United States in a mobile van with a cameraman and a sound
technician in pursuit of off-beat individuals and situations. His three-
and four-minute filmed reports were inserted as segments in the
network news programs. These vignettes were intended to bring a
smile or a tongue-cluck of admiration for the ruggedly independent
characters Kuralt filmed, unknowns who would never make news in
the traditional way but represent significant aspects of the American
character. In late 1980 he returned to an inside job as anchorman for
the "CBS Morning News."

Like many TV news performers, Kuralt came into television from a
newspaper job. He was born in Wilmington, North Carolina,
September 10, 1934, attended the state university, and became a
reporter-columnist for the Charlotte News. He left the paper in 1957
to become a writer for CBS News. After two years in that faceless
job, he was made a correspondent. Quickly he demonstrated his
knack for television feature stories.

When Kuralt and his crew took to the road, they carried tips for
stories drawn from the mail and telephone calls his New York office
received. But his instincts were always at work. Some of his best
segments—he calls them "postcards"—developed from ideas he
came across in a small town or on a rural road.

Kuralt created film stories about an 83-year-old Ohio butcher who
could hold twenty-nine eggs in one hand, three lumberjacks in a
California community who could split beer cans with logging axes
at fifty paces, and a Louisiana man who broke the world grape-
catching record at 252 feet. Along with these physical novelties were
more poignant stories about a professor of speech and dramatics
who had to retire from the faculty of a small college at seventy but
continued at the school as a janitor, and an elderly Minnesota man

who attempted single-handedly to build a two-hundred mile road because state authorities wouldn't do it.

Kuralt on the road and in his new assignment looks for stories about individuals of exceptional spirit who defy odds and those who shake their fists, figuratively if not literally, at the smothering hand of government bureaucracy.

His own homey voice and pudgy casualness on camera let the viewer know that he genuinely enjoys the stories he covers. His sense of wonder at oddities of human nature is apparent. This kindly curiosity has carried him more than a half-million miles around the United States, into remote areas, and worn out seven vans. In his trophy case he has such recognitions of his accomplishments as the Ernie Pyle Memorial Award, the George Foster Peabody Award, and a television Emmy.

DO THOSE "60 MINUTES" CRUSADES PAY OFF?
Don Kowet

One reason "60 Minutes" has had the rare distinction for a news-type show of being among the top ten popular programs in the ratings is the hard-hitting tone of some segments. This article tells what the crusading has accomplished. Ed Bradley has since replaced Dan Rather.

Easily resisting the tame adventure of *The Wonderful World of Disney* or *The Osmond Family Show*, 35 or 40 million Americans each Sunday tune in the epic jousts of four White Knights—Rather and Safer and Wallace and Reasoner—as they sally forth in search of villains, astride a dark-horse newsmagazine turned prime-time Secretariat. Ever wonder what happens off-camera to those who are speared on-camera by these *60 Minutes* Galahads?

Plenty. For instance, Dr. R.J. Rudd used to run a health clinic in Murietta Hot Springs, Cal., where "miracle" cancer cures were (supposedly) voodooed up from lemon juice and distilled water. Chancellor Ernest Sinclair used to run California Pacifica University of Hollywood, which, for a fee, issued equally miraculous degrees, unencumbered by the tedium of courses or even curricula. Only the incurably naive will be astonished to learn that Dr. Rudd earned his Ph.D. at a nonaccredited, mail-order university.

In May 1978, Rudd was convicted of bilking an arthritic woman of $25,000; he was sentenced to five years in prison and was fined

---

SOURCE: From *TV Guide*, March 10, 1979, pp. 19–22. Copyright © 1979 by Triangle Publications, Inc. Reprinted with permission from *TV Guide* ® Magazine.

\$5000. In July of that year Ernest Sinclair was indicted on 36 counts of mail fraud. He pleaded guilty to three counts of mail fraud and was sentenced to five years in prison in California. It's no coincidence that both Rudd, the previous January, and Sinclair, the previous April, had been grilled by Mike Wallace in a pair of searing *60 Minutes* exposes.

And Rudd and Sinclair are only two of scores unsaddled by Dan, Morley, Mike and Harry in mouth-to-mouth combat. Just ask Charlie Woolfolk. In 1967, Charlie had purchased the patent for an automatic flue-damper, capable, perhaps, of saving the Nation up to a billion barrels of heating oil a year. By 1976, though, Americans still couldn't buy that $10 energy-saving device. Charlie's flue-damper couldn't meet the American Gas Association's standard for flue-dampers—a blue seal of approval required in most localities; the AGA didn't have a standard.

Enter a White Knight. Morley Safer portrayed Woolfolk's plight on Dec. 26, 1976. "Within a week, I'd sold the 50 flue-dampers I had lying out in the barn," says Charlie, who now heads the Save-Fuel Corporation. Within two months, a powerful triumvirate of politicians—senators Abourezk, Bayh and Kennedy—was putting heat on the heating industry. Charlie Woolfolk got his standard for flue-dampers in early 1977.

And the concern that this *60 Minutes* segment aroused in Congress was no fluke. "One of the reasons I was eager to come to *60 Minutes*," says Dan Rather, "was that I knew from my Washington experience as a correspondent that it was a broadcast that made a difference."

It made a difference to House Subcommittee on Military Construction chairman Robert Sikes (D.-Fla.) the evening in March 1976 when Rather accused Sikes of abusing his power and influence in Congressional office for personal gain. Afterward, 45 congressmen petitioned the House ethics committee to investigate *60 Minutes'* allegations. Sikes was reprimanded. At the next session's start, he was stripped of his committee chairmanship.

"Just the mere knowledge that *60 Minutes* is doing a story can begin to have effects," says one of *60 Minutes'* producers, Al Wasserman.

60 Minutes may have been the alarm buzzing in the ears of some sleepy state attorney-generals, who for years had been yawning at the practice of selling, by telephone, commodity options on the London commodities market—at scandalously inflated rates. "So many people had been gulled by this securities fraud," says Morley Safer. "Both Massachusetts and Michigan had been looking into it for years, in the most laggardly way. Yet we had so much prima-facie evidence, I could have practically said on the air: 'Hey, these guys are damned crooks. Put them in jail!' " According to Safer, though, only when Massachusetts and Michigan learned *60 Minutes* intended to broadcast a segment called "Hang Up the Phone" were kingpin commodities con men indicted, then jailed.

Often *60 Minutes* simply pulls together jigsaw pieces scattered elsewhere in print. "In contrast," says Dan Rather, "Kepone was one of those stories where we got in very, very early, and were able to spark the action that print journalists couldn't." The first segment, telecast on Dec. 14, 1975, dealt with workers who had been contaminated by dust from Kepone—a toxic insecticide—from an Allied Chemical-controlled Kepone plant near Virginia's James River. On Aug. 29, 1976, Rather broadcast a follow-up report, repeating (in edited form) the original segment, with an addendum: Allied Chemical had pleaded no-contest to 940 counts of dumping Kepone and was subsequently fined $13.8 million . . . the State of Virginia had shut down all fishing on the James River (that ban is still in effect) . . . a group of Kepone employees were suing Allied for almost $30 million in damages (they eventually settled for an undisclosed sum).

"There's nothing automatic about follow-ups here," says producer Igor Oganesoff. "The pieces you do follow up on," he adds, "are the ones you know you've left unresolved—you only peeled back a single layer of the story, without getting to the core."

From January 1975 through October 1976, Morley Safer took three bites of an Arizona land-fraud story, spitting out more worms each time. "We started out to investigate a straightforward real-estate scam—retired people, mainly from the cold states, buying, sight unseen, worthless properties in Arizona," he recalls. "However, once we started digging out there, what we uncovered was a massive network involving organized crime and hundreds of millions of dollars." Safer's first story "named some Mr. Bigs." Safer's second story described "how the accountant of one Mr. Big was murdered the day before he left home to testify in court." The third story covered the death of Arizona reporter Don Bolles, who had been investigating Arizona land fraud for years. "Finally," Safer concludes, "a Federal Crime Strike Force went in and started throwing around indictments."

Among other *60 Minutes* successes:

□ In January 1975, Morley Safer showed how handguns, bought in quantity and legally in South Carolina, were being smuggled into New York City and sold illegally. Because of this segment, according to South Carolina attorney general Daniel McLeod, the South Carolina legislature passed the first restrictive handgun legislation in that state's history.

☐ In a piece that ran in November 1977, Dan Rather detailed supply shortages at some Navy hospitals at the same time a Navy hospital in New Orleans was operating at 25-per-cent capacity—a Navy hospital that had been built only because it was in former congressman F. Edward Hebert's district. The F. Edward Hebert Naval Hospital was closed on Sept. 27, 1978.

☐ In April 1978, Mike Wallace reported on the "invention promotion" business, in which, he alleged, companies such as the Raymond Lee Organization got inventors to spend thousands of dollars on marketing gadgets that were absolutely worthless. Three months later, Raymond Lee Organization filed for bankruptcy.

Of course, not all *60 Minutes* segments produce such definitive results. "Frances Knight, at that time head of the U.S. Passport Office, suggested to us that we do a piece on fake IDs," says Mike Wallace. "Frances wanted a nationwide ID card to be issued as a result of our piece. Well," he adds, "we did the piece." Pause. "There's still no nationwide ID card."

Producer Al Wasserman recalls a piece he did with Morley Safer on the Wilmington Ten—civils rights activists who had been convicted in 1972 in connection with the fire-bombing of a Wilmington, N.C., grocery store. "We had this couple, a reverend and his wife—both of them white, respectable—who gave direct eyewitness testimony that undercut the prosecution's whole case. We rebroadcast this story the following season. Nevertheless," Wasserman adds, "our story did not lead to the Wilmington Ten being pardoned or exonerated."

Usually, though, *60 Minutes* segments do have an impact—often with an echo that resonates through the halls of CBS itself. News generates more mail at CBS than entertainment, and 65 percent of the news mail relates to *60 Minutes*. (Through July 1978, the show had received 44,000 letters, compared with about 3500 for *The Evening News with Walter Cronkite*.) Although praise for *60 Minutes* outweighs criticism three-to-one, some complaints carry a special peril.

"In the case of a libel suit—those are handled by the corporation's lawyers," says News chief Dick Salant. "Lawsuits don't frighten us, they don't intimidate us," adds the ex-corporate lawyer. "They're just part of the territory."

The most recent case to litter that litigatory landscape was initiated by Billie Young, a Long Island publisher. Miss Young's $25-million suit against CBS and Morley Safer accuses Safer of "distortion" and "misrepresentation" in a *60 Minutes* segment done in January 1979. Other cases include:

☐ Herbert v. Lando: Col. A.B. Herbert says his reputation was damaged in 1973 by a *60 Minutes* segment raising doubts about his claim that Army officers covered up U.S. atrocities in Vietnam. The U.S. Supreme Court has been asked to review a U.S. Court of Appeals decision that journalists (in this case, CBS producer Barry Lando) cannot be forced to disclose their thought processes even when being sued for libel.

□ Greenburg v. CBS et al.: During a *60 Minutes* broadcast on Nov. 7, 1976, a woman related her experiences as a patient of Dr. Greenburg, a physician specializing in weight-reduction treatment. Greenburg claims that the statements made to Mike Wallace were defamatory.

□ Brown v. CBS: Arising from "Patient Beware," on April 3, 1977: Brown, a prominent plastic surgeon, claims that statements regarding the malpractice suits filed against him, and the nature of his practice, are defamatory. . . .*

However, *60 Minutes* manages to settle lawsuits as well as spark them. Jack Harris and his Bing Crosby—like baritone had been heard for 16 years on radio station WJR in Detroit, before Harris migrated to California in 1972 to do voice-overs in commercials. In 1975, Harris did a commercial for a tire company. Bing Crosby's lawyers then pulled the plug on his career, advising the sponsor that the Harris ad was "an unauthorized and deceptive" intentional imitation of Bing, and could lead to a lawsuit.

For the next two years, Harris was unable to get work doing voice-overs anywhere. Although Harris had filed a $2-million suit against Crosby in November 1975, it seemed as if it were going to languish in the courts forever.

Then Harris wrote to *60 Minutes*. In October 1977, Mike Wallace flew to London to play a Harris tape for Crosby himself. After learning that Harris hadn't been able to work for two whole years, Bing told Mike: "When I get home I'm going to look into this and see it's straightened out. . . ." Bing never did get home. On Oct. 14, he died.

60 Minutes decided to broadcast the segment anyway. "What happened after that was just unreal," says Harris. "The following week I got offers from all over the United States—the Tropicana in Las Vegas . . . the Riverboat in New York . . . a record deal."

---

*Asked about the disposition of these cases, the CBS Law Department in August 1980 reported that no action had yet been started in *Young* v. *CBS*; the Supreme Court had reversed the decision of the appeals court in *Herbert* v. *Lando* and pretrial discoveries of evidence were being made; *Greenburg* v. *CBS* had resulted in the plaintiff, at trial, withdrawing all allegations of negligence and the court discontinuing the action with prejudice (meaning that the contested issues could not be relitigated); and *Brown* v. *CBS* had been dormant, with no activity occurring since the service of the complaint.

However, the offer he couldn't refuse came nine months later, enclosed in a letter from Bing's widow, Kathryn Crosby. The Harris lawsuit was resolved in an out-of-court settlement.

"Now," says an elated Harris, "I am free to star in the movie I've been offered. Of course," he adds hastily, "it has nothing to do with Bing."

"That movie," says Mike Wallace, arching his eyebrows the way he does when someone tells him lemon juice and distilled water can cure cancer, "is called 'The Crooner'."

ARE THOSE POWERFUL DOCUMENTARIES GONE FOREVER?
Douglas Bauer

While the episodic "60 Minutes" grabs high ratings, the hour-long documentaries, many of which now are relatively bland, have been dropped into a secondary position by the networks.

At the end of the hour, Edward R. Murrow summarizes the outrage. Cigarette smoke, like the drawnwork of the mood, rises against a black backdrop. "These people have the strength to harvest your food," Murrow says, "but they do not have the strength to influence legislation." As he talks, images of migrant workers, Walker Evans faces, fill the screen. "Maybe," Murrow says, "we do."

The message of "Harvest of Shame," CBS's moving depiction of migrant workers' lives, was powerfully simple, like its tone, and it hit those who watched it, the night after Thanksgiving 1960, with an unadorned force. Like other documentaries of the early 1960s, it was structurally spare, contemplatively paced and had a kind of moral innocence that might seem naive today. It was also enormously effective craft.

However, although "Harvest" remains, even now, unarguably strong television, it's ironic to learn that it was originally shown during a period when documentaries were in comparative disfavor, an attitude that has been recurrent since the middle 1950s, when television news departments became functionally legitimate operations. Although figures from each network are fragmentary, they reflect in general what NBC's reveal quite dramatically: that the effort given to documentary programming seems to run in cycles. Through the late '50s, until 1961, the number of documentaries on NBC averaged roughly 10 or 11; then jumped dramatically for the

SOURCE: From *TV Guide*, July 28, 1979, pp. 3–5. Copyright © 1979 by Triangle Publications, Inc. Reprinted with permission from *TV Guide* ® Magazine.

next five or six years, to highs of 38 in 1964 and 37 in 1966; then dropped again in the last years of the decade, to 12 in 1969, 11 in 1972, 14 in 1974, and to 11 in 1978.

Whatever might explain past cycles—domestic politics, the spirit of the times, network balance sheets—the low ebb of documentary programming today seems the work of one overriding factor. For the past few seasons the skirmishing for ratings has so preoccupied the industry that one naturally fears for the well-being of the documentary and its traditionally modest Nielsens. There is the sense that fewer documentaries are being broadcast, and that those that are telecast are softer in their inquiries than models of investigative reporting such as "Harvest of Shame." Or that, if they choose hard, serious subjects, the networks see the assumed smallness of the audience as a license to be ponderous. In short, it seems that the documentary form is either changing or vanishing altogether.

Both Robert Chandler, vice president and director for public-affairs broadcasting at CBS News, and Lester Crystal, president of NBC News, believe that the reason there seem to be fewer documentaries is that the commercial networks—theirs, at least—are hiding them. Both executives talk about the incredible turbulence of the nighttime schedule, with programs being moved, new ones replacing canceled ones week after week—so that the shows are never in one time slot long enough to attract an audience.

"It's been like a tornado, everything churning and tumbling," says Crystal. He says that, like his network's newly appointed vice chairman for news, Richard Salant, he would like to see a regular time period for documentaries, but frankly doubts that it will soon happen. Salant, in fact, has recently accused the networks of hiding documentaries in a scheduling "closet," like "some poor retarded relative" who is whisked away when company calls.

Chandler adds, "The problem is that we get terrible times because we have nothing to do with scheduling our own programs. There's an uneasy tension between the news and entertainment divisions. We're a second-place network fighting for first place and the entertainment division wants to show that they can do it alone."

Only ABC, carrying the highest-rated programs and publicly committed to improving its news division, seems to be giving its documentaries any prominence. Pamela Hill, vice president and executive producer of ABC News television documentaries, says that, in fact, "our ratings are up—incrementally. And that's a healthy sign. It would not be healthy if we were doing certain kinds of shows for the sake of a rating."

Still—in a recklessly changing schedule, assigned to remote

hours, recipients of illogical audience flows—documentaries, through most of the '70s, have managed to fill 20 hours a year on CBS. ABC, except for 1976, has shown approximately 12 hours. NBC ran 26 hours in 1976, 20 in 1977 and, to date this year, 10 hours.

Comparable figures for earlier years are difficult to come by because, until the early 1970s, none of the networks kept figures for various kinds of news shows. Nevertheless, a few small and isolated comparisons are interesting. In 1962, for example, at CBS, nearly 30 hours were given to *CBS Reports* and by 1964 and 1965 the network was giving it 20 hours of broadcast time, and it still is.

How do current documentaries compare with models of the form such as "Harvest of Shame"? While it seems true that nothing genuinely controversial has been shown recently, there has been some delicate subject matter treated in the past few years. In the poignant "Any Place but Here," CBS examined how, and where, it is best to place mental patients; and ABC, in the past year, has covered the subjects of industrial cancers, urban arson, Palestinian terrorists. NBC, it seems, feels its courage lay in the sacrifice of one evening's prime-time entertainment programming—the three-hour block that, once a year, it has been devoting to one subject. But the resulting programs, especially one that recently analyzed the family structure in America, have often been terribly stiff—indeed, a justification of all the visceral responses of many viewers when they see the word "documentary" in program listings.

To the question of investigative effort, CBS's Chandler says, "Yes, there probably is less hard, confrontational reporting going on. The trouble is that *60 Minutes* has achieved that initiative. They've taken the smaller investigative things and what's left is so big and complex it defies doing." Wherever one goes in the world of television news, whomever one asks questions of, *60 Minutes* eventually takes possession of the conversation. It is the dominant occupant of documentary-style programming, a fact that means a lot of things—some good, some bad. For there is a fear that its success has so impressed a baldly imitative industry that all documentary energy may be drawn to magazine-format shows at the expense of longer, deeper efforts.

Pamela Hill at ABC has been generally applauded as the best hope for innovative documentaries on commercial television. She, for example, purchased from the Public Broadcasting Service the powerful "The Police Tapes," made by independent producers Susan and Alan Raymond.

Hill also repeatedly has encouraged the idea of buying the work of independents, most notably last year, when ABC announced that Marcel Ophuls, the brilliant filmmaker and producer of "The Sorrow and the Pity," would film a documentary about Hollywood. Recently Ophuls resigned, as he had done from CBS some years earlier, giving as his reason the restrictions at ABC, in which the network retains the right of "final cut." Hill says Ophuls' departure had to do with his going over budget and taking too long to film.

Hill's willingness to try new techniques may have contributed to the controversy that erupted last year over ABC's "Youth Terror: the View from Behind the Gun." A former employee who assisted in the filming accused the network of staging scenes involving street gangs. The network denied it, and Hill today dismisses the affair by saying: "Two sets of investigations proved the charges false. What happened was that we had a very unhappy employee."

Peter Davis ("The Selling of the Pentagon," "Hearts and Minds"), Tom Spain ("The Fire Next Door," "Any Place but Here") and the Raymonds all echo a frustration, expressed by Davis, that "the networks want form to come out of some safe place, which is like expecting light without darkness." And Tom Spain adds, "I regard my experience with the networks as good, but the primary thing is understanding that you work within their format. Expecting anything other than that is folly."

If there was any fertile middle ground between the creative richness of the independents and the subsidizing security of the networks, one might assume that it would be found at PBS, where David Loxton, director of the Television Laboratory at WNET, administers a half-million-dollar fund for independent nonfiction filmmaking. However, the problems of bureaucracy's heavy hand are apparently felt as keenly in public television as in commercial. Perhaps more keenly, if for rather different reasons. "I was sitting at a PBS meeting in a room at the Museum of Modern Art," Loxton says, "and someone pointed at a Jackson Pollock painting and said, 'I see someone was kind enough to bring along an organization chart.' And that's not far from the truth. Since I've been here, I'd say there really hasn't been a purely programmatic decision. There've been decisions sort of based on programming, sort of based on ratings, sort of based on politics and fund raising." He adds, "The distribution system to member stations is chaotic. You can make a film and have no guarantee that it will be distributed and shown."

Predictions of the future are as contradictory as conversations about the present. If opinion can be roughly drawn, it's fair to say that network executives are generally confident that the documentary will live and indeed, in some form, will flourish. An eloquent exception is Richard Salant, who, in a speech to a gathering of programmers in Washington, D.C., called the documentary an endangered species, the "snail darter or the bald eagle of our profession." He went on, reflecting his firm grounding in TV's formative days, to worry about the "new wave" of television filmmakers as somehow despoiling the purity of documentaries, citing Pamela Hill as a "semi-advocate" of that wave.

Younger independent producers strongly disagree with Salant's fear of cinematic influences. Tom Spain, for example, calls the standard prime-time documentary "a dinosaur," deserving its death on the grounds of being "just plain dull." The same producers, however, endorse to a great degree Salant's overall view.

Bill Moyers, a former CBS documentarian who now has returned to PBS, says that "at the heart of it, the culprit is television's refusal to acknowledge that reality can be more interesting to watch than fantasy." This seems a rapidly expanding truth as the networks and, also, it appears, PBS, acknowledge a single, predominant reality—the number of people watching. And ratings, since the eloquent innocence of Murrow, have been no friend of documentaries.

IT COULD BE WATERGATE OR A SPELLING BEE
William Gildea
Network reporters in Washington have frustrations, too, such as having their stories "bumped" off the air or being sent out on dull assignments. Washington newscasting is not always glamorous.

The *ABC Evening News* had already begun when Washington correspondent George Strait came up with his big story on Capitol Hill. The House had just voted on a controversial farm bill. "By God, they defeated it," said Strait, frantically phoning his office with the unexpected news. It was 6:07 P.M., but Strait still had time to do a live network report—if he hurried.

He rushed outside the House to an elm tree, with the Capitol in the background, where he would tell America the news. The camera crew set up quickly. Strait memorized his lines and adjusted his tie. "Stand by," he was told. He would be on the air any moment. It was 6:20.

Just then, another surprise. President Carter walked into the press room at the White House to thank the congressmen for their vote. ABC switched live—but to the White House, not to Strait. He was left hanging, frustrated, under the tree for another hour (the networks can update the news for some West Coast stations until 8 P.M.).

Such is life for Washington general-assignment correspondents. More often than not—much more often—their stories, good as they

---

SOURCE: From *TV Guide*, August 19, 1978, pp. 18–21. Copyright © 1978 by Triangle Publications, Inc. Reprinted with permission from *TV Guide* ® Magazine.

may be, never get on the evening news. Each network has scores of correspondents positioned around the world, vying for a few precious seconds of air time on the nightly network news programs.

"Very often," says NBC Washington news director Sid Davis, "you develop some pretty good stories and see them wither away by the end of the day. Something more important happens that blows them out of the water." Says a CBS Washington producer: "We have 25 correspondents in the bureau, and 21 of them go home unhappy on any given night."

Each network bureau in Washington has four to six general-assignment reporters, all-around "utility" people who can hustle up a story on anything from marble shootouts to Watergate. Often, these are men and women in their 30s, well-educated, with a reputation in the business for speed and dependability. They think quickly, move fast and possess the mental discipline to withstand disappointment when they don't get their stories on the air—or they don't last long in the business.

Unlike such household faces as Cronkite, Chancellor or Walters, the Washington GA correspondents can go for weeks without being seen. "I think it's the best and the worst," ABC's Margaret Osmer says. "You have great latitude, but you also get the junk."

Even the good stories often get scant air time. ABC's veteran Herbert Kaplow, covering Vice President Mondale in the Philippines last spring, came up with a piece that had everything: Mondale and Philippine President Ferdinand Marcos exchanging claims of human-rights violations, Philippine dissidents reacting and—all-important for television—dramatic pictures.

Though the story did run the next day for a minute and 15 seconds on *Good Morning America*, it was reduced to 20 seconds on the *ABC Evening News*. The reason: too many other things happened that day. Says the 51-year-old Kaplow, who thought he had seen everything in his 27 years with NBC and ABC, "I still think it was an important story."

Another veteran who knows the feeling of being "killed"—NBC's Charles Quinn—says, smiling, "Five or 10 years ago I used to get very upset, but the older I get, the more philosophical I become. In recent years, there's no anger, just resignation."

NBC's Bob Bazell says, "After the book on cloning came out ["In His Image," by David Rorvik] I did a spot on a biologist in Bar Harbor, Maine, who had done what might be called cloning with mice. I flew to Boston on a Sunday night, chartered a plane to Maine on Monday morning, got the story, flew back to Boston, rushed over to the Boston bureau and did the spot. It was killed at the last minute. It was a very depressing experience."

Says NBC's Jackson Bain, about the demise of his piece on unsafe aluminum wiring in millions of American homes: "That was the day the whole world came apart." And then there was his exclusive interview with a small-town West Virginia mayor who had sought aid from the Soviets, of all people: "The film was accidentally sliced to small ribbons about 30 minutes before air time and there was no way to put it back together. I wept openly. I came back to my office, kicked the furniture and yelled at my plants. See, they haven't recovered yet."

ABC's Charles Gibson once got on and still got "killed"—"killed in action." Gibson reported on the export of baby formula to Third World nations for ABC's first feed to affiliates at 6 P.M. But he didn't make the updated feeds that most stations get at 6:30 and 7.

If that wasn't disappointing enough, Gibson faced still another depressing day a few weeks later. Slumped behind his typewriter in his cramped office, Gibson had just returned from covering the national spelling bee. "A-b-s-u-r-d-i-t-y," one of the words in the contest, kept ringing in his ears. He simply didn't believe in this story.

"I don't know why we cover the spelling bee every year," he mumbles.

The reason, of course, was that the editors wanted it. That morning, during the ABC News morning conference call from New York to all bureaus, the voice of Av Westin, executive producer of the *Evening News*, came through clearly that the spelling bee was worth more than the "window"—a 15-second report to be read by the anchorman—that Washington was suggesting. "If it's worth anything," said Westin, "it's worth a spot"—the typical minute-and-15-second report by the correspondent.

"I bet we'll end up with a window," said Gibson, "but I'll put the piece together."

That night the first feed comes through and Gibson is right. Harry Reasoner, then ABC co-anchor, does a window on the bee. But wait! On the more important second feed, another story has been killed and now Reasoner is saying, "Here's Charles Gibson in Washington." Actually, Gibson is out on another assignment, but he comes through on tape, reporting that a Kansas girl is the new spelling champion. Whether he believes it or not, Gibson has put in a successful day. As Strait says, "That's why we do this craziness, to get on the air."

Near the bottom on the inflated network pay scale (salaries generally range from $35,000 to $50,000 a year), the GA job also ranks low in prestige. "The public probably thinks that the guy who covers the White House, State or the Hill," says Charles Quinn, "is a cut above the guy who goes down to West Virginia to cover something." And George Watson, ABC vice president and Washington bureau chief, admits that the term general-assignment reporter sometimes is used "almost in a slightly pejorative sense."

Certainly, the GA reporter is not among the networks' news "stars," who rarely if ever have to do what the GA reporters do routinely. "The greatest frustration is when you get a string of 'stakeouts'," says CBS's Jim McManus. "You will be sent to somebody's home at dawn, and you are 99 and 9/10ths per-cent sure that the person is going to come out of the house, get in his car, and say nothing. When Nixon came in for the Humphrey services, I waited for 15 hours outside a Virginia country estate where Nixon stayed, knowing that the man wasn't going to come down that driveway."

Another assignment that rarely has its good moments is the Washington hearing—"protecting" against a possible, but unlikely, news break. "That's always hard," says Osmer. "You go and sit and you know it's not going to be on."

One result of these sometimes anonymous labors is that the GA reporters are seldom in demand on the Capitol social circuit. They tend to stay at home, which is, more often than not, in some modest Washington suburb, such as Falls Church, Va., or Wheaton, Md. "I've got a car, two kids and a mortgage," says Strait. "I'm the American dream."

A GA reporter's leisure time is frequently interrupted, something that's happened to CBS's McManus enough times to prompt him to sell half interest in a 30-foot sailboat he used to enjoy on nearby Chesapeake Bay. "This business is such that you can't guarantee your weekends," he says. "It got too frustrating to have a boat over there and not be able to use it."

Only occasionally will a GA reporter get a speaking invitation, and sometimes then it's to fill in for someone else. "People," says Quinn, "want to hear from a White House reporter, or an economics-inflation guy. What can a general-assignment guy do?"

Plenty, actually, even if few people know it. The GA correspondent makes it a habit to come through, often under adverse conditions. "I like the feeling of versatility, the feeling that I can ride in like a cowboy and attack any problem," says CBS's Jed Duvall. And, adds McManus, "No matter what the conditions are in the field, bad weather or whatever, at no time do you entertain the notion that you're not going to make it."

There are even distinct advantages in being a Washington GA reporter. One is less travel than in other bureaus. "The reason I moved in Washington was not journalistic but logistic," says Duvall. "I was in the Atlanta bureau, covering the entire South. You'd get on a plane Monday morning and get back Friday night. I'd come home to sleep and I'd have a hard time waking up by Monday. I'd get up Sunday and almost fall down."

Being a GA reporter in Washington is also better than covering many beats. "I'd much rather be general assignment than on a beat I don't want," says Osmer. "If there's a beat you want, that's the best." Says Quinn, who asked to be taken off the Pentagon beat, "The Pentagon got boring. It was hard to get on the air because the stories weren't that good. I thought I'd take my chances on the street." Only 10 per cent of his Pentagon stories got on the *Evening News* but about one-third of his GA stories do.

Stories that don't make the evening news programs often make the morning shows—*Today, Good Morning America* or the *CBS Morning News*. If not, they can be used by the affiliates, which receive a great amount of material from the networks each day that can be used on local news shows. The GA correspondents also can do longer pieces for special news programs and some anchor work.

Osmer, who has anchor experience, demonstrates with her persistent reporting perhaps the best reason for working in Washington—when you hit a good story, you get the best possible exposure. Shortly after switching from CBS to ABC, she managed to get an exclusive interview with Robert Vesco. This year she gained notice for an exclusive with John Ehrlichman after he got out of prison.

While it's natural for a GA reporter to want to move up in job prestige, the wisest veterans know that just any move may not necessarily be a good one. No one, of course, would snub an anchor job. "If that were offered me," says Kaplow, his feet propped on a suitcase from still another trip, "I would consider it positively." Or, he adds, "a sort of anchor role in a weekly newsmagazine program"—something that permits more time to prepare, more time on the air.

Time—that's something the GA correspondents never have enough of. Gone are the days when McManus was a radio correspondent for Westinghouse, covering a Nixon state dinner in Los Angeles for the astronauts who made the first moon landing. He had to fill time.

"I was supposed to do a 10-minute lead-in," he says. "But the dinner was running very late. I wanted to give it back to the network, but they wouldn't take it. I had to talk for 55 minutes. I was never so glad to see Ronald Reagan stand up. By that time, I had reached back into high-school physics, talking about Copernicus."

Now that he's a Washington general-assignment network TV correspondent, McManus wouldn't mind getting 55 minutes of air time. But that's one problem he doesn't have to worry about.

THE LOCAL-NEWS BLUES

From *Newsweek*

The thousands of local television news programs are marred by superficiality, studio banter, and over-emphasis on "show biz" style, *Newsweek* contends, quoting reporters from metropolitan stations.

A few years ago, an editor at New York's WCBS-TV handed reporter Lynn Sherr what looked like a choice assignment: the local trial of Watergate figures John Mitchell and Maurice Stans for obstruction of justice, conspiracy and perjury in the Vesco case. The hitch, however, was that the station's management did not feel the proceedings were worth covering on a daily basis. As a result, Sherr was off working on another story when Nixon secretary Rose Mary Woods caused a stir by unexpectedly popping up on the witness stand. Sherr was promptly put on the trial full-time—and then, just as abruptly, was exiled to weekend duty. By now thoroughly perplexed, the reporter nosed around for some explanations. "An executive finally told me," she grimly recalls, "that another executive's wife didn't like the way I was wearing my hair."

Today Lynn Sherr is a widely respected national correspondent for ABC, but her hairy experience at WCBS still betokens the frustrations of toiling on TV's local-news beat. The hefty salary and star quality that come with being a big-city TV reporter would seem to make the job one of journalism's plummiest, and many still see it that way. But a surprising number of on-camera news people find their craft so professionally unsatisfying that they keep jumping from station to station—or drop out altogether after a few years.

Showbiz. Part of the problem is that local reporters must not only cover the story but act as producer and director of their film segments as well. But the big turnoff, particularly for seasoned print journalists who switch to the tube, is the discovery that the job is more showbiz than news biz. The promise of huge profits lies behind the let's-entertain-them approach of many local news shows. Just one additional point in the ratings may earn a major station up to $1 million in extra advertising revenue over the course of a year. Small

SOURCE: From *Newsweek*, January 16, 1978. Copyright 1978 by Newsweek, Inc. All rights reserved. Reprinted by permission.

wonder that frivolous, easy-to-digest features and studio banter tend to crowd out the information that the more conscientious pros would normally gather.

Sometimes the local-news system seems diabolically designed to prevent reporters from putting together in-depth, investigative pieces. Since many receive additional payment for each on-camera and studio appearance, it is in the reporters' financial interest *not* to take the time to research such stories. The attitude of many station managers, meanwhile, is that reporters are not earning their salaries unless they cover at least one story a day. "There's a television mentality that says the only time you're working is when you're out with a camera crew," says Lynn Sherr. "It's almost impossible to break away and do longer pieces." The advent of videotape, which does not require lengthy developing and editing, has only added to the job's hit-and-run superficiality. "You don't have time to think with tape," complains Monica Kaufman of Atlanta's WSB-TV. "At least with film, you can get your thoughts together in the car on the way back to the station."

Consultants.   Another bane of the job is the method by which on-camera performances are graded. Many stations employ outside consultants to rate their news staff through "Q-Score" tests. A group of typical viewers is shown pictures of the reporters and asked which ones they recognize and like or dislike the most. Joel Siegel of New York's WABC-TV speaks for most of his colleagues when he complains: "The problem with Q-Scores is that people are graded on the basis of how well they come over. It has nothing to do with their journalistic expertise."

Equally dismaying is the paucity of preparation given neophyte reporters before they are thrust on the air. "It's a case of pushing people into the pool and seeing if they can swim," concedes a veteran local-news editor. Trish Reilly, a former magazine journalist who switched to broadcast news, quit the business after only a three-year stint. She recalls that her entire training consisted of being told to observe another of the station's correspondents in action. That schooling lasted a mere three days, at which point the reporter snapped at her: "I'm not answering any more questions." Andy Shaw, who switched from newspaper work to Chicago's WMAQ about a year ago, remembers remaining silent during part of a live broadcast because the camera's red light wasn't glowing. As Shaw subsequently learned, the bulb had burned out. "I believed that the light was infallible," he says. "It's embarrassing to make your mistakes before 4 million people."

'Is It Funny?'   As it takes on the trappings of showbiz, the system encourages its performers to jolly up their presentations by becoming part of their stories. Everyone has seen the local news team hamming it up on a parade float or gorging themselves at ethnic street fairs. That may be forgivable for a light feature, but it becomes quite another matter when the don't-bore-them attitude is extended to serious subjects. Jerome Wilson, a former political correspondent for a New York station, recalls taping an interview with Nelson Rockefeller that yielded some highly newsworthy nuggets. Unfortunately, all his producer wanted to know was: "Is it funny?" No, conceded Wilson, it was not funny. The interview never ran, but Wilson did—all the way into a career in law.

LIFE IMITATES "THREE'S COMPANY" ON TV
Merrill R. Skrocki

One of the frothy comedies with which ABC built high ratings in the late 1970s was "Three's Company," in which two young women and a young man share an apartment. The threesome practice has spread in real life. Did TV stimulate the trend?

When the television show "Three's Company" first appeared in March, 1977, many viewers no doubt thought that the premise was totally unrealistic, a TV producer's fantasy. They were probably shocked by the idea as well: How could two women and one man live together in an apartment and just be friends?

Horrified or not, viewers tuned in by the millions. It soon became clear that the roommates Chrissy, Janet, and Jack, far from being scandalous, were simply being practical. In fact, the "Three's Company" life style has now become a small trend. An article in the New York *Times* several months ago reported on the "growing, if uncounted, number of single people across the country who are making mixed threesomes a way of life."

It's not clear whether the show itself has inspired such threesomes, or whether television is simply reflecting what real people are doing. Bea Dallas, program coordinator for the show's production company, believes that the latter is probably closer to the truth: "It's just out in the open since the show is on the air. Before, people who were doing it didn't talk about it."

The "pioneers" who tried threesomes before the days of the "Three's Company" show ran into some trouble—especially if they were outside major cities.

For the most part, however, attitudes have changed. Although she admits that the show received some "unpleasant" letters in the

---

SOURCE: From *McCall's*, August 1979, pp. 51–52. Copyright 1979 by *McCall's* Magazine. Reprinted by permission.

beginning, Bea Dallas says that the hundreds of letters that come in each week are mostly favorable. Many are from young people living in similar situations—or from their parents, who usually write to say how reassured they are to see that the relationship can work on a friends-only basis.

TELEVISION'S EXPANDING WORLD
Peter W. Bernstein

Everyone agrees that satellite transmission and the upsurge of cable and pay television will change the medium drastically during the 1980s, but no one is sure precisely how. Bernstein explores the fascinating possibilities in this prophetic 1979 article, which includes a 1981 data update.

All-pervasive as television may already seem to be, its grip on our national life is getting tighter by the day. The set itself isn't changing much, but it is going to provide its owner with a far larger choice of programs—and, before long, with an astonishing array of services as well. The $10-billion-a-year television industry is poised for a huge expansion.

Hordes of competitors, some seasoned and some new to the industry, are scrambling to keep or to carve out shares of the expanding market. In the forefront, as always, are the networks and the broadcasting stations, their leadership so far unchallenged. Coming along behind are the cable operators, whose systems are making possible a bewildering array of innovations, including pay-TV channels. Then there are videotapes and videodiscs for playing programs, and video games that can turn the television set into your adversary at chess.

With all these new developments competing to snare viewers' attention, there is a tremendous need for material to keep them glued to the tube. An army of program suppliers is forming up to provide it. In return for the monthly charge that subscribers pay—typically $7 a month—the cable systems offer not just clearer reception of network and local broadcasts, but a certain number of other programs as well, at no extra cost. Cable operators buy this added material from suppliers who get paid according to the number of subscribers. Warner Communications offers "Nickelodeon," children's programming that runs thirteen hours a day, for a fee that ranges up to 10 cents a subscriber per month. For a roughly comparable fee, UA-Columbia Cablevision relays sports

SOURCE: From *Fortune*, July 2, 1979, pp. 64–69. Copyright 1979 by *Fortune* Magazine. Reprinted by permission.

events and other spectacles from New York's Madison Square Garden. AP, UPI, and Reuters offer news services for 5 cents or less a subscriber per month.

Decoding Scrambled Signals

Riding piggyback on cable systems—and spurring their growth—are the pay-TV networks. Cable subscribers who pony up an additional fee (generally about $8 a month) get to receive the signals transmitted on pay channels. The money is divided between the supplier and the cable operator. At the moment, this part of the business is dominated by Home Box Office, a subsidiary of Time Inc. (the publisher of Fortune). HBO, supplying chiefly movies and sports events, controls nearly 70 percent of the pay-cable market, which has doubled to almost four million subscribers in the past year. HBO's closest competitor, with about 21 percent of the market, is Showtime, a joint venture by two companies with extensive cable interests, Viacom and Teleprompter. The rest is spread among a dozen companies.

In areas where cable is not available, subscription television (STV), the broadcast version of pay TV, is suddenly attracting attention. Scrambled signals are sent over the air to decoder boxes in the homes of viewers who pay $15 to $20 a month to receive movies and sports. Inasmuch as the most optimistic forecasts are that no more than 40 percent of American households will ever sign up for cable—an audience far smaller than that available to broadcast stations—STV would seem to have a bright future. Still, the physical and potential regulatory limitations on its transmissions, plus the service's cost, mean that STV will thrive only in certain markets.

There are about 4,000 cable systems in the U.S., serving 14.5 million subscribers, almost a fifth of the 74.5 million American households that have one or more television sets. The number of subscribers has been increasing at a steady clip, about 10 percent in each of the past two years, as what the operators call their "plant" grows and more viewers tie into cables already in place. Almost 27 million households are within reach of cables, and subscription lists could be almost doubled without putting in new "plant." Total industry revenues reached $1.5 billion in 1978, but most of the systems are small. Growth will have to come in the big urban centers, which are tougher to penetrate than the hamlets and towns where cable has so far had its greatest success.

Changes in the regulatory climate have helped to brighten cable television's outlook in many of the larger markets. For years, the Federal Communications Commission kept the industry on a short rein, and controlled it most capriciously. From 1968 to 1972, the FCC effectively prohibited any cable construction in the 100 largest markets while it pondered what rules should govern this burgeoning industry. Furthermore, it limited the types of programs that cable operators could run. At one point, only movies that were less than three or more than ten years old could be shown, an arbitrary rule that, in effect, reserved all the best films for broadcasters. Much to the relief of the cable operators, the courts and the commission have now swept the most onerous restrictions away.*

Programs Cost Less Than Stamps

This May, in a burst of spring cleaning, the FCC combed through its book of regulations and proposed eliminating all restrictions on the kind and number of distant broadcast signals that cable-television systems may pick up to fill empty channels. The prospect of changes in the rules governing retransmission of material has caused alarm among both broadcasters and film distributors. "The vast majority of cable operators pay more for postage stamps than for their programs," says Jack Valenti, president of the Motion Picture Association of America. Congress may soon get into the act. Hearings are now being held on a bill, introduced by Representative Lionel van Deerlin, a California Democrat, that among other things would require cable operators to get permission from the owners of the material before showing it.

While it struggled for more freedom on the regulatory front, the cable-television industry was doing some technical pioneering. One physical limitation on pay TV, for example, was that there was no way to tie local cable systems together except by microwave transmission. A transmitter and receiver had to be set up every twenty miles to fortify the signals, and every retransmission point had to be licensed by the FCC. No national cable network could exist under those circumstances. "There was no cable infrastructure, no entrenched distribution system," remembers Gerald Levin, HBO's forty-year-old chairman.

In late 1975, HBO started transmitting its programming via satellite, and it was soon operating a national distribution network that jolted the industry. Cable-system operators hurried to install earth receiving stations. About 1,500 are now in place, and almost half of all cable subscribers are signed up with systems served by satellite.

---

*Editors' note: By 1981, there were about 4600 operating cable systems, with another 2000 franchised. They served approximately 18 million subscribers, well over 20 percent of the potential cable TV homes, and reached an estimated 48 million people. More than 40 satellite services of various types were offered commercially. Industry revenues exceeded $2.5 billion. Extra-pay cable TV was reaching 5 million subscribers in 50 states. It was predicted that by the mid-1980s 30 to 35 million homes would be receiving basic cable TV.

Even supplied with a cornucopia of programming, cable operators have continued to be extremely selective in choosing new markets. To identify desirable areas, a cable operator will make a calculation based on such factors as population density, costs of construction, demographics, the number of broadcast signals available, and the size of the market. Operators who choose their markets shrewdly will generally achieve a 16 to 20 percent return on investment. Healthy as that may seem, it is slender by broadcasting standards. The return on investment of a well-run over-the-air station is usually between 20 and 30 percent and sometimes much higher.

The most attractive areas for cable are those with more than seventy-five housing units per mile, and the best spots often have at least twice that concentration. "People who live on two-acre plots are not good business targets for us," says Monroe Rifkin, president of American Television & Communications, the nation's second-largest cable company (ATC also belongs to Time Inc.). Conversely, operators would just as soon steer clear of low-income central-city areas.

The cable companies are especially fond of franchises in areas where most of the system can be built aboveground, using telephone poles. Under favorable circumstances, a system can be built at an average cost of $10,000 for a mile of trunk cable; it can cost as much as $80,000 a mile, or even more, when the cable has to be strung underground.

Generally, the density of population in cities makes the higher cost of construction worthwhile. But that is not invariably the case. In Manhattan, Teleprompter, according to its former chairman, Irving Kahn, spent about $150,000 to install each mile of trunk cable in the northern half of the borough. The company has lost $34 million there in ten years. The other cable company operating in New York City—ATC's Manhattan Cable—reports lower installation costs, of $50,000 to $75,000 a trunk mile, but only recently has it begun to break even on operations. Cable operators regard Boston, Baltimore, Chicago, Detroit, and Washington, D.C., as other unattractive places for investment.

Civic Leaders For Rent

In contesting for desirable markets, cable companies approach each franchise very much the way a politician approaches an election, mapping a strategy, outlining the key issues, and recruiting influential supporters. One of the most widely used tactics is what is known in the industry as the "rent a civic leader" approach—a large cable company will invite a group of local citizens to help it form a local cable company. Local interests usually control 20 percent of the new enterprise. The large cable company keeps the rest and agrees to build the system if the franchise is awarded. Only one of the major cable companies, UA-Columbia Cablevision, has so far refused to take in local partners. President Robert Rosecrans says: "We don't believe in giving away 20 percent."

In Fort Wayne, Indiana, ATC's local partners included the organizers of an educational-TV station and a group of black ministers. Cox Cable, which [expected] to become a subsidiary of General Electric, allied itself with a local cable company that already had the franchise for the surrounding county. Cox Cable's partners apparently had more clout—it won. Henry Harris, the former president of Cox Cable and now head of Metrovision, a joint venture with Newhouse, thinks that "having the *right* local people is 80 percent of the game."

Like politicians, cable operators are given to making big promises. These usually take the form of "giveaways," appetizing morsels to be included in the franchise proposal. Most commonly, operators will promise large quantities of local programminng, giving every citizen the chance to be a television star. They will offer to equip local television studios and urge that the cable system be hooked up with schools, colleges, police departments, and hospitals. This is partly done to serve the "public interest," but it is also an attempt to woo powerful local constituencies.

Pandering to local interests sometimes reaches absurd limits. In San Antonio, where Storer Cable and UA-Columbia were competing for the franchise, the city was anxious to complete sewage and road improvement projects and there was not enough money in the budget, so it asked both companies for a prepayment of franchise fees. Storer started the bidding at around $250,000. The city asked for a cool million. Both companies agreed to meet the city's price, but in the end UA-Columbia got the franchise.

At times, the franchising process has led to abuse. Stories about junkets for city councilmen are common. One company some years ago, for example, detoured the members of one council to Las Vegas while taking them to visit a West Coast system. Cable operators also admit that small bribes were once a common practice. In 1973, Teleprompter's Irving Kahn went to prison in connection with bribing officials in Johnstown, Pennsylvania, in order to get a franchise.

The hard-fought franchising battles will soon be a relic of the past. Within the next two to four years, industry experts expect that all the remaining desirable franchises will be snapped up. Once the nation is as cabled as it's ever going to be, expansion will depend on the programming that is offered. Says Ralph Baruch, chairman of Viacom, using the industry jargon: "Software is key." Indeed, the programming side of the business is beginning to look more attractive to the bigger companies that own both cable systems and program suppliers—Teleprompter, Time, Viacom, and Warner. Programming is not capital-intensive and, unlike the cable business, does not require heavy investments in plant and maintenance.

The program suppliers—and especially the pay-TV networks—are dependent on the cable systems to market their offerings. But the interests of the suppliers and the cable operators don't always coincide. The suppliers would like to set up more pay channels. At the moment, the operators are resisting—a position that at first glance seems strange, since they get most of the revenues. The reason for the resistance begins with the fact that three-quarters of all existing cable systems offer a maximum of twelve channels, and increasing that number is expensive. The operators want to build up their market penetration—which runs around 35 percent for most of them—before providing their subscribers with more pay-TV channels. Notes one operator: "You make as much money adding one basic subscriber as you do by adding three additional pay subscribers." Some systems are finding, however, that marketing a package that includes a pay channel in addition to the basic cable offerings can help attract subscribers.

Exactly what kind of programming subscribers are willing to pay for is only beginning to be determined. So far, viewers have ponied up for movies, and to a lesser degree sports. Only after cable's penetration substantially increases can pay channels be expected to proliferate. Nevertheless, the search for ways to market additional pay channels has already begun. In Columbus, Ohio, a "two way" cable, Qube, is being tested by Warner Cable, a subsidiary of Warner Communications. Qube allows viewers, at a basic cost of $10.95 a month, to take their pick of programs on nine pay channels, paying an additional amount for any actually viewed. It also gives them a chance to express opinions about how good a snow-removal job the mayor has done (not good) or which *US* magazine cover might have greater appeal (John Wayne won over the Incredible Hulk). One young couple even sought help in naming their baby (the viewers chose Elizabeth over May, Bernadette, and Linda). Up to now, the cable industry has been highly skeptical about Qube, because the system is expensive to operate and subscribers have proved to be highly selective about what they will pay to watch. "A $20-million disaster" is the way one executive describes it.

HBO recently initiated Take 2, a "mini-pay service" (cost: about $4 a month), which offers family-oriented entertainment, i.e., no R-rated films. Showtime, too, has come out with a second service,

Front Row. Says Jeffrey Reiss, Showtime's president: "We're not pushing it too hard." One reason for not pushing it is that cable operators fear that customers will choose the cheaper service instead of HBO or Showtime. There is some question whether that is a realistic worry. Teleprompter offers both Showtime and a $3.95-a-month service, called Uptown, in Manhattan. Directed at the adult population, the package features R-rated films like *Confessions of a Window Cleaner*. In a year, Uptown has attracted over 10,000 subscribers, many of whom get Showtime as well.

A Laser Instead of a Needle

With cable and pay television already powerful forces in the industry, two technological newcomers, videotape recorders and videodiscs, promise to bring even further changes to the business. The videotape recorder is already making its mark. In two years, more than 600,000 recorders have been sold, despite their high price tag ($750 to $1,500, depending on the model). The tapes are also expensive—$20 for reusable blank tapes, between $50 and $100 for prerecorded ones.

Only about 2,000 videodisc players have been sold so far—all marketed by Magnavox. But industry seers—with, of course, an obvious vested interest—have no doubt that the disc is headed for mass-market status. Richard Sonnenfeldt, the RCA vice president who supervised its videodisc project in its early stages, takes a particularly rosy view of the discs' promise. He expects that within the next decade a quarter to a third of all TV homes will own a videodisc machine, about the same number as will be receiving cable television and twice as many as will have signed up for pay television.

The various videodisc machines will not use compatible technology. Magnavox's player, which retails for $695, uses a laser beam instead of a needle and is equipped with such special features as slow motion. The RCA machine is simpler and cheaper, about $400, and uses a needle. The machines being developed by two Japanese companies, Japan Victor Co. and Matsushita, will not be compatible with *either* the Magnavox or RCA models.

So far, network executives haven't been losing any sleep over all this new and potential competition. In fact, a study last year by A.C. Nielsen and Young & Rubicam concluded that cable television has had very little impact on the networks or on local broadcasters. Examining four cable markets—Des Moines, Hartford, Tulsa, and San Diego—the study found that families with cable television viewed the networks at least as much as families not on the cable. Apparently, cable subscribers, by and large, are people who want to watch more (or clearer) television than they get over the air.

Among the potential threats to the networks, however, is the possibility that the cable systems will begin to try selling advertising. Young & Rubicam, the ad agency, thinks that when cable signs up 30 percent of the nation's households—10 percent more than it has today—advertisers will turn to it. So far, the major ad effort on cable has been made by Madison Square Garden, which has sought sponsors for the sports events it televises; last year it managed to take in only $550,000. The networks grossed $4.1 billion.

The networks are also still the dominant force in programming. All told, the three networks invested more than $100 million in new programs this year, backing made-for-television movies, and pilots for situation comedies and soap operas. The pay-television networks are beginning to get into that business, too. The movies that have been their mainstay cost them between 10 and 70 cents per subscriber (depending on the film), or as much as $1.7 million a program. At that price, it becomes economical for the packagers to produce their own material for showing. This year, HBO will spend about $13 million on original programming, and Showtime will invest $7 million to $8 million.

Defrosting Frozen Flounder

Newer technologies, such as fiber optics, will one day dramatically increase the number of cable channels that television sets can receive—perhaps to 100 or more. That will open up still more opportunities for new programs, including outlandish ones. Consider a few of the suggestions from Michael Dann, the former CBS programming chief, who is now a TV consultant for such companies as Warner Communications, IBM, and Walt Disney Productions. Dann foresees whole channels devoted exclusively to rock 'n' roll, and others to soap operas, game shows, or shows about such exotica as Ukrainian shoemaking, Bavarian hops-growing, sex therapy for newlyweds, the training of Pomeranians, and the proper way to defrost frozen flounder.

The television set will eventually do other things besides sit there passively, waiting to be watched. Companies are already testing data-transmission devices and energy-load management systems that will all be hooked up through the TV set by cable. If properly instructed, your set may soon be capable of turning on your washing machine at 3:00 a.m., when the demand for power is low. Indeed, as the expansion of television continues, these last thirty years may be nostalgically remembered as those days when the television set was just a television set.

Section 13

PHOTOGRAPHIC COMMUNICATION AND THE FILM

Recording facts, creating images, and telling
stories on film in both still and motion pictures
comprise a basic and multifaceted form of visual
communication. These readings describe the
work of camera experts, investigate trends in
motion pictures, and explore ways for amateurs
to make their own documentaries.

GOD THE PHOTOGRAPHER
Dora Jane Hamblin

In *Life's* glory years as a weekly picture magazine, its staff photographers roamed the world and ordered its inhabitants around with "casual arrogance" to obtain the pictures they wanted. Hamblin, a *Life* staffer, recalls the exploits and demands of these ingenious camera stars.

"The man from *Life*" became fairly well known, over the course of thirty-six years, to virtually every head of state in the world; all the best quarterbacks and movie stars; the most famous crooks, in or out of jail; astronauts and scientists; politicians, painters, and preachers; Broadway stars and chess champions; and thousands of ordinary citizens whose chief claim to fame was that (a) once they appeared in *Life* or (b) they didn't appear, after having knocked themselves out to cooperate with the photographer.

"The man"—who had some notable female counterparts in the persons of Lisa Larsen, Martha Holmes, Nina Leen—always appeared draped in cameras, bags, light meters, an air of intense concentration, and a head full of outrageous requests: "Would you please move your army back two steps for a better composition?" was actually said by Gordon Parks to the commander of Danish military forces in Copenhagen in 1950; "I know you've a ruptured hernia, but couldn't you put some ice on it or something and get into your riding pants and boots for just one more picture?" asked Margaret Bourke-White of August A. "Gussie" Busch in St. Louis in 1955; "I know it's expensive to move a whole fleet, but the ships are placed so we can't see the new plane maneuvering among them" was spoken by Ralph Morse to an admiral in the mid-sixties, off Norfolk.

These requests were often delivered through the reluctant mouths of attendant reporters, but the orders came clearly from God the photographer. Their enormity was mitigated somewhat by personal charm and generosity. Most of the men from *Life* could be beguiling, and it helped that they had virtually unlimited expense accounts. After they had finished disrupting armies, navies, and governments, they moved to assault private homes where they were likely to fuse the owner's electrical system, tip over his coffee

SOURCE: From Dora Jane Hamblin, *That Was the Life* (New York: Norton, 1977) pp. 48–54. Copyright © 1977 by Dora Jane Hamblin. Reprinted by permission of W.W. Norton & Company, Inc.

table, fill his ashtrays with burned-out flashbulbs and film cans, or spend three days instead of the "couple of hours" they had requested. After which they customarily ordered the reporter to "clean up this mess" and then invited the subject and his entire family out to dinner at the most expensive restaurant within driving distance.

Perhaps even more important than charm or money, however, the photographers epitomized the casual arrogance which permeated the entire staff. *Life* was the most important magazine in the world. Anybody fortunate enough to attract its attention should be both flattered and long-suffering. And because it was built on pictures, the lordliest of all its lordly crew was the photographer. Photographers managed to persuade a staggering number of persons that this was true.

In the process they made enormous demands upon themselves. They pioneered tools and techniques which have become standard today in television, advertising, newspaper journalism. They studied electronics and chemistry and physics to expand the limits of their medium and above all they pushed their own brains and bodies and imaginations to the limit in search of "the right picture," "a better picture," "the key picture."

The only problem was, they expected everybody within reach of their voices to do the same. At any any gathering of former *Life* researchers, reporters, correspondents and perhaps most of all subjects, the conversation eventually gets around to a semistrangled, "Do you know what that man made me *do?*"

Reporter Charles Champlin recalls the time he was sent out with photographer Ralph Crane to photograph a herd of prize bulls on the farm of Otto Schnering, president of the Curtiss Candy Company, near Cary, Illinois. Schnering had created a model farm built in the style of a Tudor village, and was making a fortune in the artificial insemination business.

"Rudi" Crane envisioned a great full-page picture of all the big money-earning bulls marching up a sloping hillside with Best Bull front and center, then two Next Best Bulls, then three. . . . He would photograph them from the top window of a farm silo. He described this concept to Champlin, who was left on the ground to translate Crane's orders to the bulls' handlers.

"The day was raw and windy, the bulls were priceless and neurotic, the handlers were contemptuous, impatient, and eventually, furious," Champlin remembers. "I was down under the silo trying to organize all this and every now and again Rudi would emerge from under his black cloth and shout something like 'Second row, back about two feet,' or 'Get the short bulls farther up toward the front.' I would clear my throat and repeat the order and handlers would say, 'Are you out of your blinking mind?' "

Crane finally got that picture, just short of insurrection.

So did Henri Dauman one day in Union Gap, Virginia, where he had gone to photograph a reunion of the Snead family. Back in the 1800s seven Snead brothers had married seven sisters, and once a year their descendants gathered in Union Gap. They were there when Dauman showed up with reporter Jan Mason from New York but there were so many of them that Dauman decided he'd have to assemble them in front of the local high school and photograph them from its roof.

Instead of being able to enjoy their reunion as they chose, the Sneads and kin were marched to the school yard and ordered to shape themselves into a family tree. Genealogy is hard enough to figure out on a piece of paper, and the Sneads got hopelessly confused trying to find their places and form a design which pleased God the photographer.

"Henri was being very French and a little Napoleonic, and the family kept not quite getting the idea," says reporter Mason. "I spent the whole day running up and down four flights of stairs to get his instructions and then push Sneads around down on the ground."

With similar insistence, men from *Life* persuaded people to chop down trees in the front yard ("We want to really see that beautiful window."), move fences, paint walls, put on their Sunday clothes when it was only Tuesday, and stand about for hours while the photographer mended a balky flash unit. Even celebrities were not immune: Actor William Holden, having been photographed in a jungle movie in Hollywood, was busy on another film in London when *Life* decided it needed a cover picture of him to go with the jungle take. A "jungle" was created hastily in London's Kew Gardens, on a Sunday, and actor Holden was persuaded to shave his chest (it had been shaved in the jungle picture), put a knife in his teeth, and crawl toward the camera. With each crawl he hissed past the knife, "I hate you, Mark Kauffman (the photographer)." Reporter Ruth Lynam had to repeat the orders on that one, but she considers if nothing compared to what photographer Gjon Mili put Igor Stravinsky through.

"Stravinsky was very ill, but still conducting, and Mili decided to set up all his strobe lights and try to recreate the mood of *The Firebird*, photographing the maestro slightly out of focus, with rainbows of light around his head. It was jolly difficult but we did it. Next day I was home, lying down, and there was a knock on the door. It was Mili. He said, 'I'm not quite sure about that last roll of film, I want to do it again.' I said, 'Darling, you're out of your mind. This man is old and ill, they had to carry him up the steps to the stage.' And Mili said, 'Well, just go and ask him.' And would you believe, he *did it again.*'"

Now and again somebody rebelled. Clark Gable once got so mad at *Life* for not publishing a story after he had cooperated for days that he refused to pose for the magazine for ten years. Beatle Paul McCartney once threw a pail over a fence at photographer Terry Spencer in England because he was so furious at having been ferreted out in a summer hideaway. And a barber in Gruver, Iowa, managed to kill a whole story because he preferred fishing to posing for pictures. That story was about an election in Gruver, pop. roughly 150, of five female town councilmen. There was no question, in the forties, of "councilpersons." Photographer Walter Sanders wanted to show the female councilmen, of course, but he also decreed that every soul in Gruver should assemble for a group shot in the local ball park.

"A *Life*-type picture in those days was everyone in town," says Hugh Moffett, who was then a reporter. "Everybody in the state would have been better, but if you couldn't get that, then everyone in town. By gosh I tried, I really tried. One man in town was a paraplegic and we arranged to have him brought to the ball park. But one guy, a barber, said 'I'll be damned if I'll show up. I fish on Sundays.' It rained so hard that day we had to move everybody to the high school gym. They waited around while we rigged up the lights and took the picture. But the barber didn't show up and the story didn't run. Gruver, Iowa, is one of those towns we can't go back to."

It is not a matter of record that "the man from *Life*" ever actually persuaded anyone to have an automobile accident, but there were some near misses. There was Rudi Crane in London, for example, shooting an assignment on "the new Europe" in the early sixties. The idea was to show prosperity, well-being, modernity. Crane had once taken a picture of traffic in Los Angeles which was a big success, with car lights blazing into his lens and creating stars in the blackness. He ordered correspondent Bacon and photographers' assistant Frank Allen to find such a spot for him in London, one with the bright yellow sulphur lights which line many heavily traveled roads around London. He further wanted a fairly busy four-lane road, on a curving hill, with some elevation from which he could photograph. Bacon and Allen drove around London for hours one night, finally found what seemed exactly the right spot. There was a four-lane road leading toward Oxford, rows of sulphur lights, and a tube station on which Crane could stand to get his picture.

"We went out about six o'clock one night. Rudi set up his cameras, everything was fine until he suddenly demanded. 'Where is all the traffic?' Ordinarily it was a very busy road, on that night for some reason the light traffic was moving smoothly. Rudi turned to me and said, 'Dorothy, go to the police and arrange a traffic jam.' I

was so stunned I just stood there, and he said, 'Go on, do something. We need an obstruction. Go cause an obstruction.' "

Crane should perhaps have brought along his own obstruction,
as did Mark Kauffman when assigned to photograph the great
Christopher Wren churches of London for a *Life* art and architecture
story. Wren's beautiful spires, built in the seventeenth and
eighteenth centuries, were all but hidden by later, larger buildings
in London, and to complicate that hazard Kauffman decided to
photograph them not on individual sheets of film but all together on
one large multiple exposure. This meant studying all the spires,
making a meticulous design on paper of how he wanted them to be
composed, then carefully masking the film itself so he could photograph first one church, then another, and end up with five or six
individual spires on one sheet of film.

It also meant getting the cooperation of the police, of the National
Electricity Board, and an immense amount of equipment. Aided by
reporter Anne Denny and Allen, he managed to rent klieg lights
from a cooperative cinema company, a powerful generator, miles of
electric wire, a flatbed truck to transport all this equipment, and a
"cherry-picker" crane in which he could be lifted up above the
intruding foreground buildings and high into the air where he could
see the Wren spires.

For two nights the team toured London, selecting sites which
provided enough space for truck, lights, crane, and a view of the
churches. Then they arranged with police to block off the space on
shooting night, redirect traffic in streets they blocked.

"It was a fantastic production line," Denny recalls. "We would set
up in one position, start the generator, rig the lights, and Mark
would sail up in his crane. When he had that picture, the light crew
and the lorry driver and the generator would move to the next
position. While Mark was packing, getting down from the crane,
coming to the next place, we'd be setting up."

The operation went on all night for two nights, with Frank Allen in
general charge of logistics, and selecting which all-night coffee bar
was best for warming up between photographs. The final picture, of
the dome of St. Paul's, was meant to be the central image of the big
multiple exposure. But when the crew got there, the dome was
dismally dark. Not even the big klieg lights would reach its towering
height, so Denny was dispatched to ring up the electricity board, in
the middle of the night, to ask if they would please turn on the dome
lights for, say, ten minutes. The board could, and it did. God the
photographer had even made light.

TWO OF *LIFE*'S STARS

Warren K. Agee

Biographical portraits of two of *Life*'s most gifted photojournalists offer another perspective on that great staff and magazine.

MARGARET BOURKE-WHITE

One of the most accomplished photojournalists in the world, Margaret Bourke-White passionately devoted forty years of her adventure-filled life to producing some of the most powerful images of the twentieth century. She was born in New York City in 1904. In 1926–1927 she worked her way through her senior year at Cornell University by taking pictures. Within three years her free-lance photographs of architecture and steel mills so impressed publisher Henry R. Luce that he hired her as an associate editor and the principal photographer of *Fortune* magazine. She photographed Russian life and industry and executed several photomurals before joining *Life*, where she provided the cover and lead article of the magazine's first issue in 1936.

In collaboration with writer Erskine Caldwell, Bourke-White worked on a study of rural poverty in the South, resulting in the memorable book, *You Have Seen Their Faces* (1937). Their sketches of life in Czechoslovakia and the United States also were published in book form. During their brief married life (1939–1942), they covered the German attack on Moscow in 1941. As an accredited photographer during World War II, Bourke-White was torpedoed and rescued near North Africa, flew a bombing mission, and photographed other war scenes under intense fire. With Patton's Third Army at war's end when it liberated death camps, she produced visual documents that speak the unspeakable.

In India from 1946 to 1948, Bourke-White mastered the spinning wheel to gain access to Mahatma Gandhi and interviewed him hours before his assassination. She reported on the agony of partition, the migration of millions to Pakistan, and the riots and bloodshed. Traveling to South Africa, she chronicled the brutalized daily lives of gold miners. Later, covering the Korean conflict, she was ambushed in a field, and in 1952 was stoned by an angry mob in a Tokyo riot.

Bourke-White survived those and other harrowing experiences only to fall victim to Parkinson's disease, a progressive neural pathology that destroys motor control of the body. She retired from *Life* officially in 1969 and died in 1971. Her courageous fight against the disease was depicted in a television play, with Teresa Wright

SOURCE: This article was written expressly for this book.

A Margaret Bourke-White cover for *Life*

playing the principal role. The story of her life is told in *Portrait of Myself* (1963), one of her six books of text and photos. She wrote four more in collaboration.

As a photojournalist with deep respect for both fact and beauty, Bourke-White joins a long line of artists—Constable, Thoreau, Van Gogh, Whitman, Eakins, Mathew Brady, Paul Strang, Alfred Stieglitz—who wove the two into the fabric of their art. Wrote one critic-historian: "With a child's sense of wonder, an adult's understanding of tragedy, and a strong impulse to share experience, Margaret Bourke-White had excellent credentials for photojournalism. Beyond this, her empathy, discerning eye, and agile mind created a body of work which establishes her as one of the great visual artists of our time."

GORDON PARKS

Gordon Parks enjoyed a distinguished career as a *Life* magazine photojournalist, roaming the world for his stories, but his candid and sensitive coverage of the Black Revolution of the 1960s in the United States earned the highest accolades bestowed upon him.

Parks was born in 1912 in Fort Scott, Kansas, where he experienced a poverty-stricken childhood before moving at the age of 16 to St. Paul, Minnesota. There he played piano in honkytonks, tried professional basketball, lumberjacked in the north woods, and waited on tables in a railway dining car before film director Robert Capa, in a chance encounter, examined his photographs and urged him to turn his talents in that direction.

The young black photographer took fashion and art pictures in Chicago and in 1942 was awarded a Julius Rosenwald Fellowship. The award enabled him to work for a year in Washington with the legendary Farm Security Administration photography unit so brilliantly directed by Roy Stryker, who taught him how to use a camera to portray the lives of the nation's poor.

During World War II Parks was a war correspondent-cameraman with the overseas division of the Office of War Information. He then rejoined Stryker and helped make documentaries for the Standard Oil Company of New Jersey. After he was hired by *Life* magazine in 1949, Parks covered major stories from Harlem gang activities to slum conditions in Brazil, where his photojournalism report of the life of a tubercular boy named Flavio attracted wide attention.

Parks' penetrating essays and forceful photographs about the various black movements during the 1960s, according to one writer, "made the misunderstandings, anger, frustrations, and violence of that period comprehensible to those who otherwise would have remained ignorantly resentful."

The journalist's work won numerous awards, appeared in publications throughout the world, and has been displayed in one-man exhibitions in major museums. Among his books are *The Learning Tree* and *A Choice of Weapons*, both autobiographical. He produced and directed for Paramount Pictures a film based on *The Learning Tree* and has followed that enterprise with several other movies in recent years, as well as continuing his photography.

On the occasion of an exhibition at the Art Institute of Chicago, Parks expressed his view of the photographer's task:

"The camera is a forthright, honest, and powerful medium of self-expression, and its potentialities are far-reaching and unpredictable. A good picture may not always be in focus or best in composition, but in it you are always aware of a specific moment, which has been recorded truthfully. As a photographer, I relentlessly search for that specific moment."

NIHILISM AT THE MOVIES
Pauline Kael

Kael, recognized as among the finest American film critics, has won many awards for her trenchant, often blunt essays and reviews. Here she laments the "blockbuster" mentality that dominates Hollywood—and movie audiences, too.

Whatever their individual qualities, such films as *Bonnie and Clyde*, *The Graduate*, *Easy Rider*, *Five Easy Pieces*, *Joe*, *M*A*S*H*, *Little Big Man*, *Midnight Cowboy*, and *They Shoot Horses, Don't They?* all helped to form the counterculture. The young, anti-draft, anti-Vietnam audiences that were "the film generation" might go to some of the same pictures that the older audience did, but not to those only. They were willing to give something fresh a chance, and they went to movies that weren't certified hits. They made modest—sometimes large—successes of pictures that had new, different perceptions. A movie like the tentative, fumbling *Alice's Restaurant* would probably be a flop now, because student audiences are no longer willing to look for feelings, to accept something suggestive and elliptical and go with the mood. Students accept the elliptical on records—the Joni Mitchell "Court and Spark," say, and some of the more offbeat Carly Simon cuts—but not in movies. The subdued, fine-drawn *McCabe & Mrs. Miller*, which came out in 1971, managed to break even, but the soft-colored *Thieves Like Us*, . . . by the same director, Robert Altman, has been seen by almost nobody. Those who might be expected to identify with Jeff Bridges in *The Last American Hero* are going to see Clint Eastwood in *Magnum Force* instead. They're going to the kind of slam-bang pictures that succeed with illiterate audiences in "underdeveloped" countries

---

SOURCE: Pauline Kael, *Reeling* (Boston: Little, Brown, 1976), pp. 309–12. Copyright © 1974 by Pauline Kael. First appeared in *The New Yorker*, August 5, 1974. Reprinted by permission of Little, Brown and Company in association with the Atlantic Monthly Press.

who are starved for entertainment. The almost voluptuously obsessive *Mean Streets*—a film that one might have thought would be talked about endlessly—passed through college towns without causing a stir. The new generations of high-school and college students are going to movies that you can't talk about afterward—movies that are completely consumed in the theatre. . . .

For many years, some of us alarmists have been saying things like "Suppose people get used to constant visceral excitement—will they still respond to the work of artists?" Maybe, owing partly to the national self-devaluation and partly to the stepped-up power of advertising, what we feared has come about. It's hardly surprising: how can people who have just been pummeled and deafened by *The French Connection* be expected to respond to a quiet picture? If, still groggy, they should stumble in to see George Segal in Irvin Kershner's *Loving* the next night, they'd think there was nothing going on in it, because it didn't tighten the screws on them. *The Rules of the Game* might seem like a hole in the screen. When *The Getaway* is double-billed with *Mean Streets*, it's no wonder that some people walk out on *Mean Streets*. Audiences like movies that do all the work for them—just as in the old days, and with an arm-twisting rubdown besides. College students don't appear to feel insulted (what's left to insult us?); they don't mind being banged over the head—the louder the better. They seem to enjoy seeing the performers whacked around, too; sloppy knockabout farce is the newest smash, and knockabout horror isn't far behind. People go for the obvious, the broad, the movies that don't ask them to feel anything. If a movie is a hit, that means practically guaranteed sensations—and sensations without feeling.

I often come out of a movie now feeling wiped out, desolate—and often it's a movie that the audience around me has reacted to noisily, as if it were having a high, great time—and I think I feel that way because of the nihilism in the atmosphere. It isn't intentional or philosophical nihilism; it's the kind one sometimes feels at a porn show—the way everything is turned to dung, oneself included. A couple of years ago, I went with another film critic, a young man, to see a hard-core movie in the Broadway area, and there was a live stage show with it. A young black girl—she looked about seventeen but must have been older—did a strip and then danced naked. The theater was small, and the girl's eyes, full of hatred, kept raking the customers' faces, I was the only other woman there, and each time her eyes came toward me, I had to look down; finally, I couldn't look up at all. The young critic and I sat in misery, unable to leave, since that would look like a put-down of her performance. We had to take the contempt with which she hid her sense of being degraded, and we shared in her degradation, too. Hits like *The Exorcist* give most of the audience just what it wants and expects, the way hard-core porn does. The hits have something in common: blatancy. They are films that *deliver*. They're debauches—their subject might almost be mindlessness and futurelessness. People in the audience want to laugh, and at pictures like *Enter the Dragon* and *Andy Warhol's Frankenstein* and *The Three Musketeers* and *Blazing Saddles* they're laughing at pandemonium and accepting it as the comic truth.

The counterculture films made corruption seem inevitable and hence something you learn to live with; the next step was seeing it as slapstick comedy and learning to enjoy it. For the fatalistic, case-hardened audience, absurdism has become the only accept-able point of view—a new complacency. In *The Three Musketeers*, Richard Lester keeps his actors at a distance and scales the characters down to abnormal size; they're letching, carousing buffoons who don't care about anything but blood sport. The film isn't politically or socially abrasive; it's just "for fun." At showings of *Chinatown*, the audience squeals with pleasure when Faye Duna-way reveals her incest. The success of *Chinatown*—with its beauti-fully structured script and draggy, overdeliberate direction—represents something dialectically new: nostalgia (for the thirties) openly turned to rot, and the *celebration* of rot. Robert Towne's script had ended with the detective (Jack Nicholson) realizing what horrors the Dunaway character had been through, and, after she killed her incestuous father, helping her daughter get to Mexico. But Roman Polanski seals the picture with his gargoyle grin; now evil runs rampant. The picture is compelling, but coldly, suffocatingly compelling. Polanski keeps so much of it in closeup that there's no air, no freedom to breathe; you don't care who is hurt, since everything is blighted. Life is a blood-red maze. Polanski may leave the story muddy and opaque, but he shoves the rot at you, and large numbers of people seem to find it juicy. Audiences now appear to accept as a view of themselves what in the movies of the past six or seven years counterculture audiences jeered at Ameri-cans for being—cynical materialists who cared for nothing but their own greed and lust. The nihilistic, coarse-grained movies are telling us that nothing matters to us, that we're all a bad joke.

It's becoming tough for a movie that isn't a big media-created event to find an audience, no matter how good it is. . . . People no longer go to a picture just for itself, and ticket-buyers certainly aren't looking for the movie equivalent of "a good read." They want to be battered, to be knocked out—they want to get wrecked. They want what "everybody is talking about," and even if they don't like the picture—and some people didn't really care for *A Touch of Class*, and some detested *The Three Musketeers*, and many don't like *Blazing Saddles*, either—they don't feel out of it. Increasingly, though, I've noticed that those who don't enjoy a big event-film feel out of it in another way. They wonder if there's something they're not getting—if the fault is theirs.

The public can't really be said to have rejected a film like *Payday*, since the public never heard of it. If you don't know what a movie is and it plays at a theatre near you, you barely register it. *Payday* may not come at all; when the event strategy really works, as it has of late, the hits and the routine action films and horror films are all that get to most towns. And if a film turns up that hasn't had a big campaign, people assume it's a dog; you risk associating yourself with failure if you go to see Jon Voight in *Conrack* or Blythe Danner in the messed-up but still affecting *Lovin' Molly*. When other values are rickety, the fact that something is selling gives it a primacy, and its detractors seem like spoilsports. The person who holds out against an event looks a loser: the minority is a fool. People are cynical about advertising, of course, but their cynicism is so all inclusive now that they're indifferent, and so they're more suscepti-ble to advertising than ever. If nothing matters anyway, why not just go where the crowd goes? That's a high in itself.

PRODUCING THE DOCUMENTARY
Roy Paul Madsen

Film workers often get their start by making documentary pictures, and many have enjoyed lucrative careers in the field. Madsen, a teacher of filmmaking and producer of films, explains how to go about producing a documentary.

The documentary film is usually produced by a very small team of filmmakers—writer, director, cameraman and editor. Sometimes one of these persons will perform more than one function, such as a writer-editor, or one will serve as the producer for the whole operation. In contrast to the compartmentalization typical of dra-matic film production, with a specialist as master for each phase of its development, the work of all filmmakers on a documentary team is interrelated from the first brainstorming session to the final viewing of a release print. Each person's experience and viewpoint contributes to the shape of the film as it takes persuasive form, its

SOURCE: Roy Paul Madsen, *The Impact of Film* (New York: Macmillan, 1973), pp. 331–35. Copyright 1973 by Roy Paul Madsen. Reprinted by permission.

cinematic elements become dynamic, and at last a documentary film reaches out hopefully to awaken the viewer to a clamant human need.

A documentary film idea is most frequently born from the gut reaction of a filmmaker that something he [or she] sees—some human condition—needs to be changed. Rambling and browsing is the next phase of development, because the documentarist is seeking a familiarity with the problem that will enable him to select those aspects of it that will graphically bring the issue into sharp focus. Immersion in the subject at its source is essential because no amount of library research (important as it may be) and preliminary discussions will get to the heart of the matter as will a complete personal experience on location. If the filmmaker is producing a film about the poor whites from Appalachia who have drifted to Chicago seeking work, he should join a family at their dinner of fatback and grits, stand in line for food stamps, walk the streets with them in their search for work and find out why they were refused, sleep in their ratty beds, join in their pastime of pitching pennies at a crack in the sidewalk, and stand with the men gathered around the guitar-strummer as they sing plaintively, "I want to go home."

Documentary Facts

From experiences on location, the documentary facts will reveal themselves. Documentary facts are visual facts that exemplify the problems, while arousing at the same time the empathy of the viewer: the rat-nibbled mattress; the hypodermic needle lying in a dirty dish; the silent empty house in the hills with ragweed growing up through the porch; the old migrant laborer, past the age of earning his keep, who slouches on an orange crate as he stares vacantly and twitches his gnarled empty hands. Documentary facts are those which exist in a *specific visual form*, rather than as verbal description or statistical abstraction, because life is itself specific and visual. But the filmmaker will also study stock shots, still photographs, tape recordings, newspaper and magazine clips and books; and he will interview victims of the problem, perpetrators of the problem, authorities on the problem—he will prowl down any alley or byway that may give him some form of insight that he can communicate to the viewer.

Theme

A theme will emerge from whatever subject is undertaken that forms the intellectual framework of the documentary film, a central concept that can usually be expressed in a single sentence: "Pollution is so huge a problem that we can't afford to clean it up, and can't afford to ignore it." Or, "Some fanatics are reducing our freedoms by abusing theirs." These thematic statements should come from the subjects themselves, not from an official spokesman giving out a public relations statement, or even from the filmmakers themselves. Most often, the theme will be spoken with unpretentious eloquence by some individual affected by the problem: a farmer, an unemployed engineer, a research assistant or informed social worker. By listening carefully, the documentary filmmaker will hear his subject say something that will provide the film with an intellectual framework and thematic summing up.

Story line in documentary film tends to derive from a natural sequence of events, or a logical cause and effect relationship between events, that lends itself cinematically to becoming a drama of ideas. To a large extent the story line and its cinematic rendering are dictated by the nature of the subject.

If the purpose of the documentary film is to gain support for a flood control or reforestation project, the filmed sequences would probably show the chronological progression of events that brought about the need for remedial action in the same essential sequence in which the events actually occurred: excessive lumbering; overgrazing by livestock; wasteful agricultural usages; dumping of corrosive acids into the river; growing erosion and lack of water controls. And then the inevitable results—the river is swollen by excessive water runoff and nature exacts vengeance by flooding the homes and industries of its human exploiters. The conclusion of the film would show what needs to be done to rectify the damage and tell the viewer what he can do to stimulate remedial action.

Graphic materials of all kinds may be included in the film if it helps to communicate the idea—newsreel footage, candid camera film, stock shots, still photographs given movement on an animation stand, animated films and special effects, are all acceptable if they give the viewer information and perspective. The viewer of a documentary film, by his selective exposure to that film, is indicating his willingness, to some degree, to be affected by the film's content, and therefore tends to watch with suspended judgment and look for anything that will help him to understand. The viewer comes to a documentary film with a different frame of reference than he would bring to a dramatic film; he tends to be seeking reality, not avoiding it, and he is less critical of production finesse. Where the documentary genre is concerned, anything goes in terms of what content may be included, and cinematic style and production slickness are subordinate to the graphic communication of the idea.

Cinematography

Cinematography for a documentary film should occur, ideally, when people are unaware of the camera's presence, for only then do they really behave in a manner which is completely normal and relaxed. Disconcerting realism is the goal of documentary film, the recording of those strange human moments when people are really tired or really busy, those times of stress and anguish, temptation and revelation, when the social veneers peel back and the lens may record real people being themselves instead of behaving as they want to be perceived.

The hidden camera may sometimes be used under specialized circumstances, and at other times, when the subjects are so preoccupied with their tasks that they are unaware or heedless of being photographed, the camera will function as if it were hidden.

More often, however, the documentary filmmakers must move into people's lives, homes and places of employment in order to make the film. They must set up cameras and lights and reflectors and engage in all kinds of activities which, if they are not actually disruptive of the subject's normal activities, are at the least distracting.

Disruption of the subjects' lives and environment should be kept to a minimum for three primary reasons: First, it may change or distort the subjects' normal patterns of behavior and activities and thereby distort the facts being presented in the documentary film. Second, the physical rearrangement of objects to suit the exigencies of film production may kill the spontaneity of a place where people live and work. Third, there may be a temptation to arrange subjects and objects before the camera in a way that is too satisfying aesthetically and a betrayal of the truth—to transform poverty and dirt into artistic tonal arrangements that please the eye and distract the mind from unpleasant realities. In documentary film production dissonance of content is sometimes important in order to persuade the viewer to support the filmmaker's proposed solution to the problem.

Multicamera setups are frequently advisable when retakes would lower the spontaneity of the subject, in order to capture sensitive human expressions for cinematic interpretations. And the multicamera technique is useful for obtaining overlapped, matching action for good editing technique; the need for establishing shots, medium shots and closeups is nearly as important in the documentary genre as in dramatic film, because jump cuts are a distraction from the communication of ideas.

Multicamera setups, useful though the technique may be, come at the price of consistency and quality in the lighting of the scenes. What may be an ideally lighted scene from one camera angle may mean low-key lighting from the second camera position and high-key lighting from the third, yielding inconsistencies of tonality that may seem glaring when the scenes are intercut in editing. But if the

end result is the capture of evanescent human impressions on film
footage, which may then be sensitively edited to reveal insight into
human consequences, it is well worth the price of inconsistent
lighting.

Single-camera setups are inadvisable because they frequently
require that a subject repeat his actions in order to obtain
matching-action footage, a kind of skill that few nonactors can
manage. Retakes of scenes should be kept to a minimum because
they tire the subject and wither his spontaneity. The surest way to
avoid such repetitions is to know, understand and anticipate the
real movements of the subject, and then capture the flow of his
natural actions with multiple-camera setups.

Before taking down the lights for any given sequence the
documentary filmmaker should make sure that he has photographed the beginnings and endings of the action—the times and
places where the subject normally pauses—and a cutaway or two to
take the curse off a jump cut should there be any aspect he has
overlooked.

Part Four

THE PERSUASIVE ARTS

As discussed in the selections in Part One, the mass media exercise a considerable influence over public opinion (although not as much as do the peer groups to which we belong). They do so primarily through their agenda-setting—the selection of most of our daily diet of news, entertainment, and opinion.

Except for much of the work of editorial writers, and critics and reviewers, the news media in their informational function—with perhaps a few scandalous exceptions—do not consciously try to influence our beliefs and actions.

Not so, however, with advertising and public relations people. Primarily through paid (advertising) and unpaid (public relations) communication, they endeavor to persuade us to buy goods, services, and ideas, and they work to build favorable images of their products, companies, and institutions. When the public's interest and their own coincide, this is a highly desirable and essential social function. Without doubt, our capitalistic society, including the news media, could not function without them.

Advertising in this country began in early colonial days with the placing of the first signs indicating places of business. At the same time, newspapers, posters, and pamphlets carried the first advertisements. As villages grew into cities, merchants increasingly cried their wares in print. Advertising agencies began to develop as early as the 1840s. The industrial and then the technological revolutions vastly increased trade, and advertising gradually encompassed all the media, including even the movies, and used other outlets as well.

In the selections that follow, brief biographies of two advertising people are presented as representing the lives of hundreds of advertising leaders who helped shape the business. Albert D. Lasker, through his vision and innovations, became known as the "father of modern advertising." Fairfax M. Cone served as a model for top-flight practitioners through his lifelong insistence on high ethical standards.

What is advertising? In a selection bearing that title, Sydney R. Bernstein, former editor and publisher of *Advertising Age* and a widely respected observer, provides a well-rounded answer: Advertising is mainly a form of mass persuasion that helps the individual salesman make a sale. In this role, he adds, advertising "performs an essential part in an economy of abundance: It helps develop demand for the host of products and services which are available to and within the reach of the vast majority, and by so doing it helps constantly to raise the standard of living and to keep the wheels of industry moving smoothly."

David Cook, an Emory University professor on leave to study the cultural history of American television, takes a somewhat different view, at least regarding network television. In his provocative article, "Your Money and Your Life," Cook says television robs us of our time and then bills us for the theft: "Since the costs of television advertising are passed along to consumers in the price of the advertised goods, television programming is hardly free." Moreover, "Through this medium advertisers not only command our leisure time in our homes at night, but they sell it back to us in the shopping malls on the weekends at a profit. Except that we can't really buy it back. Like American Indians trading their land to the colonists for trinkets, we are selling off our most precious and nonrenewable resource—the time of our lives—for a handful of electronic gimcracks and colored beads."

> Pepsi-Cola hits the spot.
> Twelve full ounces, that's a lot.
> Twice as much for your nickel too
> Pepsi-Cola is the drink for you.

That musical jingle, reminiscent of the 1940s, when soda pop cost far less than today and the Pepsi-Cola Company was just mounting its four-decades-long assault on Coca-Cola's preeminence in the market, is an appropriate introduction to James P. Forkan's article, "Pepsi Generation Bridges Two Decades."

> Find the right words, put them in the right order, set them in clear type, let them breathe with a little white space, give them straightforward headline treatment, invest them with the importance people automatically attach to someone who has the courage of his convictions, and watch them go to work.

That's the advice given by Norman Cousins, longtime editor of *Saturday Review* magazine, in his article, "Want to Sell Point of View? Use Advertising." Bernice Fitz-Gibbon, a brilliant copywriter and creator of sales slogans, tells the beginner how to find the right words that sell. While Cousins extols the virtues of print advertising, West Coast advertising executive and satirist Stan Freberg shows what radio can do, especially as compared to television, in his humorous and widely used one-minute script that stretches the listener's imagination.

Public relations—advertising's partner in persuasion—is largely a twentieth-century development. It has evolved from nineteenth-century press agentry, as exemplified by P. T. Barnum, through a long period when it was perceived mainly as a publicity function, to today's highly sophisticated operation consisting of evaluation, counseling, communication, and influencing management policies, as discussed in the selections that follow.

An important innovator in molding corporate public relations during the first three decades of the century was Ivy Lee; the highlights of his life are given here. Another important figure in the development of the field was Paul Garrett, the only public relations employee of General Motors when he joined the company in 1931. An exponent, along with Edward L. Bernays and others, of the Total Program of public relations, Garrett built GM's extensive public relations operation and his speeches did much to convince the managers of American corporations that they must consider the full effect of their businesses upon the public. Garrett's philosophy of public relations is related in an excerpt from L. L. L. Golden's book, *Only by Public Consent.*

Community relations ranks high among the public relations responsibilities of today's institutions and corporations, which also include modern press agentry, product promotion, publicity, lobbying, human relations, public affairs, and environmental scanning. An example of a community social welfare public relations program at work is provided in Edward B. Borden's " 'Somebody Cares.' "

The public relations strategies employed by companies in anticipating or handling crises are reviewed in a *Wall Street Journal* article originally titled, "When Disaster Comes, Public Relations Men Won't Be Far Behind." The *Journal's* own public relations program may have suffered with publication of that headline, for women today are an important force in the field—in fact, women own more than 6,000 public relations firms in the United States. In her article, "What About Public Relations for Women?," Fran Weinstein describes the work of women practitioners.

Although public relations is not a profession in the sense that medicine and law are professions (since state certification is not a prerequisite for practice and there are no prescribed standards of educational preparation nor mandatory internships), many practitioners believe that it can become a profession and are working to that end. The Public Relations Society of America, with more than 8000 members, has adopted a code of ethics and instituted an accreditation program that are both widely accepted. In his article, "Criticism, Evaluation and Professionalism," Dennis L. Wilcox urges fellow PRSA members to advance the cause of professionalism by criticizing incompetent performance and ineffective public relations strategies.

"Hyping"—the promotion of movie and television stars, books, magazines, etc., through shrewd use of the media and other devices—is an increasingly lively phenomenon in the world of public relations. Marguerite Michaels tells how it was done for Suzanne Somers.

Section 14

ADVERTISING

Advertising sends its roots back to the Latin verb for "giving attention." As so often in language, it now means "getting attention," or better, "the attempt to secure public attention for commercial reasons." The attempt is open, unconcealed, and involves bought-and-paid-for exposition.

SHAPERS OF THE PROFESSION
Phillip H. Ault and Warren K. Agee
The two biographies offered here serve to reflect the excitement of advertising's early years and to portray the growth of the modern advertising agency.

ALBERT D. LASKER

"Father of modern advertising" is the unofficial title often given to Albert D. Lasker, who did more than anyone to change advertisements from dull lists of items for sale into what he called "salesmanship in print." It was Lasker who created the first copywriting department in an advertising agency.

Many of Lasker's innovations in advertising seem routine now, because they are universally used, but at the time he put them into effect they had enormous impact on American consumer buying habits. During the period of his work, roughly 1900 to 1940, American industry produced a cornucopia of new products we regard as basic in life today; many of them became household words because of the advertising campaigns he ran for them.

Lasker was a gregarious, loquacious, emotional man with a subtle mind, and an instinctive psychologist. Born May 1, 1880, he graduated from high school at Galveston, Texas, and at the age of 18 through a business acquaintance of his father obtained a job at $10 a week with the Lord and Thomas advertising agency in Chicago. Eventually he became sole owner of that agency, acquiring great wealth from its profits. Then, almost on a whim, he dissolved the agency in 1942 and gave up the advertising business.

Catchy advertising headlines and slogans were key elements in Lasker's technique. He was responsible for such slogans as "Keep That Schoolgirl Complexion" for Palmolive soap and "Reach for a Lucky Instead of a Sweet," which probably did more to convince women to smoke than any other promotional effort by the tobacco industry. Pepsodent toothpaste, another of his client products, contained the detergent sodium alkyl sulphate; he told his copy writers to invent an easy word for this ingredient, something with three vowels and two consonants. They concocted "irium." The

SOURCE: This article was written expressly for this book.

Albert D. Lasker

phrase "contains irium" became an essential part of Pepsodent's sales messages, suggesting that the ingredient was a magic extra. "Give readers a reason why they should buy your product" was fundamental to Lasker's method.

Among other sales tools Lasker helped to develop were the use of test markets, sampling, and distribution of coupons. Words meant much more to him than pictures—Lord and Thomas advertising paid little attention to graphics. Nor did he believe much in the kind of intensive market research contemporary advertising agencies use.

When network radio developed in the late 1920s, Lasker put his agency so heavily into the business that at one point during the 1930s the agency purchased 30 percent of all network time on behalf of its clients and packaged many of the most famous evening comedy and dramatic shows as well as soap operas.

After more than forty years in the business, Lasker grew bored with advertising. He closed his agency and transferred many of its clients to the newly created Foote, Cone & Belding agency. The remaining ten years of his life he concentrated on philanthropies and art collecting. He died May 30, 1952, a legend among his peers and a pioneer with much effect on mass communications.

FAIRFAX M. CONE

As a noted copywriter, account executive, and board chairman of Foote, Cone & Belding, Inc.—one of the world's top ten advertising agencies—Fairfax M. Cone exerted a strong influence on advertising practices throughout his 48-year career.

Cone was born in San Francisco in 1903, the son of a mining engineer and a retired school teacher. He attended school irregularly until the age of 16, when he became a seaman on a freighter. In 1925 he enrolled in the University of California at Berkeley with the intention of studying English. A year later, however, with the help of a friend, William Randolph Hearst, Jr., he was hired by the San Francisco *Examiner* as an advertising salesman and writer-illustrator.

In 1929 Cone joined the San Francisco office of Lord & Thomas advertising agency as a copywriter. He became manager of that office in 1939 and by 1941 had moved to the firm's New York office as vice president in charge of creative work. He became executive vice president and manager of the Chicago office in 1942, and served the remainder of his career in that city.

After being chosen by agency head Albert D. Lasker to handle the American Tobacco Company account, Cone dealt successfully with the legendary George Washington Hill. He attained immediate success with a "Lucky Strike" cigarette campaign featuring a full-page reproduction of a Paul Sample painting of a tobacco auction. The slogan, "Lucky Strike green has gone to war" (informing the public that the company's elimination of copper-based green ink saved the metal for the war effort), also helped keep the cigarette's image and sales high.

When Lord & Thomas dissolved, Cone and two other company executives, Emerson Foote and Don Belding, organized Foote, Cone & Belding in 1943.

Cone advocated "straight-forward advertising, without comedy, gimmicks, or vulgarity." He once explained his advertising philosophy with the statement that "advertising is good in ratio to its approximation of personal selling. If you believe this, . . . use the same taste you would if you called upon people at their homes." Advertising, he said, "is neither moral nor immoral. But being a representation by individuals, it is subject to all their character traits."

Cone favored extending the magazine concept of advertising to television, thus enabling an advertiser to buy time without sponsoring a particular production.

When critics of advertising proposed that it be replaced by government-compiled consumer reports, Cone responded: "Here I

Fairfax M. Cone

must object. Surely it has yet to be proved . . . that consumers may be competent to select presidents, wives, and husbands . . . but not to pick breakfast foods, and that only the federal government can make such decisions soundly."

Cone worked consistently to keep advertising on a sound moral track that would retain public favor. In a widely quoted advertisement entitled, "The plain, short story of good advertising," the agency said:

> There is a small group of advertising people in the United States who make advertising not only as a business but also for the sheer, continuing satisfaction of pushing good products past all competition.
>
> This small group of men and women have no interest at all in either comfortable small businesses or questionable big ones.
>
> Its members pride themselves on accomplishment but they have no truck with even the slightest exaggeration or deception.
>
> They believe in the good judgment of the average adult American and they make advertising to excite this good judgment and to satisfy it. . . .

After a long and successful career, Cone died in 1977 following an extended illness. He had accumulated many honors, including admission to the Advertising Hall of Fame, the ultimate accolade of his profession.

WHAT IS ADVERTISING?
S. R. Bernstein

In this selection abstracted from a comprehensive essay, Bernstein defines advertising and its multiple roles, discusses how it works, and lists the tasks it performs in addition to the principal one of selling. He is chairman of the executive committee of Crain Communications, Inc., publishers of *Advertising Age*.

A great deal of the criticism of advertising in consumer, educational and legislative circles is based on some serious misconceptions of what advertising is and how it is supposed to function.

The first and most serious misconception of advertising's role is that it should be impartial and unbiased, serving a role very similar to a referee's role in a football game or an arbitrator in a labor dispute. But advertising is not impartial or unbiased; its function is to present the advertiser's story or product as effectively and as alluringly as possible, without overstepping the bounds of honesty, truthfulness and good taste. We shall discuss this at length a bit later.

Who Wants It?

The second misconception seems almost as widespread as the first. It is the assumption that the manufacturers, distributors, and retailers who pay the costs of advertising their products have some inherent interest in advertising as such. The fact is that their interest consists entirely in using advertising as a useful and effective tool in selling their products or services. If and when any advertiser discovers some quicker, more effective, more economical method of promoting his business, he will abandon advertising with no hesitation and no regrets. Those who pay for advertising consider it only as a selling tool, and measure its value carefully under that criterion. The only people and organizations who have a vested interest in advertising as such are the *sellers* and the *producers* of advertising, not the buyers—the various media, the advertising

---

SOURCE: From *Advertising Age*, May 5, 1980. Copyright 1980 by Crain Communications, Inc. Reprinted with permission.

agencies, the panoply of individuals and organizations involved in producing today's television and radio commercials, and so on.

Defining Advertising

Way back in 1948, the committee on definitions of the American Marketing Assn. agreed on a definition which said that advertising is *any paid form of non-personal presentation and promotion of ideas, goods, or services by an identified sponsor.* And four years later, the International Chamber of Commerce issued a dictionary of marketing terms in which advertising was defined as a *non-personal, multiple presentation to the market of goods, services or commercial ideas by an identified sponsor who pays for the delivery of his message to the carrier (advertising medium); distinguished from* publicity, *which does not pay the medium and does not necessarily identify the sponsor.*

The distinction made in these latter two definitions between advertising and public relations or publicity is most important. Because advertising, above all else, calls for an *identified sponsor*, so that the reader or viewer of advertising knows who is presenting the message, and is thereby equipped to weigh the advertiser's possible bias in the scale in which he judges the validity of the message.

More Than 'Presenting'

(This matter of an *identified sponsor* is particularly important in non-commercial advertising—in political advertising and advertising for "causes" or points of view, where the identity of the person, company or group sponsoring the message is of vital importance. In the case of ordinary commercial product advertising, the identity of the sponsor is almost always self-evident.)

The description of advertising as the "non-personal presentation *and promotion* of ideas, goods and services" is also vitally important, because advertising is more than *to make known, to publish, to inform.* Early advertising—the simplest kind of advertising—was designed to perform these simple functions, and much advertising still performs them. The sign outside a home industry or a modest store, identifying it as a grocery or a shoe repair shop or a vendor of drugs, does that. But modern advertising goes beyond the simple process of identification. It not only *presents* ideas, goods or services; it also *promotes* them.

In modern usage, that is the basic function of advertising: Not merely to catalog goods or services, nor to present them with a listing of their good points and bad, but to *promote* them so as to make them seem not only worth while but indispensable.

As we have pointed out, by definition advertising is not unbiased or objective with regard to the product or service or idea being advertised; it is a *special pleader*, hoping to surround its subject with a rose-colored aura of loveliness.

In short, advertising is, as it was defined before broadcasting was known, "salesmanship in print," a technique for *mass persuasion*—an extension and a multiplier of personal selling, and its usage and functions must be considered in this context.

Substitute for Salesman

So, in essence, advertising is a substitute for the human salesman talking personally to an individual prospect or customer across a store counter or a desk or an open door. And, as a substitute for the human salesman, advertising has pretty much the same functions, abilities and attributes as the human salesman.

It is less effective than personal selling, however, principally because it must be designed to appeal to a mass audience, in contrast with the personal salesman's ability to tailor his sales message to each individual prospect, and because, again, unlike the personal salesman, it has no opportunity to "talk back," explain, or refute objections.

This is advertising, no more and no less—a mechanized substitute for the personal salesman.

This is not the monster or the irresistible force so often portrayed in fiction. Most serious students of advertising are astounded at the image of advertising that seems to exist so widely in non-advertising minds. When they hear authors and legislators and educators and economists discoursing on the awesome all-embracing power of advertising to hypnotize America's millions, to mesmerize the dollars out of their pockets, and to turn them from the road of economic virtue and sobriety into the primrose paths of over-spending for useless, unneeded products, they shake their heads in wonderment. They know that advertising is not that good, not that powerful, not that influential.

Actually, the great bulk of advertising is really more of a salesman's helper than it is a substitute for the salesman. In most instances, the advertising, hopefully, makes it easier for a sales person to sell you something at some future time, and at some place other than the place in which you see the advertisement. Thus, when your neighborhood supermarket advertises today's grocery bargains in the daily newspaper, it hopes to induce you to shop its aisles and pick the advertised items off its shelves.

Helping to Make the Sale

Likewise, a department store which advertises the appearance of the new season's clothing hopes for the same happy result—that you will come into the store and complete the buying pattern with the assistance of a sales person. And the national advertiser who tells you how delicious his soft drink is hopes, in the same manner, to make you think favorably about soft drinks, and to pick his, rather than some competitor's, off the grocery shelf when you actually make your purchase.

So it can be said that in relatively few instances is advertising designed to take the place of the salesman and actually make the sale. In far more instances, advertising is designed to smooth the salesman's path, to make it possible for him to get his order more easily and more quickly.

There is, of course, a substantial area in which advertising is expected to perform the entire selling job.

In the case of catalogs and other direct mail and direct marketing offers, and a very small amount of print and broadcast advertising, the reader or listener is asked for a direct response; he is urged to send in an order by mail or by telephone. In such cases, advertising is used as a substitute for personal selling. The sales proposition is stated in the advertisement, the catalog or the mailing piece, and the prospect is invited to complete the buying transaction without further discussion or negotiation.

We have all made purchases in this fashion. But direct-selling advertising, as this type of advertising is called, represents only a small (but rapidly growing) fraction of the total advertising scene. The big volume of advertising is designed to make the sale easier, but the actual sale must be consummated in some other place, and at some other time, than the time and place in which the advertising makes contact with the customer.

It is true that in a great many buying transactions—notably in the purchase of food at retail—the actual salesman has disappeared, and self-service is the rule. Here advertising fills a relatively new and vastly more important role. It pre-informs and pre-sells the customer to such an extent that when she enters the place in which actual purchases are made—in this case the supermarket—the necessity for personal salesmanship has largely been replaced, and what was once a buying-selling situation now becomes a much simpler order-filling operation. Much spur-of-the-moment impulse buying still takes place, of course; but the essential elements of information about the product and confidence in its value have been developed as the customer or prospect has been exposed to advertising, and personal salesmanship is not required at the point of purchase.

In his book, "How to Become an Advertising Man," the late James Webb Young, a pioneer advertising man, said there are five basic ways in which advertising works:

"1. **By familiarizing**—that is, as the dictionary says, by 'making something well-known; bringing into common use.' This is absolutely basic value created by advertising, the one underlying all others.

"2. **By reminding**—a function that may alone, in some cases, make advertising pay.

"3. **By spreading news**—not only news in the newspaper sense, but a special kind of news that only advertising, in the commercial field, can most widely deal with.

"4. **By overcoming inertias**—the great drag on all human progress, economic or non-economic, as represented by the sociological term, 'cultural lag.'

"5. **By adding a value** not in the product—the most challenging field for creativeness in advertising."

In similar fashion, McGraw-Hill, which publishes books and a host of specialized business publications, says there are six steps to successful selling to business and industry. They are:

1. Make contact.
2. Arouse interest.
3. Create preference.
4. Make proposal.
5. Close order.
6. Keep customer sold.

"The function of advertising," says McGraw-Hill, "is to reduce the cost of selling." And with the average cost of an industrial salesman's call estimated at more than $90, says McGraw-Hill, it is essential to use advertising to accomplish the largest part of steps 1, 2, 3 and 6, and thus allow the expensive salesman more time to concentrate on steps 4 and 5, which must be accomplished by the salesman and cannot be performed by advertising.

Enthusiastic Pleading

Advertising worth its salt to the advertiser has another attribute of the good salesman—an attribute sometimes thoughtlessly criticized. That attribute is enthusiasm.

No one likes to believe his actions or his buying habits are influenced to any important degree by the persuasion exerted by salesmanship, whether it is personal selling or advertising. We like to believe that all that is necessary is to uncover the wares, so to speak, and buyers will make their free-will choices without further ado. Any "salesmanship"—whether it be personal or impersonal—we tend to equate with undue or unfair influence.

The statement often attributed to Emerson that if someone built a better mousetrap, the world would beat a path to his door, is not even a half truth. Making a better mousetrap is not enough. Someone must explain that it *is* a better mousetrap, and *why* it is better. Someone must be enthusiastic about its merits and its advantages—enthusiastic and interested enough to sell others on its merits, and to overcome inertia and unwillingness to change.

This is the function of the salesman—and of advertising. By definition, salesmanship, of which advertising is one manifestation, is special pleading, not unbiased reporting. Yet this inspires one of the great general criticisms of advertising: That it induces people to buy things they don't really want and can't afford.

No one expects a good lawyer to present an unbiased resume of his client's position, nor a politician to outline dispassionately the advantages and disadvantages of the course he urges, nor a clergyman to explain the possibility that some other faith may have more to commend it than the one *he* advocates. But a good many intelligent people seem to feel that special pleading and enthusiastic selling in advertising are somehow immoral or anti-social.

Thus far we have been discussing advertising quite literally as "salesmanship in print," or at least as the salesman's helper, making it easier for the salesman to consummate the buying-selling transaction. But the uses of advertising spread into many other areas, some of which are performed incidentally by the good salesman, and some of which cannot effectively be performed by salesmen at all, but which are general management activities.

The catalog of ways in which advertising may be used and the tasks it may be asked to perform are almost endless, but they may be categorized into three broad groups in addition to the principal one of selling, or helping to sell, the advertiser's products or services. These are:

1. Reassuring and retaining present and former customers.

2. Bolstering and increasing the confidence, enthusiasm and eagerness of the advertiser's own personnel, and of non-advertiser personnel engaged in the distribution of the product, or involved in recommending or endorsing it.

3. Projecting a useful image to one or more of the advertiser's various publics.

Provides Reassurance

It is no accident that research into advertising has demonstrated conclusively that the buyer of a particular product or service, at the conscious level at least, is as avid a follower of that product's advertising *after* he has made the purchase as during the actual purchasing cycle, and this is particularly true with regard to major purchases, such as those of an automobile, a major household appliance, the purchase of a life insurance policy, etc.

Having made a major and important buying decision, the buyer is looking for reassurances that he has bought well, and he finds it most easily and most satisfactorily, in many cases, in the advertising of the product he has just bought. He finds it, first, in a reaffirmation of the product virtues and values which induced him to buy it in the first place, and he finds it, secondly, in the continued appearance of the advertising, for here is widespread public testimony to the buyer's wisdom. The more advertising there is, and the more persuasively it extolls the virtue of the product, the more the buyer is re-sold and reassured, and the more likely he is to buy the same product under the same conditions the next time he is in the market.

Since practically no business can operate successfully without getting the vast bulk of its business from former customers who are satisfied enough to repeat their purchases, this reassurance of the buyer is the most important single thing an established business can do to insure success. And in most instances, even in the case of infrequent and expensive purchases, advertising can perform this function best.

Back-Up for Sales Force

The second "non-selling" value of advertising is its effect on the company's own employees, especially its sales force, as well as on those who do not work for the company but in one way or another handle the product or service in the chain of distribution which ultimately brings it to the point of sale. Here advertising can often help provide the indefinable difference between an enthusiastic, eager sales force, convinced of the value of its products and their intrinsic merit, and a lackadaisical, unsure organization which feels slightly on the defensive as it faces buyers and prospects.

Thus distributors, wholesalers, dealers and others in the chain of distribution are reminded that the advertiser's product should be given active support at every distribution level, and that doing so will benefit the distributor, wholesaler and dealer, as well as the manufacturer, because the product gives satisfaction, is well known and easy to sell, and provides a reasonable profit margin, among other reasons.

In the case of many products, approval or endorsement by experts of one kind or another is of great importance. Approval of Crest toothpaste by the American Dental Assn., was of major importance in skyrocketing this brand into No. 1 position in its field. In the case of many health products and the non-prescription remedies, endorsement or approval by individual doctors or dentists is of major importance. In the case of many building products, the architect's favor is almost basic. And consequently, a good deal of advertising is addressed to these and other "influentials," not to sell the product directly to them, but to familiarize them with it and to (hopefully) gain their approval or endorsement.

Selling Your 'Image'

The third broad category of additional jobs for advertising is that of projecting a useful image to one or more of the advertiser's various publics. Here we are in an area once comfortably known as "institutional advertising," which is now—after a period of relative eclipse—enjoying an important rebirth under the new title of "image" or "corporate image" advertising.

In broadest generality, it is possible to advertise one of two things: The goods or services you make or sell—or the company or people who make or sell them. It is this second category of advertising which embraces "institutional" or "corporate image" advertising. And although the term has largely been associated with the advertising of manufacturers and producers, its most important use probably continues to be in the retail field.

Every important retailer runs the two kinds of advertising we have just mentioned. He runs what the retail trade calls price-and-item advertising, to say that such-and-such a dress or chair or grocery special is on sale today, or will be on sale tomorrow, at such-and-such a price. Specific item advertising like this makes up the bulk of his advertising, in most cases.

But he also runs other advertising, which talks in more general terms about his store's place in the community, its broad selection of merchandise, its position in the forefront of fashion, its stand on pricing and other matters. He is trying to project a favorable image of his store as the best place to shop, because he knows that such an over-all impression in the long run is more important to his success than the promoted items.

The great growth of corporate image advertising, however, has resulted from the growth of great industrial complexes as businesses have sought diversification and have merged with and purchased other companies, and as advancing technology has resulted in fewer and fewer essential differences in the characteristics of competing products.

With products tending to become nearly identical in design, performance, price and other characteristics, many companies . . . have felt that the product itself is becoming a relatively minor factor in making a sale—that is to say, the buyer can get nearly identical products on nearly identical terms from half a dozen suppliers—and therefore factors outside the product itself, especially including the reputation and capability of its maker, may frequently be decisive in making the sale.

YOUR MONEY *AND* YOUR LIFE
David A. Cook

The belief that commercial television comes to viewers free of charge is debunked by Cook, associate professor of English at Emory University. He argues that the costs of reaching viewers are charged back to them in the prices they pay, and that they cannot be repaid for the time spent watching.

Most Americans believe that television entertainment comes to them free of charge, and that the only price they pay is having to endure the commercials—of which they see an average of nine-and-one-half minutes during each prime-time hour and up to sixteen minutes out of sixty the rest of the day. The notion that television is free is based upon the misconception that networks and stations are in the business of selling products to viewers.

In fact, as Les Brown of the New York *Times* has pointed out, the business of commercial television—the only business—is selling potential consumers to advertisers, in lots of one thousand, for between $2 and $12 per program minute.

Since the costs of television advertising are passed along to consumers in the price of the advertised goods, television programming is hardly free. Dividing the $5.9 billion industry revenues for 1977 by the nation's seventy-four-and-one-half million television homes produces an average annual cost per home of $79. And this, as we shall see, is but the beginning of what the medium extracts.

In the 1950s and early 1960s, all viewers were assumed to be potential consumers for the purpose of this transaction, and the networks sold them to advertisers as an undifferentiated mass. Today, thanks to modern demographic research, viewers whose age, race, or class makes them poor consumers can be effectively eliminated from the equation. Far from determining what viewers want to see, therefore, the strategic mission of the TV industry today is to deliver *precisely* the audience the advertisers want to sell.

SOURCE: From *Columbia Journalism Review*, July/August 1979, pp. 64–66. Copyright 1979 by Graduate School of Journalism, Columbia University. Reprinted by permission.

Buying the Vote

Before 1968, networks sold time to national advertisers based on statistical projections of each program's audience size provided by rating services like those of the A.C. Nielsen Company and the American Research Bureau, or Arbitron. As television became ubiquitous in the 1970s, however, extending its reach into 98 percent of American homes and delivering the entire mass market on a nightly basis, advertisers discovered that it was too expensive, and unnecessary, to buy such undifferentiated mass audiences.

As the cost of network commercial time began to climb—at an average rate of 21 percent a year beginning in 1961 and between 1961 and 1978 by a total of more than 340 percent—the one-minute commercial gradually gave way to short spots. By 1968, 80 percent of all commercials were thirty, twenty, or ten seconds long. Although the time devoted to advertising remained constant, the number of commercial messages increased dramatically, so that a viewer in 1968 could have been exposed to as many as thirty in a typical daytime hour. Paying high rates for their time, and also fearing that their messages would be lost in the clutter, advertisers and agencies began to demand more specific information about each program's viewers so that they could target those consumers most likely to buy their products.

With prime-time rates now averaging over $100,000 per commercial minute and with commercial production costs averaging $50,000 per spot, advertisers want to be more certain than ever that the right people see their messages. Thus, the producers and syndicators of television programs run full-page advertisements in *Broadcasting* and *Variety* describing the character of their audiences to potential buyers. "See how much bigger our crowd is?" Archie admonishes Edith, referring to the demographic dimensions of the audience that watches "All in the Family." A series of "Laverne and Shirley" ads which ran in *Variety* last fall successively claimed "Dominance with Upper Income Viewers" (October), "Dominance with Higher Educated Viewers" (November), and both "Dominance in Households with Youngsters" and "Dominance in Households with No Youngsters" (December).

Since market research reveals that 80 percent of all goods and services are purchased in the 300 largest metropolitan areas by adults between the ages of eighteen and forty-nine, the networks and most advertisers are seeking programs that appeal to an audience which is demographically urban or suburban, affluent, and relatively young. "In the past, there was a kind of democratic one-man, one-vote thing," said CBS Broadcast Group research director Jay Eliasberg in 1971, speaking of the changing effect of viewer preferences on programming. "Now we're saying that some people are more equal than others, on a demographic basis: if they buy more, they vote more."

The task of American commercial television, then, is to create an electronically synthesized marketplace in which the ideal consuming populace is brought together with the nation's largest purveyors of consumer goods and services. Obviously, only the very largest corporations can afford to purchase network advertising time, and only persons with a certain level of discretionary income can afford to purchase enough of the advertised goods to make the advertisers' efforts worthwhile. This, in turn, means that the scores of millions of viewers who have little discretionary income and the 400,000 incorporated American businesses which can't afford network time have little voice in contemporary American television. This situation would be disturbing even if television were free, as popular belief has it; but the irony is that the medium is subsidized by every viewer on a daily and nightly basis.

Something for Nothing?

Not long ago, a well-mannered telephone solicitor invited my wife and me to go to Preview House on Sunset Boulevard, where pilots for television series and commercials are market-tested, for some "free" entertainment. The caller implied that the "free gifts and prizes" to be distributed at the end of the evening would be compensation for our time.

Waiting in line on the night of the screening, we noticed that our 408 fellow previewers seemed to comprise a remarkably homogeneous group. All were white, well-dressed, and relatively youthful; and I subsequently learned that Audience Studies Incorporated, the market research firm which owns Preview House, recruits selectively so that each night's audience will represent a distinct demographic test market. Inside the theater, we surrendered our invitations and were asked to fill out a number of mimeographed questionnaires meant to elicit demographic data and our entertainment preferences, brand loyalties, and habits of consumption. Finished at last, we were marched into an auditorium where a professional actor explained our mission.

The arm of every seat in Preview House is wired with an electronic device called an "audimeter," he told us. It consists of a module, which fits into the palm of one hand, surmounted by a metered dial, which is controlled with the other. The dial has 360° calibration from "Very Dull" to "Very Good" and we were told to use it "precisely" to register our reactions to what we were about to see.

A computer at the back of the auditorium would record and tabulate the responses.

The program that night included the rough cut of an episode from "Operation Petticoat" and two animated shorts, interspersed, as on television, with commercials for new, nationally branded products. After each projection the lights came on, and we were asked to fill out questionnaires which tested our response to what we had just seen. A few were ten pages long and required some effort to complete, but the announcer kept assuring us that filling them out was prerequisite to the distribution of the free gifts and prizes.

At the end of the evening, in a period corresponding roughly to prime time, my wife and I had spent more time supplying market data to the proprietors of Preview House than we had spent watching the "free entertainment" which had brought us there. I began to suspect that we had been exploited; as the gifts were distributed, I became certain of it. There were four of them, all products from the test commercials: a six-box case of soap powder, an assortment of cheese snacks, a box of felt-tipped pens, and a month's supply of dry-spray deodorant.

I had just wasted three hours of my time on "free entertainment" that no one would have paid to see. I had spent the time producing something saleable for the owners of Preview House and had let my growing irritation be soothed by the promise of getting something for nothing at the end. (I later learned that Audience Studies charges its clients between $2,500 and $5,000 per pilot—on our night the take must have been at least $17,000.) Worse, I had voluntarily spent my own money on gasoline, parking, and a babysitter in order to put myself in this position.

I felt cheated and full of self-contempt, but when I noticed the bemused smiles on the faces in the audience around me, I couldn't help but admire the mastery of the deception. And I realized then that the whole Preview House episode was a paradigm for the experience of American commercial television. We are drawn to the theater of television by the promise of "free" entertainment; once we enter by turning on our sets, we usually find that the entertainment has quotation marks around it, too. Such is our fascination with the medium that we barely notice the shabbiness of the experience— the barely adequate production values, the one-dimensional scripts and characterizations.

We give the networks our time at the rate of more than four hours a day and they sell it to advertisers at net profits of millions of dollars a year. In the end, we are left very much in the condition of the Preview House audience: diverted but unfulfilled, deceived but never quite aware of the deception.

The Time of Our Lives

Where do these hours come from that 98 percent of us spend with
our sets on? And where do they go?

A recent UNESCO study concluded that television has increased
the amount of time Americans spend with mass media by 40
percent, and that three-fourths of the total is now devoted to TV. At
the same time, television has reduced the amount of sleep per day
by thirteen minutes. It has similarly reduced the time devoted to
social gatherings, radio listening, magazine- and book-reading,
film-going, conversation, household tasks, and religion. In short,
television has come to dominate all of our time—and thus all of our
experience—not spent in work or sleep.

The networks sell that time to advertising agencies at a profit. In
their profit-taking, the networks, as well as the stations, naturally
pass the costs of programming and overhead along to the agencies.

Advertising agencies buy audience time from the networks on
behalf of their clients in order to expose particular groups of
consumers to the commercial messages they have prepared. They
receive a commission based on the cost of this time, which they
apply, in turn, to cover their expenses and produce a profit.

Finally, corporate advertisers engage the services of advertising
agencies to produce and place commercials for their products
before the appropriate television audiences. They then build the
cost of advertising (which now includes the costs of commercial
production and placement, the costs of network programming, and
the overhead of both networks and agencies) into the price of the
advertised goods and pass it on to the consumer, who presumably
buys the product, at least in part, as a result of TV advertising.

So, when the consumer-viewer buys the products advertised on
television, he or she contributes to the total subsidization of the
networks, the ad agencies, and the sponsors. In effect, the national
audience *gives away* what the networks provide to the agencies at
a huge net profit annually and what the agencies procure for the
sponsors at a huge net profit annually—its *time*. And this same
audience is then charged for what it has lost in the retail price of
goods and services.

Television, then, not only robs us of our time, but it makes us foot
the bill for every aspect of the theft. Through this medium advertisers not only command our leisure time in our homes at night, but
they sell it back to us in the shopping malls on the weekends at a
profit.

Except that we can't really buy it back. Like American Indians
trading their land to the colonists for trinkets, we are selling off our

most precious and nonrenewable resource—the time of our lives— for a handful of electronic gimcracks and colored beads.

But there's more—one last cruel twist to the electronic shell game we call free television. It's that dirty little secret of the American product environment called planned obsolescence, where we are the product. Because the product life of an audience is finite, no less so than that of the automobile. And, like automobiles, audiences depreciate rapidly with age until they no longer have a market value. And that's television's final joke on us all; that, as we grow older, we must eventually enter that land of shades where consumerism becomes a rather slow-pulsed affair of purchasing food, medical care, and an occasional patent remedy. Only now, since we are no longer in possession of our youth and its worldly appetites, does the attention of American advertising and American television finally desert us.

Then, perhaps, when the time is short, we will find that we have given the tube the best years of our lives, bought the products, and gotten little in return but a certification of our own obsolescence. Then, perhaps, we will be forced to confront the cruelest indignity of all: that having stolen the time of our lives, American television casts us on the rubbish heap when there's nothing left to steal.

PEPSI GENERATION BRIDGES TWO DECADES
James P. Forkan
In this *Advertising Age* article, the writer tells how the soft drink company has for 18 years built its advertising campaigns around a catchy phrase, with great success.

With nearly every campaign theme in the past two decades, Pepsi-Cola Co. has returned to the roots of its first big mass market success, "the Pepsi generation."

As John Sculley, Pepsi's president, put it, "We haven't really changed our advertising—the Pepsi generation—in 18 years" because "we think we articulate a life style that large groups of Americans can aspire to."

The Pepsi generation was born in 1962 but Alan Pottasch, Pepsi-Cola's senior vp-creative services, said the seed actually was planted after the marketer chose BBDO as its agency in 1960. BBDO came up with "Now it's Pepsi—For those who think young."

SOURCE: From *Advertising Age*, May 5, 1980. Copyright 1980 by Crain Communications, Inc. Reprinted with permission.

That was the company's first earnest attempt to create a brand personality or image for the cola. Soon, the Pepsi generation was picked up in media and entertainment circles as a catchy, short-hand identification of the brand's target consumers, the youth market.

But gradually Pepsi execs came to perceive the phrase as much more—it was, a perfect description of this breed of innovators, not simply an age group.

Since every era has its own trend setters, Pepsi continued to zero in on them with campaigns that refreshed the basic thought.

"Pepsi-Cola hits the spot" scored in 1934 and "Be sociable, have a Pepsi" and "the light refreshment" in the 1950s. Pepsi entered the '60s with "for those who think young."

Pepsi and BBDO teams then segued into "Come alive! You're in the Pepsi generation," which ran from 1962 through 1967. "I can't point to one soul, one person" who actually came up with the durable Pepsi generation, Mr. Pottasch said. It was a matter of "a little piece here, a little piece there," said the creative exec, who went with the Pepsi International account in 1959 when it moved to BBDO from Kenyon & Eckhardt.

"The concept began, with 'for those who think young.' It became a question of labeling that group we were after," he said. As the copy expressed it in the early 1960s, the Pepsi generation was "everyone with a young view of things"—just another way of saying "for those who think young."

By 1966, one camp of Pepsi execs had become disenchanted and voted against continuing the tag line, asserting it was too limited in appeal, too youth-oriented. In 1969, they went in another direction, stressing product and taste rather than the Pepsi consumer via the theme "The taste that beats the others cold. Pepsi pours it on."

The Pepsi generation concept went stale, as William Munro, then vp-marketing for Pepsi, expressed it in late 1969. "Overnight, those tanned, frolicsome, happy-go-lucky people of the Pepsi generation began to become advertising anachronisms. They became square to the very people we were aiming at. We weren't relevant anymore."

That tack proved a mistake, however, so another Pepsi faction steered the brand to a revival of the Pepsi generation, using the phrase as a subtheme to the new theme "You've got a lot to live. Pepsi's got a lot to give." That spearheaded Pepsi's multimedia efforts through 1973.

Mr. Sculley, soon after becoming vp of marketing 10 years ago, dumped the "pours it on" campaign and saw greater potential in the Pepsi generation concept developed seven years earlier.

As Pepsi-Cola Co. learned, sometimes the best marketing strategy is to stick with a winner and build on it, rather than break radically new ground. The company has yet to find a better articulation of its brand personality, one in which it can feature the challenges of competition as well as an active family life.

Since the main influence on soft drink buyers is taste and since taste is a very personal thing, Pepsi-Cola Co. decided that "one of the best ways to separate our product from the competition was to differentiate our users," according to Mr. Pottasch.

Those users now, and then, were people on the leading edge of things—innovators—since they were choosing a cola other than the No. 1 brand. The ads, therefore, tried to showcase these people.

(Coca-Cola, meanwhile, has tended to concentrate on product-oriented themes, e.g., "Things go better with Coke," "the real thing," "Coke adds life." The two brands' divergent approaches are most visible in those themes that feature similar elements, for example, "Coke adds life" vs. "you've got a lot to live" and "Have a Coke and a smile" vs. "Pepsi people are the smilin' majority," a test approach that never was used.)

The fact that "pours it on" did not click was apparent, not in sales, which continued to grow, but in Pepsi's own research on recall and other areas, Mr. Pottasch recalled.

"Fortunately for us," he observed, "the visuals in pours print ads and tv commercials focused on pretty much the same zesty, youthful activities as always," which made the return swing smoother.

Using the words and music of BBDO's Spencer Michlin (who now heads his own music house, but continues to work on various Pepsi-Cola Co. projects) and Joe Brooks (who has graduated from songwriting to producing movies), Pepsi opted for "lot to live" as the main theme, but included a subtheme: "It's the Pepsi generation comin' at ya, goin' strong. Put yourself behind a Pepsi . . ."

Recognizing that the late '60s was the nation's most turbulent period, with racial and anti-war riots and drug woes, Pepsi execs okayed "live/give" as an upbeat, optimistic campaign suited to the times. Among the lines in that effort: "There's a new national pastime: Living, and making every second count."

And, to counter internal criticism that the Pepsi generation was too confining, Pepsi broadened the thrust to include a family orientation.

In 1972, Pepsi tested a theme—"Pepsi people are the smilin' majority"—to tap into what its execs saw as the new U.S. mood. That theme, however, was vetoed, some sources said for political reasons (too similar to President Nixon's "silent majority"), some said for legal reasons (since Pepsi was not in the majority in terms of sales), still others said it was just not the right concept.

Pepsi, which also shot down a "hip sip" drive due for the black consumer market, instead modified the "live/give" theme for use through 1973.

The "Pepsi people" part of that canceled theme, however, did survive into the early '70s, when the company and agency came up with a campaign keyed to "the me decade:" "Join the Pepsi people, feeling free."

As another exhortation to rise above everyday problems, and to experience personal independence, this campaign once again mentioned the Pepsi generation in passing. (By this time, Mr. Pottasch had become Pepsi's creative senior vp after stints as vp in marketing areas for Pepsi International in the late 1960s.)

"Have a Pepsi day" broke in 1977. The campaign—which Pepsi and BBDO worked on with the Sunday Productions music house—was aimed at the idea that "good times are worth preserving," according to Pepsi execs.

They chose such special moments as a newborn baby's arrival home, a little boy thrilled with a litter of puppies and a rural youngster's excitement over a surprise birthday present (a pony).

Cutting across various segments (black and general markets, rural and urban) without specially designated media buys, this campaign theme has proven "very successful" in recall monitoring, Pepsi execs agreed. At the same time this effort began, Coke was switching from "the real thing" to "Coke adds life."

The youth market remains the biggest consumer of soft drinks, but age is not the real focus of the many Pepsi campaigns created since the late 1960s. The Pepsi generation, signifying a state of mind, transcends age groups, as well as changing hair, apparel and music styles, as Messrs. Pottasch and Sculley see it.

"The Pepsi generation is a special breed of people—not an age group—that believes in living life to its fullest," said Mr. Pottasch.

Just as Pepsi's promotional tie-ins with such events as "Beatlemania" and Paramount Pictures' "Grease" span not only today's young people but also yesteryear's youth market, so does the "Pepsi generation" encompass those distinct age categories and beyond. Similarly, Pepsi's sports tie-ins identify with the group's "thirst for living" and interest in physical fitness.

To confirm its claim that the "Pepsi generation" defines an attitude more than an age group, Pepsi execs quote research indicating that 62 percent of men and women aged 13 to 24 identified with the Pepsi generation description—but so did 43 percent of those aged 35 to 49, the youth market of past decades.

By the end of this year, Pepsi-Cola Co. will have poured $345 million into measured media alone behind the Pepsi generation theme line and its related active life style message of the last 18 years, Messrs. Pottasch and Sculley estimate.

But Pepsi also has been translating the Pepsi generation into new areas lately. The company has, for one thing, been testing a "Pepsi generation club," complete with a plastic membership card "like Diners Club's," since last July. And it has licensed Donn-Kenny Inc., New York, to market a line of Pepsi Generation sportswear, introduced in February.

The sportswear license will bring Pepsi a royalty, said Mr. Pottasch, who added that any decision on whether to add other licensing categories will depend on how this works out in the marketplace.

After the Pepsi club card's initial placement in a four-color, four-page Sunday newspaper ad supplement, Mr. Pottasch guessed that about 370,000 people joined. An application in the ad for additional cards sparked well over 250,000 write-ins, he estimated.

These card-carrying members of the Pepsi generation can get into entertainment and sports events at discount prices and also buy scarves, mufflers and tote bags imprinted with the words "The Pepsi generation." In addition, they can buy nonlicensed merchandise from special catalogs, Mr. Pottasch explained.

Retailers have been using the cards to build traffic with special local advertising. A theater, for example, offered "buy one ticket, get one free" with the card, he noted.

The "Pepsi generation" theme is used internationally as well, he continued, although the company translates this concept to fit each non-U.S. market rather than offering a literal translation. It's never "generacion de Pepsi," he pointed out. For any given Pepsi theme, he noted, about 75 percent of the countries use "some form."

As the company sees it, the 1970s' "me decade" concept has "taken a you-turn," with the 1980s likely to be highlighted by a greater sharing and by family life taking on more importance, according to Mr. Pottasch.

The newest Pepsi drive, "Catch that Pepsi spirit! Drink it in," . . . once again features the venerable Pepsi generation line as a subtheme, he pointed out. One line of the jingle, assembled by Pepsi, BBDO and David Lucas of the Lucas/McFaul jingle house, says "And you're the Pepsi generation . . . You're the spirit of today."

This time around, the company hopes to project not only its typical upbeat message but also an underlying feeling of momentum in sales to both consumers and its bottlers, the Pepsi execs said.

In the new decade, the marketer is likely to continue refreshing each new campaign theme every three years. It also is highly likely that the Pepsi generation subtheme will continue into the '80s, since PepsiCo chairman Don Kendall is among those supporting the durable phrase and since the line turns up consistently higher scores in recall tests.

"It never lags," according to Mr. Pottasch, probably because it has run for so many years as a subtheme rather than as a headline.

With that in mind, Mr. Pottasch said, "We see endless applications of the Pepsi generation stretching into its third decade."

WANT TO SELL POINT OF VIEW? USE ADVERTISING
Norman Cousins

Mr. Cousins is chairman of the editorial board of the *Saturday Review* and its former editor, as well as a member of the Department of Psychiatry and Behavioral Sciences, School of Medicine, University of California at Los Angeles. His writing and lectures frequently are concerned with problems of the nuclear age.

It was only twenty years ago that Marshall McLuhan was attracting world-wide attention with his statements about the ascendency of electronics and the decline of print. What was most significant about these pronouncements was that when McLuhan had something really important to say he put it in print.

The continuing ascendency of electronics since McLuhan's original prediction has served mostly to dramatize the fact that print is still the most potent means yet devised for moving ideas from one mind to another. And the primacy of print will continue so long as the human brain is capable of using words with precision and power.

Fit Format to Message
The declarations that change lives and that make history are usually associated with ringing calls to action (Roosevelt, Churchill); or with declarations of conscience (Rousseau, Garibaldi, Jefferson, Gandhi, Martin Luther King); or with books that connect the individual to situations that call for reform (Hugo, Dickens, Tolstoy, Paine, Stowe, Sinclair); or with journalism that probes or exposes (Steffens, Tarbell, Lippmann, Woodward, Bernstein). The most effective use of print today, however, may be connected to an entirely different form. I refer to the dramatic use of full-page advertisements.

SOURCE: From *Advertising Age*, April 30, 1980. Copyright 1980 by Norman Cousins. Reprinted with permission.

TAKE A BITE OUT OF
CRIME
Crime Prevention Coalition
©1979 The Advertising Council, Inc.

"GILSTRAPS"

Public Service Announcements
Available in :60, :30, :10 Versions
60 SECONDS

DOG (VO): Y'know, the Gilstraps aren't really movin'...
they're being robbed.

DOG (OC): These crooks
know the Gilstraps are out of
town.

So, they're trying to move the
Gilstraps — permanently.

They figure: they look like
movers, they act like movers,
so who's gonna know?

The Joneses. They know.
JONES BOY: Dad, aren't the
Gilstraps in Toledo?

MR. JONES: I think they're
being robbed. Should we call
the police?
MRS. JONES: Call the police.

DOG: See, the Joneses know,
if they don't tell the cops
now,

the Gilstraps'll have to tell
them, later. (MR. JONES:
Hello, this is...)

DOG: Meanwhile, these fel-
lows are eating lunch—oh,
about a block away.

Hey, hot pastrami! That looks
very good.

COP: 10-4.

DOG: How 'bout that!

Know what it takes to stop a
crime? Your help. And your
neighbors'.

Find out more. Write to Box
6600, Rockville, Maryland.
And help—ahh...

Take a bite out of crime.

A MESSAGE FROM THE
CRIME PREVENTION COALITION
Ad Council
©1979 The Advertising Council, Inc.

Volunteer Agency: Dancer, Fitzgerald, Sample, Inc. Volunteer Coordinator: Edward W. Dooley, Citibank, N.A.
CNCP-0160/CNCP-0130/CNCP-0110   1179

Ad Council

The Advertising Council supplies public service messages

I am not thinking here, primarily, of institutional advertising,
although I believe that companies are wise to attach the highest
importance to the need for public support of their corporate name
and identity. The kind of advertising I have in mind is primarily
concerned with a point of view. The main requirement here is the
marriage of a dramatic format to a clearly written message. Specifically, I have in mind a full-page newspaper or magazine advertisement featuring a bold message that is written with sequence and
clarity.

Am I saying that an idea has greater effect in the form of a full-page advertisement than as an article in the same newspaper or magazine—or even as a vehicle for television? I am. Let me give you some examples drawn from my personal experience.

One of the most quoted articles to appear in the *Saturday Review* was "Man Is Obsolete," published just after the atomic bomb was dropped on Hiroshima. Within two weeks, more than a thousand letters from readers arrived at the magazine in response to the piece. The article was picked up by one major digest magazine and at least six other journals. It also was the subject of extensive comment by broadcasters. Yet nothing—not even the article in its original form—produced as much response as the piece when reprinted on the back page of the New York *Herald Tribune*. We must have received twice as many letters from that single paper as from all other sources combined. Also, requests to reprint were more than doubled. Directly traceable to that full-page advertisement was worldwide editorial comment.

Treaty Ratified

Next: In 1962, President John F. Kennedy decided to put a halt to atmospheric testing of nuclear weapons. But he also knew from the polls and the mail to Congress that most Americans were lukewarm on the issue. He called together a small group of communicators. The principal problem put to them was that of treaty ratification by the Senate. The President said that he was seven votes short. Within six weeks after the communicators went to work, the fight was won. I believe that the single most effective device in that campaign was the use of full-page newspaper advertisements. They presented the basic arguments against atmospheric testing and then called on the readers to write their senators. What was most impressive about that mail was not just its volume, but the clear evidence it reflected that the writers had absorbed the central issues and were able to present the main arguments in their own words. During the period of that advertising, the ratio of Senate mail on the test-ban issue shifted from 15 to 1 against to 3 to 1 for.

The third example does not involve the use of "message" or "idea" advertising in the strict sense of the terms. In 1972, I was involved in the start-up of a new magazine. Instead of proclaiming the virtues of the projected magazine and offering low-price sub-scription inducements, we stayed as close as possible to the straightforward but dramatic kind of full-page advertisement used so successfully in the instances mentioned above. We bought the back page of the New York *Times* for an advertisement that was captioned: *An Open Letter to Readers of the New York Times*. The letter didn't attempt to "sell" in the usual sense. It described our plans and hopes. It spoke of the difficulties in the way. It asked readers to subscribe—not for a short term at a low price but for *three years at full rate*. No money-back. In fact, readers were asked to take a chance on an idea—but the idea was made explicit. That ad brought in almost four times as many dollars as it cost.

We used the same "open letter" approach in other full-page newspaper and magazine advertisements—all with highly gratifying results. Then, as an experiment, we tried the conventional subscription sell in a few newspapers and magazines—cut-rate subscriptions, premiums, etc.—and we barely covered our costs.

Selling Ideas

Over the years I have tried to study advertising formats and techniques. I became convinced that the single most effective way of registering an idea on the American consciousness is through full-page newspaper or magazine advertising—preferably on the back page or back cover. I can understand how television can often do a superior job for product selling. The viewer makes an identification with the person on the screen who has a headache or a hangover and reaches for Bromo-Seltzer or whatever.

But if what you want to attract attention for is a concept; if what you want to do is to get people to run with an idea in a certain direction, then take to print. Find the right words, put them in the right order, set them in clear type, let them breathe with a little white space, give them straightforward headline treatment, invest them with the importance people automatically attach to someone who has the courage of his convictions, and watch them go to work.

After 6000 years, nothing has been invented that moves so swiftly in the direction of the human mind or carries more cargo in the right direction than the letter workings on paper that goes by the name of print.

TIPS FOR COPYWRITERS
Bernice Fitz-Gibbon

"Fitz" was among the most successful advertising women of her era. She was advertising director of both Macy's and Gimbel's, rival New York department stores. Here she offers a suggestion for beginners and shows what ingenuity can do in writing advertising copy.

SOURCE: From Bernice Fitz-Gibbon, *Macy's, Gimbel's and Me* (New York: Simon & Schuster, 1967), pp. 89–90, 178–79, 334, Copyright © 1967 by Bernice Fitz-Gibbon. Reprinted by permission of Simon & Schuster, a Division of Gulf & Western Corporation.

You can make yourself into an engineer. You can make yourself into a lawyer. Can you make yourself into a novelist or poet or playwright? I suspect not.

But I do believe that you can make yourself into a creditable advertising writer; because advertising writing does not require that rare kind of talent that sustained writing requires. Advertising is a craft, and a craft can be learned. Shaw's advice to would-be writers (somebody said that it was off the top of his head, but even the top of Shaw's head was better than other people's whole heads) was to the effect that a would-be writer should write a thousand words a day for five years—that he should learn to write as he'd learn to skate: by staggering about and making a fool of himself. So write something every day of your life.

Your job in a retail advertising department will make you write *every day*. That probably would not be true in an advertising agency, where, I hear, dozens of trainees are always "waiting in the wings" where they cool their heels for months before they ever get a chance to put a word on paper.

The exigencies of life in a retail store and the necessity to get out dozens and dozens of different ads every day are likely to hurl you into the fray before you are ready. That's good. And that's one reason why you move swiftly up in a store.

The materials a copywriter uses are words. His tools are a thesaurus and a large unabridged dictionary.

A copywriter should actually read the dictionary—go through it in the evenings as if it were what it is: an interesting book. He should make the job a form of recreation.

The point is to dig up fresh new words that have not been worn threadbare.

Take the phrases "bright red" or "bright blue"—isn't the effect more graphic if you say "shrill red" or "sharp blue"? Of course, the skilled writer will use few adjectives and adverbs and many verbs and pictorial nouns. He will also use little surprising words. Instead of saying "it wears like iron," he may say "it wears like pig iron." "Pig" makes it sound more durable. . . .

A couple of adjectives make all the difference in the world. All the difference between a mediocre description of an article and a description so irresistible that it makes money tumble out of wallets *fast*.

I can illustrate the power of carefully chosen adjectives by directing your attention to a brilliant advertising campaign for the KLM Airlines. Up to the time this campaign started, I was unconscious of the existence of KLM. But now I couldn't buy an overseas flight ticket on any other airline without a nagging suspicion that I really ought to take the trip with the "careful" and "punctual" Dutch.

Those are the two adjectives—"careful" and "punctual." Of course, no airline can advertise that it is safer that any other airline, but every word has connotations beyond its literal meaning—overtones that impress the reader mightily. Those two words "careful" and "punctual" run through the whole body copy of the ad and make one feel that everybody in KLM bends over backward in being careful. And what could be more irresitibly appealing when you fly than carefulness? Nothing. . . .

Whenever Bea [Rosenberg], who was merchandise manager of a good chunk of the [Macy's] soft-goods business (hats, shoes, slippers, accessories, etc.) brought up an item to be advertised, she was bursting with an enthusiasm that was infectious. This same limitless vision was a characteristic of Macy's best merchandisers. They felt that nothing was impossible, that there was no limit to what they could accomplish.

An illustration: One day Bea brought me a bedroom slipper and said, "Fitz, you must write this ad so I'll get orders from all forty-eight states." I said, "Why would a woman in Red Oak, Iowa, need to send all the way to Macy's for a pair of bedroom slippers?" Her answer, "Because nowhere else in the world can she match these slippers in looks or comfort."

So I wrote the ad with a headline saying we expected orders from forty-eight states. Bea bounced up later, triumphant but not satisfied. "We got thousands of orders from forty-six states. But, Fitz, we didn't get a single order from Utah or Nevada. Let's go back in the paper and jog those odd people that live in Utah and Nevada to send in orders."

I wasn't quite sure what I'd say; but that evening I took a pair of the slippers home with me to the suburbs. After dinner, I told the problem to my family—my lawyer husband, my son, Peter, home from Annapolis on holiday, and my high-school-age daughter. I said, "Now just suppose *you* are a woman in Utah or Nevada—what could jolt you into sending for the slippers?" Peter asked, "How bad are her old slippers?" So I said, "Wait and I'll put on my worst old slippers." I did. They were pretty bad. "They are awful," said Peter. "Your feet look like two dead rabbits."

There was my headline: "Come on, Utah and Nevada. You are the only two states who did not order Macy's unbeatable slippers. Throw out your old slippers that look like dead rabbits and get your order in. We may not have any more for another six months." Orders poured in from Utah and Nevada—as well as more orders from the other forty-six states.

RADIO STRETCHES THE IMAGINATION
Stan Freberg

Radio's ability to stimulate the imagination has never been demonstrated more vividly than in this oft-reprinted 60-second promotional spot. Freberg is a West Coast advertising executive and satirist.

Voice 1: Radio? Why should I advertise on radio? There's nothing to look at—no pictures.

Voice 2: Listen, you can do things on radio you couldn't possibly do on TV.

Voice 1: That'll be the day. . . . *(Skeptically)*

Voice 2: All right. Watch this. . . . *(Clears throat)*
OK, people. And now when I give you the cue I want the 700-foot mountain of whipped cream to roll into Lake Michigan, which has been drained and filled with hot chocolate. Then the Royal Canadian Air Force will fly overhead towing a 10-ton maraschino cherry, which will be dropped into the whipped cream to the cheering of 25,000 extras. . . . *(Pause)*
All right. Cue the mountain.
SFX: *RUMBLING, THEN SPLASH.*

Voice 2: Cue the Air Force.
SFX: *Roaring planes.*

Voice 2: Cue the maraschino cherry.
SFX: *Downward whine, then splash.*

Voice 2: OK. 25,000 cheering extras.
SFX: *Cheers.*

Voice 2: Now, you want to try that on television?

Voice 1: W—e—l—l. . . . *(Hesitatingly)*

Voice 2: You see, radio is a very special medium because it stretches the imagination.

Voice 1: Doesn't television stretch the imagination?

Voice 2: Up to 21 inches, yes.

SOURCE: Credited to Stan Freberg.

Section 15

PUBLIC RELATIONS

Public relations—more clearly stated as "relations with the public"—owes its existence as a field to mass communications. It is the business of communicating with the mass public reached by the media. It also is the business of bringing segments of that public to hold attitudes, habits, and opinions pleasing, useful, or both to the corporation, group, or individual on whose behalf the public relating is done. Here are the pioneers, the great practitioners, the successes, the failures, the compassionate concern, and the super-heated "hype" of this energetic field.

IVY LEE, PIONEER PUBLICIST
Phillip H. Ault

Ivy Lee's career stretched across the years of press agentry to the initial phase of corporate public relations. His story is one of both accomplishment and defeat.

The emergence of public relations as a skilled and specialized craft, in contrast to the fast-talking press agentry of earlier times, owes much to Ivy Ledbetter Lee.

He was born in 1877, the son of a Georgia preacher, attended Princeton University, studied briefly at Harvard Law School, and obtained a newspaper job in New York. His work in development of public relations techniques grew out of this early career as a newspaper reporter specializing in financial writing. With the knowledge of business he acquired as a reporter, he left newspapers to do public relations and promotional work for financial firms.

Lee built his reputation representing the Pennsylvania Railroad during the early 1900s. Then in 1914 he became adviser to the Rockefeller family. A fatal mining strike in Colorado had put John D. Rockefeller, Sr., in a bad light. In the public mind, the Rockefellers were heartless exploiters to whom money meant more than human life.

It was Lee's task to humanize the Rockefellers and convince the public that the family used its wealth for constructive, humanitarian purposes. One device he used to build Rockefeller's image as an everyday fellow was having the multimillionaire give shiny dimes to strangers he met. John D.'s dimes became a national joke.

As a pioneer in corporate public relations, Lee had a double role: to show managements that for their own good they must explain themselves to the public, and to convince the media and the people that the companies operated with concern for the public's interest. The tasks were of equal difficulty; many firms had a chronic conviction that their affairs were none of the public's business, and citizens felt a deep distrust of the large companies.

Among the tools Lee developed was the written handout. By distributing these printed sheets officially stating company policies and explaining company operations, Lee made the routine work of reporters easier. More important to him, he increased the likelihood

---

SOURCE: This article was written expressly for this book.

Ivy Lee

of positive information about his client getting into print. His assign-ment, as he saw it, was to put his client's situation in the best possible light. He insisted that company officials avoid talking to the press unless he gave prior approval and controlled the cir-cumstances. Critics of Lee's methods argued that he stifled access to important news about his clients and blocked the investigative efforts of diligent reporters.

As head of his own independent firm, Lee was immensely successful in handling public relations for nonprofit organizations, including the Red Cross in World War I, as well as for corporations. However, his own public relations failed and his public image suffered in the period before his death in 1934. At that time he was criticized extensively because he represented I. G. Farben, the German industrial complex, during the early years of Adolf Hitler. For this he was perceived by the public as an adviser to the Nazi movement, a charge he denied, but did not outlive.

A PHILOSOPHY OF CORPORATE PUBLIC RELATIONS
L. L. L. Golden

Paul W. Garrett developed the public relations department of the gigantic General Motors Corporation and headed it for 25 years. Here Golden summarizes the philosophy Garrett followed so successfully in building the automobile maker's image.

What was [Paul] Garrett's philosophy of public relations? What was his view of the function of management in its relations with the various groups which make up the public as a whole? What, in Garrett's belief, makes for good corporate public relations? An analysis of his views, based on interviews with executives, conversations with Garrett, and a study of his speeches, articles, and programs, provides one of the most useful outlines of how a corporation ought to conduct itself. What Garrett said, wrote, and did for twenty-five years is as fundamentally valid today as it was during the period when he was developing his theories. These were based on close observations of his own company and of the often wildly changing moods of the public.

Garrett made scores of speeches and presentations. . . . Yet the single speech that best explained what he thought business ought to do, in fact had to do, for survival, was made before the American Association of Advertising Agencies at its twenty-first annual meeting in 1938. The surprising thing is that it was given only seven years after he joined General Motors. It remains one of the best documents for those who want to know what public relations can do, what it cannot do, what it is, and what it can never be. Even though Garrett had another eighteen years in harness at General Motors he most simply explained his views in this speech, which he titled: "Public Relations—Industry's No. 1 Job." It received wide distribution at the time he made it. Sloan had it sent to every stockholder. The newspapers gave it exceptional coverage. . . .

To Garrett, if business is to survive it must interpret itself by deeds and words that have meaning to those outside the company. That management thinks it is worthy of public support—that it is certain it makes a contribution to the economic advancement of the country—is not enough. Business's future depends not on the return on the capital invested, nor the wages it pays, but on the benefits to those outside the company, particularly the consumer, who is both inclusive of all groups directly affected by the company and so

SOURCE: From L. L. L. Golden, *Only by Public Consent* (New York: Hawthorn Books, 1968), pp. 106–109. Copyright © 1968 by L. L. L. Golden. Reprinted by permission of Hawthorn Properties (Elsevier-Dutton Publishing Co., Inc.).

280

Paul Garrett

larger in number than any. Business has to learn that people are interested in more than the product and the price. They are interested in the way things are done, in what he calls the "social by-products" of business.

Garrett believed "public relations" is a synthetic term which to many is nothing more than a tony appelation from common press agentry. To some it is putting over insidious propaganda; to others its function is to present only the "favorable" side of business. To gain some understanding of public relations is to think of it as an institution's relations with the public. It is not something that can be applied to a particular phase of business. It is not a panacea. It is rather a fundamental attitude of mind, or if you will, a philosophy of management, which deliberately and with enlightened selfishness puts the broad interest of the consumer first in every decision, not just key ones, affecting the entire operation of the industry. Nor can good relations with the public be achieved through publicity or though what one particular department of a corporation can do.

To Garrett, what really counts is removing the causes of trouble, not putting out fires of public antagonism caused by bad corporate policies. Press agents, hack writers, publicity hounds, lobbyists, psychoanalysts, pseudo-scientists, straw vote experts—none of these can change public opinion. Public relations is not a program of defense or experiment in mass psychology, but a philosophy of management which must concern itself with satisfying the public's wants.

Garrett felt that the public means people who are members of many overlapping groups. They include those who build the product, distribute it, buy it, own the business, live in a plant community, supply the materials, and also those who do not directly fall within these categories but who, with the special groups, make up the entire consuming public. Public relations does not turn on the needs of industry, but the needs of the consumer. In its broad sense, public relations is not a specialized activity like production, engineering, finance, or sales. It cuts through all these as the theme for each. It is an operating philosophy that management must apply in everything it does and says. Patching up past mistakes or providing temporary or soothing substitutes for sound management policies will never do the job. Industry will only solve its public relations problems if it puts as much serious effort into their solution as it does in solving financial, engineering, and production problems. And business must stand "for" some things and not so often only be "against."

Garrett stated that good relations outside a company can only grow from good relations inside. If you want to be well thought of in the plant community the beginnings must be in the plant. To be favorably regarded throughout the nation the beginnings have to be in the plant community. If those who work for the corporation are not happy, those whom they meet outside the shop will not be friendly, for outsiders judge a corporation by the people they know who work for it. Nor do high wages alone assure good internal relations, important as good wages are. What the employee needs is the feeling that he is being fairly treated. Grievances, even if they are imaginary, must be met. The failure to explain company policies and why they were adopted can cause trouble. This is true for both the white- and blue-collar worker. In addition, management, while explaining its policies to its employees, must provide machinery for communication upward as well.

Garrett maintained that a company's public relations must always be firmly rooted in its plant community. This is where it lives and this is where the employees and their neighbors notice and talk about what is going on. Employees are the most articulate spokesmen for the company's policies. But being a good employer is not enough. The company, since it gets the benefits of the community, must shoulder its community responsibilities. Here again two-way communication is important: local management must make certain that the community understands what the company is doing and why, and must at the same time understand the community's wants.

Garrett believed that living right, however, is not enough. People must know you live right. To let them know, there must be communication that is effective. All media must be used to tell the corporation's story clearly and simply, without blurring facts. This demands a system of informing people who are directly involved and reaching beyond them. It demands the proper use of all means of communication to mulitply the effect of good policies. Whether it be through stories in the local press or in a national magazine, or through films, speeches, brochures, open house for visitors to the plants, or round tables with teachers and editors, communication is vital. But the impact of all this is meager unless the basic policy of sound practices in the public interest is there to begin with.

Garrett insisted there is no place for public relations that connives, distorts facts, squirms, or is not frank and honest. It must have vigor, be open, and pervade the entire business from top to bottom. And it must interpret the practices and beliefs of industry in terms of benefits to others, not to itself. Public relations can only serve its purpose if it convinces the public as a whole that the public's good is being served at all times.

"SOMEBODY CARES"
Edward B. Borden
A significant aspect of public relations work is promoting the activities of social agencies, both governmental and volunteer, in communities. This is an example of how it is done.

How does a juvenile corrections agency gain community acceptance and support?

That was the thorny problem facing the South Carolina Department of Youth Services when I became its first public information director in 1974. Community support is necessary for a juvenile offender to return successfully to society. Without public acceptance a delinquent child may well turn into an adult criminal.

In South Carolina, any child under 17 years old found guilty of committing a crime is committed to our agency. He or she usually receives an indeterminate sentence and may stay until age 21. If the

SOURCE: From *Public Relations Journal* December 1979, pp. 36–37. Copyright 1979 by the *Public Relations Journal*. Reprinted by permission.

HAVE YOU HUGGED YOUR KID TODAY?
S.C. DEPT. OF YOUTH SERVICES - YOUTH BUREAU DIVISION
©S.C.D.Y.S. 1977

crime is a felony, he or she receives a determinate sentence and is remanded to the South Carolina Department of Corrections between ages 17 and 21.

When we started our campaign for community awareness, the Department's image wasn't all that bad. Mostly it was just there. Nobody seemed to care that the agency had limped along for more than 70 years with minimal public support. The prevailing opinion seemed to be that juvenile offenders should be locked away and forgotten.

For this reason, agency Director Grady A. Decell and I agreed that the primary theme of our public information program would be "Somebody Cares."

We decided to focus on the positive side of incarceration—that rehabilitation works. Our aim was to show our students as human beings—with faults, to be sure—but progressing towards their return to society. We have our share of failures, of course. But the examples of success, even partial success, abound.

The public relations program was centered around the premise that human concern, together with the proper psychological and social behavior techniques, would help shift Johnny or Jane from a delinquent social dropout to a viable, loving person.

With staff members from the Youth Bureau Division of the agency (our newest arm, aimed at working with children in the community before they become delinquent), we developed the now internationally famous bumper sticker, "Have You Hugged Your Kid Today?"

The bumper sticker was designed to give recognition to the Youth Bureau as well as remind even good parents that their children need love and praise. We have been astounded at the response. Letters have poured in from as far away as Australia. A writer from New Hampshire told us: "This is probably one of the dumbest inquiries you've ever had, but I have just chased a man about three miles to find out where he got the bumper sticker on his car. . . . " And a mother from New York wrote: "I, for one, will try my best to remember not only to hug my children, but also to say I love them."

Informing Various Publics

An effective public information program depends a great deal on an informed, dedicated staff. We revamped the agency's internal newsletter, *We Care*, to make it more informal and newsy. Its focus was changed from birthdays, marriages, etc. to spotlighting agency policy and goals. Staff members were recognized for their involvement in agency affairs.

At the same time, a quarterly publication, *The Youth Advocate*, was created. It tells the general public, the legislature, and youth-oriented professionals about our agency. The six-page newsletter carries photos and feature stories on agency events.

Through the South Carolina Educational Television Network, we produced a 12-minute slide-tape on the Youth Bureau. The emphasis was on personal involvement, and showing that the children were loved, not rejected.

The next project was to get a display board for fairs and conventions. A lightweight metal frame with fabric panels in agency colors was purchased. Illustrations, messages, and other items can be attached to it and removed with ease.

We took 8 × 10 color photos for the board, concentrating on people. We wanted to show the world that delinquent kids, eat, sleep, laugh, play, and have the same hopes that "other" children do.

I shot a lot of close-ups—the more involved the staff and student, the better the photo. One of my favorites is a teacher leaning over a student at his desk. The photo was taken from behind the student, but you can see love and concern in that teacher's expression and the pupil's trusting response.

We concentrated on placing staff and students on TV and radio programs. Though we must guard against identifying them, the children can talk and they can tell their stories. Thus, they helped us get across to the public an agency objective: the understanding that delinquency is caused by many factors—home environment and peer pressure, among others. By recognizing that delinquents are human, too, adults can begin coping with the causes of delinquency.

Radio spots featured children from one of our Youth Bureau projects. They talked about parental love and what it meant to them. What made the discussion more poignant and real was that in many cases the children had terrible home environments. Another message also came through: the Department of Youth Services was doing something concrete to help them.

Through Educational Television we also designed a series of six TV promotions for the agency. We created a cartoon character, J. Arthur Hugbug, who personifies the selfless giving and receiving of love. Hugbug runs the Hugbug Manufacturing Company—it manufactures hugs, of course—and he laments that his company is not doing well. "People just aren't giving hugs these days."

Each public relations program reinforces the message that delinquent children deserve society's best if they are to become useful citizens. Implied in each message is that delinquent children, through the Department of Youth Services, are salvageable and are being rescued.

Our campaign has been generally successful. We've had to overcome public suspicion of governmental agencies, a phenomenon of our times. Respect for agency treatment programs has grown, and many identify with our bumper sticker, feature stories and ads.

More recently we've been involved in a model leadership program based on Boys' State. National publicity, because of American Legion sponsorship, is just around the corner.

We're also considering a statewide magazine that will help parents and professionals deal with children who have behavior problems, and are discussing a short movie and additional slide-tapes on our treatments. Another bumper sticker has been created and may soon be distributed. We feel it will have just as much impact on parents as the first.

Seventy years of neglect is hard to overcome in a short period of time but we're making inroads. It's an exciting period because we know we're doing something positive to help juvenile offenders.

Public education in the field of juvenile corrections is just beginning. There's a lot of history just waiting to be made—and publicized.

WHEN DISASTER COMES—CRISIS PR
Thomas Petzinger, Jr.
Reportage on the mishandling of public relations at the Three Mile Island nuclear accident leads into an examination of how large companies manage their public relations strategies in time of crisis.

During the panic-filled week that followed the first release of radiation from the damaged Three Mile Island nuclear reactor, the plant's beleaguered public-relations officials huddled in a nearby motel room.

With them were representatives of Hill & Knowlton Inc. The big PR firm had been called in to help Metropolitan Edison Co. and its parent, General Public Utilities Corp., handle the throngs of repor-

---

SOURCE: Thomas Petzinger, Jr., "Crisis PR: When Disaster Comes, Public Relations Men Won't Be Far Behind," *The Wall Street Journal*, August 23, 1979. Reprinted by permission of *The Wall Street Journal* © Dow Jones & Company, Inc., 1979. All rights reserved.

ters arriving on the scene. To the utility men, the accident was a PR nightmare: The press was getting hostile; the public was edgy and the rest of the nuclear-power industry seemed to be looking the other way. What should the utility do?

A few beers and a few hours later, suggestions began to emerge. Met Ed could hold a press conference with "experts" who would show that the accident wasn't serious. Reporters seeking interviews with executives could be placated with "press kits." The media could be given a special list of "Met Ed communications numbers" to call for official information; the phones, however, would be taken off the hook.

Publicity Disaster

None of those suggestions were used, but the motel-room group wound up getting the sort of publicity that it had sought to avoid. Outside the door that night, pencils and pads in hand, were two Philadelphia *Inquirer* reporters, Jonathon Neumann and Julia Cass. The following Sunday, the *Inquirer* ran a detailed report of the strategy session under the headline: "A Secret Utility Meeting About Public Relations."

Today, Howard Seldomridge, Met Ed's PR director, says the suggestions at the meeting were made only facetiously by tired and frustrated men. And Richard C. Hyde, a Hill & Knowlton senior vice president who attended the meeting, contends that while much of what the *Inquirer* reported was indeed said by the PR men, the newspaper took their remarks out of context and "twisted completely what the purpose of the meeting was—to develop a plan, a strategy, a mechanism to get information out to people."

So it sometimes goes with "crisis PR," the term that public-relations practitioners apply to the handling of disasters. When a nuclear plant fails, an airliner crashes, a car turns up with a dangerous flaw or a supertanker sinks, the company involved is placed on trial in the press and in the public mind long before regulators or juries get around to finding legal fault. And, many PR veterans say, how the company reacts in this period can mean the difference between a temporary loss of public good will and the permanent loss of business.

When disaster strikes, "the first thing that comes into your mind is, 'Do we talk or don't we?' " says Melvin Boeger, manager of public affairs at Shell Oil Co. "But you have to be candid. There just literally is no choice."

A PR Success

As a result of this practice, Mr. Boeger says, Shell was able to turn a 1971 disaster into a PR success. In the Gulf of Mexico, a fiery blowout on a Shell drilling platform had killed four people and threatened the water, wildlife and shores of the area for more than four months. Rather than stonewall or cover up, Shell during this period issued 150 press releases, arranged 50 interviews and six press conferences, and took reporters to the site in boats, planes and helicopters. These "techniques of communication," as Mr. Boeger calls them, successfully directed the media's attention to Shell's diligence in putting out the oil-well fire.

But at many companies, "the first tendency of executives is to say, 'Let's wait until all the facts are in,' which is dignified with the phrase 'low profile,' " says Thomas G. Leighton, a PR consultant in New York. "The fallacy is that in trying to say nothing, (a company) has already made a decision which excites the press, and that compounds the problem," Mr. Leighton adds.

Some corporate critics aren't so enthusiastic about crisis PR. "You may come out with a half-baked product and literally weigh the chances that it'll be faulty or murderous. Your fallback, your cover-up, your cosmetics, is the PR contingency plan," contends Thomas Mechling, a former PR official at International Business Machines Corp. and later at Xerox Corp. who is writing a book called "The Covert Communicators." When companies rely on a PR man's talents as a substitute for good business practices, Mr. Mechling says, "they're figuring that by sheer weight of money and words they can build a credibility that their actions don't warrant."

Painting Out the Name

Years ago, of course, most companies caught up in a disaster sought, and got, the lowest possible profile. One veteran airline public-relations executive recalls that as recently as the 1950s, "one of the PR man's first responsibilities when a crash occurred was to paint over the company's name" on the wreckage, preferably before news photographers arrived.

Today, such tactics are risky at best. The consumer movement, the spread of government regulation and the media's heightened sensitivity to companies' roles in catastrophes that once were passed off as acts of God all mean that even though a company might refuse to answer questions, it surely will be asked them.

If the American Airlines DC10 crash had occurred 10 years ago, "we would've just gone to American and to the FAA to cover the story, whereas now we've been all over McDonnell Douglas," says Av Westin, producer of ABC's "World News Tonight" program. The networks, he says, no longer are content to merely cover a disaster itself. "We're far more aggressive and far more cynical now," he says. (As for aggressiveness in the print media, the *Inquirer*'s Miss

Cass terms the eavesdropping epidode at Three Mile Island "guerrilla journalism.")

Today, fooling the press and the public isn't easy; so PR specialists contend that companies should plan before a crisis for controlling the flow of information. All U.S. airlines, for example, have elaborate policies designed to reduce unfavorable news coverage. Trans World Airlines' "Red Book," a pocket-sized manual to be used after a crash, is typical. It says airline spokesmen should "avoid being led to speculate, even off the record," and not use "hard verbs such as slammed, careened, plowed, etc." in talking to reporters. Such practices, it explains, will help "minimize sensationalism and the prominence with which the story is treated" by the media.

Corporate fears of bad publicity also have led to increasing reliance on outside PR agencies, which can assemble a team of "crisis-management" specialists within hours. McDonnell Douglas, for example, recently hired Carl Byoir & Associates, a big New York PR firm, to help it through the DC10 mess. Previously, when McDonnell Douglas was handling post-crash PR on its own, it pursued a mixed assortment of techniques, assailing the government for grounding the plane, for instance, while at the same time withdrawing all DC10 advertisements and stonewalling reporters.

Basic Choice Remains

Whether staffers or high-priced outside specialists, PR men still must choose whether to hunker down, say little and hope the public memory is short, or to take the offensive and push the company's point of view.

Until the Federal Aviation Administration recertified the DC10 last month, McDonnell Douglas and Carl Byoir chose the first approach. "McDonnell Douglas would like to clear the air, but feels as though it can't," Robert Kelly, a Carl Byoir official, explained at the time. Only after the recertification, Mr. Kelly added, would the PR firm work with the company to "restore the flying public's confidence in the plane, if, indeed, any's been lost."

Passengers are, in fact, packing into the DC10s pretty much as before, but McDonnell Douglas wants to take no chances. It has commissioned a ridership survey and plans to begin a multimillion-dollar advertising blitz extolling the plane. The company also has "become active in putting our story across" to shareholders and reporters, now that the plane is flying again, a spokesman says.

Other companies have taken a somewhat different approach: telling the media more than they want to know in hopes of dampening their enthusiasm for the story. At the Department of Energy's Rocky Flats Research Center near Denver, which is managed under contract by Rockwell International Corp., the PR policy is to notify local media within 30 minutes of any mishap even hinting of danger.

Four years ago, when there was no such policy, recalls Felix Owen, a Rockwell PR man, the Denver newspapers gave Rockwell "quite a bit of flak" in front-page stories when the company neglected to disclose that a building had been quarantined after a minor radiation accident. But when a fire broke out at the complex, Mr. Owen followed his full-disclosure policy and, as a result, the news stories appeared "not on page one, but page 26," he says, even though the fire was "far more critical from the community's point of view" than the earlier incident.

Taking the Offensive

Other times, companies go a step further and take the offensive. Last year, the PR department at Chrysler Corp. learned 15 hours ahead of time that the publishers of *Consumer Reports* magazine were planning to publicly blast the steering mechanism of the new Omni and Horizon cars and label both models "not acceptable." In that 15 hours, the auto maker's PR men made their own videotapes demonstrating how well the cars handled and taped interviews with company officials defending the autos.

When the *Consumer Reports* press conferences were held in Washington and New York, Chrysler's PR men and engineers were ready to give the auto company's position. The fast action, contends Frank Wylie, Chrysler's PR director, not only prevented a slump in sales but also proved that "crises can be avoided by anticipation."

(Although Chrysler denies that it changed the steering mechanism because of the flap, *Consumer Reports'* April edition said that the cars' steering response was "much improved" in the 1979 models and that they shouldn't any longer be considered unsafe.)

Yet other companies have found that aggressive action sometimes creates more problems than it solves. For example, the PR department at Westinghouse Electric Corp., the world's largest maker of nuclear reactors, issued a strong statement shortly after the Three Mile Island accident insisting that the plant's safety features had proved just how safe nuclear power was. But a day later, after the danger had suddenly heightened and pregnant women and children were evacuated from the area, Westinghouse not only refused further comment but also said its earlier statement "doesn't apply anymore."

Seeking a Delicate Balance

Consultants say the delicate balance between stonewalling and saying too much can best be achieved if corporate executives, attorneys and PR and marketing officials plan together in advance for even the most unlikely disasters. Such plans, they say, should include channels of communication within companies so that spokesmen are supplied with reliable, timely information. Indeed, Met Ed's Mr. Seldomridge acknowledges that "internal communications problems" contributed to the confusion at Three Mile Island.

But even the best-prepared companies can't anticipate everything. When the Amoco-Cadiz supertanker ran aground off France and polluted beaches, the vessel's owner, Standard Oil Co. (Indiana), responded in textbook fashion: PR officials from London, Belgium and the U.S. were dispatched to the scene, a French-speaking company attorney was flown in from Geneva to translate, and daily media briefings with company engineers were held in the hotel where most of the reporters stayed.

The unexpected problem: A national election in France made the wreck a political issue in addition to the environmental one anticipated by company officials. "That actually escalated the (news) interest in the thing beyond what it would've been otherwise," recalls Carl Meyerdirk, Indiana Standard's director of corporate media relations. "The European papers carried some pretty sensational stuff."

WHAT ABOUT PUBLIC RELATIONS FOR WOMEN?

Fran Weinstein

From data on the strong presence of women in public relations this article goes on to explain the attributes, talents, and practical steps needed by women who seek to enter the field. It concludes with a first-rate set of unisex guidelines.

Public relations was one of the first professions to open its doors to women, but until recently, those women who did enter remained within traditional, stereotypical boundaries—"woman's page" interests, such as food, home furnishings, cosmetics and fashion. Business, banking, finance, insurance, publishing, petroleum, radio, even television and movies were largely off-limits.

SOURCE: Fran Weinstein, "What About Public Relations?", *Working Woman*, March 1978, p. 20. Copyright 1978 by *Working Woman*. Reprinted by permission.

Then, too, although PR gave women the opportunity to compete with males in terms of job position, that equality did not extend to salary.

Now, things are changing. The trend toward a more up-to-date approach to social concerns—consumerism, ecology and the environment—and the need to protect industrial credibility in the eyes of the public, has enlarged the scope of public relations and made it more feasible for women with intelligence, skill and experience to move ahead. Salaries for women, while substantial, are still about $2000 lower on the average than their male colleagues', but the high incomes possible from a privately-owned PR firm are encouraging an increasing number of women to open their own agencies.

According to Denny Griswold of *Public Relations News*, "Public relations is the management function that evaluates public attitudes, identifies the policies and procedures of an individual or an organization with the public interest, and plans and executes a program of action to earn public understanding and acceptance."

The latest figures from the US Department of Commerce—Bureau of the Census show that over 6101 public relations firms are now women-owned. Rea Smith, executive vice-president of the Public Relations Society of America (PRSA), recently reported that women account for more than 20 percent of the society's membership, representing a sharp increase in the last few years. The PRSA, the largest national organization of its kind, serves as a communications center for PR people and offers an accreditation program to maintain high professional and ethical standards.

"It's not an easy business," said Amelia Lobsenz, chief executive officer and chairman of the board of Lobsenz-Stevens, Inc., a top public relations firm based in New York City. "It's a service business, and you've got to give your all. But there are so many compensations; there's no other field where you can experience so much variety, you can use your full potential."

Lobsenz, originally a free-lance magazine writer, started her own agency about 20 years ago because, "I like to follow my own instructions." She found that her talents as a writer were transferable and she put them to work for corporations in need of magazine coverage. Consequently, her firm now specializes in print media placement, and the business was built—right out of her own apartment—around it. Today, Lobsenz-Stevens is among the country's top 25 public relations firms in billings. An all-service agency with clients in virtually every field, it has a staff of 25—with a healthy mixture of men and women.

A public relations business can be nourished with a small capital input: There are no licensing requirements, overhead is limited and, to start, you are your chief hired hand. Willingness to work hard and a firm sense of determination are the most important ingredients for success. Press parties may seem glamorous but, Lobsenz stressed, "It's not enough to have a nice smile. You need skill, technique and a lot of backbone."

Lobsenz strongly believes in "women's intuition" and regards it as an important implement in dealing with clients—sensing whether they are happy with what you've done and where you can proceed from there. For would-be entrepreneurs, she passed along her formula: 1. *Specialize*—Find an area of public relations for which you possess a special knack; something to set yourself apart from the rest. 2. *Study*—Take courses in the field and be familiar with all aspects of PR. Acquire new techniques as they come along. 3. *Be a sponge*—Cultivate the ability to soak up information that can be put to practical use by asking how, what, when, where, who and why; and 4. *Read*—Everything.

Since PR is an extension of the management process, you have to *think* like management and be fully equipped to understand the client's needs. Carol Boswell of Boswell Frantz Associates, said, "The key to getting that account is a good, strong, lengthy proposal. If you can explain what public relations can do for them and identify their problems with full knowledge of the workings of that particular organization, you will gain their confidence." The proposal should be interesting, well-written and as specific as possible, without offering "freebie" secrets until the agreement is signed.

With public relations, you can make a liberal arts education pay off. Necessary skills range from English composition to psychology. The important thing to learn when contracting out your time, said Gina Frantz, co-owner of Boswell Frantz, "is how not to be too nice. As a woman, you've got to be just a bit tougher. Stick to the deal and, if a contract runs overtime, re-negotiate. You've got to love your clients but you've also got to set a limit."

Boswell and Frantz echo the Lobsenz story—they, too, started their business in an apartment. With a total of $800 ($400 cash plus a $400 phone bill), they set up shop—a desk, a file cabinet, a rented typewriter. Both emphasize the importance of building a wide contact network in order to service clients more effectively. Prior to establishing their own firm, Boswell and Frantz had been employed in various areas of the public relations departments of major publishing houses. With this experience, they were able to establish important connections in TV, radio and newspapers. Their specialty today: servicing the publishing industry.

Lobsenz, Boswell, Frantz—they share the enthusiasm and dedi-

cation necessary to their work, as well as the readiness to go out on
a limb for their clients and for themselves. As a result, they have
succeeded in breaking into a predominantly male stronghold.

You'll need:
1. An ability to understand all aspects of the media.
2. Extensive knowledge of English useage and journalistic writing. How to make news.
3. An ability to investigate and research.
4. A sense of psychology or insight into personalities and what
makes people tick.
5. An understanding of the running of a business—legal responsibilities, accounting, budgeting, costs, etc.
6. A good lawyer and accountant, if you can afford them.

CRITICISM, EVALUATION AND PROFESSIONALISM
Dennis L. Wilcox
Dr. Wilcox, of San Jose State University, contends that the public relations
community, in order to improve its work and prestige, should examine its
practices and admit errors and shortcomings when they occur.

"Thou shalt not criticize" seems to be evolving as a new axiom in the
public relations community, and it is being touted that it is "unprofessional" for a public relations practitioner to publicly criticize the
public relations operations of another person or organization.

Denny Griswold, APR, for example, recently wrote in *PR News*
that public criticism by a public relations practitioner of the performance of a colleague is a dangerous practice because it
downgrades public relations in the eyes of the public. She adds, "PR
practitioners might well remember that it does little good to talk
about being professional unless one acts like a professional."

Lawrence Tavcar, senior vice president of Carl Byoir &
Associates—the agency now handling Firestone Tire Co.—wrote a
critic of Firestone's public relations activities during the recent tire
recall controversy and said, ". . . it is unprofessional and unfair to
denigrate the performance of the public relations department without being fully aware of the facts, circumstances and conditions
affecting the department."

Even Leo Northart, editor of the *Public Relations Journal*, has
found it necessary to speak out. He chastised public relations

SOURCE: From *Public Relations Journal*, November 1979, pp. 56–57. Copyright
1979 by the *Public Relations Journal*. Reprinted by permission.

practitioners in a recent column for their "self-flagellation ritual" over the effectiveness of public relations during the Three Mile Island nuclear accident. He noted, "One mark of unprofessional conduct is shooting from the hip—passing judgement or issuing critical comments before one has all the facts."

In other words, one gets the distinct impression that public relations practitioners are supposed to keep silent about the fire raging in their own house until a full investigation of the fire has been made. It is not our place to yell "fire" until "all the facts are known" and that might not be until the house is completely destroyed—given the massive hesitancy of public relations practitioners to simply say "we goofed."

There is something ironic about the idea that the mass media can devote columns of space to Firestone's stonewalling of accurate information about defective radial tires, or the conflicting statements of officials at the Three Mile Island nuclear power plant, while public relations practitioners—those most qualified by experience to evaluate the situation from a public relations standpoint and add perspective—are supposed to assume the position of the proverbial three monkeys.

One wonders if the credibility of public relations would improve drastically if qualified and respected public relations practitioners made public comment about the outstanding features or shortcomings of a company's public relations strategy, especially if the issue has caused national attention already. At least this approach would inform the media and the public that effective public relations consists of truth and candor, and that a lot of company strategies are misnamed as public relations.

A Deafening Silence
In most cases, the silence of the public relations community is deafening. This creates the problem of letting unqualified critics get all the headlines. Vermont Royster of *The Wall Street Journal* sees this as a major problem in terms of the Three Mile Island accident. While politicians and anti-nuclear critics were getting national attention with their comments, managements remained silent. Mr Royster writes, "Where were the chief executives of the companies that design and build power reactors, or of the utility companies that make and sell the electric power, speaking out to defend and explain nuclear power as a source of energy. Again, silence."

The libertarian concept of the press provides for the marketplace of opinions; managements and the public relations community aren't participating.

The idea most disturbing is the faulty concept that "thou shalt not criticize" is an integral part of what constitutes professionalism.

Duloney. This is akin to the old propaganda technique of legitimacy through association. No description of professionalism includes the idea that one should not speak up if one sees incompetent or unethical behavior. Silence has nothing to do with professionalism—it is merely a self-serving device to preserve the clublike atmosphere of most professions, including law and medicine. It is preservation of the *status quo* and a "don't rock the boat" mentality.

Although it has never been considered polite for members of a club (profession) to criticize each other, one can argue that conscientious professionals have an obligation to speak out on behalf of the public interest. To not do so is to place the public relations community in the position of condoning shoddy practices and giving tacit approval by silence.

The public gets the impression—and this is where credibility is most eroded—that the profession is more interested in preserving the *status quo* than serving the public interest. Indeed, public confidence in the professions of law, medicine and accounting has suffered in past years because one is not supposed to evaluate the performance of a colleague. The result has been a new blizzard of consumer activism and more government regulations because the professions show no desire to police or publicly censure their own members. Will public relations come under the same pressure in the next decade?

Ron Aaron Eisenberg, senior vice president of Marston and Rothenberg Public Affairs, Inc., recently wrote in the New York *Times*, "It is time for the business community and those of us in public relations to take the lead, to talk 'straight' with the American people and government and the media and *ourselves* [emphasis added]."

The idea of talking straight, however, is under attack by those who have a mind set about the unprofessionalism of it all. Indeed, the Public Relations Society of America's "Code of Professional Standards" gives some solace by stating, "A member shall not intentionally injure the professional reputation or practice of another practitioner." This can be interpreted several ways. One should not call another public relations person a liar or an idiot (that's slander), but the public performance of a public relations department or agency, in this author's mind, is fair game for comment.

Lack of Public Accountability
The PRSA Code suggests that complaints about practitioners should be brought to the attention of the proper authorities within the Society for possible action. This is a nice concept but not really worth much since all proceedings are kept secret and no public an-

nouncements are made. One even has trouble getting the proper authorities to acknowledge to a letter writer that they have even received his or her complaint. Again, we preach public accountability to our employers and clients but don't seem to have much use for it in the conduct of our own affairs.

One wonders if we are really advancing the cause of public relations professionalism by burying our heads in the sand whenever we see incompetent performance or ineffective public relations strategies—especially when the situation has become a *cause célèbre* in the media already. One also wonders if we are advancing the profession by being so thin-skinned about criticism of public relations. The public relations newsletters, usually Pollyannas regarding the practice of public relations (Did you ever read a case study of a program that flopped?) marshal all the defensive mechanisms when *The Wall Street Journal* or the New York *Times* prints a critical story. We seem to take it personally when the *Times* satirizes the Environmental Protection Agency's new name for public relations—Office of Public Awareness. Perhaps we need a better sense of humor and less of an inferiority complex about public relations.

What the public relations community really needs is a healthy, robust discussion of contemporary practice. Some will say that we don't need any self-flagellation, but we do need some insightful, critical analysis of how public relations is practiced today. Perhaps we should take a tip from the format of the *Columbia Journalism Review*—a publication that serves as part educator, part watchdog, and yes, even part self-flagellator.

It might also improve public confidence in public relations if PRSA took an active, vocal role in enunciating standards relating to current situations. This would give the profession more visibility than the somewhat fruitless exercise of mouthing platitudes that can easily be applied to any number of occupations, including used car and insurance salesmen.

We advise trade groups to have a hot line for citizen complaints, but none really exists for public relations. It might even be somewhat interesting to have an organization like the National News Council. A respected, qualified panel of public relations practitioners could investigate situations where the mass media or the public feel that a company's public relations staff engaged in activities not beneficial to the public interest. A finding could be made and publicized without getting into the problems of libel or slander. Such a panel would protect public relations from unjustified criticism, and, at the same time, be a strong voice for high performance standards.

All this might be a bit heady for the "yes" persons of public ɪʋlutions who just follow management or client wishes—whether it's in the public interest or not—but it all depends on the desired function of public relations in the 1980s. None of us will become a true professional until we are willing to have a sense of responsibility and ethics that is answerable to a standard higher than mere loyalty to the employer or client of the moment.

SUZANNE SOMERS GETS A BUILDUP
Marguerite Michaels

A relatively minor but colorful facet of public relations is the "hype" promotion of individuals into sudden celebrities, especially in the entertainment field. In this excerpt is a glimpse of how the buildup is done.

[Into the office of Jay Bernstein, publicist and manager, last spring walked] Suzanne Somers—5-foot-4, 106 pounds, blonde and blue-eyed. At the time, she was playing the dumb, helpless, underdressed Chrissy in ABC-TV's menage à trois sitcom "Three's Company." That part might have satisfied some Hollywood actresses, but not Suzanne. "I want it all now," she announced. In her early 30's, Suzanne had previously played only a few bit parts in movies and television.

So her agent, Edgar Small, sent her to Bernstein "to get heat, because publicity is the difference between success and giant success."

Bernstein put one of his team of publicists, Stu Ehrlich, on the account and undertook to manage Suzanne himself. Ehrlich began to phone magazines, like *People* and *Us* about "Three's Company," while Bernstein put her on programs like ABC's "The Battle of the Network Stars."

By last November, Somers had her first magazine cover story, establishing her in the public mind as an individual in her own right, or as Ehrlich puts it, "separating the smart Suzanne from the dumb Chrissy.

"She had a real Hollywood story," adds Ehrlich. "Pregnant at 16, married at 17, divorced at 18. Carried the baby on her back to college classes. Waited tables, did modeling, lots of struggle. Published two volumes of poetry. Wonderful homemaker, wonderful mother."

A slight image problem arose when Ehrlich got word that a national newspaper was about to reveal that Suzanne had been

---

SOURCE: From *Parade*, July 23, 1979, p. 4. Copyright 1979 by *Parade* magazine. Reprinted by permission.

arrested a few years previously for passing bad checks. Ehrlich was equal to the occasion. He promptly called other news media and arranged for several "exclusive" interviews where Suzanne explained "her side" of the story—she had been broke and hungry at the time, the rent had been due, and her little boy was ill. The result: a flood of sympathetic stories on the air and in the press.

Jay Bernstein, meanwhile, was busy signing deals for Suzanne "to let everybody know about her." These included four episodes on "The Six Million Dollar Man" and a big deal with CBS for six movies over six years. The CBS deal was widely reported to be worth $1 million, but that's just hype. Actually, it's a guarantee of three movies for three years at a total of $150,000, with an option for the next three years and for a second movie each year should another network come through with an offer.

Bernstein also made an outside television deal with Pro Arts, Inc., a company in Medina, Ohio, that makes posters and starts fan clubs . . . .

By now "Three's Company" had become television's No. 1 show, topping the ratings after *Newsweek* magazine put Suzanne on a "Sex and TV" cover, calling her "the queen of jiggly." "If you've got it," Suzanne said, "bump it with a trumpet."

"It doesn't matter if the hype is vulgar or dumb," says agent Small. "It only matters that it works. In this business—and it's a business no different from GM selling cars—the bottom line is winning."

Jay Bernstein says that Suzanne is winning. A year and a half ago she was glad to make $300 for a guest spot on "Starsky and Hutch." Last month alone, says Bernstein—who has been known to exaggerate—her earnings ran into six figures.

"There is a formula," explains Bernstein, "but I'm not going to tell you what it is because everybody would use it."

As for creating a blonde superstar: "You have to get the right makeup people, the right hair people. You have to have a way of working with the press to help you. For instance, you don't do 'at home' interviews. People want to see Suzanne on a beach in a bathing suit, not at home with her husband [Canadian talk show host Alan Hamel].

"What you do," sums up Bernstein, "is build a transparent bubble around a client to keep everybody at arm's length. The client is inside the bubble and I—just me—travel back and forth. I don't like to use words like control or manipulation, but it's 15 percent of the take against 100 percent control."

He's now got the full 100 with Suzanne: Bernstein recently squeezed out agent Small and Ehrlich.

Part Five

RESEARCH AND EDUCATION

During the past half century there has been a steady increase in the volume of research involving communication theory, the processes and effects of mass communication, and the individual mass media. Education for journalism and mass communication has grown even more dramatically. Selections in this part examine research techniques and specific studies in uses and gratifications research, agenda-setting, communication effects, news diffusion, and content analysis. A final reading reviews the growth of educational philosophies and programs through sketches of four formative educators.

When the focus of communication research shifted from the "hypodermic" theory of planned messages exercising quick effects on audiences to studies of more sustained effects, Elihu Katz emerged as a leading scholar. This distinguished Israeli research psychologist approached the problem as the study of the individual's utilization of mass communication. The "uses and gratifications" theory, involving information seeking, became a major research area in the 1960s. Lazarsfeld, Berelson, and other pioneers noted long-range gratifications as a point for audience research, but it remained for Katz and his associates to dramatize this conclusion, as they do here. Dr. Katz holds a professorship in the Communications Institute, Hebrew University, Jerusalem.

The concept of an agenda-setting function of the press was developed in the early 1970s from research reevaluating the effects of mass communication in election campaigns, in public information campaigns, and on general public attitudes. In the popular view—shared by historians, politicians, and journalists—mass communication could achieve major social and political effects. But by 1960 Joseph Klapper had concluded in his *The Effects of Mass Communication* that "Mass communication ordinarily does not serve as a necessary and sufficient cause of audience effects, but rather functions among and through a nexus of mediating factors and influences. These mediating factors are such that they typically render mass communication a contributory agent, but not the sole cause, in a process of reinforcing the existing conditions. . . ."

This widely accepted conclusion was based on quantitative studies of small samples measuring changing voter attitudes during election campaigns. Scientific research workers now conclude that only very small numbers of voters ever desert their traditional political preferences, thus to expect the mass media to have large-scale quick effects on voting was wholly unrealistic.

Yet it remains clear that people do become aware of information about public affairs primarily through the mass media, and that the general public

302

identifies issues and individuals primarily through exposure to print and broadcast media. What agenda-setting theory suggests is that the audience also learns how much importance to attach to an issue, topic, or person from the emphasis placed by the mass media. Thus the choosing and displaying of news—gatekeeping—by print and electronic news reporters and editors becomes a crucial matter. An issue or candidate not on the "agenda" will fare badly in public awareness and response. Two University of North Carolina journalism professors, Drs. Maxwell E. McCombs and Donald L. Shaw, made the pioneering study of agenda-setting during the 1968 election, a study extended by their later findings reported in their article here.

Newspaper editorials had some effects on "swing" voters in the 1968 and 1972 elections, according to two studies of national probability samples by John P. Robinson of the University of Michigan's Survey Research Center. Robinson's 1974 report of his findings helped to restore the image of the mass media as active agencies in the formation of public opinion. The 1968 election was full of contradictions, but Dr. Robinson found that voters perceived the editorial stand of their favorite newspaper on Humphrey vs. Nixon. In 1972, independent voters reading an editorial supporting McGovern were twice as likely to vote for him as were independents reading newspapers endorsing Nixon. McGovern's only trouble in this regard was that almost no newspapers endorsed him.

A dramatic example of a news diffusion research study is offered by Wilbur Schramm, leader in mass communication research, who was on the Stanford University faculty when President Kennedy was assassinated in 1963. In "Communication in Crisis" Schramm relates the roles played by communicators and the media in moments of crisis, and then gives details of how people learned about John Kennedy's death. Within half an hour two-thirds of Americans heard the news that Kennedy had been shot, even before his death had been announced. Half heard the news by television or radio, and half by word of mouth. Dr. Schramm also gives data from other major studies and examines concepts of news diffusion.

Content analysis is a major area of mass communication research, and its techniques are widely used by mass communications students. These techniques are best learned through study of one of several basic guides to content analysis. Here John W. Windhauser and Guido H. Stempel III present a case study of the reliability of six techniques for content analysis of local coverage in newspapers. The authors suggest time-saving techniques to use when their reliability is sufficient for the area under study, and they analyze some of the common problems faced by content analysts. Dr. Stempel, Ohio University journalism professor, is editor of the *Journalism Quarterly* and a nationally recognized expert on content analysis research. Dr. Windhauser is on the University of Mississippi faculty.

The effects of television on children has been one of the major topics for communication research during the past decade. Two authorities on television, Drs. Jerome and Dorothy Singer, codirectors of the Yale University Family Television Research and Consultation Center, offer a review of the research trends in this area and a summary of their findings. A final reading on the role of journalism education presents the philosophies and contributions of four early leaders in the field: Walter Williams, founder of the University of Missouri School of Journalism; Willard G. Bleyer, founder of the University of Wisconsin's journalism school and historian of the American press; Ralph D. Casey, first director of the School of Journalism at the University of Minnesota, who expanded Bleyer's concept of integration of journalism education with the social sciences; and Frank Luther Mott, winner of the Pulitzer Prize for his history of American magazines and journalism head at the universities of Iowa and Missouri. In this essay, Warren K. Agee finds a thread of continuity in the precepts and accomplishments of these and other mass communication educators.

Section 16

COMMUNICATION RESEARCH TRENDS

The six readings presented in this section explore
the current major areas of communication
research and theory development. They also
demonstrate how specific studies were planned
and conducted by mass media researchers.

UTILIZATION OF MASS COMMUNICATION BY THE INDIVIDUAL

Elihu Katz, Jay G. Blumler, and Michael Gurevitch

In this selection from their comprehensive paper the authors point out that from the earliest studies of mass communication, certain underlying assumptions guided research. Later work recognized these assumptions and developed them into the "uses and gratifications model." The selection ends with a summary of important elements of this model.

Suppose that we were studying not broadcasting-and-society in mid-twentieth-century America but opera-and-society in mid-nineteenth-century Italy. After all, opera in Italy, during that period, was a "mass" medium. What would we be studying? It seems likely, for one thing, that we would find interest in the attributes of the medium—what might today be called its "grammar"—for example, the curious convention that makes it possible to sing contradictory emotions simultaneously. For another, we would be interested in the functions of the medium for the individual and society: perceptions of the values expressed and underlined; the phenomena of stardom, fanship, and connoisseurship; the festive ambience which the medium created; and so on. It seems quite unlikely that we would be studying the effects of the singing of a particular opera on opinions and attitudes, even though some operas were written with explicit political, social, and moral aims in mind. The study of short-run effects, in other words, would not have had a high priority, although it might have had a place. But the emphasis, by and large, would have been on the medium as a cultural institution with its own social and psychological functions and perhaps long-run effects.

We have all been over the reasons why much of mass communication research took a different turn, preferring to look at specific programs as specific messages with, possibly, specific effects. We were social psychologists interested in persuasion and attitude change. We were political scientists interested in new forms of social control. We were commissioned to measure message effectiveness for marketing organizations, or public health agencies, or churches, or political organizations, or for the broadcasting organizations

SOURCE: From *The Uses of Mass Communication: Current Perspectives on Gratification Research*, Sage Annual Reviews of Communication Research, vol. 3, J. G. Blumler and Elihu Katz, eds. (Beverly Hills: Sage, 1974), pp. 20–22. Copyright 1974. Reprinted by permission of the publisher, Sage Publications, Inc.

themselves. And we were asked whether the media were not causes of violent and criminal behavior.

Yet even in the early days of empirical mass communication research this preoccupation with short-term effects was supplemented by the growth of an interest in the gratifications that the mass media provide their audiences. Such studies were well represented in the Lazarsfeld-Stanton collections (1942, 1944, 1949); Herzog (1942) on quiz programs and the gratifications derived from listening to soap operas; Suchman (1942) on the motives for getting interested in serious music on radio; Wolfe and Fiske (1949) on the development of children's interest in comics; Berelson (1949) on the functions of newspaper reading; and so on. Each of these investigations came up with a list of functions served either by some specific contents or by the medium in question: to match one's wits against others, to get information or advice for daily living, to provide a framework for one's day, to prepare oneself culturally for the demands of upward mobility, or to be reassured about the dignity and usefulness of one's role.

What these early studies had in common was, first, a basically similar methodological approach whereby statements about media functions were elicited from the respondents in an essentially open-ended way. Second, they shared a qualitative approach in their attempt to group gratification statements into labelled categories, largely ignoring the distribution of their frequency in the population. Third, they did not attempt to explore the links between the gratifications thus detected and the psychological or sociological origins of the needs that were so satisfied. Fourth, they failed to search for the interrelationships among the various media functions, either quantitatively or conceptually, in a manner that might have led to the detection of the latent structure of media gratifications. Consequently, these studies did not result in a cumulatively more detailed picture of media gratifications conducive to the eventual formulation of theoretical statements.

The last few years have witnessed something of a revival of direct empirical investigations of audience uses and gratifications, not only in the United States but also in Britain, Sweden, Finland, Japan, and Israel. These more recent studies have a number of differing starting points, but each attempts to press toward a greater systemization of what is involved in conducting research in this field. Taken together, they make operational many of the logical steps that were only implicit in the earlier work. They are concerned with (1) the social and psychological origins of (2) needs, which generate (3) expectations of (4) the mass media or other sources, which lead to (5) differential patterns of media exposure (or engagement in other activities), resulting in (6) need gratifications and

(7) other consequences, perhaps mostly unintended ones. Some of these investigations begin by specifying needs and then attempt to trace the extent to which they are gratified by the media or other sources. Others take observed gratifications as a starting point and attempt to reconstruct the needs that are being gratified. Yet others focus on the social origins of audience expectations and gratifications. But however varied their individual points of departure, they all strive toward an assessment of media consumption in audience-related terms, rather than in technological, aesthetic, ideological, or other more or less "elitist" terms. The convergence of their foci, as well as of their findings, indicates that there is a clear agenda here—part methodological and part theoretical—for a discussion of the future directions of this approach.

Some Basic Assumptions of Theory, Method and Value

Perhaps the place of "theory" and "method" in the study of audience uses and gratifications is not immediately apparent. The common tendency to attach the label "uses and gratifications approach" to work in this field appears to virtually disclaim any theoretical pretensions or methodological commitment. From this point of view the approach simply represents an attempt to explain something of the way in which individuals use communications, among other resources in their environment, to satisfy their needs and to achieve their goals, and to do so by simply asking them. Nevertheless, this effort does rest on a body of assumptions, explicit or implicit, that have some degree of internal coherence and that are arguable in the sense that not everyone contemplating them would find them self-evident. Lundberg and Hultén (1968) refer to them as jointly constituting a "uses and gratifications model." Five elements of this model in particular may be singled out for comment:

(1) The audience is conceived of as active, that is, an important part of mass media use is assumed to be goal directed (McQuail, Blumler and Brown, 1972). This assumption may be contrasted with Bogart's (1965) thesis to the effect that "most mass media experiences represent pastime rather than purposeful activity, very often [reflecting] chance circumstances within the range of availabilities rather than the expression of psychological motivation or need." Of course, it cannot be denied that media exposure often has a casual origin; the issue is whether, in addition, patterns of media use are shaped by more or less definite expectations of what certain kinds of content have to offer the audience member.

(2) In the mass communication process much initiative in linking need gratification and media choice lies with the audience member. This places a strong limitation on theorizing about any form of

straight-line effect of media content on attitudes and behavior. As Schramm, Lyle and Parker (1961) said:

> In a sense the term "effect" is misleading because it suggests that television "does something" to children. . . . Nothing can be further from the fact. It is the children who are most active in this relationship. It is they who use television rather than television that uses them.

(3) The media compete with other sources of need satisfaction. The needs served by mass communication constitute but a segment of the wider range of human needs, and the degree to which they can be adequately met through mass media consumption certainly varies. Consequently, a proper view of the role of the media in need satisfaction should take into account other functional alternatives—including different, more conventional, and "older" ways of fulfilling needs.

(4) Methodologically speaking, many of the goals of mass media use can be derived from data supplied by individual audience members themselves—that is, people are sufficiently self-aware to be able to report their interests and motives in particular cases, or at least to recognize them when confronted with them in an intelligible and familiar verbal formulation.

(5) Value judgments about the cultural significance of mass communication should be suspended while audience orientations are explored on their own terms. It is from the perspective of this assumption that certain affinities and contrasts between the uses and gratifications approach and much speculative writing about popular culture may be considered.

THE AGENDA-SETTING FUNCTION OF THE PRESS
Maxwell E. McCombs and Donald L. Shaw

It is easy to assume, as both the general public and mass media professionals always have, that the press has major influence through its decisions of what to cover, how strongly, from which point of view. But it is quite difficult to document the influence of its agenda-setting function, as this excerpt from a landmark study shows.

The general notion of agenda-setting—the ability of the media to influence the salience of events in the public mind—has been part of our political culture for at least half a century. Recall that the

---

SOURCE: Maxwell E. McCombs and Donald L. Shaw, *The Emergence of American Political Issues* (St. Paul: West Publishing, 1977), pp. 5–6, 8–11. Copyright © 1977, West Publishing Company. Reproduced by permission. All rights reserved.

opening chapter of Walter Lippmann's 1922 book *Public Opinion* is titled: "The World Outside and the Pictures in Our Heads." As Lippmann pointed out, it is, of course, the mass media which dominate in the creation of these pictures of public affairs.[1]

More recently this assumption of media power has been asserted by presidential observer Theodore White in *The Making of the President, 1972.*

> The power of the press in America is a primordial one. It sets the agenda of public discussion; and this sweeping political power is unrestrained by any law. It determines what people will talk and think about—an authority that in other nations is reserved for tyrants, priests, parties and mandarins.[2]

The press does more than bring these issues to a level of political awareness among the public. The idea of agenda-setting asserts that the priorities of the press to some degree become the priorities of the public. What the press emphasizes is in turn emphasized privately and publicly by the audiences of the press. . . .

This concept of an agenda-setting function of the press redirects our attention to the cognitive aspects of mass communication, to attention, awareness, and information. While there was justification for earlier emphasis on attitude change,[3] it was precisely that emphasis on the affective aspects of mass communication that led to the law of minimal consequences. However, the history of mass communication research from the 1940 Erie County study to the present decade can be viewed as a movement away from short-range effects on attitudes and toward long-range effects on cognitions.[4]

Attitudes concern our feelings of being for or against a political position or figure. *Cognition* concerns our knowledge and beliefs about political objects. The agenda-setting function of mass communication clearly falls in this new tradition of cognitive outcomes of mass communication. Perhaps more than any other aspect of our environment, the political arena—all those issues and persons about whom we hold opinions and knowledge—is a secondhand reality. Especially in national politics, we have little personal or direct contact. Our knowledge comes primarily from the mass media. For the most part, we know only those aspects of national politics considered newsworthy enough for transmission through the mass media.

Even television's technological ability to make us spectators for significant political events does not eliminate the secondhand nature of our political cognitions. Television news is edited reality just as print news is an edited version of reality. And even on those rare occasions when events are presented in their entirety, the television experience is not the same as the eyewitness experience.[5]

Our knowledge of political affairs is based on a tiny sample of the real political world. That real world shrinks as the new_ decide what to cover and which aspects to transmit in their repo_. and as audiences decide to which news messages they will attend.

Yet, as Lippmann pointed out, our political responses are made to that tiny replica of the real world, the *pseudoenvironment*, which we have fabricated and assembled almost wholly from mass media materials. The concept of agenda-setting emphasizes one very important aspect of this pseudoenvironment, the *salience* or amount of emphasis accorded the various political elements and issues vying for public attention.

Many commentators have observed that there is an agenda-setting function of the press, and Lippmann long ago eloquently described the necessary connection between mass communication and individual political cognitions. But like much of our folk wisdom about politics and human behavior, it was not put to empirical test by researchers for over half a century.

Empirical Evidence of Agenda-Setting

The first empirical attempt at verification of the agenda-setting function of the mass media was carried out by McCombs and Shaw during the 1968 U.S. presidential election.[6] Among undecided voters in Chapel Hill, North Carolina there were substantial correlations between the political issues emphasized in the news media and what the voters regarded as the key issues in that election. The voters' beliefs about what were the major issues facing the country reflected the composite of the press coverage, even though the three presidential contenders in 1968 placed widely divergent emphasis on the issues. This suggests that voters—at least undecided voters—pay some attention to all the political news in the press regardless of whether it is about or originated with a favored candidate. This contradicts the concepts of selective exposure and selective perception, ideas which are central to the law of minimal consequences. Selective exposure and selective perception suggest that persons attend most closely to information which they find congenial and supportive.

In fact, further analysis of the 1968 Chapel Hill survey showed that among those undecided voters with leanings toward one of the three candidates, there was less agreement with the news agenda based on their preferred candidate's statements than with the news agenda based on all three candidates.

While the 1968 Chapel Hill study was the first empirical investigation based specifically on agenda-setting, there is other scholarly evidence in the mass communication/political behavior literature which can be interpreted in agenda-setting terms. Let's briefly consider several examples.

The first example comes from the 1948 Elmira study, research which cemented the strong role of interpersonal rather than mass communication in the election process. For an optimum view of the agenda-setting influence of the press, one should examine those Elmira voters with minimal interpersonal contact. As Berelson, Lazarsfeld, and McPhee noted:

> . . . about one-fifth of our sample did not know the politics of any of their three closest friends in August. Such people have so little political content in their normal social interaction that what little they do learn about politics is largely independent of their social surroundings most of the time. Therefore, they are more likely than their fellows to be 'blown about' by the political winds of the times, in a way especially independent of their social surroundings.[7]

In other words, for those voters the political agenda suggested by the media is not mediated, interpreted, or confronted by interpersonal sources of influence. These voters would seem especially open to the agenda-setting influence of the press.

And the influence was there. These Elmira voters moved with the trend of the times more than did the other voters. Like the national Democratic trend that mounted during the 1948 campaign, these Elmira voters moved rapidly into the Democratic column. The cues were there in the media for all. But persons without the conservative brake of interpersonal contacts moved most rapidly with the national trend reported in the media.

The second example of agenda-setting comes from a study of county voting patterns in an Iowa referendum.[8] In this example it is easy to see the agenda-setting effects of both mass media and interpersonal news sources.

The question before the voters was calling a constitutional convention to reapportion legislative districts. Since large counties stood to gain and small counties to lose from reapportionment, the study anticipated a strong correlation between county population and proportion of votes in favor of the convention. In short, it was hypothesized that counties would vote their self-interest. And, overall, this was strikingly the case. Across all counties, the correlation is +.87 between county population and vote.

But now let us consider whether this pattern is facilitated by the presence of agenda-setting institutions. Two sources of heightened awareness were considered: a citizens' committee in favor of the convention and a daily newspaper in the county.

In the 41 counties where the citizens' committee was active, the correlation was +.92 between vote and population. In the 58 counties without such a group, the correlation was only +.59. Similar findings are reported for the presence or absence of a local daily newspaper. In the 38 counties with a local daily, the correlation was +.92. In the 61 counties without a daily, the correlation was only +.56.

Each agenda-setting source made a considerable difference in the outcome. What about their combined impact? In 28 counties with both a local daily and a citizens' committee the correlation was +.92. Where only one of these sources was present, the correlation declined to +.40; and when neither agenda-setter was present, the correlation declined to +.21.

Self-interest may have motivated many voters. But unless the issue was high on the agenda—placed there via the newspaper and local citizens' committee—this motivation simply did not come into play.

A similar "necessary condition" role for agenda-setting is found in a study of the distribution of knowledge among populations.[9] Generally, there is a knowledge gap between social classes concerning topics of public affairs, typically documented by a rather substantial correlation between level of education and knowledge of public affairs. That is to say, as level of education increases, so does the amount of knowledge about public affairs. But as communication scientist Phillip Tichenor and his colleagues discovered, the strength of this correlation, at least for some topics, is a direct function of the amount of media coverage. They found a monotonic relationship between media coverage and the strength of the education/knowledge correlation. The more the press covers a topic, the more an audience—especially audience members with more education—learn.

Notes

1. Walter Lippmann, *Public Opinion* (New York: Macmillan, 1922).
2. Theodore White, *The Making of the President, 1972* (New York: Bantam Books, 1973), p. 327.
3. Maxwell McCombs and Thomas Bowers, "Television's Effects on Political Behavior," in *The Fifth Season*, ed. George Comstock et al. (Santa Monica: Rand Corp.)
4. Maxwell McCombs, "Mass Communication in Political Campaigns," in ed. F. Gerald Kline and Phillip J. Tichenor, *Current Perspectives in Mass Communication Research*, vol. 1 (Beverly Hills: Sage, 1972).
5. Kurt Lang and Gladys Engel Lang, *Politics and Television* (Chicago: Quadrangle, 1968).
6. Maxwell E. McCombs and Donald L. Shaw, "The Agenda-Setting Function of the Mass Media," *Public Opinion Quarterly* (Summer 1972), 36: 176−87.
7. Bernard Berelson, Paul Lazarsfeld, and William McPhee, *Voting* (Chicago: University of Chicago Press, 1954), pp. 138−39.
8. David Arnold and David Gold, "The Facilitation Effect of Social Environment," *Public Opinion Quarterly* (Fall 1964), 28: 513−16.
9. G. A. Donahue, Phillip J. Tichenor, and C. N. Olien, "Mass Media and the Knowledge Gap: A Hypothesis Reconsidered," *Communication Research 2* (Beverly Hills: Sage, 1975), pp. 3−23.

THE PRESS AS KING-MAKER
John P. Robinson

The effect of newspaper endorsements of political candidates in national elections was dismissed by 1960s researchers. But a University of Michigan Survey Research Center staff member studied afresh. The results analyzed here were based on two contrasting elections, yet they show a significant and substantially equal influence of newspaper endorsements on voters in both 1968 and 1972.

That newspaper endorsements can and do influence voter decision in *local* elections seems a well-accepted part of conventional wisdom, and it also has received empirical support.[1] However, the classic research on voting behavior in *national* elections has so well documented the pervasive influences of personal factors, such as one's political party identification or the political orientations of one's peers,[2] that the likelihood of newspaper endorsements having any influence has been dismissed almost out of hand.

Nevertheless, research on the 1968 national election uncovered a curious and persistent relation between newspaper endorsements and voting behavior.[3] While voters were generally confused about or unaware of the partisan stands of reporting in television, radio or magazines, they accurately perceived where their favorite newspaper stood on the election. Moreover, these newspaper endorsements were clearly associated with how people reported they voted on election day, even after such personal factors as party identification and pre-election vote intention were taken into account. However, the highly abnormal character of the 1968 election—with its third-party candidates, resignations and highly divisive internal conflict—made one cautious about generalizing too far from this particular election. The 1972 election, while not entirely free of these elements, might be seen as providing a more normal context in which to examine the possible influence of newspaper endorsements. Indeed, it may be argued that 1972 provided a rather unexciting presidential campaign, in which most matters were settled long before the newspapers made their endorsements.[4] Thus, the nature of the campaign could have minimized the possible impact of newspaper endorsements.

Data Bases

As in our 1968 study, the data come from a national probability sample of American adults interviewed by the Center for Political

SOURCE: From *Journalism Quarterly*, 51: 587–94. Copyright 1974 by the Association for Education in Journalism. Reprinted by permission.

Studies (CPS) of the University of Michigan after the election about their voting behavior and mass media usage *during* the campaign. Of this cross-section of 1,119 adults, which was also interviewed during the campaign about their political attitudes and vote intentions, a total of 501 reported both having voted and having followed the campaign in a newspaper. In general, this sample reported levels of mass media usage similar to that found in earlier CPS election studies,[5] indicating that, if in fact 1972 did provide a relatively unexciting campaign, attention to the media did not seem diminished by it.

In contrast to our 1968 study, respondents who read newspapers were not asked about their perceptions of where the newspapers stood but merely the name of the newspaper they read most closely about the campaign. The actual endorsements of these newspapers were then verified through listings in *Editor & Publisher*,[6] or by the CPS field staff in cases where a newspaper's endorsement was not reported in *Editor & Publisher*. By *Editor & Publisher's* calculations, some 93% of newspapers making endorsements in 1972 had endorsed Richard Nixon, with only 7% for George McGovern. Projected by circulation figures, 10 times as many Americans were exposed to a pro-Nixon as a pro-McGovern newspaper, with less than 15% of the readers being exposed to a paper that remained uncommitted.

Results

The results, outlined in Table 1, indicate a basic replication of the results obtained for the 1968 study.[7] Independent voters exposed to a newspaper endorsing McGovern were twice as likely to vote for McGovern (50%) as independent voters exposed to a pro-Nixon newspaper (26%). However, this 24% differential in 1972 was matched by a 25% differential (71% vs. 46%) by newspaper endorsement among voters with Democratic party identification. In 1968, no such differential was found among Democrats, a point

TABLE 1 Percentages of Voters Voting for the Democratic Candidate by Newspaper Endorsement and Party Identification, 1972

Voter's Party	Newspaper Endorsement		
	Democratic (N = 53)	Neither (N = 197)	Republican (N = 251)
Democrat (N = 207)	71	61	46
Independent (N = 152)	50	34	26
Republican (N = 142)	0	6	5

which will be discussed in more detail below. Consistent with the 1968 results, no such differential was found among Republican party—identifiers in Table 1.

Table 1, of course, fails to take into account the several other factors beyond party identification that predict the vote and which may also lie behind the predictive power of exposure to newspapers of differing endorsements. Table 2 presents the voting differentials obtained after 12 such predictors are taken into account, predictors such as opinion giving, interest in the campaign, feelings of political efficacy, as well as age, education, religion, urbanicity and sex. Also included *as a control variable* in Table 2 is vote intention expressed in the pre-election interview, a variable that may be considered an "overcontrol" since its correlation (.84) with actual reported vote in the post-election interview approaches unity. The combined statistical effects of these variables in Table 2 has been assessed by Multiple Classification Analysis (MCA), a computer program that provides estimates of the effects of single variables simultaneously controlled for the effects of several other variables.[8]

Table 2 indicates that introduction of these 12 variables does indeed substantially reduce the differentials in Table 1. Instead of 25% differentials, Table 2 indicates newspaper endorsements contribute a 7% difference (40% vs. 33%) in voting behavior after the other variables have been controlled. This is practically identical to the 6% differential found after a parallel MCA run was performed on the 1968 election data.[9] Such a finding is but one piece of evidence supporting the persistence of the newspaper endorsement effect that we shall encounter.

MCA is strictly a linear model and cannot detect differentials in which strong interaction effects among variables are present. We suspected a strong interaction effect would occur for the variable of region, particularly for the difference between voters in the South compared to those in the rest of the country. Thus, the traditional Democratic loyalties of Nixon-voting Southerners (who were over-overwhelmingly exposed to pro-Nixon newspapers) might very well lie behind the differentials noted thus far. In other words, one might well expect Southerners to defect from the Democratic party candidate whether any stimulus from the mass media was present or not.

However, the figures at the bottom of Table 2 show that the differential holds almost as well in the South as it does in the rest of the country. Moreover, among Democratic and Independent voters (for whom the differential is at a maximum in Table 1), the newspaper endorsement "effect" is even stronger in the South than elsewhere. This provides a second support for the presence of a real difference in voting behavior attributable simply to exposure to newspapers of different political orientation.

TABLE 2 Percentages of Voters Voting for the Democratic Candidate by Newspaper Endorsement, 1972 (after correction for 12 leading explanatory factors, including party identification)

| | Newspaper Endorsement | | |
	Democratic Candidate	Neither Candidate	Republican Candidate
All voters (N = 501)	40	36	33
South (N = 140)	37	31	30
(Dems & Indeps only) (N = 102)	57	43	42
Non-South (N = 361)	45	38	35
(Dems & Indeps only) (N = 257)	69	63	60

A third feature of the data in Tables 1 and 2 that bolsters confidence in this conclusion is the voting behavior of individuals exposed to uncommitted newspapers whose endorsement was unknown or could not be ascertained (i.e., the "neither" category of Tables 1 and 2). To be consistent with the results thus far, these voters should exhibit voting behavior that falls somewhere between readers of pro-McGovern newspapers and readers of pro-Nixon newspapers. While voters exposed to uncommitted or unknown newspapers do not generally fall at the expected midway point in the Table 1 and Table 2 calculations (except for the most important row for all voters at the top of Table 2), their voting behavior does not fall outside the interval defined by readers of pro-McGovern and pro-Nixon newspapers.

Moreover, this middle position is maintained when the "neither" group is decomposed in Table 3, which contrasts readers exposed to an uncommitted newspaper with readers exposed to a newspaper whose allegiance was unknown or could not be ascertained. More

TABLE 3 Percentages of Voters in the 'Neither' Category of Table 1, and of Voters Who Did Not Read Newspapers, Voting for the Democratic Candidate by Party Identification, 1972

| | Readers in Neither Category | | | Non-readers |
Voter's Party ID	Total Neither (N = 197)	Newspaper Uncommitted (N = 74)	Newspaper NA or DK (N = 123)	(N = 277)
Democrats (N = 87)	61	67	63	60
Independents (N = 61)	34	31	40	33
Republicans (N = 49)	6	5	0	8

powerful corroborative evidence is provided by the "non-readers" category in Table 3, which may be more akin to a "control group" than the neither group. As such, this group should also maintain a middle position. In fact, Table 3 shows their voting patterns to be practically identical to that of the total neither group.[10] In brief, the basic rank order of voting behavior, running from exposure to pro-McGovern endorsements to exposure to "neutral" or no messages to exposure to pro-Nixon endorsements, is impressively preserved when rather subtle distinctions are drawn within the middle of these three groups.

Notes

1. See, for example, William Mason, "The Impact of Endorsements on Voting," *Sociological Methods and Research*, 1: 463−95 (May 1973); Maxwell McCombs, "Editorial Endorsement: A Study of Influence," *Journalism Quarterly*, 44: 545−48 (Autumn 1967).

2. Paul Lazarsfeld, et al., *The People's Choice* (New York: Duell, Sloan and Pierce, 1944); Angus Campbell, et al., *The American Voter* (New York: Wiley, 1960).

3. John Robinson, "Perceived Media Bias and the 1968 Election: Can the Media Affect Behavior After All?," *Journalism Quarterly*, 49: 239−46 (Summer 1972).

4. Irving Crespi, "1972 and the American Voter," *Public Opinion Quarterly*, 37: 441−42 (Fall 1973).

5. John Robinson, et al., *Measures of Political Attitudes* (Ann Arbor, Michigan: Survey Research Center, 1968), pp. 616−21.

6. *Editor & Publisher*, November 4, 1972, pp. 9−12.

7. Robinson, op. cit. It must be noted that the data are not exactly comparable, since the 1968 data refer to reader perceptions and the 1972 data refer to the actual editorial stance of the newspaper.

8. Frank Andrews, et al., *Multiple Classification Analysis* (Ann Arbor, Michigan: Survey Research Center, 1967).

9. Robinson, op. cit., p. 244. To the extent that the pre-election intention does represent an "overcontrol," the reader may well feel more comfortable with a figure closer to the *overall* 15 percent differential in Table 1 than the 7 percent differential in Table 2 (or the 6 percent differential in 1968). The 15 percent differential does take into account the factor of party identification, which explains most of the variance in vote after the pre-election intention variable is taken into account.

10. The middle position of the group is also maintained after application of MCA.

COMMUNICATION IN CRISIS

Wilbur Schramm

In a major crisis, such as the assassination of President Kennedy in 1963, the news is far more likely to leave the media and be spread by word of mouth. In this excerpt from a classic news diffusion study are the analysis and data that change the preceding statement from a supposition into an observation of fact.

The Part Communication Plays in Crisis

When a crisis interrupts the slow, ongoing rhythms of communication—scanning the environment, disposing of the day-to-day needs and problems of the system, filing away and sharing the increment of experience—the rate of information flow is enormously increased. A message signals the emergency. Information rushes to and from the point of crisis, which becomes a new focus of attention as the system strives to adjust to the problem.

This is the case regardless of the size of system. A message that unusual heat is being felt on a finger will alert a human system to move the finger, check the situation visually if possible, take steps to repair the damage, and so forth. A message that one member of a group is deviating will interrupt the usual humdrum communication of the group for a great flow of persuasion to the deviant until he is restored to loyal membership or the cause is seen to be hopeless. So in Dallas on November 22 in 1963 the reporters, broadcasters, photographers, and their equipment were operating routinely until 12:30. They were providing routine coverage of a chief executive. Then came the bulletin that roused the men and facilities of communication to such efforts that it was many days before information from Dallas and the coverage of the American chief executive could again be called routine. . . .

Systems theory would describe the response to crisis as a sudden imbalance in the system, followed by emergency steps to restore balance, and then a gradual restoration of normal functioning around whatever new balance is achieved.[1] This comes closer to describing what seems to have happened in the case of the Kennedy assassination. We can identify three periods. First came the time when the news had to be told. Then followed a period when society staggered under the blow but struggled to restore equilibrium—the shocked response of ordinary men and women, the shocked but disciplined response of officials striving to maintain

SOURCE: From *The Kennedy Assassination and the American Public*, edited by Bradley S. Greenberg and Edwin B. Parker (Stanford: Stanford University Press, 1965). Copyright © 1965 by the Board of Trustees of the Leland Stanford Junior University. Reprinted with permission of the publishers.

WEATHER

Today: Sunny and cool.
Tomorrow: Cloudy, milder.

TEMPERATURE RANGE

HUMIDITY

Reports and Maps—Page 16

NEW YORK
Herald ⚓ Tribune

Established 122 Years Ago. A European Edition Is Published Daily in Paris

VOL. CXXIII No. 42,613   MONDAY, NOVEMBER 25, 1963   TEN CENTS

THE
CITY

A Nation Appalled

Monday, Nov. 25, 1963

IN THE NEWS
THIS MORNING

[FROM THE HERALD TRIBUNE'S WORLD-WIDE SOURCES]

TOPIC A—

¶The body of John Fitzgerald Kennedy was borne from the White House to the Capitol Rotunda yesterday. An estimated 300,000 watched the mournful procession along Pennsylvania Avenue when the flag-covered coffin was lifted from the black caisson and placed inside the Rotunda. Mrs. Jacqueline Kennedy, dressed in black and wearing a black veil, knelt and kissed it. In a brief ceremony, government leaders mixed their eulogies with pleas for an end to bitterness, violence and hatred in the land. And then the people began to file past. (Page 1)

IN DALLAS—

¶In the same Dallas Hospital under the hands of the same doctors who had labored to save President Kennedy, Lee Harvey Oswald, the accused assassin, died at 1:07 p.m. One bullet fired point-blank from the nickel-plated revolver of nightclub owner Jack (Ruby) Rubenstein cut down Oswald as an army of Dallas detectives ushered him out of City Hall jail for transfer to County Jail. Within an hour, Rubenstein was charged with Oswald's murder and Dallas homicide chief Will Fritz said the case of the assassination of the 35th President was "closed." (Page 1)

¶Rubenstein was not regarded as a criminal type although he was arrester six times for minor incidents. Un-married, he lived with a roommate who said he showed "a terrible grievance" over the President's assassination and lamented. "That poor family." He was a physical-fitness enthusiast reportedly well acquainted with Dallas police and newspapermen. (Page 2)

IN WASHINGTON—

¶Fresh from the melancholy experience of the cortege, President Johnson turned immediately to the country's No. 1 foreign policy problem—the shooting war in Viet Nam. In a conference with top security officials and Henry Cabot Lodge, his Ambassador in Saigon, President Johnson heard a "hopeful" report on a bold Communist move against a training center 20 miles from Saigon. (Stories on Page 5)

¶The late President's widow and two young children followed directly behind the horse-drawn caisson that brought Mr. Kennedy's flag-draped coffin from the White House to the Capitol. Caroline, nearly six, occasionally looked up at her mother's tear-stained face as if to comfort her. John jr., who will be three today, waved a small American flag. Other members of the Kennedy family followed. The President's father, Joseph, was unable to travel to Washington because of illness. (Full story, Page 4)

¶Leaders from all parts of the world began to assemble in Washington to pay last respects to the late President Kennedy. Sixty-seven nations indicated they were sending representatives. The U. S. told foreign governments the presence of regular envoys would suffice, did not encourage the mass influx of heads of state. President Johnson will receive heads of state and other dignitaries at 5:30 p.m. today on the eighth floor of the State Department Building. (Reports on Page 7)

IN THE NATION—

¶The single shot that cracked in the basement of the Dallas City Hall yesterday closed forever the story of the man who the police believe committed one of the century's most incredible crimes. His motives, his preparations, his reasoning will never be known exactly. The bizarre shooting bewildered and angered people across the nation. (Story on Page 4)

¶Unprecedented radio and television coverage of the events in Dallas and Washington continued into a third day. It appeared there would be no return to normal broadcasting schedules until tomorrow morning. White millions of Americans continued the coverage the medium's finest hour, both the White House and the networks reported receiving calls from people around the country annoyed that their favorite programs had been deleted. (Page 13)

¶Of the problems suddenly placed on Lyndon Johnson's shoulders, one of the first he must deal with will be the threatened national rail strike. Tomorrow, a board set up by Congress to avoid the strike by compulsory arbitration of the key issues will deliver its decision to the new President. (Details, Page 20)

IN THE CITY—

¶Clergymen of all faiths eulogized the late President Kennedy and church attendance increased throughout the city yesterday. A typical response: the Rev. Peter Chase, canon pastor of the Cathedral of St. John the Divine, told his congregation "This is a great country with a great mission to lead us on." (Story on Page 13)

BULLET STRIKES VITALS of accused assassin Lee Oswald as night club owner Jack Ruby pulls the trigger, detective recoils, in crowded corridor of city hall basement.

Nightclub Owner
Silences Assassin

By Maurice C. Carroll
Of The Herald Tribune Staff

DALLAS

Lee Harvey Oswald met an assassin's death yesterday just 48 hours and seven minutes after the bullet he was accused of firing killed the President of the United States. With much of the nation watching on television, Oswald was shot down amid a crowd of reporters, photographers and policemen as he was to be taken from the Dallas police station to the county jail. He was rushed to Parkland Hospital and gasped out his final breath in the same emergency ward, Just 10 feet from the room where John F. Kennedy died Friday.

At the Dallas police station, detectives were mounting guard again over their newest killer, nightclub owner Jack Rubinstein, alias Jack Ruby. Dallas District Attorney Henry Wade, who had vowed to seek the death penalty for Oswald, said he would even it for Oswald's killer.

Last night police barricaded parts of downtown Dallas to help control the crowds which have been increasing at the scene of the President's assassination and the Oswald shooting.

The chief of the Texas Highway Patrol ordered 20 extra men into Dallas to guard Gov. John Connally, still recuperating in Parkland Hospital after being wounded in the second killing, Texas Gov. John Connally, who is recovering from his wounds. The room is across the corridor from the room where President Kennedy died.

The shooting was witnessed by millions of Americans on all three television networks which had set up cameras to view the President's accused assassin as he was transferred from the police station to the county jail.

This reporter was within eight feet of Oswald when he was shot I may have shouted the last words he was ever to hear.

The prisoner, hands cuffed in front of him, was led into the cavernous garage under the station. Seconds before...

¶...parently feel that the violence of the last three days has disgraced the city's good name. No one is sure the violence is over yet.

Oswald died without ever having changed his statement that he was innocent of the murder of President Kennedy. Authorities had said that they had an overwhelming case prepared against him.

The bullet that killed the admitted Communist sympathizer pierced Oswald's spleen, pancreas, aorta, kidney and liver.

The same physicians who had treated President Kennedy at Parkland were unable to save Oswald, even though they administered heart-peated transfusions and used an electronic Pacemaker to attempt to bring his heart back into action.

He died in Emergency Room Two, the same room where physicians had worked over his second victim, Texas Gov...

ON THE WHITE HOUSE STEPS, the woman the slain assassin widowed, Jacqueline Kennedy, appears with her children, John jr. and Caroline, to escort the President's body to the Capitol where it lay in state in the Rotunda.

MOURNING
IN CAPITAL

By David Wise
Washington Bureau Chief

WASHINGTON.

Under an American flag and a bright autumn sun, to the roll of muffled drums, the body of John F. Kennedy, 35th President of the United States, was borne along Pennsylvania Ave. to the Capitol rotunda yesterday, and rested there overnight. Pleas for an end to bitterness, violence and hatred in the land were voiced in eulogies.

In an unforgettable scene, Mrs. Jacqueline Kennedy, in black and veiled, stood in the rotunda in sorrowful dignity, holding the hands of her two children, Caroline and John jr. Then she and her daughter knelt and Mrs. Kennedy kissed the flag-draped casket.

At the very moment that Sen. Mike Mansfield, the Democratic leader of the Senate, stood at the bier and decried "the hatred, prejudice and the arrogance which converged in that moment of horror to strike him down," there was new horror in Dallas, Texas. At 2:07 p.m. as Sen. Mansfield spoke, Lee Harvey Oswald, accused of assassinating the President, died in an emergency room of Parkland Hospital in Dallas.

He had been shot with a single bullet fired point-blank by a man police identified as Jack Ruby, the owner of a dance hall and a strip-tease club.

All day and into the night, thousands of people filed past the bier of the dead President as the nation and the world paid tribute to his passing. Today, he will be buried in Arlington National Cemetery after a requiem mass.

The leaders of the world converged on Washington to attend the funeral today.

President Lyndon B. Johnson rode in the cortege from the White House to the Capitol, but then sped back to the Executive Office Building to deal with a new crisis in Viet Nam.

Thousands of spectators, many wiping tears from their eyes, watched as seven white horses carried the body of the President to the Capitol on the same caisson that once bore the body of President Franklin D. Roosevelt, 18 years ago.

The rain that had poured for hours in Washington Saturday was gone Yesterday dawned bright, cloudless and crisp. The sun shined off the black wooden wheels of the caisson, accompanied by a military honor guard, as it moved slowly to the capitol, to the mournful rhythm of the muffled drums. The procession took just 40 minutes.

As it began, wind spread among the throngs that the man charged with the assassination of President Kennedy had been killed. It added a new nightmarish twist to the horror of the past 48 hours.

In brief, muting ceremonies in the rotunda, pleas for unity and an end to violence were voiced by Sen.

More on MILLIONS—P 1

More on MOURNING—P 4

A climactic newspaper page

law, order, and government. And finally came a period of social reintegration: the government closed ranks around a new chief, and the people overcame their shock, expiated their grief, and returned to old responsibilities in a new situation.

Each of these periods, as we have suggested, made its own special demands for communication. At 12:30 on November 22 the machinery of newsgathering was suddenly jarred out of its routine. The first staccato bulletin from Dallas was followed by a veritable ocean of telephoned news, wire copy, radio, television, and film, until all sides of the monstrous events had been filled in, and the chief actors had moved or been moved elsewhere.

This roused two great waves of communication in response. About one of these we know relatively little, and probably shall continue to know little until the autobiographies and the "now it can be told" articles begin to appear. This was the great and urgent flow of administrative communication, beginning in front of the Texas School Book Depository and the Parkland Hospital, and speedily involving the local and national police agencies, the White House, and Congress as officialdom took the actions required to protect the new President, bring the murderers to justice, and arrange a farewell to the leader and an orderly transition of leadership. The Warren report has told us a little of what went on during that time, and it is possible to piece together other bits. For example, there was for a time a question whether the killing of the President was an isolated act or was part of a conspiracy that might strike other leaders in an effort to take over the government. Unlikely as it may seem, still this was a possibility that had to be recognized and guarded against.

About the other wave of response to the crisis news, however, we know a great deal. This was the great ground swell of grief aroused in the American people and to some extent in people of other countries. There were incredulous questions, as we know; there was anger, but less of it than one might have expected; there was a certain amount of anxiety and withdrawal, and a considerable feeling of need to "talk it over." There was apparently a compulsive need to glue oneself to television and thus vicariously take part in the events and the farewells. About this response of nonofficial America we know a great deal, and what we know is documented by the articles in this volume.

After the news of the crisis and the shocked official and unofficial responses, there was the longer period of reintegration, when society closed ranks again, resolved most of its doubts and questions, worked out its grief, and returned more or less to normal. Much of this, but by no means all, was accomplished by the end of the day when John Kennedy was laid to rest in Arlington. Some of the scars lingered. The enormous sale of the memorial books and pictures, and of the Warren Commission report nearly a year later, testifies to how long the memories and the questions have lingered. . . .

How Was the News Circulated?

There are some remarkable figures in the Nielsen report on television viewing for November 22–25.[2] During these days the average home in the Nielsen sample had a television receiver tuned to the Kennedy report for a total of 31.6 hours. During that time, Nielsen estimates, approximately 166 million Americans in over 51 million homes were tuned at some time to the Kennedy program, and in one-sixth of those homes people had their television on for the big story for more than 11 hours per day! These figures are supported by the NORC survey, for which people estimated that they spent, on the average, 8 hours Friday, 10 Saturday, 8 Sunday, and 8 Monday watching television or listening to the radio.[3]

Undoubtedly no event like this, where so many Americans have concentrated vision and hearing on the same story at the same time for so long a period, has ever occurred before. It is difficult from existing records to estimate the amount of listening to and viewing of the Roosevelt story, but at that time radio and newspapers carried the burden of news diffusion and there was no such concentration on one story as there was in November of 1963.[4] A very rough estimate suggests that for an average family the television viewing of the Kennedy story was greater than the radio listening to the Roosevelt story by a factor of perhaps five to eight times.

One result of the enormous flow of information on the events in Dallas, and the extraordinary public attention to this information, was that there was apparently in this case no hard core of know-nothings. It is a rule of thumb in survey research that 10 to 20 percent of a national sample will probably be unaware of almost any news event. But 99.8 percent of the NORC national sample reported having heard the news by 6 p.m. on Friday—five-and-a-half hours after the President was shot. Furthermore, the news traveled with almost unbelievable swiftness. Two-thirds of the people seem to have heard it within half an hour, even before the President's death was announced. Table 1 gives comparable figures for four of the studies made at the time.

There are no entirely comparable figures from earlier events in this class. A sample of students attending one college at the time of Roosevelt's death showed that 83 percent of them heard the news within 30 minutes and 93 percent within an hour, but these young people were living in close contact in dormitories.[5] Eleven hours elapsed before 90 percent of a university community heard of the death of Senator Taft, and fourteen hours before 90 percent of the eventual knowers in a housing project heard it.[6] Samples of the general public on previous occasions have usually returned much lower figures than those obtained in 1963, although it must be noted that these earlier stories have not had the news value of the Kennedy story. For example, 26 percent of the persons in two samples in different parts of the country reported that they had heard of Eisenhower's stroke within an hour of the time the news became available, 43 percent knew of the first Explorer satellite within an hour, and only 6 percent had heard of the voting of statehood for Alaska within an hour.[7]

How was the news heard? The studies are in general agreement: a little less than half heard by television or radio; a little over half heard from another person, either face to face or by telephone. Table 2 gives comparative figures from the same four studies just reported upon. Here again we have no strictly comparable figures from the past. The telegraphic survey at the time of Roosevelt's death indicated that 47 percent of people had learned the news from radio or the press, 53 percent from interpersonal sources. Of the college students in dormitories studied by Miller, 88 percent reported they had heard the news from another student.

Table 3 gives figures for lesser stories. These figures suggest a pattern as to how fast and by what means a news story reaches the public. The two chief variables would seem to be news value and the time of day when the story breaks. Greenberg was able to show that when a story has narrow interest so that it receives little or no mass media treatment, it is likely that more people who hear about it will hear from other persons.[8] When news value is perceived to be sufficient that the mass media generally carry the story, then, other things being equal, the greater the news value, the more the story is passed on by word of mouth and therefore the higher the proportion of persons who hear it from interpersonal sources. Thus, if the neighbor's child has measles, that news is likely to be heard, if at

TABLE 1

Sample[a]	Proportion of people who heard news within			
	15 min.	30 min.	45 min.	60 min.
National		68%		
Dallas	67%	84	89%	93%
San Jose, Calif.	42	62	81	90
Iowa City, Iowa		70		91

[a]The national sample is reported on by Sheatsley and Feldman; the San Jose sample by Greenberg; and the Iowa City sample by Spitzer and Spitzer. The report on diffusion in Dallas is in R. J. Hill and C. M. Bonjean, "News Diffusion: A Test of the Regularity Hypothesis," *Journalism Quarterly* 41:336–42 (1964).

TABLE 2

	First source of news			
Sample	TV	Radio	Personal	Newspaper
National	47% (TV + radio)		49%	4%
Dallas	26	17%	57	
San Jose	20	28	50	
Iowa City	19	25	55	

all, by word of mouth. If Alaska is voted statehood, that news may be passed around a great deal by word of mouth in Alaska but will be heard mostly by mass media in the rest of the country. Stories like the death of Taft, the launching of the first American satellite, President Eisenhower's stroke, and his decision to seek a second term are of generally higher news value and therefore more likely to be passed on by word of mouth. We find that about three times as many people heard about these stories from interpersonal sources as heard from such sources about the vote on Alaska, but still about four out of five persons heard these news stories first from the mass media. But when we have a story of the highest news value, like the assassination of a president, we find that as many as half the population hear the news from other persons rather than the media.

TABLE 3

	First source of news			
Event[a]	TV	Radio	Newspaper	Personal
Launching of Explorer I, 1958	41%	23%	18%	18%
Eisenhower's stroke, 1957	38	32	12	18
Alaska statehood, 1958	29	27	38	6
Eisenhower decides to seek second term, 1956	14	39	27	20
Taft's death, 1953	15	49	11	26

[a]The source for the first three of these events is Deutschmann and Danielson. The source for the fourth is W. Danielson, "Eisenhower's February Decision: A Study of News Impact," *Journalism Quarterly*, 33:433–41 (1956). The source for the fifth is Larsen and Hill.

Notes

1. For example, L. Bertalanffy, "General Systems Theory: A Critical Review," *Yearbook of the Society for General Systems Research* 7:1–22 (1962) and K. E. Boulding, *The Image* (Ann Arbor, 1956).

2. A. C. Nielsen Co., *TV Responses to the Death of the President* (New York, 1963).
3. However, Nielsen found Monday—the day of the funeral—the day of heaviest television viewing.
4. A telegraphic poll taken after Roosevelt's funeral indicated that about 88 percent of American adults had listened to the radio at *some* time during the three days following the President's death.
5. D. C. Miller, "A Research Note on Mass Communications," *American Sociological Review*, 10:691–94 (1945).
6. O. M. Larsen and R. J. Hill, "Mass Media and Interpersonal Communication in the Diffusion of a News Event," *American Sociological Review*, 19:426–33 (1954).
7. P. Deutschmann and W. Danielson, "Diffusion of Knowledge of the Major News Story," *Journalism Quarterly*, 37:345–55 (1960).
8. Bradley S. Greenberg, "Person-to-Person Communication in the Diffusion of News Events," *Journalism Quarterly* 41:489–94 (1961).

RELIABILITY OF SIX TECHNIQUES FOR CONTENT ANALYSIS OF LOCAL COVERAGE

John W. Windhauser and Guido H. Stempel III

Content analysis is a basic communication research tool. This valuable study compares the results of six techniques used to analyze the content of twelve newspapers as means of establishing their political leanings in local elections. The authors evaluate each technique for the results obtained, comparative usefulness and reliability, and the effort required.

Studies comparing different content analysis techniques have generally found that results are nearly identical. Lasswell *et al*[1] found that varying coding and context units had only a moderate effect on results. Markham and Stempel[2] found that space measurement, symbol coding and headline classification produced highly similar results. Price[3] and Budd[4] suggested systems for weighting content that despite their somewhat different emphases yielded results that were similar to those obtained from space measurement.

The content covered by these studies has varied widely, but the greatest interest has been in ways to code political campaign coverage. The political content in question has been coverage of national or state campaigns. This study explores the question of coding local campaign coverage.

Stories of presidential national or state campaign races may be reported in combined stories, but usually separate stories are written on those races or on each candidate. Those stories are

SOURCE: From *Journalism Quarterly*, 56:148–52 (Spring 1979). Copyright 1979 by Association for Education in Journalism. Reprinted by permission.

available to newspaper editors from staff writers, and from national, state and regional news bureaus, and from wire and syndicated services.

For the most part, local campaigns are reported by a newspaper's own staff or by news releases about the candidate. As a result, available copy for coverage of local campaigns may be more contingent upon an author's style of writing than in a story written about only one campaign race, such as the presidential. But more importantly, the use of different content analysis measures for coding local campaign coverage in newspapers might result in different performance evaluations of the local races studied.

Consequently, the purpose of this investigation was to describe and to compare alternative procedures and to suggest the best uses of those techniques for the description of news and editorial content. Another was to refine some of the existing measures as they could apply for evaluating local press coverage.

Method

Local political news and editorial coverage of the Democratic and Republican parties by 12 Ohio metropolitan dailies[5] was analyzed for a 35-day period from Sept. 28 to Nov. 1, 1971. Every issue of the newspapers was studied.

Six content analysis techniques were compared. They were:

1) *Article:* All news and editorial articles concerning the campaigns of Democratic and Republican candidates were coded and classified as either a Democratic or Republican article.

2) *Space Measurement:* All political campaign stories were measured for length to the nearest one-fourth inch, and then classified as either Democratic or Republican.

3) *Statement:* All statements[6] within a campaign article were coded and classified as either Democratic or Republican.

4) *Issue Single:* Every time an issue[7] was found in a campaign story, it was recorded and classified as either Democratic or Republican, but it was coded only once in any given story for either party.

5) *Issue Multiple:* All issues[8] found in a campaign item were recorded and classified as either Democratic or Republican.

6) *Headline:* All headlines for local campaign items of either Democratic or Republican candidates were recorded and then classified by party and by type.[9]

All campaign content recorded in each of the six content areas also was classified as either favorable or unfavorable.[10] No attempt was made to measure the intensity of the directions. Neutral content and items lacking an association for either party, were excluded from this study.

Local election items concerned only those campaigns for a

municipal office by Democratic or Republican party candidates. Election content excluded from this study included political advertisements and those referring to the election campaigns in general, or to non-campaign activities of the candidates or their parties. Coverage of local races not within the main circulation area of each newspaper studied also was eliminated.

An issue was considered as a reference which was associated with a municipal candidate of either the Democratic or Republican party and could be considered as a matter of public discussion. A list of 11 campaign issues was used.[11]

Results

All six measures correlated highly with each other for the description of combined news and editorial content, for only news content and for only editorial content. But more importantly, the six also correlated highly with each other in describing both news and editorial coverage of political campaigns by local Democratic and Republican candidates. All those correlations were significant beyond the .05 level. Equally important was the significantly high degree of association (W) among the six measures for each of the independent variables studied.

The total number of content units generated by the six different procedures is reported in Table 1. The pattern was the same for all

TABLE 1 Totals of the Six Content Analysis Measures by Newspaper

	Space	Article	Issue Single	Issue Multiple	Headline	Statement
Akron						
Beacon Journal	312	24	65	556	15	599
Canton						
Repository	281	17	49	1040	10	1218
Cincinnati						
Enquirer	873	45	170	2474	13	2796
Cincinnati *Post*						
& Times Star	1313	102	302	3598	68	3994
Cleveland						
Plain Dealer	1115	88	262	2043	61	2432
Cleveland *Press*	1136	99	305	2936	62	3234
Columbus						
Citizen-Journal	306	15	55	982	6	1066
Columbus *Dispatch*	1885	151	639	5605	102	6473
Dayton						
Journal Herald	336	18	69	856	9	1055
Dayton *Daily News*	339	19	65	797	8	1155
Toledo *Blade*	772	51	225	2454	35	2952
Youngstown						
Vindicator	527	67	177	1061	56	1168

papers, with the Statement coding procedure producing the most units and the Headline classification the least. Both the Issue Single and the Issue Multiple measures had nearly identical distribution subject patterns among the newspapers in the sample.

The rank-order correlations in Table 2 indicate that the six measures resembled each other for obtaining news content distributions in the individual papers. Highest agreement was between the Article measure and Space (+.97), followed by the Issue Single and Space (+.965). The lowest rank-order correlations were between the Statement and Headline measures (+.685), and between the Issue Multiple and Headline measures (+.692). The uniformly high positive relationships between Space and the other measures implied that the Space measurement provided nearly the same political content information. Other evidence of similarity among the six variables studied was shown by a significantly high Kendall's Coefficient of Concordance ($W = +.88$, $x^2 = 58.1$, $p < .001$). Similar results were obtained for editorials only, and for news and editorials combined.

When we took directional coding into account, we found slightly lower, but still substantial and statistically significant correlations, as shown in Table 3. The basis for these correlations was the percentage of Democratic content with neutral content excluded.

As might be expected, the highest correlations were between Issue Multiple and Statement (+.972), Issue Single and Statement (+.938), and Issue Single and Issue Multiple (+.91). The lowest was between Space and Issue Multiple (+.618). As was the case with the measures of total content, highly similar results were obtained for editorial content, and news and editorial combined. The correlations for these were in fact somewhat higher than those for news content alone. That probably reflects the stylistic character of editorials in that they tend to be one-sided. Any measure will pick up the direction rather clearly.

TABLE 2 Rank-Order Correlations of All News Content Units in Each Newspaper by the Six Content Analysis Procedures

	Space	Article	Issue Single	Issue Multiple	Headline	Statement
Space	—	—	—	—	—	—
Article	.970[c]	—	—	—	—	—
Issue Single	.965[c]	.949[c]	—	—	—	—
Issue Multiple	.888[c]	.792[b]	.846[c]	—	—	—
Headline	.899[c]	.921[c]	.951[c]	.692[a]	—	—
Statement	.860[c]	.753[b]	.808[b]	.916[c]	.685[a]	—

[a] $p < .02$
[b] $p < .01$
[c] $p < .001$

TABLE 3 Rank-Order Correlations of All Democratic Percentage Scores of News Content Units in Each Newspaper by the Six Content Analysis Procedures

	Space	Article	Issue Single	Issue Multiple	Headline	Statement
Space	—	—	—	—	—	—
Article	.760^c	—	—	—	—	—
Issue Single	.778^c	.833^d	—	—	—	—
Issue Multiple	.618^a	.778^c	.910^d	—	—	—
Headline	.799^c	.757^c	.674^b	.694^b	—	—
Statement	.660^b	.819^c	.938^d	.972^d	.708^c	—

^{a}p<.05
^{b}p<.02
^{c}p<.01
^{d}p<.001

Discussion and Conclusions

All six measures in this investigation had highly significant correlations with each other regardless of the type or slant of the content. But more importantly, all six measures provided similar results for differences in political content with high degrees of predictability.

Of the six, the Statement and the Issue Multiple procedures were the most time consuming. Each statement and issue for the appropriate categories took from one to five minutes to be analyzed and recorded because these items required a more careful and detailed reading of the content. When seeking coverage patterns as to daily frequencies and trends during local election campaigns among and between candidates by political party and by political office, these two measures could be used together. Both also could be applied for all variations and types of content. The time involved to code the information, however, makes both measures impractical when seeking only coverage patterns, including directional, that could be gathered by a simpler method.

Besides the Issue Multiple measure for political propaganda issues in news and editorial patterns, a quicker method is by the Issue Single method. It was the quicker of the two issue procedures and provided similar information, including distributions of issues in various subject areas.

An even quicker way of coding the content was the Headline technique, but it was the least desirable for coding either news or editorial content by party affiliation. The measure had high associations with the other five procedures for overall, for combined news, and for combined editorial content, but when the content was sorted by political party those associations were much lower.

One explanation for those low associations was the low number of headlines having a direction for either political party. Of the 696 articles published, only 64% had headlines with a reference for either party, and for only editorial content only 43% of the editorial stories had a headline for either the Democrats or the Republicans. Part of this again reflected the large number of candidates—202 candidates in eight municipal election races seeking a local political office—and the way that local campaign stories were written.

It seemed that in stories, especially editorials, of many candidates, a make-up editor chose a general, neutral headline rather than a specific one for any of the candidates or for either party mentioned in the article. Other studies evaluating content analysis procedures used in presidential[12] and in other political campaigns,[13] along with some unpublished measurement results of all races in a state,[14] suggest that this may be unique to local races. Results of these studies showed that the headline method correlated highly with the other content analysis techniques studied.

For determining only party differences in local campaigns, either the Article or the Space measure could be used. Both can be easily and quickly applied to determine both the volume and the slant of both news and editorial content for the Democratic and Republican parties. More importantly, they both had high degrees of predictability with each of the other four measures. The Space procedure is the best-known, commonly-used, basic method, and it includes every other type and kind of content in an article. The Space measure should be used, rather than the Article one, because it shows the emphasis in terms of length for a story. That emphasis usually reflects both the headline size and content. After the Headline measure, the Space and Article techniques are the fastest ones to use in coding data, followed by the Issue Single, the Statement, and the Issue Multiple measures.

Overall, this study suggests that the Space measurement technique is the best measure for evaluating party coverage of local election campaigns, and that the Space measure, when used with the Issue Single and Headline measures along with subject categories, will provide a more complete description of coverage patterns. A person might want to use other methods, such as the Statement or the Issue Multiple measure, only because of the selected information they yield. In the final analysis, this investigation provides evidence that the simpler method of Space measurement is the quickest and easiest technique for significant results.

Notes

1. Harold D. Lasswell and Associates, "The Politically Significant Content of the Press: Coding Procedures," *Journalism Quarterly*, 19:12–23 (March 1942); A. Geller, D. Kaplan, and Lasswell, "An Experimental

Comparison of Four Ways of Coding Editorial Content," *Journalism Quarterly*, 19:362–70 (December 1942).

2. James W. Markham and Guido H. Stempel III, "Analysis of Techniques in Measuring Press Performance," *Journalism Quarterly*, 34:187–90 (Spring 1957).

3. Granville Price, "A Method for Analyzing Newspaper Campaign Coverage," *Journalism Quarterly*, 31:447–58 (Fall 1954).

4. Richard W. Budd, "Attention Score: A Device for Measuring News Play," *Journalism Quarterly*, 41:259–62 (Spring 1964).

5. The 12 newspapers studied were Akron *Beacon Journal;* Canton *Repository;* Cincinnati *Enquirer;* Cincinnati *Post & Times Star;* Cleveland *Plain Dealer;* Cleveland *Press;* Columbus *Citizen-Journal;* Columbus *Dispatch;* Dayton *Journal Herald;* Dayton *Daily News;* Toledo *Blade;* and Youngstown *Vindicator,* See: *1971 Editor & Publisher International Year Book* (New York; *Editor & Publisher,* 1971).

6. John W. Windhauser, "Reporting of Ohio Municipal Elections by the Ohio Metropolitan Daily Press," *Journalism Quarterly*, 54:552–65 (Fall 1977).

7. Windhauser, "Reporting of Campaign Issues in Ohio Municipal Election Races," *Journalism Quarterly*, 54:332–40 (Summer 1977).

8. *Ibid.*

9. Stempel, "The Prestige Press Covers the 1960 Presidential Campaign," *Journalism Quarterly*, 38:157–63 (Spring 1961); Stempel, "The Prestige Press in Two Presidential Elections," *Journalism Quarterly*, 42:5–21 (Winter 1965); Stempel, "The Prestige Press Meets the Third-Party Challenge" *Journalism Quarterly*, 46:699–706 (Winter 1969).

10. Windhauser, "Reporting of Ohio Municipal Elections by the Ohio Metropolitan Daily Press," pp. 556–57.

11. Windhauser, "Reporting of Campaign Issues in Ohio Municipal Election Races," pp. 333–34.

12. See: Notes 1, 2 and 3.

13. Lasswell, op. cit.

14. Windhauser, "Metropolitan Press Coverage of the General Election Campaigns in Ohio," unpublished paper prepared as a research project for Dr. Guido H. Stempel III, Ohio University, 1973.

COGNITIVE AND EMOTIONAL CHARACTERISTICS OF THE FORMAT OF AMERICAN TELEVISION
Jerome L. Singer and Dorothy G. Singer

These two Yale University television research specialists undertake the difficult task of correlating younger children's behavior with their television-watching habits. Surprisingly, the pace of a program may be one of its most influential factors. Also, educating children to the nature of the medium may be very productive, according to these findings.

SOURCE: Dr. Jerome L. Singer and Dr. Dorothy G. Singer, Codirectors of the Yale University Family Television Research and Consultation Center, based upon a paper presented at the Tenth Broadcasting Symposium, University of Manchester, England, February 1979. Copyright 1979 by J.L. and D.G. Singer. Reprinted with permission.

The Special Appeal of the Television Medium

We believe television has introduced something into the American home that has never existed before in human history. The picture box with its moving and dancing forms, its music and its liveliness far surpasses in immediacy the appeal of any other communication medium.

We can gain some perspective on understanding the impact of television if we remember that just a little over a century ago the monthly appearance of a new chapter of a book by Dickens was a matter of intense excitement in homes all over Great Britain. For a rising middle-class and even for some increasingly literate working class groups this regular availability of entertaining and informative material appearing more or less simultaneously around the nation was novel and thrilling. As a matter of fact, lacking any competition from other popular media, Dickens was the closest thing in those days to a rock star today.

But now consider the greater immediacy of the television set. Reading is after all more demanding and somewhat more difficult. Television gives you the material right at once, all of a piece. A careful analysis of what we call the characteristics of the medium suggests that its rapid movements make it almost impossible to resist. As human beings we are "wired up" to respond to novel movements in the environment even from earliest infancy. This so-called "orienting reflex" is of course an important adaptive development from evolution but it makes us especially susceptible to the peculiar qualities of television. Whenever there is a TV set in a

THE FAMILY CIRCUS   by Bil Keane

"I hope we're not votin' for HIM. He pre-empted our cartoons!"

THE FAMILY CIRCUS®   By Bil Keane

"Between the dark and daylight,
When the night is beginning to lower,
Comes a pause in the day's occupation
That is known as the children's hour."

room it is difficult for a viewer to restrain from staring at the moving objects no matter how dull the program may be. In our occasional visits to the offices of television executives they usually have television sets which are continuously turned on. It is quite difficult to carry out an effective conversation under such conditions since one's eyes keep straying to the moving figures.

This tremendous attractive power of a little box that sits in the home has increasingly been relied upon by American parents as the means of keeping the children in place and relatively quiet. In some recent research we carried out at Yale University we were interested in obtaining indications of how children become initiated to the television set. We thought it would be a good idea to start with three and four year olds. To our dismay we found after following these children for a year that the three year olds were already long-term initiates to the medium. Most of them were watching four or five hours a day on the average in the winter and, taking into account seasonal variation and opportunities for outdoor play, our sample of 140 preschool children averaged over three hours a day through the year of television watching. Indeed a sizable minority of our children were watching as much as 50 hours a week. These, by the way, were middle-class children of fairly well-educated parents. There are indications that children from less-well-educated or working class homes watch even more extensively. A current study we are carrying out with 200 children from such lower socioeconomic status families seems to bear out this indication.[1]

Thus we are finding that in a certain sense television is a member of the family. Children grow up from earliest ages watching these moving figures. Clearly they may not understand very much of what is going on but they cannot resist the pull of the changing patterns of stimulation.

American television has a special property that is not found in many other countries of the world. It is paced with a rapidity because of assumptions of the producers and the demands of commercial interruptions that pile new information on top of new information. Even a program like "Sesame Street," developed for public television with the intention of stimulating early cognitive development and particularly aimed at the masses of children who might be receiving much less encouragement to recognize letters and numbers at early ages, built its format around the rapid pace of commercial television. As a matter of fact, one of the major methods employed by the psychologists developing "Sesame Street" was to use a competing set of flashing lights and slides to see if their program with its rapid changes of sequence could hold the child's attention better than a competing stimulus resource.

American television producers often seem to behave as if the viewer will switch the dial to another channel if there is not some novel sequence introduced within every two or three minutes. Perhaps there is "in-house" research that supports this notion although we must confess that we are not aware of extensive scientific evidence for this notion. Certainly in our observations of children watching television it is clear that their attention wanders from the set when material is presented more slowly but it does not preclude their obtaining information even when they have looked away. As a matter of fact this raises an extremely important question that needs to be studied much more extensively. To what extent is the very emphasis placed upon piling new material upon new material preventing individuals from processing what they have seen in a way that will allow them to grasp relationships, to shift the material from what we call the short-term to the long-term memory system and increase their chances of really remembering and comprehending what they have seen? There is a real danger that the very rapidity of presentation may create a kind of "mindless" watching. At the end of the program there may be little genuine comprehension of what has been watched, indeed often scarcely any memory.

In the research we have carried out we have watched children watching "Sesame Street" and compared their response to that program with that of a much more slowly-paced show, "Mr. Rogers' Neighborhood."[2] We found that children remembered quite as much of Mr. Rogers as "Sesame Street" even though their attention wandered much more from the screen. What was characteristic of Mr. Rogers was his quiet repetition of words, his speaking directly to the child and his encouraging the child to pause and think. And indeed that's what the children did. Only our brightest and most mature children seemed to do well with "Sesame Street." The less imaginative, the less intellectually-gifted children seem to profit more from the "The Mr. Rogers' Neighborhood " show. If a program has a didactic purpose embedded in an entertaining format it seems important that it avoid extremely rapid pacing. We have all kinds of psychological research to suggest that new material piled upon new material leads to difficulties in memory. A good deal of the way human beings function is to replay what they experience mentally and replay it again in the form of fantasies or elaborations of the experience. Extremely rapid paced television prevents such activities at the same time as it holds the viewer's eyes on the screen.

Some Research Approaches to Early Television Watching in Children

We would like to describe briefly some of the research methods we have been employing in trying to study the effects of television in relation to the early childhood development of American preschoolers. Our methods involve watching the children at play in the nursery schools. Pairs of observers who have been carefully trained to record precisely what the children do and say, watch a child for ten minutes at a time on two occasions. Then a few months later they watch the child again on two occasions and so on for over a year. These carefully written protocols are then rated for variables such as imaginativeness of the children's play, indications of positive emotionality, the degree to which the children concentrate during their play on particular tasks, the evidence of overt aggression, that is, attacks on other children or property, the degree of cooperation the children show with each other or with the adults at the school and so on. During the same period that the children are being observed in the nursery school parents at home are keeping daily records following forms that we have provided them of what the children were watching at home for a two week period. We repeat this process every few months so that by the end of a year we have samples of the TV-viewing patterns that children have shown for two weeks at a time four different times during the year. We collect additional evidence such as the children's intelligence, their imaginative play at home and so on. We have also gone into the homes of selected children and interviewed the parents in detail about the family's daily routines, evidence of the difficulties or problems in the family, indications of violence between family members, etc.

A major finding which has emerged from these studies is that children by the ages of three and four are already habitual TV watchers and are spending a significant portion of their waking time in front of the television. In addition, we find that by and large they are watching programming that comes on during the afternoon and evening and that is primarily designed for adult audiences even though there is the so-called Saturday morning children's ghetto in which four or five hours of cartoons are presented. They watch at that time also but the major portion of their watching is in the afternoons and evenings.[3]

Our data based on tracking the children for over a year, which after all is a major portion of the life of the three or four year old, suggests that there is a statistically reliable correlation between heavy television viewing and overt aggressive behavior by the children displayed in the nursery school. In addition it is also clear that children who watch the so-called action-adventure or detective shows are especially prone to being aggressive in the nursery school but there are also indications especially for girls that those who watch highly pressured situation comedies in which there is much loud shouting and a good deal of "sight gags" are also likely to show aggressive behavior. In addition, we found a relationship between the watching of game shows, those embarrassing programs in which the winners leap up and down screaming hysterically, and those children who show a lot of aggression in the nursery school. By contrast those children who watch a good deal of a slower-paced carefully developed program like "Mr. Rogers' Neighborhood" are much less likely to be overtly aggressive.[4]

Of course it could be argued that we are dealing here with selective viewing patterns. We have tried by various statistical methods to eliminate alternative explanations. In general, we have been led to conclude that our findings of the association between aggressive behavior and TV watching in such young children cannot be explained simply by preferences in viewing of the already aggressive children nor by the fact that these children come from homes that are already characterized by violence. Actually our high television viewing, high aggressive children come from conventional homes in which the family lifestyle is built around a great deal of television watching as a major form of recreation. People in these families watch even during mealtime and their only outside recreation is an occasional visit to the movies or supermarket taking the children along. Families in which there is a considerable laxity of control of the TV set but where there is at least some emphasis on the children watching public television programming and where there also is some parental input through storytelling and reading to the children at night tend to be significantly less aggressive despite the high viewing patterns.

In general we also find indications that imaginativeness as stimulated by parental reading and interaction with the child tends to be somewhat negatively associated with the likelihood of aggression in the children and also with the emergence of some of the more deleterious effects of the television situation. As a matter of fact those children who have developed imaginery playmates at home are often less drawn to the TV set and are also prone to imitation or arousal by the violence and hyperactivity presented on the screen.[5]

Unfortunately our data suggest that women's liberation, which has now brought to the screen increasing examples of aggressive women in shows like "Police Woman," "Charlie's Angels," "Bionic Woman," and "Wonder Woman," has led to girls becoming more physically aggressive in school.[6]

Our research suggests that the children exposed to a program like Mr. Rogers which values imagination, encourages sharing, and avoids support for aggressive behavior actually behave more cooperatively after just two weeks of watching the program.[7] They also increase in their spontaneous imaginative play and in general seem to be happier and nicer children. The tragedy its seems to us is that we have so little of such programming available for children. We personally would be willing to allow stations to continue their advertising to children (subject under scrutiny now by various U.S. government agencies) if they would plough some of their vast profits back into a higher quality of thoughtful programming for children.

It is apparent that children can increase their capacities for understanding things about the world, for learning how to share and cooperate, and for developing a more private imagination through appropriate programming. We think here lies an important challenge for producers in the future.

One of the consequences of our experience in studying behavior of very young children with respect to the television set has been to lead us to look at other possibilities of the medium and also ways in which one might be able to shift children from being relatively passive consumers of television fare towards becoming more active and discriminating in their response to the medium. We have been in various research studies exploring ways in which parents and teachers can use material from television to stimulate greater learning by the children, to encourage them to pay attention to concepts that they need to acquire, to help them understand new vocabulary and in general to encourage them to approach the set as a way in which one can learn things as well as simply sit back passively and stare with glazed eyes. We have special lesson plans being taught by nursery school teachers that include snippets from television to exemplify points that teachers are making about sharing, cooperation, concepts such as large and small, up and down, new words that can be introduced, etc. It remains to be seen how effective these will be but it is already clear that the children value this opportunity to see the television in a somewhat different perspective.[8]

In addition we have attempted to bridge the great gap between the television medium and the elementary school system. In the past American teachers have tried to act as if television simply doesn't exist. This flies in the face of its obviously great attraction to the children. We have developed lesson plans for third, fourth, and fifth grade children (ages eight, nine, and ten) to be taught by classroom teachers.[9] These include discussions of the nature of the television medium, the various genres of television from documentary through fiction and fairytale, the ways in which special effects such as disappearances are produced, the differences between reality and fantasy as represented on the screen, the nature of commercials and the intention of commercial messages, the nature of violent material on television and its limitations, the various cultural stereotypes fostered by the medium about women or racial groups, etc. As part of this effort we have also produced brief segments of television that can be shown in the classroom to exemplify some of the points made in the teacher's lesson. Associated with these lesson plans are written assignments for the children and reading assignments so that we are attempting to foster growth of reading and writing through the use of the inevitable excitement produced in the children about material from television. The evidence from our statistical evaluations of the effectiveness of these lessons suggests that children do indeed learn the material and they have then distinct advantages over comparable control children who have not been exposed to this training.

Third graders who viewed a specific program and then had an opportunity for discussion in the classroom and who were pre- and post-tested on friendship patterns and moral reasoning questions made significant gains on specific items of the tests compared to children who viewed the programs without the subsequent classroom discussion, or to children who watched neutral films. These children were able to increase their understanding of why they chose particular friends and were able to decrease their use of concrete reciprocity or the notion to only help those who help you. The fifth graders who watched programs and had discussion time also made significant gains in their willingness to accept parents interacting with children of the opposite sex, and to accept more positive views of parent—child interaction in general. The group of children who watched the programs with no discussion or who watched neutral films did not make such gains. These changes in attitude persisted when we again tested the children four months later.

Our work, too, with high school students has demonstrated the importance of discussion as an adjunct to TV viewing. We found that 13, 14, 15 year olds who watched six special programs designed for this age group, and who discussed the content after each program with two trained leaders, made significant gains in their degree of communication with their parents, became more selective in their viewing habits, and increased their homework time. These young people were able to discuss their feelings concerning death, prejudice, stealing, friendship as a result of watching programs of a serious nature, and given ample time to relate these incidents to their own experiences.

Television thus has the power to influence children and adolescents to develop prosocial patterns of behavior such as sharing, cooperating, taking turns. It has the power to enable children to change their attitudes, to think more deeply about their feelings concerning friends and family, to imitate behavioral patterns and gestures. Fortunately in the last year there has been some reduction of violence on prime time in American television. We hope this continues. Mindless programming such as the hyperactive game shows persists and we fear may still be producing some negative effects. What is clear is that children can benefit from the television medium, they can acquire new concepts, they can be stimulated imaginatively, they can be stimulated to be more socially cooperative and sharing beings. We think there is a real challenge for producers to pay careful attention to developing programming that directly communicates with children, that incorporates constructive elements and that recognizes the tremendously important socialization power of the medium. We believe we owe it to children who are growing up in an environment never before experienced in human society. The moving picture box in every home can become a form of mindless distraction or a rich source of constructive stimulation.

NOTES

1. Singer, J. L., & Singer, D. G. *Television-viewing and imaginative play in preschoolers: A developmental and parent-intervention study.* Unpublished progress report (#4), Yale University, 1979a.
2. Tower, R. B., Singer, D. G., Singer, J. L., & Biggs, A. Differential effects of television programming on preschoolers' cognition, imagination, and social play. *American Journal of Orthopsychiatry*, 1979, 49:265–81.
3. op. cit.[1]
4. Singer, J. L., & Singer, D. G. "Television-viewing, family style and aggressive behavior in preschool children." In M. Green (Ed.) *Violence in the family: Psychiatric, sociological and historical perspectives.* Washington, D. C.: American Association for the Advancement of Science Symposium Series, 1979b.
5. Caldeira, J., Singer, J. L., & Singer, D. G. *Imaginary playmates: Some relationships to preschoolers' spontaneous play, language and television-viewing.* Paper presented at the meeting of the Eastern Psychological Association, Washington, D. C., March 1978.
6. op. cit.[4]
7. Singer, J. L. & Singer, D. G. "Can TV stimulate imaginative play?" *Journal of Communications*, 1976, 26:74–80.
8. op. cit.[1]
9. Singer, D. G., Zuckerman, D. M., & Singer, J. L. "Teaching elementary school children critical television viewing skills: An evaluation." *Journal of Communications*, 1980, 30.

Section 17

EDUCATIONAL GOALS IN JOURNALISM

Schools and departments of journalism began as
training grounds for those entering professional
careers in the media. How they assumed
responsibility for the creation of a discipline in
mass communication theory and research is told
in terms of their early leaders.

JOURNALISM EDUCATION: HOW FOUR PIONEERS INFLUENCED ITS GROWTH

Warren K. Agee

Journalism education is a relatively young academic discipline, but it has grown rapidly. Few, if any, fields have been faced with the simultaneous problems of defining and implementing a coherent policy and of adapting that policy to rapidly changing demands. That both definition and adaptation could proceed at the same time is due to the clarity of vision exemplified by these four extraordinary leaders.

The relatively brief, 75-year history of university journalism and mass communications education in the United States is a record of slow but steady, even remarkable progress. It has been characterized by a gradually increasing acceptance on the part of the academic community and the mass media industries and professions, and by an equally gradual understanding by its own faculties—many of them, at least—of the full dimensions and responsibilities of their educational function.

After a "trial and error" period, during which the first instructors in the main tried only to provide practical training for newspaper work, far-sighted pioneers laid down a blueprint for full development that, perhaps surprisingly, remains virtually as valid today as then.

Ever-changing social and technological conditions have, of course, altered techniques and added such new perspectives as the vastly increased role of research, but essentially the same basic philosophy undergirds journalism and mass communications education, that of emphasizing broad cultural background study as an essential part of professional curricula.

Through these decades a score or more of teachers and administrators have loomed as "giants" in the field, upgrading standards and guiding journalism and mass communications education to the high plateau of instruction, service, and research that marks today's foremost schools. Representative of these leaders are four educators whose contributions may be especially noted. They are Walter Williams, Willard G. Bleyer, Frank Luther Mott, and Ralph D. Casey.

Walter Williams was born in Boonville, Missouri, in 1864. He rose

---

SOURCE: This article was written expressly for this book.

Walter Williams

Willard G. Bleyer

Frank Luther Mott

Ralph D. Casey

from printer's devil in a newspaper in his hometown, through high school and 18 years of newspaper work, to become dean of the first formally organized school of journalism at the University of Missouri in 1908. He served as president of the university during five years prior to his death in 1935.

Professional education for journalism was Williams' abiding interest, but by no means his only one. He worked hard to develop an international point of view among journalists of the world as a force for preserving peace. He also sought a more honest press reflecting an impartial, objective kind of journalism that, as he once said, "will have the public for its client and will accept fee from no lesser source." In describing the ideals toward which journalists should strive, he wrote "The Journalist's Creed," whose principles were incorporated into codes of ethics later adopted by various journalism organizations.

Williams' personal influence, and that of his school, were enormous. The Missouri school's practical approach to journalism education, laced with a strong infusion of liberal arts studies, set the pattern for scores of other schools and departments of journalism headed by Missouri alumni, thus influencing thousands of future journalists and teachers.

"My theory," Williams once said, "has been, and is, that the successful school of journalism should do three things. First, it should afford an opportunity for the pursuit of those subjects every man aspiring to a liberal education should be grounded in; second, it should emphasize special subjects that are of the most value to the journalist—say, an emphasis on the study of politics over the study of geology. And, third, it should instruct in the practical side of newspaper making. Let it teach the student how to write and present in print (and there is the crucial point: *in print*) the principles learned in those other courses."

Willard G. Bleyer's lifetime, influence, and philosophy of journalism education roughly paralleled that of Williams . Bleyer, a Wisconsin native, instituted the first courses in journalism at the University of Wisconsin in 1905 and became, successively, chairman and director of the Course in Journalism and finally director of the School of Journalism from 1927 until his death, also in 1935.

"Daddy" Bleyer, as he was known to students and associates, exercised a great influence not only in his own university but also on the thinking of others charged with educating prospective journalists. He is credited with being the first to emphasize the integration of journalism and the social sciences, and he was among the early leaders who sought to stress the importance of upper-division journalism courses containing values not directly bearing upon technical procedures.

Bleyer was born in Milwaukee in 1873 into a family associated with the press for three generations. Unlike Williams—"the first college president who never went to college"—Bleyer earned three degrees at Wisconsin, capped by the Ph.D. degree in English in 1904, while simultaneously working for newspapers.

Bleyer saw the need to provide journalists with the perspective of history; thus he gradually formulated a program of study closely linked with history and the social sciences. His formula for combining journalism with undergraduate studies in these fields also characterized the Wisconsin curricula for graduate students, many of whom later established similar programs of study elsewhere.

"Daddy" Bleyer headed all the national journalism educational organizations. Among them was the National Council on Education for Journalism, which brought editors and publishers into closer cooperation with the schools and, 20 years after Bleyer's death, evolved into the current Accrediting Council on Education in Journalism and Mass Communications. In setting accreditation standards, the council now "suggests about one-fourth, three-fourths as an equitable ratio between courses in journalism and mass communications, and courses in the arts and sciences." This concept is rooted in the thinking of journalism's educational pioneers.

Bleyer's prolific writing included six journalism texts, the most notable of which was his 1927 volume, *Main Currents in the History of American Journalism*. The first chapter of this book remains unsurpassed in delineating the English forerunners of American journalism.

When Bleyer outlined his views on journalism education in 1930, he concluded that:

> A well-organized four-year course of study in preparation for journalism, in which required and elective courses in history, economics, government and politics, sociology, psychology, science and literature are being pursued at the same time that students are taking courses in journalism, gives purpose and direction to the students' work and shows them what these other studies mean in relation to the life and work of the world. Personally, I should be willing to pit the average journalism graduate against the average liberal arts graduate, not on the basis of his fitness to enter upon a journalistic career, but on the basis of his ability to think straight and to apply what he has learned to present-day social, political, and economic problems. That, after all, is the final test of the value of a college education, and that is the test that I believe the average school of journalism graduate is ready to meet.

The scholarly quality of Bleyer's work is reflected also in the productive life of Frank Luther Mott. After 15 years' service as director of the University of Iowa School of Journalism, Mott occupied the dean's chair at Missouri from 1942 to his retirement in 1951. In addition to his administrative efforts, Mott taught memorable courses in "History and Principles of Journalism" and "The Literature of Journalism" and wrote or edited an exhaustive total of 30 volumes.

Mott was born in Iowa in 1886, the son of a weekly newspaper editor. He attended Simpson College and was coeditor of a weekly before earning an M.A. degree at Columbia University in 1917. He taught English at Simpson College and the University of Iowa, turning to journalism in 1927. Columbia University awarded him a Ph.D. degree in English a year later.

Dean Mott's most masterful accomplishment was a five-volume *History of American Magazines*. He won a Pulitzer Prize for the second and third volumes, and was near completion of the fifth at his death in 1964. His equally well-researched and well-written *American Journalism: A History*, published in 1941 and revised in 1950 and 1962, served as the foremost text in the field for many years.

As is true with Williams and Bleyer, Dean Mott headed numerous journalism organizations and worked prodigiously to improve standards of teaching and practice. He was perhaps most influential, however, in his historical writing, his informed lectures, and his direction of the Iowa and Missouri schools.

In an address to the Press Congress of the World at Columbia, Missouri, in 1959, Mott outlined six broad steps that, he said, "make up a short staircase of reasoning leading to the edifice of education for journalism." In essence, he stated, "It is essential today, and will be even more essential tomorrow, to prepare men and women to inform our peoples fully and honestly in order that they may know about current situations and events and thus be competent to rule our nations and the world. Without a communication system thus formed and thus functioning, we and our children may not look forward to any conceivable future of worldwide peace and welfare."

As journalism and mass communications education moved more closely into an alliance with the social and behavioral sciences, one of the principal exponents of that concept was Ralph D. Casey. Under his direction the journalism program at the University of Minnesota became another prime source of distinguished journalists and teachers after he assumed its leadership in 1930.

Casey, who was born in Aspen, Colorado, in 1890, obtained his A.B. and M.A. degrees at the University of Washington, worked then as a reporter for the Seattle *Post-Intelligencer* and New York *Herald*, and taught at the universities of Montana, Washington, and Oregon before accepting the Minnesota position.

Casey was the first person to include journalism study at the Ph.D. level, which he did as a political science doctoral candidate.

He was a student of Willard G. Bleyer at the University of Wisconsin, where he received his degree in 1929. When the Minnesota journalism department was elevated to the status of a school in 1940, Casey was named director. During his tenure he organized the first research division for the study of mass communications at a school of journalism. Working with other scholars, he wrote and edited several books and bibliographies. His class in "Public Opinion and Propaganda" was a cornerstone of the Minnesota program. He received numerous honors before and after his retirement in 1958. He died in 1977.

Casey exerted strong leadership in journalism accreditation and the development of notable graduate schools, attracting to Minnesota one of the foremost faculties in the nation. He insisted that all teachers, even crafts people drawn from the mass media, should undertake research, either of a qualitative nature or along behavioral, quantitative lines; or at least, he said, they should plow back into their teaching some synthesis of important findings developed from systematic and disciplined communications investigations.

In the best journalism schools, Casey contended, well-prepared faculties will maintain a high level of performance, will conduct and use research on a level equal to that of their colleagues in the behavioral sciences, will attract students of superior intelligence, will establish an organic program of instruction, and will know precisely the goals that they seek to achieve both individually and as a school. Most of all, Casey said, schools must give students "a sense of the worth and dignity of the profession of journalism," adding that, "To make known to students the fundamental significance of the role of the press in our society is the *sine qua non* of any journalism teaching program."

These pioneers—Williams, Bleyer, Mott, and Casey—and other far-sighted leaders of equal stature, all sharing similar philosophies and goals, marked the path and established the standards of today's education in journalism and mass communications.

Williams and Bleyer lived during the early stages of the communications revolution that has transformed, and been transformed by, American life. Mott and Casey saw the beginnings of the impact that television would bring and observed, as well, the structuring of many schools, after World War II, to provide teaching, research, and service in virtually all areas of media activity and in mass communication itself.

The increasing complexities of society and communication systems have since placed even heavier demands upon educators and the communications professions and industries, sharpening the role of research in problem-solving. Even so, the philosophy of integrating practical training with background liberal arts studies, set forth at the beginning of this century, remains a primary ingredient of journalism and mass communication education today.

References

Journalism Quarterly 4,4 (1927); 5,1 (1928); 8,1 (1931); 9,1 (1932); 12,3 (1935); 12,4 (1935); 13,1 (1936); 14,1 (1937); 15,1 (1938); 21,1 (1944); 24,1(1947); 32,1 (1955); 35,2 (1958); 37,4 (1960).

Journalism Educator 32,3 (1977).

Editor & Publisher 68,12 (1935).

Sutton, Albert A., *Education for Journalism in the United States From Its Beginning to 1940.* (Evanston, Ill.: Northwestern University Press, 1945).

Part Six
CRITICISMS AND CHALLENGES

Because the media of mass communication have an intense impact upon the lives and thinking of everyone, inevitably they are the objects of public scrutiny. Media practitioners freely criticize other institutions of our society, especially government, so it is only fair that these critics should be examined to determine how well they exercise the responsibility and power that have been given them.

Unfortunately, too many craftsmen and leaders of the news media are thin-skinned about accepting criticism. They tend to brush it off as the complaints of cranks or cynics. Much of the criticism of their daily operations is indeed ill-informed, failing to recognize that the media are primarily messengers bearing information from other sources—in simplest form, charging a newspaper with incompetence because rain fell after it had published a weather bureau forecast promising sunshine. Nevertheless, there exist significant areas of attitude and performance where the media are vulnerable and open to criticism.

Criticism at times is politically motivated. No more flagrant example of this can be found than the campaign by the Nixon administration to depict the television networks and large Eastern newspapers as biased, indeed evil, because their correspondents and commentators frequently put a bad light on President Nixon's policies and personality. Vice President Spiro Agnew opened the attack with a speech denouncing the networks, in effect accusing them of a conspiracy against the President. This section includes an excerpt from the Agnew speech. Other examinations of television, on a much higher plane, are by Charles Ferris, long the chairman of the Federal Communications Commission, and Benjamin DeMott in "The Trouble With Public Television." Similar scrutiny of newspapers comes from Louis Banks in "Memo to the Press: They Hate You Out There" and from Norman Isaacs in "Values."

Although many media leaders were reluctant to recognize the fact, the Agnew attack attracted a substantial following. As demogoguery often does, it exploited a latent uneasiness among the people. A feeling had grown among Americans that the television networks and the large newspapers, even the smaller ones, were too powerful, self-serving, and out of step with their listeners and readers. A gulf had developed between media and audience without the media operators recognizing that it existed.

Almost until the moment of Nixon's resignation to avoid impeachment, after his misconduct in office had been documented beyond doubt, some Americans were inclined to believe claims by Nixon men that he was the victim of a press "conspiracy." A few still do.

The caustic bitterness of the Watergate confrontation contributed to a distrust of the news media that is still extensive today. In their fight to break down the self-protective secrecy that often surrounds news sources, especially in government, news people see themselves acting as the eyes and ears of the public. They are shocked to discover that some Americans believe the First Amendment gives the media too much protection, which should be curtailed.

This is the counsel of ignorance, of course. Those who think this way fail to comprehend that the First Amendment was put into the Constitution not to benefit newspaper proprietors but to provide a weapon with which the press can search out and publish the truth for the benefit of the people. Contemporary application of the First Amendment is examined here by Jules Feiffer in "Love/Hate & the First Amendment," by Tom Wicker in "Our All-Too-Timid Press," and by Erwin Knoll in " 'National Security': The Ultimate Threat to the First Amendment."

Recently the media have encountered a formidable new foe in their effort to gather and report the news: the courts. Judges have banned the press from certain proceedings, such as preliminary hearings. They have sent reporters to jail for refusing to disclose their news sources, ordered television stations and networks to submit to the court taped material that their reporters gathered but didn't put on the air, and in other ways sought to curb the reporting power of the press. Protecting the right to report from the chilling effect of excessive judicial zeal is one of the most urgent challenges facing the media in the 1980s. Henry Grunwald, editor in chief of *Time*, discusses the problem in "The Press, the Courts and the Country."

Public discontent with the media is furthered by a frequently heard criticism that the electronic media and newspapers are the tools of Big Business, excessively concerned with making large profits. The phenomenal growth of newspaper chains and the predominance of one-newspaper cities are cited as evidence of this. More alarming are the conglomerate corporations that have taken over cross-media ownership of radio and television stations, book publishers, and magazines, along with cable television systems. They have created a fear that the media are not as free as their spokesmen assert, that hidden masters control the media and "tell us only what they want us to hear."

This conspiracy theory is greatly exaggerated. It is as unrealistic as the opposite romantic notion that newspapers in particular are quasi-public institutions that somehow should go along publishing forever without soiling their hands with the "dirty" business of making a profit. Nevertheless, the growing concentration of media ownership is just cause for deep uneasiness, a worry shared by many thoughtful individuals within media ranks. The problem is examined here by John B. Oakes, former editorial page editor of the New York *Times,* and in articles about the Gannett Company, largest of the newspaper groups, and its head, Allen Neuharth.

In "The Future of the Fourth Estate" Anthony Smith discusses effects of the new technology on the press.

For many years the Western nations have dominated the flow of information throughout the world, including news, business data, and cultural products such as movies and television. The advent of satellite and computer technology and the increasing disparity between rich and poor nations have heightened fears, particularly in the Third World, that the old shackles of political and economic colonialism have been replaced by an even stronger dominance based on control of the flow of information.

Consequently, a growing number of nations, led by Socialist and Third World countries, are seeking to impose a "New World Information Order" that would put governments in control of the flow of information, including news. Increasingly, the developing nations have come to view communications as essential support for their development efforts. Some have placed severe restrictions on the gathering and transmission of news by Western reporters and many have urged the United Nations Educational, Scientific, and Cultural Organization (UNESCO), in which the Third World nations hold majority voting power, to issue a declaration opposed, in many respects, to the Western concept of a free press and the free flow of information.

In their article titled, "Foreign News Flow and the UNESCO Debate," Professors Robert L. Stevenson and Richard R. Cole of the University of North Carolina School of Journalism summarize the essential points of this East–West, North–South controversy, the outcome of which will have a profound effect upon the world's politics and business.

The Third World position has been cogently argued by Mustapha Masmoudi, former Secretary of State for Information in Tunisia. Excerpts from Masmoudi's detailed litany of complaints are provided so that readers may grasp the intensity of the Third World argument. Meanwhile, the number of United States foreign correspondents has declined dramatically in recent years, a fact deplored by one of them, Don Cook, in "Trench Coats for Sale."

Section 18

THE MEDIA, THE COURTS, AND THE PUBLIC

Spiro Agnew's attack on television network news opens this section, followed by discussion of media rights and responsibilities under the First Amendment by Henry Grunwald, Jules Feiffer, Tom Wicker, and Erwin Knoll. Finally, two legal authorities debate the use of television cameras in the courtroom.

SPIRO AGNEW ATTACKS TV NETWORK NEWS

Vice-President Agnew's speech created national controversy. This excerpt gives the essence of his charges and his accusatory style. The underlying assumption throughout is that the press is an adversary of government—exactly the intention of the founders of America, including Jefferson and Hamilton.

Monday night a week ago, President Nixon delivered the most important address of his Administration, one of the most important of our decade. His subject was Vietnam. His hope was to rally the American people to see the conflict through to a lasting and just peace in the Pacific. For 32 minutes, he reasoned with a nation that has suffered almost a third of a million casualties in the longest war in its history.

When the President completed his address—an address, incidentally, that he spent weeks in the preparation of—his words and policies were subjected to instant analysis and querulous criticism. The audience of 70 million Americans gathered to hear the President of the United States was inherited by a small band of network commentators and self-appointed analysts, the majority of whom expressed in one way or another their hostility to what he had to say.

It was obvious that their minds were made up in advance. . . .

The purpose of my remarks tonight is to focus your attention on this little group of men who not only enjoy a right of instant rebuttal to every Presidential address, but, more importantly, wield a free hand in selecting, presenting and interpreting the great issues in our nation.

First, let's define that power. At least 40 million Americans every night, it's estimated, watch the network news. Seven million of them view ABC, the remainder being divided between NBC and CBS. . . .

Now how is this network news determined? A small group of men, numbering perhaps no more than a dozen anchormen, commentators and executive producers, settle upon the 20 minutes or so of film and commentary that's to reach the public. This

---

SOURCE: Speech delivered to the Mid-West Republican Committee, Des Moines, Iowa, November 13, 1969.

selection is made from the 90 to 180 minutes that may be available. Their powers of choice are broad.

They decide what 40 to 50 million Americans will learn of the day's events in the nation and in the world.

We cannot measure this power and influence by the traditional democratic standards, for these men can create national issues overnight.

They can make or break by their coverage and commentary a moratorium on the war.

They can elevate men from obscurity to national prominence within a week. They can reward some politicians with national exposure and ignore others.

For millions of Americans the network reporter who covers a continuing issue—like the ABM or civil rights—becomes, in effect, the presiding judge in a national trial by jury. . . .

Now what do Americans know of the men who wield this power? Of the men who produce and direct the network news, the nation knows practically nothing. Of the commentators, most Americans know little other than that they reflect an urbane and assured presence seemingly well-informed on every important matter.

We do know that to a man these commentators and producers live and work in the geographical and intellectual confines of Washington, D.C., or New York City, the latter of which James Reston terms the most unrepresentative community in the entire United States.

Both communities bask in their own provincialism, their own parochialism.

We can deduce that these men read the same newspapers. They draw their political and social views from the same sources. Worse, they talk constantly to one another, thereby providing artificial reinforcement to their shared viewpoints. . . .

The American people would rightly not tolerate this concentration of power in Government.

Is it not fair and relevant to question its concentration in the hands of a tiny, enclosed fraternity of privileged men elected by no one and enjoying a monopoly sanctioned and licensed by Government?

The views of the majority of this fraternity do not—and I repeat, not—represent the views of America. . . .

Now I want to make myself perfectly clear. I'm not asking for Government censorship or any other kind of censorship. I'm asking whether a form of censorship already exists when the news that 40 million Americans receive each night is determined by a handful of men responsible only to their corporate employers and is filtered through a handful of commentators who admit to their own set of biases. . . .

Tonight I've raised questions. I've made no attempt to suggest the answers. The answers must come from the media men. They are challenged to turn their critical powers on themselves, to direct their energy, their talent and their conviction toward improving the quality and objectivity of news presentation.

They are challenged to structure their own civic ethics to relate to the great responsibilities they hold.

And the people of America are challenged, too, challenged to press for responsible news presentations. The people can let the networks know that they want their news straight and objective. . . .

The great networks have dominated America's airwaves for decades. The people are entitled to a full accounting of their stewardship.

THE PRESS, THE COURTS, AND THE COUNTRY
Henry Grunwald

Grunwald, editor in chief of *Time*, examined this complex relationship in an address to the annual conference of the Second Judicial Circuit in Buck Hill Falls, Pennsylvania in 1979. This version of his speech was published later as a *Time* essay.

Are courts going too far in what is beginning to look like a campaign to curb the press?

Most journalists would not yet agree with Allen Neuharth, head of the Gannett newspaper chain, that in this respect, the Supreme Court has moved "above the law." But the trend is clear and alarming, from the denial of confidentiality of sources to surprise newsroom searches. . . . Not only the press is affected. The search decision can send the cops into psychiatrists' or lawyers' offices as well. The latest court ruling that pretrial hearings and possibly trials themselves may be closed to press and public is reprehensible, among other reasons because it could lead to collusion—behind closed courtroom doors—between judges, prosecutors and defendants. This ruling more than any other shows that the conflict is not just between the courts and the press but the courts and society.

Tension between power centers is useful in America. But the judiciary ought to reflect about what it is doing. In important respects, judges really are in the same boat as journalists, and ultimately in the service of the same ideals. People who cheer the courts' moves against the press are quite ready to condemn the

---

SOURCE: From *Time*, July 16, 1979, pp. 74–75. Reprinted by permission of *Time*, The Weekly Newsmagazine; Copyright Time Inc. 1979.

courts in other areas. If the press is seen as having too much power, so are the courts, and then some.

The monstrous regiment of lawyers has rarely been more resented. In a recent Harris poll about public confidence in various institutions, law firms ranked eleventh on a list of 13. Even when lawyers are miraculously transformed into judges, they do not regain total trust. In the same poll, the Supreme Court came in sixth, while TV news (somewhat surprisingly) ranked first and the press in general ranked fifth, thus nosing ahead of the august court. . . .

On the frontier, tarring and feathering editors was a popular pastime. Symbolically, of course, it still is. The press, its reach almost infinitely expanded by electronics, has come a long way since those days. Yet, the public, despite its daily if not hourly intimacy with the press, does not really understand it very well. That lack of understanding is reflected in the courts, although it goes far beyond matters of the law. In part, this is inevitable because the press is indeed a peculiar institution, full of paradoxes. To understand and judge—even to criticize it for the right reasons—a few broad points might be kept in mind.

▶The American press is better than ever. Yellow journalism persists, but largely on the fringes of the press and is pale compared with what it was in the heyday of William Randolph Hearst. One episode: Drumming the U.S. to war against Spain, Hearst sent Artist Frederic Remington to Cuba. When Remington cabled that all was quiet, with no war in sight, Hearst fired back: "You supply the pictures, I'll supply the war." Arrogance of such magnitude is unheard of today. The sensationalist Joseph Pulitzer declared that accuracy is to a newspaper what virtue is to a lady, but the fact is that journalism today takes that maxim far more seriously than did the papers of Pulitzer's time.

True, the press still features triviality, gossip, scandal. It always will. Charles Anderson Dana of the New York *Sun*—like Hearst and

Pulitzer quite a phrasemaker and an exemplar of the era—declared that the *Sun* could not be blamed for reporting what God had permitted to happen. That was only partly a copout. While the press should not pander to base or grisly appetites, or merely "give the people what they want," neither should it be expected to change human nature (if that concept is still admissible). America's mainstream publications today, for all their faults, are far more broad-gauged, responsible, accurate—and self-critical—than ever before, or than any other in the world.

▶The press should not be expected to be what it is not. Literary critics chide journalism for not being literary enough, historians for lacking historical accuracy, lawyers for not marshaling facts by the rules of evidence. But journalism is not literature, not history, not law. Most of the time it cannot possibly offer anything but a fleeting record of events compiled in great haste. Many news stories are, at bottom, hypotheses about what happened. Science, of course, works by hypotheses, discarding them when errors are discovered, and it does so, on the whole, without blame, even when a mistake costs lives. The press, which lays no claim to scientific accuracy, is not easily forgiven its errors. Admittedly, the press often rushes into print with insufficient information, responding to (and perhaps creating) an occasionally mindless hunger for news. A utopian society might demand that the press print nothing until it had reached absolute certainty. But such a society, while waiting for some ultimate version of events, would be so rife with rumor, alarm and lies that the errors of our journalism would by comparison seem models of truth.

The press was not invented by and for journalists. It is a result of mass literacy and the instrument of a political system in which, for better or worse, all literate people—indeed even the illiterate—are considered qualified voters. So the hunger for news is a hunger for power—not power by journalists, as is often suggested, but by the public. The press is a child of the Enlightenment and those who inveigh against it also attack, sometimes unconsciously, the values of the Enlightenment. It is no accident that the press grew as the concept of revealed truth declined. The press as we know it could not (does not) exist in societies that in all things accept the voice of authority.

▶Profits should not make the press suspect. Many people (including journalists and judges) are troubled by the fact that the press performs a public service and yet makes profits. But this is nothing the press should apologize for; on the contrary. The press as a business is the only alternative to a subsidized press, which by every conceivable measurement would be worse. True, there are serious risks in the commercial aspects of the press, but these are relatively minor compared with the situation a few generations ago, when weak and insecure newspapers all too easily succumbed to the checkbooks of political or business pressure groups. Henry Luce argued that the press was not really taken seriously and, in a sense, did not really become free until it became a big business. Enterprising journalism is expensive. (It costs more than $100,000 to keep a correspondent in Washington, D.C., for one year. Paper, printing and distribution cost *Time* magazine $120 million. The newspaper industry spends $3 billion each year on newsprint alone.)

Questions about profits lead to questions about size. The spread of newspaper chains and one-newspaper cities is, to be sure, a cause for concern. Yet smallness as such is not necessarily good: it guarantees neither quality nor independence. Bigness as such is not necessarily bad: in most cases, large resources improve a publication. Nor does the size of some enterprises keep new publications out. The number of small publications is growing and their diversity is dazzling. The really remarkable phenomenon of recent years is not so much the growth of communications companies, but the spread of highly organized special interest groups that have had considerable success in making themselves heard and seen.

▶The press is not too powerful; if anything, it is not powerful enough. Those who want to curb the press point out that it is no longer the "fragile" thing it was when the First Amendment was written. But neither is the Government. When Franklin Roosevelt took office, the federal budget, in 1979 dollars, amounted to about $38 billion. In fiscal 1980, it will be around $530 billion. When Roosevelt took office, the federal bureaucracy consisted of 600,000 people. Today it adds up to 2,858,344. Such figures can only suggest that the growth of Government has been far more dramatic than the growth of the press that attempts to cover·and monitor it. With innumerable Xerox machines and printing presses, through tons of publications, reports, tapes and films, countless Government flacks churn out enough information, and disinformation, to overwhelm an–army of reporters. To a lesser extent this is true of other large institutions: corporations, unions, foundations, all of which try to manage the news and use the press for their ends.

The fact that the press is not accountable to any other power except the marketplace clearly agitates a lot of people. This often takes the form of the hostile question to editors: Who elected you anyway? But some institutions in our society simply should *not* be subject to the usual political processes. As for the courts, whatever their intentions may be, they are not the place to cure the undeniable failings of the press.

Do recent court actions really make much of a difference to

journalists in practice? Many judges doubt it, but let them try an experiment and take on a tough reporting assignment. Let them try to get complicated and controversial information from resisting sources and amid conflicting claims—without the judicial power to subpoena documents or witnesses—and have to testify under the disciplines of contempt or perjury. Let these judges then see how far they will get with their assignment if they are unable to promise an informant, who may be risking his job, assured confidentiality, or if they are hit by subpoenas, now said to be running at the rate of 100-plus a year, many of these mere "fishing expeditions."

To say this is not to claim an absolute privilege for journalists. Newsmen should not ask the same standing that a lawyer or doctor has in dealing with clients or patients; lawyers and doctors after all are licensed, which is precisely what journalists will not and must not be. Obviously, the American journalist enjoys unusual latitude and he must, therefore, bear unusual responsibility. He must expect a certain rough-and-tumble in his trade, and not wrap himself in the Constitution at every setback. By no means were all recent court rulings unmitigated disasters. The court in effect allows the press to print anything it can get its hands on. When the Supreme Court held that a newsman's state of mind and his preparations for a story were legitimate subjects of inquiry, this evoked visions of thought police; and yet it was only a consequence of an earlier pro-press ruling that a public figure, in order to be able to sue for libel, must prove "actual" malice and gross neglect on the part of the journalist. Most newsmen do not demand confidentiality of sources automatically, but only when naming sources or delivering notes is not strictly necessary to meet the specific needs of a defendant. (Many judges in fact agree with this view.)

No serious journalist questions the need to balance the rights of a free press against other rights in society, including the rights of defendants. But the degree of balance is what counts, and the balance is tilting against the press. As a result, a backlash against the courts has begun in Congress, with the introduction of many bills designed to shore up the rights of journalists. That is a mixed blessing. Spelling out rights that were assumed to exist under the general protection of the First Amendment may very well result in limiting those rights. Most of the press would much rather not run to Congress for protection against the courts. Yet if the courts continue on their present course, journalists will have little alternative.

Perhaps it is not too late for judges to restore some balance and to discover that they do share with the press certain common interests, if not a common fate. As New York's Irving R. Kaufman, Chief Judge of the Second Judicial Circuit, has written: "Different as the press and the federal judiciary are, they share one distinctive characteristic: both sustain democracy, not because they are responsible to any branch of Government, but precisely because, except in the most extreme cases, they are not accountable at all. Thus they are able to check the irresponsibility of those in power . . ."

Ultimately the question of freedom of the press comes down to the question of freedom, period. Freedom exists both for good and bad, for the responsible and the irresponsible. Freedom only for the good, only for the right, would not be freedom at all. Freedom that hurts no one is impossible and a free press will sometimes hurt. That fact must be balanced against the larger fact that this freedom does not exist for the benefit of the press but for the benefit of all. In the majority of countries, judges are in effect only executioners and journalists are only Government press agents. This reality should be kept in mind as the courts deal with the American press and its rare and fragile rights.

LOVE/HATE & THE FIRST AMENDMENT
Jules Feiffer
Feiffer is known for both his cartooning and his writing about contemporary mores. His speech to the American Civil Liberties Union National Convocation on Free Speech was adapted later as this article in *The Nation.*

Something must be seriously wrong with the First Amendment with so many newspapers suddenly in favor of it. The pathetic truth about the love/hate relationship Americans have with the Bill of Rights is that we tend to support it only when it supports us, when it favors my interest group against your interest group, or his, or hers. Most of us, and polls again and again show this to be so, are in basic disagreement with the first ten amendments to the Constitution except when it comes to special pleading.

I have long wondered what stand this nation's press would have taken on the Pentagon papers if Daniel Ellsberg had seen fit to release them not to the New York *Times* but to the *National Guardian* or even *The Village Voice.*

The Communists didn't see much point to civil liberties until the late 1940s, when a sizable segment of the ACLU stopped seeing much point to them. A sizable segment of the ACLU membership today sees no point in civil liberties for Nazis; so 20 percent have

SOURCE: From *The Nation*, July 1, 1978, pp. 19–20. Copyright 1978 by Jules Feiffer. Reprinted by permission.

chosen to quit, stirring up the same argument used against the far Left in the '40s and '50s. "How can you defend the freedom of low lifes who, if they gained power, would take your own freedom away?" The unstated clause in that argument is: "And watch, if civil liberty fanatics and nudicks like you have your way, the Nazis *will* gain power. And crush us all!"

The knee-jerk assumption is that, in an argument between an authoritarian cult and a democratic society, the authoritarians can nought but win; that, given a fair chance, bad guys always win. Given a choice, a free people will prefer to be enslaved every time, just so long as they are given a guarantee that groups they hate will be enslaved worse. I find this to be a scary assumption; although I must admit at times not a totally disagreeable one, because over the years I've had my own checkered reaction to civil liberties.

I don't like civil liberties any better than the average American. I would say that more than half the people whose First and Fourth and Fifth Amendment rights I've vigorously defended I wouldn't care to have to my house for dinner. I wasn't crazy about defending all those "card-carrying" Communists in the '40s and '50s, for example. I didn't morally approve of their use of my Constitution to protect their freedom. . . .

I often wondered in those days and after why we couldn't come up with a better class of victims—victims I could identify with instead of simply patronize, or feel somewhat sorry for, somewhat fearful of, somewhat contemptuous of. Whatever became of victims like Eugene Debs? Whatever became of *mythic* victims? Victims whom you could hang around with, who enhanced your stature? Today there is no question but that we have some terrific victims. We have Indians and Chicanos and blacks and government whistle blowers, all very reassuring to those of us who prefer not merely to believe in civil liberties but would also like to like them. But we also have *bad* victims, victims who are not nice guys, who are not sympathetic, who are Nazis, who are Kluxers, who are pornographers, who are even crooks. Should crooks have civil liberties? I don't like it.

But I do think it worth closer examination, this Pandora's-box argument. You give rights to your enemies, and they use them against you. You give rights to your enemies, and they'll eat you for breakfast. This attitude speaks volumes about our national self-doubt, about our belief only in our own fragility, our own vulnerability. Any repugnant idea, given half the chance, is bound to take over. So say the Pandora theorists. Certainly it's the argument behind Skokie. Just as it's the argument behind obscenity prosecutions or, for that matter, the argument behind the Supreme Court's recent decision to outlaw the First Amendment.

The Court would have seen no need to allow police the uncivil liberty to raid newspaper files ten years ago. This is obviously a post-Vietnam, post-Watergate decision. The press mainly stayed in line before Vietnam and Watergate, faithfully publishing publicity handouts disguised as news by whatever government agency. The sources, whose anonymity it sought most to protect in that time, were generally named Walt Whitman Rostow or McGeorge Bundy or Henry Kissinger.

The news media came to be seen as an enemy of government, and eventually of the Court, only when it abused its privilege of freedom of the press by exercising it: by publishing the Pentagon Papers, by turning against the war, by waging Watergate. Not that the press today doesn't behave a good deal of the time like an arm of government. It surely does. But it's become an unpredictable and—dare I say it?—a disloyal arm. Give it an inch, and it may well take over the country. The Fourth Estate will become the First Estate. The Court, checking its balance, acted accordingly. In its eyes, it had no other choice, so it sent in the cops.

Government operates, just as individuals operate, on the assumption that whoever differs seriously with it is out to get it, and is therefore a threat to internal security. Consequently, defensive measures must be taken. All vicious laws are explained and truly understood by their proponents to be defensive measures.

We, no matter who the we of we are, see ourselves as perennially innocent, perennially put upon, perennially helpless before ceaseless hordes of swiftly changing predators. In foreign affairs Russians turn into Chinese, turn into Vietnamese, turn into Cubans, and then back into Russians. At home surly Irish turn into greasy Italians, turn into devious Jews, turn into lazy blacks, turn into screeching Puerto Ricans. The single remaining idea that unites all Americans today, regardless of race, creed or previous conditions of servitude, the single belief of every man- and woman-jack of us, is in our own group's powerlessness. . . .

People convinced of their own powerlessness aren't interested in across-the-board civil rights and civil liberties. They are interested in selective civil rights and civil liberties. They want laws to stop this and start that, and bring back this and fix that. They want less government interference and more laws that say so. Increasingly, they lust in their hearts for Frank Capra movies; for good old American innocence; for women who support their men only morally and emotionally, not financially; for homosexuals who know their place—namely oblivion; and for blacks and Indians and other foreigners who know theirs.

That judge in Madison, Wis. who freed a teen-age rapist on the ground that the girl was asking for it because she wore tight jeans was not an isolated nut; he was the stifled and stifling voice that cannot bear the idea of change, crying out in his frustration: "Say it ain't so, daughter." . . .

Our national affinity for powerlessness makes us yearn for a return to the good old days of capital punishment, for getting even. And why not? I've often yearned for it myself—thirty or forty times a day. Not in the case of convicted murderers or terrorists, people like that. I yearn for it in the case of theatre critics, my book publisher, my landlord, Con Edison, taxi drivers, motorcycle thugs who wear swastikas, any teen-ager on a city bus playing a transistor radio. If there existed such a thing as justice in this country, no one would be going around free who disagreed with me, displeased me, or who hurt my feelings.

But we do not have justice. All we have is law, and the law tells me that I cannot sentence people to death on a whim, or close down their businesses on whim, or blacklist them from their jobs on whim. . . .

Civil rights and liberties were hot issues, "sexy issues," as the press likes to describe these things, during the days of Nixon and his plumbers, but recently they've come upon hard times. We are as bored with hearing about the rights of women and homosexuals and Native Americans and blacks and Hispanics as we are bored with the latest cancer-causing discovery in our daily diet.

A growing number of people have come to look on civil liberties, on human rights for Americans, as cancer-causing and self-destructive, as taking all the fun, all the individualism—our freedom of choice—out of life.

It seems to me that, among its other functions, this conference could well put aside time to work out the groundwork for a massive education campaign to sell the Bill of Rights to the people it was created for, not excluding their police and their courts.

A campaign to explain—to the various and sundry groups who see themselves as constantly being threatened, eaten away at—that, nonetheless, there is a place in their lives for a free press, despite its distortions and special relationships; that there is a place in their lives for free speech, despite how outrageous or just plain disagreeable or wrong others who practice it may be; that there is a point to protecting even those we hate from unreasonable search and seizure; and that, despite the fact that civil liberties often prove to be unpleasant, inconvenient and even painful, still they are of momentous value and make enormous practical sense.

If we wait till that day, surely coming, when the Bill of Rights becomes a document of radical chic, it will be too late. So I think that pretty soon we'd better look for ways to let our fellow Americans in on its secrets.

OUR ALL-TOO-TIMID PRESS

Tom Wicker

Wicker is a columnist for the New York *Times* and the author of numerous books, both fiction and nonfiction. Here he argues cogently and eloquently that any restriction of freedom or monitoring of performance of the press, no matter how well intended or well designed, whether external or internal, will be more damaging than productive.

The First Amendment does not say anything about "responsibility." This observation, which I have offered to hundreds of disbelieving and usually disapproving audiences, invariably brings some challenger to his or her feet with something like the following inquiry (usually varied more in its degree of choler than in wording): "Do you mean to say that the press has a right to be irresponsible?"

I mean to say nothing of the sort, although it's true—just to be argumentative—that irresponsibility does not appear to the layman's eye to be a constitutional violation. But it's just as well for journalists in particular to recall the skeptical judgment in *The Federalist* of Alexander Hamilton—who opposed as unnecessary a Bill of Rights for the Constitution:

> What is the liberty of the press? Who can give it any definition which would not leave the utmost latitude for evasion? I hold it to be impracticable; and from this I infer that its security, whatever fine declarations may be inserted in any constitution respecting it, must altogether depend on public opinion, and on the general spirit of the people and of the government.

Just so. And with that in mind, no journalist should advocate to the public the idea that the press has "a right to be irresponsible"; no one could agree to that. Nor should any journalist wish the press or broadcast news to *be* irresponsible. Aside from their pride in their craft and its institutions, their desire to do their personal work well, and their concern that the public should be informed, all journalists know that popular contempt for and fear of press irresponsibility are as grave threats—and more justified ones—to a free press as are government attempts to silence it. And, as Hamilton foresaw, that part of the First Amendment might not long survive a hostile, determined public opinion.

Granting all that, a certain case for tolerance of irresponsibility still has to be made. That is to say, if the American press is to remain free—even in the somewhat limited sense that necessarily results

SOURCE: From *Saturday Review*, March 4, 1978. Copyright © 1978 by Tom Wicker. Reprinted by permission of Paul R. Reynolds, Inc.

from the conflict of this freedom with the other equally guaranteed freedoms in the Constitution and the Bill of Rights—it cannot have responsibility imposed on it by legislation, judicial interpretation, or any other process.

Freedom contains within itself the possibility of irresponsibility. No man is truly free who is not permitted occasionally to be irresponsible; nor is any institution. Responsibility, it goes without saying, is profoundly important; and the highest freedom of all may well be the freedom to conduct one's life and affairs responsibly— but by one's own standards of responsibility. It's a mean freedom in which a mere failure of responsibility brings a jail term or a fine or some other societally imposed penalty—and no freedom at all if standards of responsibility are uniform, designed to prevent rather than to punish failures, and set by higher authority.

Yet some of the most sweeping restrictions on the freedom of the press have been proposed in the name of preventing press irre- sponsibility. What is lost sight of is that if responsibility can be imposed, freedom must be lost; and of those who advocate various means of ensuring the responsibility of a supposedly free press, two questions should be asked:

Who defines responsibility? In numerous instances, the difficulty editors and reporters have in determining a responsible course in disputed circumstances has, I believe, been demonstrated—notably in the case of the New York *Times's* treatment of the Bay of Pigs story. In literally thousands of other instances—most of them less important but many on the same level of seriousness—editors have no hard-and-fast rules to follow, save those of experience, ethics, and common sense—all of which vary from person to person. Editors may, and often do, differ on what is responsible—even as *Times* editors differed among themselves on handling the Bay of Pigs story. There simply is no certainty, in most instances, as to what constitutes a responsible course in an enormous number of cases that editors and reporters have to face.

Most journalists believe that the multiplicity of editorial decisions likely to result in any given case is a major safeguard against irresponsibility and misinformation. All editors won't make the same decision based on the same set of facts—a story played on page one by the *Times* may be printed inside the Washington *Post*, a quota- tion in the one story may not appear in the other; different lines of interpretation may well be taken by the two papers and by any number of others, with the result that the same story appears in many versions and with a greater or lesser degree of prominence. This rich diversity not only works against the possibility that any story can be covered up or manufactured but it also offers a reasonable guarantee that differing viewpoints on the same events will reach the public.

Not only, therefore, would the imposition of standards of responsibility on the press move it away from diversity and toward uniformity of presentation but it would require an instrument big enough and comprehensive enough to define responsibility in an immense number of instances, for a huge number of publications and broadcasters. No such instrument exists, save the government.

Who enforces responsibility? This is a simpler problem. Once responsibility is defined, obviously nothing of sufficient power and scope exists to force the defined responsibility on the entire press— again save the government.

Thus, if we are to be *sure* of a responsible press, the only way is through a government that both defines and enforces responsibility. Not just Richard Nixon would have leaped at *that* opportunity. It need scarcely even be pointed out that in such circumstances, the condition of the American press would be a far cry from freedom.

Would that matter?

Obviously, a totally government-controlled press would make much difference to liberty in America; but that is not what most of those who demand greater press responsibility have in mind. They more often set forth a supposedly middle course—yielding a little freedom in a beneficial trade-off to gain some responsibility.

The middle-course argument is respectable. It cannot be maintained by the most ardent First Amendment advocate that democracy is not reasonably healthy in Britain, where the press is under much greater restraint than it is in the United States. Libel laws that sharply restrict publication and broadcasting; a heavy bias toward privacy rather than publication in laws governing press reports on criminal justice proceedings and other actions of the courts; the Official Secrets Act that governments of both parties frequently invoke, apparently not always in matters of indisputable national security; and the quasi-governmental Press Council to monitor and criticize press activities—have these stifled the larger British democracy? From my side of the Atlantic, I cannot say that they have.

For whatever reasons, the history of British politics is by no means as marked by venality and corruption as is that of the United States, and governing ethics and traditions there appear so settled that serious violations of them—for example, a power grab such as that represented by the Watergate complex of offenses—are far less likely. Secrecy by the British government has been widely accepted for centuries. Profound policy miscalculations—the Suez War, for example—bring quick political retribution, Official Secrets Act or no, while more egregious American blunders in Vietnam and Cambodia for years produced in the United States mostly a "rally-round-the-President" effect, until the press—primarily television—finally turned the public against the war (by printing and broadcasting *news*, not editorials).

Therefore, press restraints perhaps amenable to British democracy—although not many British journalists really consider them so—would not necessarily be fitting in the United States. Should a Watergate occur in the United Kingdom, colleagues in the British press say, the governing party plausibly accused of conniving in the burglary of opposition party headquarters and then of obstructing justice to conceal the crime would soon be turned out of office, despite restrictions on reporting such a story. But it was a challenging American press that kept Watergate in the public eye and ultimately forced the various actions that led to Richard Nixon's resignation—at that, two years after the offense.

But the existence of restrictions on the British press, together with the evident survival of the essential British democracy, leads many serious and reasonable persons to suggest not government control of the American press but similar instruments of responsibility in this country's journalistic practice.

When the Senate in 1977 established an oversight committee for the so-called intelligence community, for example, one of the committee's first studies was of the need, if any, for a limited form of Official Secrets Act in the United States—an effort to protect the CIA from the public rather than the public from the CIA that stood the committee's supposed responsibility on its head.

The discussed act's reach would ostensibly have been limited to barring disclosures of "source methods" of gathering intelligence—"ostensibly" because although "sources and methods" describes an arcane art and is a term therefore supposedly capable of being strictly defined and narrowly applied, both the FBI and the CIA have in the past shown themselves capable of slipping large abuses through tiny loopholes. It was, for example, supposedly to protect sources and methods that some of the CIA's mail-opening and surveillance operations were illegally pursued.

Whatever the situation in Britain, in this country—as I hope I have demonstrated—secrecy has too often been used to shield blunders, crimes, and ineptitude. Alert citizens should not accept without sharp questioning a secrecy law designed to give a secret agency even greater powers of covering up its operations than it already has. And unless Congress were to show an uncharacteristic willingness to include a "shield" provision for reporters—which it has never done in other legislation of less importance and which would be of dubious constitutionality—a likely consequence would be about as follows:

The leak of a secret protected by the act would appear as a news story in a newspaper or on a broadcast. An inquiry would be launched; but as usual, the identity of the leaker (who could be prosecuted under the new law) would not be learned. The reporter-recipient of the leak would be subpoenaed to appear before a grand jury and would be asked the identity of his source, with a view to prosecuting the leaker. It would be made clear that no other means existed of obtaining this information vital to enforcement of the Official Secrets Act and the orderly administration of government.

The reporter would abide by his professional code of ethics and would refuse to answer. He would then be held in contempt and ordered to jail—although there might be no evidence of any damage to national security as a consequence of his or her story. A lot of reporters would have a lot of second thoughts—chilling indeed—about accepting leaks of so-called security secrets under such a threat.

Would that serve the cause of responsibility? Once again, the answer depends upon who defines responsibility in any given case; but those who place a high value upon a "robust and uninhibited press" and who have learned to be skeptical of the government's assertions of "national security" are not likely to think so.

But even if no such drastic step as instituting an Official Secrets Act was taken, why not more restrictive libel and privacy laws? Would they limit press freedom so severely as to threaten the public's right and need to know? And what about a non-governmental press council, at least to criticize—constructively, as well as punitively—press performance, even if the council had no real power to punish or penalize?

The question of more severe libel and privacy laws requires, essentially, a value judgment. There isn't much doubt that greater protection from press charges than is now provided for public officials would limit the ability of the press to act as a check on the power of government; but some reasonable persons believe the press has too much latitude to criticize government, expose its workings, penetrate needed confidentiality, and hinder its effectiveness. Similarly, no one should be in doubt that stricter protection of individual privacy from searching press inquiry would frequently prevent needed public exposure and discussion of personalities, institutions, and processes; but few in the press would deny that the power of the press has too often been the instrument by which have come unwarranted personal humiliations, embarrassments, misfortunes, and losses of reputation and livelihood.

As for a U.S. press council, the National News Council has been financed and supported by the Twentieth Century Fund, which is neither conservative nor antipress. Neither have been the first workings of the council, which is supported by many in the press and broadcasting and which has no connection with the government. Its purpose is to conduct quiet private investigations of controversial press or broadcasting decisions and to report publicly on whether or not those decisions were taken responsibly and on reasonable grounds. The council has no power, other than the force of its disapproval, to penalize news organizations.

Concerned journalists have argued that the press and broadcasting ought to cooperate wholeheartedly with the News Council. Most news organizations, they say, would have nothing to fear; and it would be better for those who might be culpable to be censured by a private group with press interests at heart than by unsympathetic courts or legislatures. Besides, say the advocates, by certifying in most disputed cases that editorial decisions had been responsibly and reasonably taken, the council would more often reassure the public than threaten the press.

In short, these journalists view the News Council as a good public relations instrument for the press. Not only would news organizations appear to be trying to police their own work and that of colleagues but most would periodically be given a good bill of health by a respected panel of citizens, while irresponsible publications and broadcasts would be sternly reprimanded by a council backed by the press itself.

But there is another underlying reason why there has been considerable press support for the News Council. Seldom stated outside newsrooms, journalism classes, or press club bars, it is that the News Council ideas offer a safe way to "clean up the press before the government comes in and does it for us." This suggests that even many who are themselves deeply involved in American journalism believe that there are so many excesses and malpractices that need to be cleaned up that the press really does face possible governmental control. And that points straight to the fundamental reason why I personally am opposed to the News Council, to more restrictive privacy and libel laws, and to all other schemes for enforcing the responsibility of a supposedly free press—reasonable as some of these schemes undoubtedly appear in their proposals for only limited sacrifices of freedom.

The overwhelming conclusion I have drawn from my life in journalism—nearly 30 years so far, from the *Sandhill Citizen* to the New York *Times*—is that the American press, powerful as it unquestionably is and protected though it may be by the Constitution and the laws, is not often "robust and uninhibited" but is usually timid and anxious—for respectability at least as much as for profitability. Those whose idea of the press is bounded by the exploits of Woodward and Bernstein on the one hand and by the Pentagon Papers on the other do not usually understand that such remarkable efforts as these—whether or not they are viewed as necessary or excessive—are limited exceptions to long-established practice.

Undoubtedly, in the more than a decade since Dwight Eisenhower roused the Goldwaterites with his attack on "sensation-seeking columnists," the press has become more activist and challenging, particularly in covering politics and government—though *not* business and financial institutions. On the evidence of press performance in that decade—the disclosure of duplicity and ineptitude in Vietnam; the exposure of political corruption in the Nixon administration; the demonstration of grave threats to American liberty by the "Imperial Presidency," the FBI, the CIA, and other security agencies—I assert the necessity to encourage the developing tendency of the press to shake off the encumbrance of a falsely objective journalism and to take an adversary position toward the most powerful institutions of American life.

By "adversary position," I don't mean a necessarily hostile position; I use the word in the lawyer's sense of cross-examining, testing, challenging, the merits of a case in the course of a trial. Such an adversary is opposed only in the sense that he or she demands that a case be made; the law stated, the facts proven, the assumptions and conclusions justified, the procedure squared with common sense and good practice. An adversary press would hold truth—unattainable and frequently plural as it is—as its highest value and knowledge as its first responsibility.

Such a press should be encouraged on its independence, not investigated—even by its friends—when it asserts that independence. A relatively toothless News Council that nevertheless could summon editors and reporters, notes and documents, film and outtakes, in order to determine publicly whether editorial decisions had been properly made *by the News Council's standards* would be bound to have an ultimately inhibiting effect on editors, publishers, and broadcasters—not all of whom would therefore be dismayed. Most, it's safe to say, would rather be praised for someone else's idea of responsibility than risk being questioned or criticized for their own independence.

Somewhat similarly, tighter libel and privacy laws would surely narrow the area open to editorial judgment—and some editors and publishers might welcome such laws just for that reason. Some might even yearn privately for an Official Secrets Act because its proscriptions would relieve them of having to decide such difficult questions as whether or not to publish so-called national security stories and of the loud accusations of irresponsibility that inevitably follow such decisions, no matter how they are made.

My belief is that the gravest threat to freedom of the press is not necessarily from public animosity or mistrust, legislative action or court decision. Certainly, even though absolute press freedom may sometimes have to accommodate itself to other high constitutional values, the repeal or modification of the First Amendment seems unlikely. At least as great a threat, I believe, comes from the press itself—in its longing for a respectable place in the established political and economic order, in its fear of the reaction that boldness and independence will always evoke. Self-censorship silences as effectively as a government decree, and we have seen it far more often.

In the harsh sunlight of a robust freedom, after all, nothing stands more starkly exposed than the necessity to decide and to accept the responsibility for decision. If the true freedom of the press is to decide for itself what to publish and when to publish it, the true responsibility of the press must be to assert that freedom.

But my life in journalism has persuaded me that the press too often tries to guard its freedom by shirking its responsibility and that this leads to default on both. What the press in America needs is less inhibition, not more restraint.

"NATIONAL SECURITY": THE ULTIMATE THREAT TO THE FIRST AMENDMENT
Erwin Knoll

The problem of "national security" being invoked to obtain a prior restraint injunction is reviewed by the editor of *The Progressive* magazine, against whom such an injunction was issued in 1979. He spoke at a 1981 conference at the University of Minnesota celebrating the fiftieth anniversary of the landmark *Near* v. *Minnesota* decision.

"Depend upon it, Sir," Samuel Johnson observed, "when a man knows he is to be hanged in a fortnight, it concentrates the mind wonderfully."

Being subjected to a prior restraint on utterance and publication has much the same effect. Fortunately, very few Americans have had the experience. As one of those very few, I can assure you that I never gave the First Amendment such close attention, or such deep devotion, as during the six months and nineteen days when I was deprived of its full protection by court order.

Obviously, most of us respect the First Amendment (or at least pay lip service to it) as the cornerstone of our freedom. Journalists, in particular, are swift to sing its praises and invoke its protection. But I suspect few of us can appreciate the constitutional guarantee of freedom of speech and of the press as fully as one who has been directed by a court, on penalty of fine and imprisonment, to refrain from "publishing or otherwise communicating or disclosing in any manner" some words, sentences, paragraphs, facts, or ideas.

Full particulars of the case called *The United States of America v. The Progressive, Inc., Erwin Knoll, Samuel Day Jr., and Howard Morland* are available elsewhere. In this presentation, I will confine myself to those aspects which have a direct bearing on my thesis that governmental claims of "national security" constitute the ultimate threat to the First Amendment. As it happens, those are the aspects which relate directly to the historic case we are commemorating, for I believe it is important to recognize that the Supreme Court's 1931 decision in *Near* v. *Minnesota*, which we celebrate quite properly as a great victory for the First Amendment, also helped lay the groundwork for potentially the most injurious assaults on freedom of speech and of the press.

I am referring, of course, to the narrow exception stipulated by Chief Justice Hughes in *Near*, when he observed that in time of war "no one would question that a government might prevent actual obstruction to its recruiting service or the publication of the sailing dates of transports or the number and location of troops." That passage was cited by the Government of the United States in 1979, as a basis for restraining *The Progressive*, and it was embraced enthusiastically by Federal District Judge Robert W. Warren: "Times have changed significantly since 1931 when *Near* was decided," he ruled. "Now war by foot soldiers has been replaced in large part by war by machines and bombs. No longer need there be any advance warning or any preparation time before a nuclear war could be commenced. In light of these factors, the court concludes that publication of the technical information on the hydrogen bomb contained in *The Progressive*'s article is analogous to publication of troop movements or location in time of war and falls within the extremely narrow exception to the rule against prior restraint."

What Judge Warren concluded, in other words, was that the "extremely narrow exception" in *Near*, which Chief Justice Hughes had explicitly reserved for time of war, must also apply in time of peace because of the exigencies of the nuclear age. It must, in fact, apply at all times.

According to Federal statute—the Atomic Energy Act of 1954—the narrow exception must also apply to all nuclear data. The law states: "The term 'Restricted Data' means all data concerning (1) design, manufacture, or utilization of atomic weapons; (2) the production of special nuclear materials; or (3) the use of special nuclear material in the production of energy." Such data are "restricted" not only if they originate within the Government, but also if they originate within the mind of a private citizen. And unless they have specifically been "declassified or removed from the Restricted Data category," such data may not be published, according to the Atomic Energy Act. These are powers of censorship far more sweeping than those embodied in the "official secrets" laws of some nations that make no pretense of observing freedom of the press.

In arguing *The Progressive* case before the U.S. Court of Appeals for the Seventh Circuit (which, unfortunately, never was given an opportunity to rule on the merits), the Government carried the narrow exception still further, contending that "technical information," presumably including but not confined to nuclear information, is not covered by the First Amendment at all, but is—like obscenity, presumably—a form of unprotected speech. The potential consequences of such a doctrine in our highly technological society are mind-boggling.

I do not mean to hold the *Near* decision and its narrow exception responsible for all of these unforeseen and unfortunate consequences. I do mean to suggest that even the narrowest of exceptions have a way of attaining horrendous breadth, and that an exception based on considerations of "national security" can create truly pernicious results. My experience suggests, in particular, four especially serious considerations:

1. The invocation of "national security" makes it extraordinarily difficult—and perhaps impossible—to apply First Amendment principles.

2. In attempting to impose censorship on grounds of "national security," the Government is able to wield sweeping powers of selective prosecution and to exert a severe chilling effect.

3. When prior restraint is sought to protect "national security," the judicial process itself becomes a mockery.

4. Once prior restraint is imposed for reasons of "national security," the infringement of other freedoms is a logical and inescapable consequence.

The invocation of "national security" makes it extraordinarily difficult—and perhaps impossible—to apply First Amendment prin-

ciples. Chief Justice Hughes exaggerated only slightly when he assumed in *Near* that "no one would question" infringement of the First Amendment to protect military secrets in time of war. Very few would question such censorship a half century ago, and I suspect even fewer would do so today. In fact, most of us seem to have accepted the narrow exception of *Near* as an unwritten addendum to the First Amendment. Even in legal and journalistic circles, the narrow exception tends to be taken for granted, and anyone who challenges it is likely to be dismissed as an "absolutist"—that is, as one who naively believes the First Amendment actually means what it plainly says.

But whenever anyone finds it necessary (or expedient) to weigh freedom in the balance against any other consideration, freedom is likely to be found wanting. That is certainly the case when freedom of speech and press is balanced against considerations of "national security." The logic is irresistible: Who would not gladly permit a trivial and temporary incursion against the Bill of Rights when the alternative might be a military defeat—or even a nuclear holocaust? That was precisely the logic Judge Warren articulated in *The Progressive* case: "You can't speak freely when you're dead," he said.

In the nuclear age, striking a balance between freedom and "national security" becomes a task charged with emotion that approaches, and sometimes attains, hysterical proportions. Judge Warren said, "I want to think a long, hard time before I'd give a hydrogen bomb to Idi Amin," and the statement made headlines everywhere. (Some reporters actually asked me whether we had any subscribers in Uganda. When Judge Warren acknowledged, some time later, that there was no way *The Progressive*'s suppressed article could "give a hydrogen bomb to Idi Amin," hardly anyone paid attention.)

Confronted with Government allegations that "national security" was at stake, much of the press abandoned not only its principles but also its minimal standards of accuracy. A headline in the Lansing *State Journal* blared, YOU TOO, CAN BUILD H-BOMB, and an editorial in the San Francisco *Chronicle* described our article as "a handy guide to building your own H-bomb." The Washington *Post*, with no more to go on than a Justice Department news release, editorialized that it was "John Mitchell's dream case—the one the Nixon administration was never lucky enough to get: a real First Amendment loser."

In the atmosphere created by such reporting and commentary, and against the background of fully justifiable public apprehension about nuclear dangers, predictions of a "judicial climate" hostile to the First Amendment are almost certain to become self-fulfilling prophecies. (Judge Warren made a point of noting that "even the press" wasn't supporting the First Amendment in *The Progressive* case.) Any case that pits the First Amendment against official assertions of "national security," no matter how ludicrous or cynical those assertions may be, is likely to turn out "a real First Amendment loser."

In attempting to impose censorship on grounds of "national security," the Government is able to wield sweeping powers of selective prosecution and to exert a severe chilling effect. An example that has become all too familiar in recent years is the Central Intelligence Agency's punitive litigation against dissident former employes who have attempted to publish books about the Agency. No such action has been taken, of course, against former high officials who have drawn freely on classified materials for their published works.

Where nuclear "secrets" or other scientific or technical matter is concerned, the potential for abuse is even greater, for the "restricted" knowledge is widespread within the scientific community, and even outside it. Dr. Edward Teller, often described as "the father of the H-Bomb," has said of his offspring, "When a secret is known to a million people, it isn't a secret any more." Where some of those million are allowed to disseminate the secret while others may be subjected to prior restraint or prosecution, the potential for intimidation is enormous.

In the course of *The Progressive* case, our attorneys submitted to the courts more than two dozen publications or broadcast transcripts that contained some or all of the allegedly "secret" material that we had been enjoined from publishing. (One of them was a Soviet journal we obtained from a Swedish library.) A Milwaukee *Sentinel* reporter, after a week's work in the public libraries of Milwaukee and Waukegan, Illinois, came up with the "secret" of the H-Bomb and published it in his newspaper. Dr. Teller himself gave the "secret" away years ago in an article for the *Encyclopedia Americana.* Yet *The Progressive* alone was singled out for prior restraint.

When the Government invokes "national security" to protect technical or scientific "secrets," it is probably lying; there are few secrets in science that last for more than a few months. But the notion of "atomic secrecy" is so deeply imbedded in public consciousness, that even the most spurious Government claims are likely to be believed. And even if the Government's secrecy rationale can eventually be exploded—as it was in *The Progressive* case—the costs can be so formidable as to constitute a chilling effect against publication. Before the Government dropped its censorship attempt against *The Progressive*, we had incurred almost $250,000 in legal costs—a huge sum for a small, financially unstable political magazine. We are still a long way from paying off our indebtedness. The pressures on our small staff—and, of course, on our budget—came close to putting us out of business, and might easily dissuade another publication from pursuing its First Amendment rights.

When prior restraint is sought to protect "national security," the judicial process itself becomes a mockery. For the sake of consistency, if for no other reasons, the Government must insist on maintaining in court the same sort of secrecy that it is trying to enforce in print. The results can be both ludicrous and ominous—part Lewis Carroll, part Franz Kafka.

These perversions of the judicial process help illustrate why prior restraint has always been held in particular contempt by those who value freedom. Prior restraint is, perhaps, the most obnoxious form of governmental abuse precisely because it puts the Government's own conduct beyond public scrutiny. In the absence of censorship, any other offense against liberty is, at least, visible to the people; prior restraint provides its own blanket of concealment. The Government needs to offer no public justification for imposing secrecy: The justification itself is secret.

Once prior restraint is imposed for reasons of "national security," the infringement of other freedoms is a logical and inescapable consequence. In this respect, censorship on grounds of "national security" carries implications that are unique and extremely disturbing—especially to those who are being censored. It was only gradually, during the half year we were under court-ordered restraint, that we became fully aware of those implications.

During that half a year when my mind was wonderfully concentrated on the First Amendment, I came to believe that when it comes to matters of fundamental freedom—and the First Amendment *is* our most fundamental freedom—even the narrowest of exceptions is too broad. And when that narrow exception is based on claims of "national security," the likelihood of abuse is so great as to be unavoidable.

There was a reason, I suspect, for the First Amendment to be written without exceptions of any kind—even those "no one would question." There was a reason for it to be written so simply, so clearly, so—absolutely.

SHOULD TV CAMERAS BE IN THE COURTROOM?

From *U.S. News & World Report*

Photographing trials in progress by still and television cameras is permitted in some courts, often on an experimental basis, but argument continues as to the wisdom of the practice. Here two veterans debate the issue in *U.S. News & World Report.*

YES—Letting public see what's going on "may improve the courts"

Interview With Judge Jack Weinstein

U.S. District Court, Brooklyn, N.Y.

Q Judge Weinstein, why do you favor allowing television news coverage of trials?

A Because the people are entitled to know what goes on in this important segment of their government.

The courts are one of the three great branches of government. The court system serves an educational function in deterring criminals. In their work in civil rights, courts attempt to educate the people on what the Constitution and our ideals require.

In short, I don't think the public is getting the information it needs through the written media alone.

Q But wouldn't TV cameras affect what goes on in court?

A Yes, they would. I think television would improve matters. Putting the eye of the public into courtrooms, so to speak, may improve the work of courts at every level—even the U.S. Supreme Court, where I think it's perfectly clear that arguments ought to be televised.

Many of the arguments before the Supreme Court are substandard. A city or state official who wants the publicity and prestige of arguing a case before the Supreme Court when he's not competent to do so would be seen on television. People back home would see what's going on, and there would be pressure to let the best-qualified make arguments at the Court.

Q Is there a danger that judges, witnesses and lawyers might be tempted to ham it up before the cameras?

A Yes, and that possibility has to be guarded against. But the experience we have had in the six states that permit televised trials—Alabama, Colorado, Florida, Georgia, Texas and Washington—indicates that this is not a substantial problem. [In a seventh state—Montana—new rules allowing TV in courtrooms took effect on April 1.]

Cameras today are very

SOURCE: "TV Cameras in the Courtroom?" *U.S. News & World Report*, April 17, 1978, pp. 51–52. Copyright 1978 by *U.S. News & World Report*, Inc. Reprinted by permission.

small. Very quickly in a trial you forget about everything else and concentrate on the trial itself. There are incompetents who would use television for publicity, but I think they can be dealt with.

Q How about claims that television would broadcast only the most sensational court news?

A There is that danger, but we have public-broadcasting systems that would tend to give the courts more time. And I think that the media, over time, tend to give the average citizen a fair idea of what's going on.

Take the Bakke appeal on so-called reverse discrimination: You had people from all over the country standing out in the street trying to get a seat for the arguments before the Supreme Court. These were young people interested in a major issue and the future of the country. It seems to me that there was so much interest in the Bakke case that televising the full argument, even with some editing, would have given the public a much better appreciation of what was really involved.

Q Should the defendant be permitted to veto TV coverage of his trial?

A Yes. The defendant should have this right—at least at the outset—until we acquire experience.

Q Should the judge have veto power, too?

A Again, I think I'd tend to move slowly and give any of the three parties involved—defendant, prosecutor and judge—the right to veto television. I think that ultimately we would reach the point where we are now in the case of print media, where certain fixed rights are involved in covering trials. But initially, since there is so much objection—ill-founded objection, in my view—it would be politic and sensible to limit use of TV.

Q Should the camera be required to always focus on whoever is speaking, or could it pan the courtroom at will?

A I wouldn't be too tight about restricting the camera. Trials get awfully dull. Everything that goes on in the courtroom is part of the total scene, and the reaction of a defendant or juror sometimes is quite revealing.

But there are myriad of those kinds of details that must be worked out. Given good will and good sense, which I think exist in both the media and the law, I see no reason why they couldn't be worked out.

I have a lot of confidence in television people, just as I have in the press. I think generally they're very sensible and they appreciate the problems of the courts. They don't want to complicate our ability to give people due processs of law.

Q Should any court procedures be excluded from television coverage?

A Deliberations by the jury would have to be excluded. I would not have them open to anyone. You want the jurors to feel perfectly free to say anything they want so they can be candid with each other.

Q When could televising start?

A As to appeals hearings, I think television coverage of them ought to start forthwith. I just can't see any valid objections to that. Rules will have to be developed for trial coverage.

Q Chief Justice Warren Burger opposes TV in the courtroom. Will federal courts allow television as long as this is so?

A No. The Judicial Conference makes the rules for federal courts, and the Chief Justice pretty well dominates the Judicial Conference for very good hierarchical reasons. But the Chief Justice is a very sensible, flexible person, and now the American Bar Association is starting to take a positive view toward televising trials.

The states where television is allowed have encountered no serious problems.

At the very least, trials should now be videotaped for use in the training of trial lawyers. That's something that might appeal to the Chief Justice, who is critical of the quality of trial work by many lawyers.

As it becomes clear there was no more to fear from this modern device than from the telephone, we would be more sensible and expand the use of TV.

Interview With John Sutro
Attorney in San Francisco, Calif.

NO—"Trials are not for public entertainment"

Q Mr. Sutro, why do you oppose television coverage of trials?

A Because the purpose of trials is to provide a forum for the administration of justice. Trials are not for public entertainment. They aren't a drama to be played for the public, but are held to ascertain the truth.

Q But wouldn't television, by showing what goes on in court, thereby educate the public?

A No. There isn't a television station that would show a court proceeding from the moment the judge takes the bench until the jury is discharged. That could take from a day or two to a matter of weeks.

The only portions that are going to be televised are those that are dramatic—where the accused takes the stand or where the principal witness testifies or when some lawyer is making a big speech.

If you're going to educate the public with respect to how justice is administered, the public must know exactly what transpires from the moment the judge takes the bench until the jury is dismissed.

Q The public doesn't see that now, does it?

A Courtrooms are open to the public. A person attending a trial sees exactly what goes on in the courtroom. If you're looking at TV, you see only what the camera pictured, and there's no camera that can show you everything that goes on in court.

Q Don't newspapers summarize what happens in a trial, and often distill the dramatic aspects?

A Yes. But the newspaper reader knows he is reading only the reporter's appraisal of what happened. If you look at a television program, you're purportedly looking at what actually took place. By televising only a part, however, the picture is distorted.

Q Why not allow televising of Supreme Court arguments, at least in important cases?

A I agree with Chief Justice Burger, who I understand disapproves of televising appellate arguments. I don't think arguments on technical legal points are appealing to the public generally. If there were a murder of a well-known person and there was a trial, that's what would interest the television viewer.

Q Would trial participants be affected by television?

A Yes. It would upset witnesses; it would upset jurors; lawyers wouldn't act like themselves, and judges would be placed in an undesirable position. If a witness has to be subpoenaed to testify because he is unwilling to volunteer, then the presence of television would scare him to death.

The judge's job is to do whatever is necessary to see that a trial is handled properly. If the judge is conscious he is being televised, his attention might be diverted from that task. Also, judges are human; some would inevitably ham it up.

As for the lawyers, a lot of them would conduct themselves differently if they were on television. They may try to create a public image for themselves.

Q Don't lawyers dramatize the case for the jury anyway?

A Sure, there are some lawyers who are actors. They are the ones who get written up in books and articles. But there are an awful lot of lawyers whose demeanor is very calm and not a bit that of an actor. It would be very unfortunate to have the public evaluate the capability of lawyers based on the way they appear on television.

Q Why not let the judge decide whether he wants TV in his courtroom?

A That would be terrible. Most state judges have to stand for election. If a judge turned down television, he'd be as popular with the TV stations and the press as a case of the measles. The judge would be placed in a most undesirable position.

Q Would federal judges, appointed to lifetime terms, be subject to pressures, too?

A If you were a federal district judge and you turned down the televising of a criminal case of great public interest, I don't think that either the TV stations or the press would give you any kudos.

Q Some broadcasters argue that the First Amendment's guarantee of freedom of the

press gives them a right to tele-
vise courtroom proceedings—

A There is nothing in the First
Amendment that does that.

Under the Constitution, anybody connected with a television
station is as welcome in the court
as any newspaper reporter. The
television editor or newsman
can sit in court and observe
what goes on and get on the air
that night to say whatever he
wants—within the area of rea-
sonableness.

Q As technology becomes
more pervasive in our daily
lives, isn't it almost inevitable
that television will come into
the courtroom?

A Definitely not. A television
news program is entertainment
in the broad sense. It isn't like
looking at a comedy program,
but the news show does aim to
entertain.

But a trial's most important
goal is to determine if a person
accused of a crime did or didn't
do it. Television has no place in
that.

Section 19

THE MEDIA AND SOCIAL ISSUES

The shortcomings of television, both commercial and public, in providing programs of social value are examined by Charles D. Ferris and Benjamin DeMott. Louis Banks and Norman Isaacs talk about the need for greater accountability and higher values among newspapers.

THE NEW TELEVISION: CHANGING THE MEDIUM, ENRICHING THE MESSAGE

Charles D. Ferris

Ferris, long the chairman of the Federal Communications Commission, has been a frequent critic of television practices. Here he calls provocatively, and logically, for greater variety in television fare created by new technological opportunities, rather than by the decrease of commercial influence so frequently demanded by critics.

In a very short period of time, television has become a dominant force in our society, if for no other reason than that it touches so many millions each hour of every day. What other form of mass communication is considered unsuccessful if it does not attract a share of the audience representing tens of millions of persons? A musical group is honored by a gold album if it sells the latest L.P. to a million buyers. A novelist reaches the top of the best seller list if a mere half-million persons buy his or her book, while a very few newspapers can claim a daily readership even approaching this number. With the notable exception of *Reader's Digest*, the only magazine that comes close to the audience television claims is a magazine about—what else—television. Yet even *T. V. Guide's* circulation figure—an impressive 18 million worldwide—would bring embarrassment and quick cancellation to a prime time network show.

The incredible reach of television—from studios in Hollywood and New York into the homes of almost all Americans—is an awesome extension of the power of communication. This is an astounding reality. But it is also a depressing one, because you and I know that unless the message can capture a 30 percent share, none of the networks would take a chance on it.

You operate under a wholly different set of constraints than artists who communicate in any other way. On a medium where every second means revenue, you must face extreme time limits. An author of books or articles may feel free, within very broad limits, to expand on an idea in many different ways. Television often seems to

---

SOURCE: This address was presented to the Academy of Television Arts and Sciences, Los Angeles, May, 1979.

imitate an idea, or to repeat it over and over in series that clone one another, but seldom to expand on ideas in a meaningful sense.

You must engage a viewing audience predisposed to passivity, an audience that has come to expect relaxation and accept escapism, rather than even mild intellectual challenge. You are asked to create a new reality for viewers who are exhausted by their own, who are often already too aware of the agonies and ironies of life.

But perhaps your most oppressive burden is the state of cold war that exists between you and those who ultimately control your creativity. You must deal not only with artificial lead time, deadlines, and schedule changes, but with market researchers and network executives whose goals are fundamentally different from your own. Your best work may be rejected simply because it is too innovative, too daring—in short, too good.

Some might say that these complaints come with the television turf—that this is simply the way things are and necessarily must be. I strongly disagree, and I am committed to proving that the pessimists are wrong. It may be the way things are today, but that is only because we have chosen this way among the many possible ones of structuring the industry.

Maybe I am still too fascinated by the world of science fiction, but I believe that the future offers us a better way, a way out of the sterile box that confines your creativity, a way to develop the still latent possibilities of television. This prospect is the promise of communications history.

Each dramatic revolution in communication technology—from the development of language and script to television broadcasting—has stimulated new forms of thought, expression, and even experience. Advances in one medium have not only opened a new path of creative communication, but have forced as well other media of communication to respond to new competitive circumstances. When television reached maturity, the movie industry was forced by the growing popularity of television to make better films, to narrow the gap between the art films once aimed only at a small audience and the general run of motion pictures.

The revolution of the 1980s will not break with this historical trend. It too will expand the opportunities for artist and audience alike. As technologies like satellites, fiber cable, and videodiscs become widely available, the opportunities and the rewards for creativity will multiply. There will be room and incentive for many more hours of new programming on new channels and limitless hours on videodiscs. There will be room and incentive within these hours for experiments in new formats, for more fulfilling and effective ways to depict the ironies, the agonies, and the joys of our experience.

Those of you who have seen your best ideas sacrificed upon the altar of the ratings competition soon will find room for risky and controversial ventures—and you will find a market willing to reward your efforts.

But if we are to grasp this opportunity for the coming decades, we must make the proper policy choices today. The proper choice is not always the easiest to perceive or to carry out. Some have urged the Congress and the FCC to require the networks to provide certain types of programs at certain hours.

To be frank, I have grave concerns about government second-guessing of specific network programming decisions. We must remember the simple truth that government power over programming most often becomes the power to impose conformity.

What *can* the government properly do to promote the public's interest in diverse and meaningful programming? If it cannot, and should not, directly ban or prescribe specific programs, then we must depend primarily on the pressures and incentives of the market to elicit what we want and need from television. Yet the broadcasting market has had precisely the opposite effect: it has encouraged sameness and rewarded caution. We have asked for inspiration, and we have received the moral equivalent of "The Gong Show." The potentially chilling effect of government regulation is more than matched in practice by the chilling effect of the Nielsen ratings.

It is now becoming clear that free speech can be surrendered to market pressures as easily as it can be subverted by government. Today, commercial competition for the broadest possible audience has stilled divergent voices and left us largely with the monotone of commonly held values and viewpoints.

I believe that the First Amendment means much more than the right of each sit-com to be endlessly spun-off. It means that dignity and human worth come from the open exchange of controversial ideas and criticism. It means that the human spirit should be refreshed by thoughts and ideas contrary to the conventional wisdom, by criticism that is effective because it sometimes angers and enrages. It means that the majority must not only respect the minority but learn from it as well. It means that artists have not only an abstract right but real access to free expression.

It is not the heavy hand of government but the all too visible hand of a conforming market that today limits your talents. Yet, if we make the proper policy choices today, you can become freer artists in a freer market with greater diversity and responsibility.

There are many examples of television's excellence, from "Roots" to "Holocaust" to "60 Minutes." But we also need to ask how often in the daily average of seven hours of viewing we are called upon to search our souls and our minds, to rethink old ideas and prejudices, to reconsider and reshape our understanding of the world. Sadly, it is not often.

There is ample room on the airwaves for relaxation and pleasure. But we must have a broader vision of television, a vision of a time when television will offer a genuine choice—for the artist who seeks to explore new insights and techniques—and for the viewer who seeks a program suited to his or her individual needs, tastes, and schedule.

I know you share this vision. Yet the choices do not exist for you, and so they cannot exist for viewers. Ninety percent of broadcast time continues to come from three networks locked in a battle for the attention—or the half attentive glance—of the "average viewer."

Let me say something about this average viewer. No such individual exists, except as a construct suited to the current structure of broadcasting. The real viewers are people who want something interesting on television but will settle for what is on. They are people increasingly dissatisfied with current programming but who watch out of habit. The average viewer is a concept created by the commercial compulsion to capture 100 percent of the audience, down to the last decimal point. This mindless pursuit has led the networks to round off to the lowest common denominator, to deny the diversity of which we are otherwise so proud, and to justify it all by the law of averages.

Instead of a system that thrives on the rich differences among us, we have chosen a broadcasting system that denies viewers their distinctiveness and your community a chance to create rather than imitate. Creativity lies in seeing things differently, not in seeing averages.

We are becoming more creative at the FCC, because we see things differently than we have in the past. The new technologies offer us a chance for a new television of competition, innovation, and diversity.

In the face of aggressive competition from other programming sources, success may come to mean a 10 percent share of the audience, an audience that would still be over 20 times as large as the readership of *Harper's* or *Atlantic*. But it will be a share earned by imagination and thoughtful programming decisions, not by dominant market power. Networks and other programmers will have to become much more sophisticated *and* selective in their choice of audience.

In short, I believe we can have diversity in the market by allowing the structure of the market to encourage diversity. Then and only then will American television become a fertile field for fresh programming.

THE TROUBLE WITH PUBLIC TELEVISION
Benjamin DeMott

In this article DeMott argues that nonprofit television programming, intended to provide varied cultural offerings, often is narrow, timid, and pretentious. He also explores the methods and attitudes that lead to these failings and calls for the freeing of individual talent to vitalize public television.

The forces of light are coming on strong again for public broadcasting. Throughout most of the past year the heads of Common Cause and Columbia University and Quaker Oats, Bill Moyers, and selected light-bringers, organized as the second Carnegie Commission on the Future of Public Broadcasting, worked together to decide how Congress and the President ought to proceed on this front. The minor (if tricky) task confronting the commissioners was that of clarifying the power structure of the public broadcasting industry. The major job was to tell the policy-makers and the rest of us what can be done to improve the quality and increase the impact of public broadcasting all across the land. And the report the commissioners have just completed (its nickname is Carnegie Two) recommends a massive infusion of new government funds into the country's nonprofit TV system.

By enthusiasts of WNET, WGBH, WETA, and scores of other public stations, that recommendation will be warmly received. Public TV fans compose only a small fraction of the total viewing population, and they're not going to become a majority overnight, regardless of what Congress does. (A recent Corporation for Public Broadcasting poll disclosed that many viewers who avoid public TV do so because they are unfriendly to what it offers, not because they are unaware of its existence; the common complaints are that stars, serial comedy, and sports spectaculars don't appear on the non-profit channels, and that most public TV programs are amateurishly staged.) But the fans' devotion is intense, compounded of gratitude for escaping hard-selling commercials and attachment to favorite performers such as Julia Child, Thalassa Cruso, Dick Cavett, and MacNeil and Lehrer. (A few seasons back, when members of the cast of "Upstairs, Downstairs" made themselves available at station open houses as TV fund-raisers, the parties were—decorously—mobbed.) The 2.7 million families who anted up $50 million last year to keep individual stations alive are sure to see nothing but justice in the notion that all taxpayers should join in the contributory act.

SOURCE: From *The Atlantic*, February 1979, pp. 42–47. Copyright © 1979 by The Atlantic Monthly Company. Reprinted with permission.

NOVA

The Mbuti Pygmies of Africa still hunt the elephant with bow and arrow as they have done for hundreds of years. _____ night NOVA takes a look at the unchanging world of the "BaMiki BaNdula: Children of the Forest" at _____ on Channel ____, PBS.

A Public Broadcasting System series

Whether the notion is in fact just, though, isn't by any means clear. . . .

On occasion, public TV leaves an impression of energy, excitement, or daring, but it's far more often predictable and mild, even downright prim.

At one level this is a matter of social accent and interest. The announcer who lets fall that "Mahsterpiece Theatre is made possible by a grahnt from Mobil" and the gourmet lady who recommends a *petit* Chablis with the chicken suprême both speak in voices full of unearned increment and a dozen other regulars have Grottlesex marbles in their mouths. What's more, the attitudes nicely match the accents. Public TV seems obsessed, for instance, with Edwardian England, especially with the class system and The Help—perfect cooks and ladies' maids. It is perpetually inviting the viewer to think how splendidly the aristocrats used to live: smashing crystal in the Russian officers' mess, suiting up in heavy satin for St. Petersburg court gavottes; sniffing luxo snuff, sipping Madeira—Chippendale furniture, silver by Revere—while serving as Founding Fathers.

And there are comparable social dimensions in public TV's depiction of life nowadays. In "our" world, as shown on the nonprofit channels, "people" play tennis, never bowl. Their hobbies embrace fancy food, gardens, and chess, not lathes in the cellar or twin overhead carburetors in the garage or chickens or pigs in the back yard or homely pickling operations on the kitchen stove. "People" are, furthermore, totally reverential toward the High Arts (I've seen poetry programs on the public channels whose solemnity is unmatched except by funeral Masses), whereas "people" conde- scend to the Popular Arts, concerned about grading them up. It seems to help just a little, for example, if jazz musicians assemble on shiny white, beauty-salon-like sets. (In fairness, it should be noted that the sanitized jazz settings used on public TV are but another version of the cute "African" village that turned up in ABC's "Roots" and that resembled some impeccable lane in Brookline, Mas- sachusetts.) . . .

Lots of class, in a word, in this quarter of the tube. Much embryonic snootiness. If public TV were our only means of com- munication we (and it) would long ago have drowned in a sea of corporate mayonnaise. From the very first, indeed, the makers of what we've come to know as public TV have behaved as though their prime duty was to coat the land with a film of what can best be described as distinguished philistinism, lifelessly well-meaning, tolerant, earnest, well-scrubbed—and utterly remote from what is most precious and vital in the soul of this nation.

But we're in no sense dealing with a plot. If public TV is what it is because it's not free to be anything else, the reason lies neither in an effort by the top five hundred corporations to sell upper-class values to a mass audience, nor in more general forces such as elitism, Anglophilia, and the like. The reason lies—to judge from the results of my inquiry into how the medium works—in the peculiar politics of public TV's address to creativity itself.

Creativity—a hard word and an embarrassing subject. How much, if anything, is really known about fostering creativity? When writers and artists dogmatize on the matter, startling exhibitions of self-pity usually ensue. And when ordinary folk enter the game, they do so only to elevate themselves.

But painful as the subject often is, we're not in total darkness concerning it. We know something—not everything, but something—about the circumstances under which creativity has flourished in the past. We know about the structures and practices of institutions with good records for encouraging creativity. We know that works in different genres, in different periods when creativity was at a peak, resemble each other; the creators—whether of lyric poems, chase choruses in jazz, documentary photographs, repre- sentational novels, torch songs—worked in a spirit of hopeful liveliness, and the results were debated or praised by their contem- poraries (artists and audiences alike). We're aware, further, that the merits of these works derive from a seemingly inexhaustible freshness—a deeply interfused sense that when the object was made, the act of creation was touched by love of the medium, joy in discovering new possibilities within a form.

One or two corollary principles are also obvious. The creators believed in their pivotal importance in the production of the work, believed that the structure of the forms they worked in was pliant to their will, believed that an audience existed for the work and that competence in an art didn't necessarily entail death by hunger or exposure.

Absolute freedom was seldom in the equation, admittedly. The jazz trumpeter who learned to trim his improvisational chorus to the patterns set by a three-minute 78 rpm disc was hardly in complete control of his form. Neither was the novelist who had to adapt his story for serialization in magazines. Yet while a hundred constraints could be cited, the balance wasn't hopelessly tipped, in the memorably creative environments, against the creator. Institutions knew that if they wanted good work, they had to pay for it, had to grant a measure of autonomy to the creative artists, had to develop a sound "selection process."

And the truth is that time and again institutions—repeat, *institutions*: organizations managed by bureaucrats, occupying office space, communicating on printed letterheads—have proven that not only can they sponsor first-class work, but they can do this without sinking either themselves or their audience in Establishment hoity-toity. . . .

Obviously, significant talents are often neglected. No method of peer review has ever eliminated logrolling and back scratching. Selection systems have to keep reminding themselves that nobody is infallible at recognizing creativity.

Still, it equally bears repeating that we're not helpless on this front. We know that certain procedures, emphases, modes of encouragement work better than others. And these historically effective procedures and emphases have a fundamental plausibility. None is in conflict with the most pertinent truth, which is that in our time, achievement in the arts is highly individualistic, dependent upon the artist's ability to believe in the possibilities and significance of personal choices of subject, form, and means.

Why this refresher course on creativity? Because public broadcasting behaves as though the truths just reviewed don't exist. The structures and arrangements of the Public Broadcasting Service (PBS), the Corporation for Public Broadcasting (CPB), and the rest are wholly oblivious to the nature of past environments of creative achievement. Public TV's patterns and procedures are well gauged to bakery chains or fuel wholesalers or meat-packing plants, or to any established nonprofit organization bent on confirming old beliefs rather than on adding to the possibilities of life. But they are remote from the methods of organizations that have dealt success-fully with artists. Putting it more bluntly, on five major organiza-tional fronts public TV deserves indictment as nothing other than a straight-out enemy of talent. The charges against it are the follow-ing:

First, *the arrangements by which individual broadcasting sta-tions produce or buy programs are ingrown, clogged, and unim-aginative.* Who invents most program ideas? Public broadcasting station staffs—administrators preoccupied from day to day by sta-tion housekeeping and budgetary details. They conceive schemes for TV series that can be offered for purchase to the staffs of other stations like their own. An organization called the Station Program Cooperative functions, through rounds of voting on sample pieces produced by individual stations, as producer of a smooth-edged consensus market. . . . In this market the individual program or artist has small standing, or none; neither has the series that reflects an individual style, angle of approach, or sense of new possibilities in the medium. What has worked will work again; innovators keep out. A living culture (so goes the assumption) can be created by poll and committee. . . .

Second, *procedures by which independent talents are paid for their work are invariably unrealistic and demeaning.* Now and then an independent video artist, as opposed to a station executive, manages to interest the public broadcasting bureaucracies in an idea. But those bureaucracies, both at the national level and among the larger producing stations, seem persuaded that paying indi-vidual artists over and above the cost of material (that is, paying the artist's general living expenses) would be an inconceivable in-dulgence. Nearly all programs by individual producers are pur-chased as single items, not as series. These programs are "ac-quired" at a rate of payment for a completed film or videotape that averages about $200 to $250 a minute, or $12,000 to $15,000 an hour. Even in those rare cases where the decision-makers consent to go higher, the total never approaches full production costs—the money the artist has to spend to create the product. And the situation is even worse when an artist seeks a return on his own investment from local stations, which often pay as little as $250 for a half-hour program. . . .

Third, *procedures by which individual creators are chosen for support are arbitrary and frivolous.* The very few institutionally funded programs designed to help independent talents are man-aged with no reference to what's known to be necessary if competi-tions are to be fair—and be seen to be fair. The Corporation for

Public Broadcasting's TV Activities Department last year had a budget of well over $10 million to spend on awards to independent artists, and it spent every penny. But it operated under a procedure by which no guidelines for applicants were ever published, nor any application forms, nor any deadlines, nor any information whatever about the selection process. Furthermore, rejections and approvals by the CPB department's staff were often challenged—sometimes overturned—by applicants who were in a position to go above the heads of the presumably professional staff to members of the politically appointed CPB board. . . .

Sample case: A young filmmaker I know, a man with a reputation among his peers and a talent for demythologizing the film media, sought for a year to interest the Public Broadcasting Service in a series of documentaries about the television business itself. (There were to be six one-hour programs focused on the daily lives of a sit-com producer, the head of a commercial network's operation, a daytime-soap producer, a children's TV producer, and so on.) In time, enough enthusiasm for the project developed to make it seem plausible for him to approach the TV Activities division of CPB. He waited months for an answer to his letter, and received a one-sentence dismissal, no reasons adduced except that the series "would not be a prudent expenditure of public funds." Perhaps that was the right decision, but in the absence of any visible procedure for selection, my friend surely deserved a fuller—and faster—answer.

Fourth, *the hierarchies of program value and importance are established in the public mind, as well as among insiders, in ways that discount the significance of the individual creator.* Masterpiece Theatre and its cousins are offered free to all stations by the Mobil Corporation, the underwriter. This fact, together with Mobil's PBS ad budget and the certified Establishment-academic credentials carried by Shakespeare, Tolstoy, the Founding Fathers, and the BBC, confers highest status on corporate-financed public broadcasting projects. What station manager could avoid concluding that the best shows are Mobil shows? The idea instilled is that vigorous cultural life—serious creativity—means primarily reperforming the great works of the past, and that financing the work of individual unknowns is culturally counterproductive. Dickens and Tennyson forever, who needs anything new?

Fifth, *attempts by public broadcasting stations to acquaint themselves with the views and tastes of the living American public are spiritless and cynical.* It's not inconceivable that an individual creator assured of deep public concern with a subject, could commit himself to it unreservedly. But as matters stand, efforts by public broadcasting stations to seek out the actual feelings of their constituencies are perfunctory at best. . . . The point is clear enough. There is virtually nothing in the arrangements of public TV that is on the side of individual creators. In the eyes of this medium, the talented independent video artist is, in truth, The Enemy.

Suppose things were different: What would public TV look like? Endless programs on fast-food franchising? Endless Frederick Wiseman documentaries?

The skeptical edge in such questions is understandable, and the only fair answer to them has to seem evasive. The fair answer is that predicting the future of a vital medium is a mug's game. I can imagine an interviewer interrogating Sackville and Norton, authors of *Gorboduc*, the first blank-verse tragedy in English, which appeared in 1561, three years before the birth of Shakespeare;—Er, gentlemen, what will happen if we have a rash of scribblers writing plays in the vernacular, people without Culture or University Backgrounds, people without Latin, Greek, or titles? People who don't know about the Unities, etc.? Gentlemen, what will *happen*? The last answer, probably, that the creators of *Gorboduc* would have made was that just ahead lay the Globe Theatre, *Hamlet* and *King Lear*, and the emergence of the greatest literary artist in the long history of the West. Yet Sackville and Norton would have been right if they had answered that way.

As for ourselves, it's wise to bear in mind that in the late twentieth century, noncommercial film and video is a significant nascency in the arts. Nobody can be sure what the young and not-so-young will finally make of the cinematic forms that now enthrall them. . . .

Light-bringers and, ultimately, legislators could, if they had sufficient will and imagination, speak intelligently to the emergent situation. They could encourage serious and disciplined work in the chosen new form, helping to lay out a future in which this country's most gifted video artists would learn to trust themselves and relish their inventiveness, assured that art isn't a lottery but a struggle on decent ground for true creation. The United States could renew its vision of itself as a society that appreciates both the capacity to see individually and the ingenuity that finds, through a labor of craft, ways of accommodating personal vision to the fraternity of millions. But precisely the opposite result will be obtained if the light-bringers and legislators continue to assert that the prime need in public broadcasting is simply more money to produce essentially the same programs now being offered. . . .

We need new ambitions. We need a clearer, sharper understanding of the overall mission of mass communications in the nonprofit setting. Once these are in hand, we need voices speaking out boldly and persuasively to the Congress on behalf of those major structural changes that alone can assure a future for creativity in public broadcasting. But until then, says this old-time contributor to Channel X's auctions, bargain sales, and what-have-you, not another nickel to public TV.

MEMO TO THE PRESS: THEY HATE YOU OUT THERE
Louis Banks

As a former managing editor of *Fortune* and as adjunct professor of management at the Alfred P. Sloan School of Management, Massachusetts Institute of Technology, Banks was in an excellent position to discuss the antagonism he perceived between business and the media.

Do you remember the "invisible shield"? That was in the TV commercial which demonstrated that all kinds of baseballs, footballs, slings, and arrows (i.e. germs) would be stopped dead by a transparent barrier just short of the toothy smile of the fellow who brushed with Colgate toothpaste. Well, I realize now that most of my friends who write, edit, publish, or broadcast the news work behind an invisible shield something like that—a shield of righteousness, defensiveness, and self-protection which blocks out germs of conflicting judgment or thoughtful criticism from other elements of our world. During my thirty-odd years on newspapers and national magazines I saw no shield at all, and joined my colleagues in looking outward with a clear vision, a sense of mission, and perhaps an occasional wink. Not until I went in search of a second career as an academic did I really get outside, and perceive the shield for what it is.

The frustrating, nightmarish aspect of that perception is that I now have an urgent message to send back, and I am having a very hard time getting through. The message I try to convey is this: *"Be careful! They hate you out here!"* But they can't or won't hear me, and the best response I can ever get is a momentary slip in the Colgate smile to the sad sweetness of martyrdom.

Of course my message is somewhat oversimplified—like most headlines or TV news items. There are different "they's," and different degrees of hate, perhaps a certain amount of love–hate, and even a few great exceptions of respect and admiration. But by and large the people who are trying to get things done in this country have a growing contempt for mass journalism, and it is visceral, pervading, and, in the words of the chairman of a $2 billion

---

corporation, full of "dangerous emotions [which] should not be left unattended."

After nearly five years on the outside I've learned to hear some of the sounds that the shield shuts out. Here are two examples:

Time magazine nominates the top 200 young leaders of America and invites them to a Washington conference to meet each other and discuss leadership. On the second day of the panel sessions, antimedia bitterness breaks out spontaneously in nearly every group. In my own session (I was an observer, not a leader), four of the most impressive, attractive young political leaders we could ever hope to elect to office agreed without a quibble that the press was a totally negative influence on their attempts to advance positive programs of reform. "I have to live two lives," said one young governor whose name is cherished by Common Cause. "One to work on my programs and another to cope with the irrelevant, personal, frequently trivial interests of the press. They don't care very much about what I'm really trying to get done." This spontaneity of criticism so stunned Hedley Donovan, the host and editor in chief of Time Inc. publications (and a man quite sensitive to alien sounds), that he later remarked: "I thought it was particularly striking that a group of people who on the whole have prospered from the attention the press has given them, and indeed had been brought together by an organ of the press . . . were quite emphatic in their concerns about, as they saw it, superficiality in the press, unexamined power in the press, problems of accountability in the press, and the press's general place in American life."

In a virgin attempt to teach something about business–media relations to a class of senior corporate executives at the Harvard Business School, I was stopped cold after the first five minutes. One hand went up, and then another, and in a kind of anarchy student after student poured out tales of media perfidy in the coverage of business. Many of them admitted later, over coffee, that they would not have dared to level like that before a working journalist for fear of retaliation. (As former Senator William Fulbright said of some of his fellow politicians: "They have seen the media's power and few are disposed to trifle with it.") Inured by now to such corporate executive emotion, I was surprised again last summer to find the same deep anger from a group of thirty social service managers from around the United States—many of them men and women up from hardscrabble backgrounds themselves, and trying to salvage young lives in their respective cities.

Perhaps I should declare right here that my particular interest is in business–media relationships, because I see business and the media as two essential elements of voluntaristic activism in American life—and, in my view, quite a lot that is central to enterprise, individualism, imagination, ethical performance, material well-being, and even political liberty depends on the successful workings of that voluntarism. I do not expect business and the media to lie down together. They play very different roles, and an adversary relationship on a certain plane provides an essential check-and-balance function. Journalistic history is rich with instances of robber barons of various sizes and guises being brought to justice by diligent reporting—and there is still enough evidence around to sustain that legend. Even so, from my neutral territory I have concluded that it is time for the mass media to pay close attention to the business bill of complaints, to the very end that the check-and-balance function can maintain its effectiveness.*

Since my first traumatic experience I have spent considerable time over the last three years in trying to explain the media to business achievers of various age levels in the benign atmosphere of business school. I have learned that the only way to get on with a rational discussion of the relationship between the media and the rest of society is to exorcise as much emotional anger as possible in the first session. This I do by asking innocently some neutral question about media performance and then listing the responses on the blackboard. This is the way such a list usually runs—these are literal, unprovoked quotes from taped sessions:

"Always sensational. Always looking for the negative."

"Doom-criers."

"The liberalism of most reporters and editors may be way out of whack with the norm of society."

"Some reporters have preconceived answers and merely go through the motion of checking the facts. They have the story written before they come in."

"We can explain our side of the story and think we are on the right side and then a reporter tells his version of that, and what the public thinks about us is going to depend on that reporter."

"The press has a very inflated opinion of its role in society—'the right of the public to know.' They push their way into things and justify really obnoxious, ignorant behavior, sometimes on the argument of the public's right to know."

"They're insulated from the real world."

"As far as TV is concerned my attitude is forgive them for they know not what they do."

---

*As a matter of definition, by "business" I refer to the influential corporations of the Fortune 500 or Business Roundtable caliber unless otherwise indicated. By mass media I mean television, radio, the wire services, and general circulation daily and weekly newspapers—as distinguished from business publications. By "general assignment reporter" or "editor," I refer to those who handle the general run of the news, as distinguished from business specialists.

"They're a closed monopoly. They even monitor criticism of what they write."

"They're a business like any other business, except in some perverse way they profit by being against the rest of us."

"They're a bunch of whores."

Of course such statements are heavy with emotion, such group fault-finding tends to be contagious, and the most opinionated critics always out-talk the most reticent "not quite sure" people.* But for all of the variations in quality of assertion, the basic and reportable fact is that the passion increases year by year.

A Blow to Widows and Orphans

It is not easy to get to the bottom of these pent-up business feelings about the mass media, nor indeed to separate emotion from rational thought. However, I believe it is possible more or less to pinpoint three distinct levels of antagonism. The first involves everyday operational relationships, i.e., the specific reactions to specific encounters in which the business executive or his company has been involved. The second is attitudinal: a businessman's conviction that the great power of the media is used selectively to sour the body politic on corporate product, profit, and practice. The third is societal: a gut feeling that, behind a facade of constitutional right-eousness, First Amendment guarantees are being misused at the expense of other institutional rights no less basic, with a net loss to the American system.

Operationally, the business bill of particulars tends to be a litany. Careless news stories present business executives as saying things they never said, or corporations as doing things they never intended to do. In the reporting of figures, apples are compared to oranges, and decimal points slide back and forth. In the corporate view, sensationalism ignores the 99 percent of constructive progress and gives headline attention to the bizarre, odd, inconsequential, or exceptional. Chronic negativism fortifies this tendency so that the "good news" story or the positive TV footage does not see light of day in the mass media, while the accident, or the competitor's slur, is surefire copy—and usually wrong in detail. Ignorant reporting tangles business complexities into erroneous conclusions, or ducks the complexities in favor of power struggles and personality clashes, real or imagined.

Fred Hartley, the feisty chairman of the Union Oil Company of California, became a sort of business legend in the 1960s when he

---

*In a show of hands at the end of my most recent group discussion, eighteen voted that "the major impact of the media is sensationalism disregarding consequences," and ten voted that it is a "legitimate fulfillment of its informational function in a democratic society." Two abstained.

claimed he was misquoted in a touchy senatorial hearing on the infamous Santa Barbara oil spill. He produced a transcript of the record to back his case. *Newsweek*'s investigation revealed that a New York *Times* reporter had made a direct quotation out of a paraphrased fill-in on Hartley's testimony, provided by the *Christian Science Monitor*'s man. Once printed in the *Times*, the quote turned up as fact in the innumerable newspapers that use the New York *Times* service, in the *Wall Street Journal*, on network television, and in *Time*. Hartley demanded—and got—apologies from nearly everybody involved.

Few business executives see themselves as that lucky. A Boston supermarket chain howled in vain when the Boston *Globe* head-lined the news that its profits were "up 200%" at a time when consumers were very upset about supermarket food prices. In fact the chain was recovering from a *loss* the previous year, and was earning, overall, less than a paltry one percent after taxes on gross revenues. . . .

Handling the Egomaniacal Executive

In truth, the business case probably is weakest at the operational level. Anecdote for anecdote it can be matched by editors, corre-spondents, and camera crews who have tried to get at the facts of business news under deadline pressures, and failed (they hold) through no fault of their own.

To begin with, journalists prove to themselves every day that too many corporate executives want things printed their way—or not at all. "The first thing we have to teach a reporter is to get behind those press releases," says Robert Healy, executive editor of the Boston *Globe*. Since New England businessmen feel somewhat persecuted by this policy at the *Globe*, perhaps they should hear the same thinking from Laurence O'Donnell, the managing editor of their favorite newspaper, the *Wall Street Journal*. "As a young reporter for the *Journal*, I soon learned that the press release was the start of the conversation," he says. "What *aren't* they saying? And what do they mean by this? What has the lawyer told them to put in here? Why does what they say disagree with their 10K reports to the Securities and Exchange Commission?" . . .

When a corporation is in trouble or bedeviled by its lawyers, the press release syndrome can deteriorate to actual lies. A Detroit correspondent of the *Wall Street Journal* carries a flaming scar because, many years ago, American Motors flatly assured him that, contrary to rumor, the company had no intention of selling off its appliance division. He flashed the news to brokerage offices on the Dow-Jones "ticker." One hour later the company announced just such a sale. "One hour later! You don't forget!"

Perhaps the most common editorial grievance is that reporters cannot get to responsible executives when they need information. Instead they are shunted to public relations people who are afraid to say anything except on the word of the boss. And the boss is probably "out of town" when needed most. So deadlines loom, and stories get written on information from best available sources (sometimes competitors). The corporate executive's next-day call to the publisher is predictable: "Your people never even bothered to call me to check the facts." If interviews with top managers are finally granted, the PR person frequently goes along to monitor the conversation. Newspeople see this as meddling just short of prior restraint, and the practice fortifies the journalist's inherent distaste for the authoritarian structure of corporate business in general.

Privately, some corporate PR men commiserate with newsmen at the nearest bar, particularly when trying to "handle" that not uncommon genus, the egomaniacal chief executive. The latter is inclined to believe that he hires a public relations expert to *control* what is printed about the company. Such a president of a middle-sized New England firm thought he was worthy of an interview in a metropolitan daily. Wondrously, his PR man was able to bring it off—only to be fired the day after the story appeared because the interviewer had described the executive as "swarthy."

Add to the media's litany the prayer for the soul of a corporate boss who uses the company's economic power to forestall a story or retaliate for one already printed. In *Fortune*'s earlier days AT&T canceled a lucrative advertising campaign in the magazine after a writer had trenchantly criticized the company's financial strategy (which was subsequently modified). In the celebrated battle between the Detroit bureau of the *Wall Street Journal* and General Motors, in 1954, the *Journal* refused to abide by release dates on stories about new models. GM pulled its advertising until it was badly bruised in the *Journal*'s editorial columns and in publications sympathetic to the *Journal*.

Every editor who assigns a story on a corporation in trouble knows that he or his bosses are in for a certain amount of pressure. In a recent issue of *New York* magazine, Chris Welles reported that hard-hitting stories, directed by a gutsy editor named Lew Young, had provoked "many major corporations, such as Westinghouse, First National Bank of Chicago, and Braniff Airways" to cancel their advertising in *Business Week*. Few are the corporate executives willing to march behind the banner of Stanley Marcus, who built the Neiman-Marcus department store chain into an international name by adroit public relations. "A businessman can make no worse mistake than to try to use the muscle of his advertising dollar to try to influence the news," he says, and adds that one of his first moves at Neiman-Marcus was to separate totally the advertising and public relations departments.

Yet there is a certain amount of hope that trouble at the operational level can be eased somewhat by confrontation and discussion among parties concerned. I have found, in business—media conferences and panel sessions, that this usually means that businessmen are supposed to understand that journalists are 1) really nice people (which they generally are), 2) dedicated to impartial truth, 3) serving their readers or viewers with unwavering professionalism, 4) hampered at every turn by corporate secrecy or deceit, 5) hounded by deadlines and technical problems beyond imagining, and 6) motivated by some indefinable compulsion to get "the story" in print or on the tube at whatever cost, before anybody else. The editors may confess that most general assignment reporters find business dull. Often they will claim aggressively that a journalistic state of original ignorance makes it easier for them to explain matters to an audience that is equally ignorant. (This is particularly a ploy of television newspeople.) But there is a recent heartening tendency for publishers, editors, and even TV news executives to risk sending a few specialists off to short courses in business school, and in most cases this practice has resulted in more effective reporting—if the reporters can get through the layer of editors above them who still believe that business is dull.

For their part, business executives at the panel sessions rarely get much through the shield about the problems of making corporate decisions under intense and conflicting pressures from governments, shareholders, labor unions, environmentalists, consumerists, and competitors. Or about the importance to the neighborhood of a thriving, prosperous business operation. But being quintessential pragmatists, they learn to recognize the media as one more difficult constituent to be dealt with, and they go home to give increasing support for, and new sympathy to, the vice president for public affairs. So all is not lost. . . .

Easy Mark for the Leak

The difference between the operational and the attitudinal states of mind is revealed in what happens after the last drink and the last first-name farewells of the panel sessions. The media people tend to drift to their own gatherings to have a nightcap and swap old stories about the last war or the last presidential campaign—i.e., anything but business coverage. The business executives slam their doors and write notes to themselves about "those arrogant bastards." . . .

Basically most ranking editors of mass media see business as suspect until proved innocent. At the attitudinal level this means a greatly overweighted coverage of antibusiness pronouncements. The average editor of print or tube becomes an easy mark for the leak from governmental or public interest agencies, some of which have a vested interest of sorts in being antibusiness. Political candidates are eternally running against privately owned public utilities; usually their campaign charges are faithfully reported, but the media are rarely moved to ask why the issues fade away after the election. Congressman Les Aspin of Wisconsin, a member of the House Armed Services Committee, generally has a release blasting some aspect of the military–industrial complex ready for the Monday morning papers; the statements invariably get wide coverage, but I have yet to see a story reporting this careful regularity as something newsworthy in its own right. (I noted with interest, while attending a conference in Colorado with the affable Congressman Aspin, that the Monday morning stories kept coming under Washington datelines despite the fact that he was some 2000 miles away.)

The latest vogue in business reporting is consumerism. Newspapers and wire services that previously have carried little more business news than the stock and bond tables find room for lengthy reports by their consumerist investigative teams. Even local television stations are conducting a daily search for bait-and-switch advertising, spoiled vegetables, or tainted hamburger. Now executives of consumer goods corporations may be willing to admit reluctantly that the original reformists probably had a case, but today they see themselves as victims of a media epidemic more virulent than botulism. Here again the print is not the accuracy or inaccuracy of specific stories, or whether some businesses may deserve all the investigatory attention they can get, but the fact that consumerism is attitudinally antibusiness by definition, and the media are coming to have something of a vested interest in pushing coverage which, on net, provides a distorted view of reality.

One cannot help but note the irony in coverage of a recent major development in the automobile industry. Whereas we are well informed about alleged auto industry foot-dragging in matters of pollution control and air bags, there was no visible consumerist reporting praising General Motors for its risky leadership in chopping down the size of its principal cars in the 1977 and 1978 model years to aid energy conservation. Instead, the story slipped over to the business pages, where the question was whether stupid old GM would suffer lower sales because it wasn't providing consumers with the big gas-guzzlers they loved and wanted.

Given this general attitude, both industrial and consumerist corporations are terrified at the persistent and often careless linkage of industrial or commercial processes to nearly all of the world's woes, including the state of the ozone layer and the spread of cancer. In the business view, the big danger lies in the mass media's uncritical acceptance of fragmentary or half-baked claims. It is one thing to report findings carefully considered by competent professionals, and quite another to shout "fire" in a crowded theater by giving space or air time to speculative theories propounded in raw research.

Business has its list of horrible examples of distortions that proved to be disastrous to responsible producers (cranberries, swordfish, cyclamates, spray adhesives, and even nuclear power), while the media can counter with an equally long list of missteps or cover-ups (Kepone, B.C.M.E., thalidomide, and some aspects of nuclear power). Doubtless environmentalism and toxicity are areas where the check-and-balance process has worked to social advantage. News coverage spurred passage of various environmental protection measures (along with their excesses) and of the Toxic Substances Control Act of 1976. Fear of news coverage, biased or fair, also has something to do with prompt corporate attention to potential trouble areas. . . .

Where Is the Public Interest?

Not far beneath these feelings about media attitudes lies a pervading suspicion among those achievers, the businessmen, that the repetitive effect of mass media coverage is to denigrate achievement itself. This is another way of saying, in societal terms, that the mass media has somehow lost track of one of the basic drives of the country. James Ferguson, the chairman of General Foods, is one of the handful of corporate leaders who have wrestled seriously with the business—media problem—not only because his company has been burned by exaggerated alarms about food processing, but because he is concerned about the potentially dangerous emotions building up in the society against the media. He argues that "by their current pattern of behavior the news media in America are telling us that they are suffering from an identity crisis."

". . . As is true of other institutions, technology and economic trends have presented them with tools of enormous power," he writes. "Like most institutions they have not yet fully learned to cope with the new environment, nor to understand and control the new tools. In fact it could be argued that they are on something of a binge with the new tools."

(I never saw the invisible shield so clearly as when Ferguson's thoughtful statement was brought up for comment at a panel session of award-winning reporters in Manhattan in late 1976. With almost no discussion, the young prizewinners dismissed it as "just like Spiro Agnew," and that was the end of the subject.) . . .

It goes without saying that corporate executives see the American business system as fundamental to national development. Yet they are all too aware that business functions in a capitalist democracy, and in the final analysis will rise or fall in accordance with public opinion and resultant political pressure. In their view the persistent drumbeat of media oversimplification, exaggerated fault-finding, and antagonistic news selection is providing a perverted picture of the nation's principal achievement. They see business being burdened, as a result, with an overload of indirect taxes, restrictions, and social obligations to the point of net loss in its ability to function economically in the development of new resources, new markets, and new "breakthrough" research. When this state of affairs becomes evident it will probably be documented, with Walter Cronkite severity, as a business failure "to meet our needs," and will be viewed politically as evidence that only additional governmental intervention can put things right. In these terms it will be very difficult indeed to keep alive the yeast of corporate enterprise and the rate of growth and creation of wealth to which society has become accustomed. And when those are gone, according to this worst possible scenario, we will be in for a period of social upheaval that could even involve damage to the First Amendment.

In reply the media could argue that such "worst possible scenarios" have been the standard prediction of businessmen since the advent of the progressive income tax or the reform legislation of the New Deal; yet for all of those imagined horrors, the United States today offers the most hospitable business climate in the world. A give-and-take between the demands of business enterprise and the community's changing social standards—which the media reflects—has been with us since the founding of the Republic. All this can be argued without putting so much as a dent in the invisible shield.

Yet what is involved in the basic business—media antagonism today is the serious question of whether the press itself should adjust to new social responsibilities. In its ferocious drive to maintain audience ratings, to cater to populist fears and prejudices, to entertain instead of enlighten, is the mass media perhaps sacrificing editorial leadership? Is it ducking the complex explanations for terse simplistic bulletins that provide villains and heroes and feed a public hunger for high drama?

The message we have to get through the shield is that business and other social sectors have a legitimate right to ask such questions. There is nothing in the First Amendment that makes the media immune to the same kind of critical examination it administers to the rest of society. A first step toward answers might involve a responsible collegial corporate group, such as the Committee for Economic

Development, the Conference Board, or the Business Roundtable, in just such an audit, at the three levels of criticism and frustration. To this a group of responsible editors could draft a considered reply, only this time on someone else's territory. Somewhere in the process the media people might discover that a significant part of the seething anger out there reflects a yearning for constructive collaboration in finding a way through the multiple variables of uncertainty that seem destined to afflict the decades ahead.

There is no question that even when the system is working well there will be tension between business and the media. The corporate executive, by definition, deals primarily with specific decisions under the risk–reward mechanism of the marketplace. Responsible editors have the function, as Henry Fairlie reminds us by way of Matthew Arnold, "to see life steady and see it whole." They will, and should, sit in judgment on the causes and effects of important corporate decisions in terms of the whole. But the question that business criticism has provoked—and which is reflected by others who themselves claim a share of responsibility for American life—is whether the mass media are in danger of abrogating that very function by its current behavior.

VALUES

Norman Isaacs

Long a combative figure in journalism as editor, critic, and educator, Isaacs is now chairman of the National News Council. He sees a lack of underlying values as being the root danger to journalism today. This leads, he claims, to the arrogance that refuses to see faults and to make conscientious corrections.

Not long ago, I was in Washington, where hundreds of editors gathered for their annual series of discussions and debates over the state of journalism. Underlying all that they examined was the core issue never mentioned out loud—not because anyone is trying to hide it, but simply because nobody really knows how to get a handle on it.

That core issue is journalism's values.

There are a number of risks involved in tackling the subject of professional values. One risk is that what I may consider a violation of a decent ethical code, another may regard as a professional duty.

SOURCE: Sigma Delta Chi Foundation Lecture, University of Minnesota, 1978. Reprinted with permission.

Also, one risks tarring everyone with the same sweeping brush strokes. I think there is an ethical code that all journalists ought to abide by and any number of good professionals follow. Unhappily, there are more who find excuses not to follow a code. So I don't mean to besmirch the good while trying to pillory those who deserve it.

There are all kinds of journalists. They represent a vast range of views about life. There are intellectual giants among them and a lot of pygmies. There are the dedicated and industrious. There are the sloths, who don't even merit rank under the "Peter Principle." There is journalism that touches on near-greatness. But there are many more evidences of a mindless, tunnel-visioned journalism that torments all of us who see communications as the most vital of all callings.

In years past, I conducted guerrilla war against publishers, separating good guys and bad guys in a broad Jehovah-like manner. Subsequently, I came to realize that while many of my rockets were well-intended, there was also lack of decent understanding on my part.

Now approaching what Fred Friendly quips as being the springtime of senility, I recognize that the main troubles with most of the journalistic enterprise are weak leadership from managers, and what so many editorial writers so love to denounce—a resistant bureaucracy in newsrooms.

There are, of course, among publishers and editors, the types one editor I knew loved to brand as "JOURNALISTIC STINKERS." But I also know publishers and editors of conscience and integrity who are often frustrated by the bureaucracies that operate on news, copy and city desks, in other departments, and among reporters.

A number of intelligent approaches were advanced at the Washington meeting. Many editors left, intending to put some of the new concepts into practice. The track record suggests, however, that they will struggle to get the messages across, but that these messages will be tortured out of rational purpose in the substrata of enterprises. And finally weary of the endless stonewalling and alibiing, the key executives will grudgingly accept a few minor and really meaningless compromises.

R. Peter Straus, director of Voice of America, has been telling an amusing story about Henry Kissinger.

Kissinger's brother Walter, one year younger than Henry, is a highly successful business executive in New York. They came to the United States together, refugees from Germany. Their American educations were strikingly similar. Yet, while Henry's speech has a notably Germanic accent, there is not the faintest trace in Walter's speech. Asked about it, Walter laughed and said, "Well, you know, Henry was never a very good listener."

I relay the story because it seems to me to relate to many of this country's journalists, young and old. It is relevant to ask whether enough of them listen to new ideas, whether they read adequately about the society. To ask how many of them stop once in a while to ponder about journalism's function, or, at the least, to weigh whether any of the many criticisms have any merit.

This is an important part of the equation because there is no escaping the fact that journalism is held in low esteem by many Americans. In a recent issue of *Atlantic* magazine there is an article by Louis Banks, a former editor at *Fortune* and now a professor at MIT. It is headlined: "Memo to the Press: They Hate You Out There." Banks writes about the attitudes of businessmen, but he could just as well have broadened it to include most segments of the society.

There are many in the press who argue that the journalist has no business hoping to be liked, that the only needed response is respect. I agree. But it poses another question: Isn't there something wrong, terribly wrong, when there isn't even respect?

Now mind you, some news organizations and some journalists do command respect. But it is far from general.

In the spring issue of *Nieman Reports*, Professor Chris Argyris, the Harvard scholar who is expert in organizational behavior, has written about what he considers journalism's astonishing predilection for self-destruction.

Both the Banks and Argyris articles, in my opinion, are thoroughly accurate. But Banks does not tap a new vein. For years now, the polls have been reporting deep resentment on the part of many people toward the press.

This is where the lack of respect comes in. It is not basic news judgments people quarrel with. The main criticisms are about inaccuracy, about stories perceived as biased, about defensive and arrogant behavior.

Out of a lifetime of experience in journalism, I see these charges are largely true. Argyris expresses astonishment over the defensiveness. He has studied all kinds of enterprises and professions and he hasn't found one that matches the journalist's defense mechanisms, which the good professor concedes are amazingly skilled.

Here is where my arguments about values enter. I hold that all these things of which we are charged, and of which I say we are too often guilty, stem from the fact that the majority of those in journalism refuse to accept any concept of enduring values, and, therefore, override as inconsequential any and all criticism.

This may stem from the fact that for almost all its history, our press has been reactive, operating by instinct. In moments of crisis—the accident of fate or of major confrontation between antagonists—coverage can be superbly efficient. There is nothing like a visible emergency to galvanize the journalist to skilled, factual coverage of an event, with remarkable ingenuity and sense of pursuit.

But absent emergency, our press has too often lapsed into being habit-prone in coverage patterns, obtuse about complex issues and always exhibiting the standard resistances to self-examination.

Those news organizations and journalists who have been thoughtfully self-conscious about the public's low rating of the press have changed course. There is today more and better examination of important issues than ever before. But the best in American journalism is, unhappily, atypical.

I know editors who say, "What others do is not my business. I run my newspaper for my readers. If somebody wants to be a stinker, that's his business." I can't swallow that. It seems to me both capricious and condescending in reasoning. All of us owe it to ourselves to try to move the society forward all the time. We need better doctors, better lawyers, teachers, engineers, businessmen, politicians, public servants, and, vitally, better journalists, because we are the ones who feed the minds of people.

From square one there are automatic, immense responsibilities that fall on the journalist. What is selected for coverage, how it is written and presented, can alter the course of life, in tiny ways and in giant ones. A wrong diagnosis by a journalist does not affect just a single patient, it can run like a contagion through an entire city. If any calling demands a sense of values, this is the one.

Earlier, I mentioned managerial weakness as one reason for some of the softness about newsroom values. There has been, and there is, too much reliance on the "learning-by-doing" pattern. It might be acceptable at a cub level, but it is crippling when applied to supervisors, the heart of newsroom bureaucracy—a bureaucracy that in too many places crushes initiative, imagination and enterprise.

Reporters operate their own bureaucracy, one fed by what I see as ever-present peer-group pressure. I concede that often it is not pressure as such at work, but the desire of people to be popular. Heaven knows how many young journalists with sound potentials will never rise much above pedestrian levels because of this curious urge to be well-thought of by colleagues. I am not suggesting that the way to the top is by being tough and abrasive. I am saying that the desire to be popular all too often becomes a form of self-suppression of talent.

One good, young reporter was recounting recently how things operate at his paper. He was aghast at the prevailing mind-set that treats every complainant as a kook. There may be a call about a mistake in a city hall story, or in an obit, or anything else, and the desk person taking the call will cup a hand over the phone mouthpiece and announce, "I've got a crazy on the line." Everybody's crazy, you see, except us.

Not until publishers and top editors recognize the vital importance of investing in training people for supervisory responsibility and advancing an honest and valid value system will the evil be cured.

A rational value system need begin with only four goals:

- To do all possible to be accurate.
- When we fail in that, to correct our errors promptly.
- To recognize the responsibilities we carry.
- To abandon all arrogance about what it is we do.

Given the speed at which journalists have to work, error is bound to occur. The fault may lie with a news source, or it may be thoughtlessness or weariness, or some odd electronic error. Whatever the cause, isn't it simple virtue to correct the record—clearly, cleanly and without trace of embarrassment?

Yet the record is that wherever an ombudsman—or people's editor or advocate—is named to deal with these sins of commission or omission, battle lines are drawn immediately by desk editors and reporters.

This fault of refusing to correct error is arrogance of the worst kind. There would never be a need for ombudsmen or press councils if only this elemental principle of fairness were to be accepted by newspeople as a given.

Arthur Miller, the brilliant Harvard law professor, spoke at the editors' meeting in Washington on the subject of privacy. He was stunned by the quotes attributed to him in the subsequent press coverage. For the first time in his career, he read absolutely the reverse of what he had told the editors.

He expostulated immediately. Correction? None.

I suppose Miller goes down on the chart as a "crazy." That, my friend, is journalistic arrogance and it's precisely what led Louis Banks to write "Memo to the Press: They Hate You Out There."

One reason the people Banks talked with hate the press is the fault James Reston of the New York *Times* put his finger on years ago: "The American newspaperman would rather break a story than understand it."

I don't know where in the list of many arrogances this fits, but it ranks very high. One such episode that comes to mind still galls me.

In the 1960s, the late Sen. Everett Dirksen (R-Ill.) mounted a national campaign to try to overturn the Supreme Court's one-man/one-vote decision. Dirksen wanted, finally, the ultimate: a constitutional convention.

I'm still not sure many newspaper people really tried to understand that fight. If they didn't, I'll never know why. The only such convention we ever had was the one called in 1787 under the Articles of Confederation. It was summoned to propose amendments to the Articles, but it proceeded to write an entirely new Constitution. And, given the torments and stresses of our present time, can you not imagine the mischief that a constitutional convention could bring this republic?

There was no obligation for news people to build any emotional campaign. All that was required was reporting the news. But there was no such reporting. Dirksen's drive took on the appearance of a soundless avalanche.

The number of state legislatures that adopted resolutions for a constitutional convention grew to 31. But coverage came in bits and snippets—a couple of graphs now, a couple in a week or two. Not even the American Bar Association, which had become deeply concerned, could determine how many states had passed resolutions, and some key members of the Bar began to set up an informational network to find out.

Chief Justice Earl Warren made some speeches, trying to highlight the importance of what was going on. He said that if the Bill of Rights were to come to a popular vote, it probably would fail, given the public's perceived temper. Those speeches were reported, but customarily minus any broad view of what Warren's purpose was in using such strong terms.

As I say, either the journalists around the country didn't understand, or they didn't care.

Because of my involvement in press/bar matters, I was asked if I felt it proper to try to capture the attention of some leading editors. Feeling that it was, I wrote urgent letters, enclosing detailed information. You can perhaps understand how embarrassed I was to receive only the most casual of responses. I had about as much effect as a gnat on an elephant's behind.

The country was saved the trauma because the bar associations went to work. They had the muscle to lobby enough legislatures to retract their calls, but even that series of recalls drew less attention in the press than a row within some mayoral office or zoning board.

We've improved some. At least, the conflict over the Equal Rights Amendment draws adequate regular attention. It is of far less consequence than a full constitutional convention, but it does have some sex to it and, I suppose, for some troglodytes in journalism, it makes a big difference, even if they don't understand this one either.

And yes, there is a good deal of excellent investigative journalism going on. But how many in the craft have paused to assess whether there is a consistent thread of true-value purpose in all the investigating? Some of it is certainly in order, vitally necessary. About some others, there is room for question, if not doubt; and I say this as the chairman of the jury that passed the investigative category of the Pulitzer Prizes this year.

Might there be some merit to the charge that surfaces here and there that journalism in some aspects is serving as one of the prime destroyers of values—that it is so gripped by the passion to expose that it is on the way to tearing down everything in the society?

All of it rests on values. And the values for journalism are there if only we build equal passion for responsibility. Out of this will come devotion to accuracy. That devotion will see to it that what errors we make are quickly corrected. And in the doing, we cannot help but lose some of the arrogance.

If journalism is going to come to general acceptance of higher ethical standards, the change is not likely to come from within the existing ranks. The good organizations already hold those standards. The resisters are not able to shake off the built-in habits of looking on everyone outside as "crazies."

The changes nationwide are going to have to come from the new generation of journalists and, if we have the time, the generation next.

There are publishers and editors hoping for the emergence of young people with a sense of conviction about journalism—who are determined to try to get the facts straight, who welcome having error corrected, who believe that news and opinion belong in properly labeled separate compartments, who scorn the freebies, who aspire to be thoroughly responsible professionals.

If that kind of partnership can come—a partnership of the new, committed, young journalists with the editors of conscience—then we can have journalism with the touch of greatness upon it.

At the heart of it, this is the kind of value system the true journalist needs: To be aware of the pressures and the temptations, but know that this is a calling demanding men and women ever conscious of the power within their hands to do good or evil—who choose to use that power serving a citizenry that to survive needs the most faithful picture of life and its problems—to the end that the decisions made are based upon rounded knowledge and not sullied by narrow internal or external pressures.

Section 20

WHO OWNS
THE MEDIA?

The rapid growth of newspaper groups and
cross-media ownership is scrutinized in this
section. So is the technological revolution in
newspaper production, which has greatly altered
the economics and traditional methods of
publishing.

THE GROWTH OF MEDIA CONGLOMERATES
John B. Oakes

Oakes, former editorial page editor of the New York *Times*, makes a critical examination of media ownership trends, correlating them to a perceived loss of public confidence in the press. He sees this confidence as the ultimate protection of a free press, and its loss as the greatest danger.

The American press has changed completely in character, in structure and even, to a considerable extent, in purpose not only over the past two hundred years, when the First Amendment was written into the Constitution, but over the past twenty years; and it is changing at an accelerated pace every day.

It isn't the press alone that is changing. It is the audience, too. With a change in character and in audience has come a change in public attitudes toward the press, a weakening in that public understanding and support of the First Amendment in "the general spirit of the people," that is the rock on which its protective power ultimately rests. Unless we establish a new relationship between press and public, we are eventually going to see the basic Constitutional guaranty outmoded in the public mind, and therefore, because the courts do indeed eventually follow the election returns, weakened by courts or legislature if not ultimately destroyed.

Hardly a hundred years ago, we were in the golden age of personal journalism. It took little capital to start a newspaper, little readership to keep it alive. What it did take was a strong, articulate editor who had a distinct point of view and was willing and able to express himself with force and cogency. This was the era of the partisan personalities of American journalism, whose names— Greeley, Bennett, Dana, Pulitzer—were synonymous with their newspapers.

As industrialization developed, education broadened, and means of communication improved, the limited audience to whom the editors of the nineteenth century were addressing their message, changed both qualitatively and quantitatively. Publishers and editors discovered that the new mass audience was interested in a wider spectrum of news and information than had been the

---

SOURCE: From the Frank E. Gannett Memorial Lecture presented at the Washington Journalism Center, Washington, D.C., May, 1978. Reprinted with permission.

norm for the relatively rarefied elite of earlier decades, a point Adolph Ochs demonstrated in two ways when, to save his tottering newspaper at the turn of the century, he broadened and deepened its content and at the same time lowered its price.

The old-style, highly competitive personal journalism began to give way to the journal of information; and throughout this century, through two world wars and on to the present day, American newspapers, *reflecting* and at the same time *stimulating* existing trends in American industrial society, have increasingly moved toward a kind of standardization and away from the peculiar and often erratic individualism that had once been their characteristic.

They have also become Big Business, a development that has already had and will doubtless continue to have a subtly adverse effect on both public and judicial perception of the First Amendment's protection of press freedom. What has happened is that there has been a massive concentration of control of larger and larger numbers of newspapers in fewer and fewer top managerial hands; huge corporate conglomerates are replacing private or individual ownership; and along with this trend there has been a corresponding reduction of competition to the point where less than 50 of the 1,550 cities of this country with daily papers have two or more under competing ownership.

It's easy to say that these developments have been inevitable, paralleling similar developments in many other areas of commerce and industry; but it is just because the free working of the press, both print and electronic, is of such peculiar importance in our democratic society that the consequences of this kind of evolution take on a special significance, threatening to undermine Constitutional protections that we now take for granted.

Press freedom is not something to be taken for granted simply because that one phrase was written as an afterthought into the Constitution. . . . .

The First Amendment as it applies to the press is clearly designed to protect a public rather than a vested interest; our Constitutionally protected purpose is essentially one of public service rather than private profit.

Only a few days ago, the Chief Justice of the United States wrote a concurring opinion in which he went out of his way to state, in effect, that he could see little if any distinction between the First Amendment rights of a newspaper corporation and those of any other kind of corporation. It is clear that Mr. Justice Burger believes that the Constitutional guarantee of freedom of the press does not necessarily involve protection of the press as a unique kind of institution requiring the special institutional protection that Mr. Justice Stewart, for example, attributes to it. The point is important not only because

Mr. Burger is Chief Justice, but because he has put his finger on a Constitutionally tender spot in the anatomy of huge press corporations.

While he spoke against "limiting the First Amendment rights of corporations as such," Mr. Burger seemed at the same time to be suggesting a reinterpretation of First Amendment protections in light of—and here I quote—"The evolution of traditional newspapers into modern corporate conglomerates in which the daily dissemination of news by print is no longer the major part of the whole enterprise. . . ."

The converse of Mr. Justice Burger's opinion implicit in this recent Massachusetts case fits, I believe, a growing public perception of press conglomerates replete with built-in conflicts of interest. I think this perception may lead to a questioning of the need for special protection of the press *as such*, under a First Amendment that was in fact designed to ensure the free flow of information and opinion, and not the accretion of corporate power.

As the capital investment required to produce and publish newspapers has increased, three distinct but related economic developments have taken place, affecting the industry and its relationship to the public: the formation of "media conglomerates" linking under one ownership a wide variety of large enterprises; the establishment of enormous newspaper and broadcasting chains; and the development of both conglomerates and chains into publicly-held stock corporations. When to the already great power of a quasi-monopoly in a given city is added the greater strength of chain ownership, some troublesome questions of public policy are inevitably raised.

While many chains operate in such a way as to leave editorial independence in the hands of individual components, and use their vast resources to upgrade their papers—as has happened in a large number of cases already—this is not true of all chains and there is no guarantee that it will always be true of any. The potential threat of centralized, remote control, of concentrated economic and editorial power, is always there. . . .

Yet today the ten largest newspaper chains control one-third of the country's total readership—20 out of 61 million. . . .

As the mad race within the communications industry toward bigger combinations and conglomeration goes on, we are going to see intensified moves to extend anti-trust and other kinds of restrictive legislation, which will of course be fought on "free press" grounds, much as the efforts to break up industrial trusts and combines early in this century were also fought—and with the probability of just as little success.

As recently as 15 or 20 years ago, no newspaper shares were traded on the stock market. Today there are at least a dozen, including some of the largest newspaper corporations, controlling in all about 20 percent of national circulation. There are perfectly sound economic reasons for this trend, but there are also inherent dangers. . . .

What essentially worries critics of the growing concentration of power in the news industry in the hands of relatively few communications companies—publicly and privately held—is that the more concentrated power becomes, the more likely it is to move the focus of print journalism away from its original goals and purposes into becoming a mere money-machine, as has happened in the television industry. It is this potential threat that inevitably colors the public perception of the press as an independent institution.

That perception is further altered—and not for the good—when the press lobbies for special privileges and exemptions from, for example, the anti-trust laws—as it did in connection with the Failing Newspaper Act a few years ago, and from the child labor laws a good many years before that. To use the battle cry of "Freedom of the Press" as a shield on every possible occasion for special economic benefits is to debase the currency of freedom whose integrity we desperately need to preserve.

Meanwhile, the newspaper audience has been changing, and we have to face the fact that, relatively speaking, it has also been declining, especially among younger readers. The reason? It's too simplistic to blame it all on TV—though TV has undoubtedly given them a taste for the "quick fix" in news rather than for in-depth reporting. More deep-seated causes may be found in the new mobility of the American family and its resultant loss of deep-seated roots; the growth of leisure time and of affluence, affording in both respects a wider choice of interests to compete with the daily newspaper; but above all, the loss of credibility in all institutions, including the press.

These are among the factors that have affected in varying degrees the responsiveness of the American reader to the daily newspaper and have already led to profound changes in the attitudes and contents of newspapers themselves. These changes have been taking place in a society that seems increasingly to be turning in to itself, more interested in problem-evasion than in problem solving, more concerned with style than with substance, more self-indulgent than self-critical.

Newspapers are now desperately trying to recapture the attention of their readers, as broadcasting has always done to its viewers and listeners by supplying, in Henry Geller's felicitous phrase, "Chewing gum for the eyes." The press is now moving in that direction, emphasizing "chewing gum for the brain." Service-oriented journalism is the word today, to grab the reader who, it is confidently believed, is more interested in "what will it do for me?" than in "what do I need to know?"

In the effort to win back readership in the suburbs, among youth, from the TV audience, American newspapers have been shifting their emphasis away from what the editor thought the reader ought to have, to what they now believe the readers want. The press has been increasingly catering to shallowest taste, increasingly forgetful of its Constitutional obligation to inform the democracy. . . .

Last January, the *Times* of London was briefly shut down because one of the printers' unions within the plant refused to permit publication of one issue containing an article highly critical of the union. In a magnificent editorial discussing the problem, the *Times* of London had this to say:

> Those who wish to maintain the freedom of a nation must stand behind the editorial freedom of the press, even though they know that it will sometimes be abused and often be wrong in its judgments. Those in the press who want to maintain its freedom must also try to raise the standard of its news reporting, its sense of responsibility, its willingness to report all sides and its essential fairness. *Only a fair press will retain the public confidence that is needed by a free press.*

Once the American public loses faith in the press as an institution of prime importance to the democratic process, the most fundamental protection of the press—far greater than that embodied in the First Amendment—will have been lost. I think there are ominous symptoms today that we of the press are indeed in danger of losing that public confidence.

The growing number of attacks on press freedom in the courts is, I believe, a reflection of that development in the public mind. The tidal wave of gag rules, of subpoenas, of efforts to force revelation of confidential sources, and now the new vogue of closing off pre-trial hearings, are all part of this trend, which is clearly subversive of First Amendment guarantees and must be resisted as much in the public interest as in the Press's interest.

But I think the institutionalized press would place itself in a better position to fight the real encroachments on its freedom if it acknowledged, more readily than it is now prone to do, that when competing constitutional rights collide—as often happens especially between First and Sixth Amendments—it is not necessarily true that the press in every case must prevail. I don't think we are very convincing when we take—as we tend to do—an even more absolutist position than Justice Black would have done, by regarding the First Amendment as automatically overriding every other provision of the Constitution, not to mention common sense. . . .

A great deal has been heard in recent years about the right of newspapers' access to the records, documents and files of government. But although we newspapermen are generally highly articulate on the public's right of access to government, as we should be, we are not usually quite so strong on the public's right of access to ourselves.

Governmentally enforced access to the press is not the answer. Far from it. To force a newspaper to publish an item is no less an infringement on its freedom than to forbid it from publishing one, as the Supreme Court has pointed out. . . . Nevertheless, the public demand for greater accessibility to the press is not to be laughed off—and I believe that in one form or another, the threat of governmentally enforced access will remain, just as long as there is a public perception that newspapers tend to operate less in the public interest than in their own interest. We need to cut away from our characteristic arrogance, and to open ourselves much more than has been the custom in the past to accessibility *by* the public as well as accountability *to* it. . . .

In a sense, the American newspaper is an unregulated public utility, and that's the way we want it to be maintained— unregulated, unlicensed and free. But this is an era when every value is being reexamined and every right is under question, even the Constitutional protection of freedom of the press. In defending itself from that attack, it seems to me the press has to be accountable to something more than our own business offices and our stockholders; we have to be accountable in the narrowest sense, and first of all, to our own consciences, of course; but in the broadest sense to the public interest as we see it.

THE GREAT PRESS CHAIN
N. R. Kleinfield

The Gannett newspaper group is the largest in the country and plans further expansion. In this article Kleinfield examines its operations, and especially its policies of leaving editorial control to local management. In passing, he also names the other national newspaper chains and gives basic data about them.

In Tarentum, Pa., the newspaper office is a small building of Colonial design in the middle of town. "Valley News Dispatch" is written on its facade. On a recent afternoon, a pair of hounds was

SOURCE: From *New York Times Magazine*, April 8, 1979, p. 41. Copyright © 1979 by The New York Times Company. Reprinted by permission.

snoozing in front of the ramshackle V.F.W. headquarters next door. Except for the hounds, there wasn't a sign of life. Inside the cramped newsroom, though, the very air crackled and smoked with an undercurrent of aliveness. Copy paper was in motion, reporters were hugging telephones, and there were sporadic bursts of typing.

The afternoon's paper had just rolled off the presses. The front page was given over to, among other things, a story about a gubernatorial candidate demanding Federal dollars to finish the Allegheny Valley Expressway, and a dispatch on a wildcat strike at a nearby auto plant. There was a three-paragraph item on radioactive waste being discovered on Interstate 80. Inside the paper, things were happening all over. The "Hospitals" column noted that 42 people had been admitted yesterday to area hospitals; 49 were discharged. The lead editorial railed against legalized dog racing in Pennsylvania.

Inside his snug office, Paul Hess, the laconic managing editor, leaned back in his chair and plonked down some papers he was scanning. "There has been a load of improvements since Gannett bought this paper several years ago," he said. "Our circulation hasn't moved much; it's still around 45,000. But the newsroom has been totally reorganized. We used to have two managing editors, and nobody knew whom to report to. The paper is packaged better. And did we increase our local coverage! I don't want to pass on the image that *The Valley News Dispatch* was the worst paper on earth and now it's the toast of the profession. Gannett didn't come rolling in here and pull off a modern-day miracle. This was a good paper before. Now it's a better one."

Out in the newsroom, John O'Donnell, a rumpled feature writer, shared similar feelings. "It's a more professional paper. Some of these small-town papers are real rags. We did lose some of the family atmosphere around here when the big guy moved in. I had my fears about casting my lot with him. But we've been given local autonomy. I think all Gannett does is look at the bottom line. Each of us is like a little gold mine. As long as the golden stuff keeps pouring out, they leave us be."

Now approaching the age of 74, the Gannett Company has gone from its position as a one-paper operation to its status as the biggest newspaper chain in the United States. There are 1,764 daily papers in the country. Gannett owns 78 of them. Its short-term objective is to publish an even 100. Several other newspaper groups—Knight-Ridder, Newhouse, Scripps-Howard—own a slew of papers, but it would take an Everest climb for them to catch up. Spaced out from Guam to New Jersey, Gannett's papers thud on the doorsteps of three million readers a day, more than the combined daily audience of the New York *Times*, the Los Angeles *Times* and the Washington *Post*. The chain has doubtlessly done more to change the nature of how America's newspapers are owned than any other company. Not that long ago, most papers were independently owned; today, all but around 500 belong to one or another of 167 newspaper groups. Independents are being bought out by chains rapidly, at a clip of 50 to 60 papers a year.

The trend is well established. With few exceptions, newspapers in this country are more desirable investments than ever. There are bidders enough for them, and the gavel is being brought down for some pretty sums. As with the auto industry, as with the supermarket industry, the likelihood is that there will be fewer and larger newspaper empires in the future. Already, the bigger chains are turning their attention from individual newspapers to entire groups. The building of newspaper chains is not a phenomenon that everybody is happy with. It raises sticky issues of monopoly ownership, the concentration of power, and whether newspaper excellence suffers when competition dwindles. Deeper than all this, it brings up the matter of how, in fact, people get the news that informs their decisions.

Many of the country's daily newspapers fall short of the standards that most journalists aspire to. And other papers, sadly, do not even try to reach those standards at all. Throughout the United States, too many readers are given a smattering of canned local stories crammed in among a flurry of wire-service dispatches and a mass of advertisements. Ben Bagdikian, a longtime press critic, sees little evidence that these papers are going to get any better; indeed, they may get worse. With mounting pressure to show high profit margins, some newspapers seem to have discovered that it is cheaper not to gather, edit and print the news than to perform these functions. "I'm convinced that we're not going to see any more great papers, at least not any coming out of chains," Mr. Bagdikian told me. "It takes five or six years or more of pouring money into a paper to make it really distinguished. No modern corporation is going to wait that long for good dividends. There's real danger that the number of distinguished papers will decline, because they're part of chains now, too, and the pressure is great on them to produce the dollars."

Gannett's magnitude and its role as a management trend-setter make it the very model of a modern American chain. Gannett has become a publishing empire that grossed $690.1 million in 1978, and routinely has added 10 or more papers every year. In addition, the Gannett Company interests have spread to include radio and TV stations, a scattering of 19 weeklies and the Louis Harris pollster organization. Gannett is also in the midst of wrapping up one of the biggest media deals of all time, the acquisition of the huge Combined Communications Corporation, owner of seven television and 12 radio stations, an outdoor advertising group and two good-sized newspapers, the Oakland *Tribune* and the Cincinnati *Enquirer*.

This deal has not escaped the notice of the Justice Department's Antitrust Division, nor of some members of Congress who are perturbed by the trend toward concentration of news media power. Also, the sheer size of Gannett, and some of the other newspaper chains, has stirred fears among those who feel that, in becoming vulnerable to government interference through possible antitrust action, the chains also make the nation's press itself susceptible to government encroachment and possible control.

Curiously, though, despite Gannett's ranking as the mammoth in the press industry, with seemingly immense power to inform or misinform or omit to inform, the chain commands practically no national influence, as influence is usually measured. The reason for this obscurity is that it owns no big-name papers. It has got to the top by purchasing papers situated in towns like Battle Creek, Mamaroneck, Freemont, Ossining, Port Chester, Bridgewater, Elmira, Tarrytown, Santa Fe, Boise, Pensacola, Lansing, Honolulu, and Saratoga Springs. The papers are a mixed bag of editorial voices (from arch conservative to obstinately liberal), and Gannett makes no effort to bring them into chorus. "It's like a choir where everyone sings something different, and so the effect is that nobody pays any attention," an observer of the industry suggests. At least from the point of view of the profits-and-loss column, this policy seems to have paid off. Since going public a decade ago, Gannett has never had to report a down quarter.

Few people expected such big doings when Frank E. Gannett founded the company in 1906. He was a bulldog-faced, garrulous man, born on Gannett Hill, N.Y., to a father who flopped both at farming and as a hotel keeper, and to a mother who set maxims before him like stepping stones ("Little strokes fell big oaks," "You don't get nowhere by making enemies"). After working his way through Cornell, Mr. Gannett climbed to the editorship of the Ithaca *Daily News*, before he bought a half-share of the floundering Elmira *Gazette* in 1906 for $20,000. He later merged it with the competing *Evening Star* and had the slender makings of a newspaper company. He at once started shopping for other money-losing propositions to buy and merge.

From Rochester, where he merged the *Union and Advertiser* with the *Times*, he proceeded to combine Utica's *Herald-Dispatch* and *Observer*, Elmira's *Telegram* and *Advertiser*, Ithaca's *News* and *Journal*. He bought with an auditor's eye. Before he was done (after 51 years of buying dailies), he would acquire 30 papers, plus a string of radio and television stations. He took over more papers than any other United States publisher ever acquired without the aid of inheritance.

Instead of taking on a deadening conformity, papers in the Gannett "group," as the publisher liked to call it, were urged to vary their typography, select their own features and shape their editorial policies to suit their own communities. It is a hands-off policy that continues to this day. Mr. Gannett always sent his political pronouncements to his editors with the notation scrawled on them: "For your information and use, if desired"—and editors were free to ignore them, as many of them did. As a result, the papers taken together came to be known as the chain that isn't. It has been officially called the "World of Different Newspapers."

The papers were not altogether dissimilar. Most of them were (and still are) staid organs with a Rotary-Kiwanis conservative bent. Exposés or stories of sex and crime rarely turned up in their pages.

In 1940, Mr. Gannett interrupted the shepherding of his papers to run as the highly unsuccessful "businessman's candidate" for the Republican Presidential nomination. Shrugging off the loss, he continued to direct his empire until 1955, when he fractured his spine in a fall. He died in 1957, at age 81.

On Oct. 24, 1967, the Gannett Company went public. Then, it consisted of just 28 papers in five states, with a total circulation of 1.3 million. Soon afterward, the company initiated a shopping spree that continues with gusto. The man doing all the buying was Paul Miller, once Washington bureau chief of the Associated Press and later its chairman, who took over as Gannett's president in 1957. He subsequently became chairman, before stepping down at the end of last year at the age of 71; he remains active as a director and chairman of the executive committee. Gannett's earnings have routinely improved 15 to 20 percent a year, up to $83.1 million last year, and the price of its stock has spiraled from $6.87 a share in 1967 to over $43 today. Wall Street newspaper watchers have long gushed at Gannett. "The company is one honey of an investment," one securities analyst told me. "It's got to be the premier newspaper stock," said another analyst.

The main man at Gannett today is 55-year old chairman and president Allen Neuharth. He has silver, wavy hair combed back, a movie-star smile and the confident air of a man who is good and who knows it.

I spoke with Mr. Neuharth in his starkly modern Manhattan office, situated high in the Pan Am Building. Sipping a Coke, he casually laid out the elements of the Gannett philosophy: Basically, the company goes after papers with circulations of between 25,000 and 100,000 that are located in cities free of competition—meaning that there are no other papers and no dominant television or radio stations. The average circulation among the 78 dailies is no more than 38,400. Only four circulate above 100,000 copies a day, and those lie in less than big-time cities—Rochester (two of them), Honolulu and Camden, N.J. What accounts for the company's huge success is that it is, in effect, a chain of small monopolies. Since they are the only papers in town, the papers do not feel inhibited by competitors' ad rates and newsstand prices. The papers are therefore less reliant on help-wanted classified and national advertising than their big-city counterparts. Gannett has found that the smaller the town, the faster the paper tends to grow. And the faster the paper grows, the faster its profits grow, since in the newspaper business editorial and makeup costs increase much less sharply than the rate of circulation. As one observer sums it up, "Gannett has basically built a cathedral out of pebbles."

Mr. Neuharth doesn't like just to sit around. He spends much of his time traversing the country in the corporate jet, wooing newspaper magnates. He is paid a salary of $390,000. He glows like an ember when he describes the deals he has brought off. To acquire a paper, he has bargained for as little a time as a few weeks and for as long as 12 years. Some critics contend that Gannett is given to absurd speculation, sometimes laying out a stiff 40 or 50 times earnings for a newspaper. Mr. Neuharth scoffs that balance sheets are not always what they appear to be, and that family owners rarely are crafty businessmen, and that all that matters is how much black ink Gannett figures it can get out of a paper. Mr. Neuharth's greatest disappointment, he says, was one of the few papers that failed. It stands as a perfect illustration of why Gannett doesn't buy into two-paper markets. Gannett had long owned the Hartford *Times*, but it steadily began to lose ground to the Hartford *Courant* in a classic case of an afternoon paper succumbing to a morning paper. Gannett sank a lot of money into the operation, including enough dollars to start a Sunday edition. Nothing worked. The newspaper was sold in 1973 to The Register Publishing Company. It had no more success, and folded the paper three years later.

As energetic as Gannett is, it has stiff competition. Knight-Ridder, the owner of 32 dailies, reaches the biggest combined circulation of any chain (3.5 million), and, in stark contrast to Gannett, it operates in some or the large cities, with papers like the Miami *Herald*, the Philadelphia *Inquirer* and the Detroit *Free Press*. Prosperous and well-managed, the chain posted revenues of $879 million last year. Many in the business maintain that Knight-Ridder's commitment to editorial excellence qualifies it as the best chain of all. Like the other giants, it grants its papers local autonomy.

The Newhouse combine, the personal preserve of Samuel I.

Newhouse, is known as the money factory. It publishes for the most part small papers—29 of them (3,281,000 circulation)—in addition to the Condé Nast publications (*Vogue, Mademoiselle, House & Garden, Glamour, Bride's*). Knowledgeable analysts put revenues at about $1 billion and profits somewhere near $100 million.

A mighty fortress and bulwark of conservatism is The Tribune Company, owner of the Chicago *Tribune*, the New York *Daily News* and seven additional dailies (3.1 million circulation). Revenues last year amounted to $967 million. Recently, the group has emerged as an aggressive acquirer of small monopolistic papers. Another chain interested in acquisition is Scripps-Howard; its collection of 17 dailies is read by 1.8 million people in sizable cities like Cincinnati, Cleveland and Denver. Sources of income include United Press International and *The World Almanac*. Financial statements aren't made public, but an informed source puts revenues at about $425 million. Of late, it has been purchasing weeklies.

No longer the cynosure it once was, the Hearst Corporation is still an important owner of newspapers and has been reviving its empire with mixed success. Its interests include 10 dailies (1.4 million circulation) and a batch of magazines (*Harper's Bazaar, Good Housekeeping* and *Cosmopolitan*, among others). Knowledgeable sources put Hearst's revenues at $400 million. Notorious in earlier days for forging its papers into political weapons, Hearst has lately been more magnanimous in letting its editors take charge.

Other powers include the well-fixed Dow Jones & Company, which, fueled by the wealthy *Wall Street Journal*, has been expanding fast; Times Mirror, the mighty parent of the Los Angeles *Times*; The Washington Post Company; and, of course, The New York Times Company, which has five weeklies and nine dailies in Florida and North Carolina in addition to the *Times*. (The total circulation for all 10 daily newspapers is 1,055,400). The newspapers and the company's other interests (magazines, broadcasting, books) took in $491,558,000 last year.

As the big chains continue to increase in size, where does this leave the readers of newspapers? What about "the people's right to know"? To some extent, this has to do with the editor's right to edit, which brings up the matter of centralized control. Yes, most large groups claim they grant local autonomy. However, some of them hold editorial conferences annually, or more frequently, to exchange ideas—and, some say, to exercise control over policy. Some smaller chains are more overt about telling editors what to do.

Anyway, as the chains start to increase in size, the specter of monopoly looms larger and larger, to some observers. Representative Morris Udall, a Democrat from Arizona, worries a lot about all of this. "I really shudder to see the day down the road when you have four or five organizations that have a hammerlock on what Americans read," he told me late one afternoon. Mr. Udall doesn't quibble with the contentions of many chains that they've improved a good many papers. "But you strike a bargain with the devil," he went on. "I know the folks who run these chains and they're nice people and they love their kids and all, but the day may come when you have some leaders who hunger for political power. The power is there. It's not comforting to know that it isn't being used." . . .

Virtually every week, a paper comes up for auction. Bid. Bought. Sold. As the papers get assigned to their various chains, what about individual differences between newspapers? John Morton, a veteran student of the newspaper business for John Muir & Company, the investment firm, suspects that papers will become homogenized. They will look alike, and read alike, and may differ no more than a Big Mac bought in Keokuk does from a Big Mac bought in Brooklyn. Mr. Morton says, "There'll be fewer papers that print and raise hell. You'll see fewer gadflies. Newspapers, I think, are going to have less distinctive personalities. All papers are becoming more service oriented, and the chain-owned papers, with their sophisticated market-research techniques, are most aggressive in this area." . . .

To figure out where the Gannett newspapers fit into the spectrum of American journalism, you have to look at the diet that average daily newspapers feed their readers. A recent study conducted by Arthur D. Little, the consulting outfit, carved up the average paper this way: Local news, 4.5 percent of the total column space; foreign and national news, 7.5 percent; leisure time, 5 percent; people, entertainment and opinion, 6.5 percent; sports, 4.5 percent; data and listings, 8 percent; retail advertising, 36 percent; national advertising, 8 percent, and classified advertising, 20 percent.

Gannett itself has never tried to cook up a comparable profile of its chain. To get some notion of how it stacked up, I combed through more than a hundred copies of several dozen Gannett papers, and chatted with a number of Gannett editors and publishers. Some of the papers were pretty much in line with the composite. A number differed in providing somewhat greater percentages of local coverage, noticeably more service material and a more generous dose of sports news, which are things Gannett readership studies indicate are in demand.

More often than not, changes are made in a paper after Gannett buys it, though they are often slow in coming, and are not always as galvanic or profound as readers would like. John Quinn, Gannett's low-keyed senior vice president for news, is the master blacksmith who takes new purchases and attempts to remake them, if not into brilliant journals, at least into respectable ones. Most papers, he finds, are horridly organized. He suggests that they split things into several sections and create departments. Modern makeup is introduced.

"We operate community newspapers," Al Neuharth explained to me. "We stress local- and regional-interest news. We get from other sources the amount of foreign news we feel our readers want. Basically, we respond to reader studies. Whatever diet the readers want, we custom-tailor the paper for that diet."

What, then, ought the reader to get in the way of vital news?

"We give readers what they want, because we are in the business of selling news," Mr. Neuharth said. "If we meet the wants of the audience in a community—as we try to—successfully, then we can also give readers a percentage of what they need. But that isn't what sells. And if we tried to give people more of what they need, we wouldn't be successful. If the readers in Ithaca want to know the school menus for all the schools in the area, we'll give them that. That's no great practice of journalism, but it's what the readers want. You can't ram an unwanted object down an unwilling throat, no matter what business you're in." . . .

The Gannett News Service (G.N.S.) . . . consists of a Washington bureau made up of 19 reporters, along with 17 additional reporters scattered in 10 state capitals and in New York City. All told, figuring in the filings from staffers at member papers, G.N.S. sends about 70 stories a day clacking over the wire. However, the philosophy of G.N.S. is to leave all the major breaking stories to the Associated Press and United Press International and to deploy its people to file analyses, background pieces, stories with a regional angle that might perk the interest of, at most, a couple of Gannett papers, and occasional enterprise stories.

To know a newspaper chain, you need to know its newspapers. One of the biggest and most flourishing, and possibly the best, in the Gannett stable is the Camden *Courier-Post*. The paper is housed in a low-slung building with a well-barbered front lawn in Cherry Hill, N.J., a community of some 75,000 with one of the heaviest concentrations of warehouses on the East Coast. Gannett bought the *Courier-Post* in 1959 for $5.5 million. It was fairly lackluster then and had a circulation of 76,000. Its readership has since increased to 124,000, while other papers in the area, notably the Philadelphia *Inquirer* and the Philadelphia *Bulletin*, have suffered dwindling circulations. . . .

The *Courier-Post* has billed itself as "New Jersey's Really Great Newspaper." Nobody can really say whether it is or isn't, though some of the credentials are impressive. It rakes a lot of muck. It has a three-member investigative team that pursues scandal with the exhilaration of a pack of beagles on the trail of a fox. Recent unearthings have included a seven-month study of the municipal court system that triggered closer monitoring of the courts and that provoked bills to be introduced into the State Legislature.

However, the *Courier-Post* tries to be the town billboard as well as the town scold. "Lorelei's List" runs down upcoming yard sales and fashion parties. Until recently a "Trouble Shooter" column solved problems and tried to "make dreams come true." . . .

Gannett never dickers with the editing of the paper, it was agreed by everyone. "I've been with Gannett for 13 years and not once—I mean not once—have I heard a directive from headquarters telling me how to do something," managing editor Phil Bookman said. "They don't hold a gun and say, 'Run this, don't run that.' "

Later, I was told by N. S. (Buddy) Hayden, then the publisher of the *Courier-Post*: "I used to own my own paper, so I think I'm pretty well qualified to compare independent ownership to Gannett ownership. The Gannett management is just like the board of directors at the bank I used to go to for loans. I don't have any less freedom, and there is the beauty that Gannett people understand the newspaper business."

Like other chain members, the *Courier-Post* picks up almost all of its office supplies from Gannett's wholly owned subsidiary, the Empire Newspaper Supply Company. Everything from newsprint (325,000 tons of it a year) and ink to typewriters and pencils are bought by Empire, all at hefty discounts. A national advertising headquarters is situated in New York, with regional offices spotted around the country. Package deals among papers bunched close together can be arranged.

Despite all its profits, though, one wonders whether the exponent of the small-town daily can ever rest easily without the benefit of prestige. I asked Mr. Neuharth if there were ever days when he wished he owned just one big-name newspaper, one Detroit *Free Press*, one St. Louis *Post-Dispatch*, one Chicago *Tribune*.

Mr. Neuharth smiled. "I don't miss the prestige and influence of a big-city paper," he answered. "I've been there and a lot of the allure is myth. I think I have as exciting a job as exists in the newspaper business."

Did he dislike fighting, I asked.

The smile widened.

"I don't dislike fighting," Mr. Neuharth said. "I just like to win."

ALLEN NEUHARTH, THE NEWS MOGUL WHO WOULD BE FAMOUS

David Shaw

This thumb-nail sketch from Shaw's article describes the energetic leader of Gannett. It also adds another detail to the portrait of the Gannett chain and shows it in a slightly different light.

Al Neuharth, at fifty-five, is president, chairman, and chief executive officer of the Gannett Company, the largest newspaper chain in the United States. Neuharth is not widely known outside the newspaper business, even though he is one of the most powerful, controversial, fascinating and enigmatic figures in publishing—a $390,000-a-year executive whose loud wardrobe, blunt language, and movie-star looks (Florida suntan, carefully swept-back, silver-black hair) have aroused as much attention in the business as his aggressive pursuit of new acquisitions and big profits. He is known also for elaborate practical jokes. He once sent his first wife and a friend to a football game in his rented car, reported the car stolen, and left town on a business trip; his wife was subsequently stopped by the police and taken to the local precinct house for questioning.

Neuharth grew up poor in a small town near Sioux Falls, South Dakota. His father died when Neuharth was two, and his mother took in washing and sewing to pay the bills. By the age of thirteen, Neuharth was working in the composing room of a weekly newspaper. When he graduated from college, he started a weekly sports newspaper—SoDak Sports—financed with $50,000 he had raised among hundreds of friends and relatives. The paper folded. Neuharth was so humiliated that he packed all his possession in a U-Haul trailer and fled to Florida—"the farthest I could go without leaving the country."

Thus, it was one of the biggest thrills of Neuharth's life when he was able to return to Sioux Falls in 1977 to buy the Sioux Falls Argus-Leader for Gannett. It was his proudest acquisition; he had returned triumphantly to the scene of his ignominious defeat.

In the years between failure and success in South Dakota, Neuharth built quite a reputation for himself as a newspaperman. Unlike most publishers, he began as a reporter—and still thinks of himself as one. Reporters who worked with him in Miami twenty-five years ago remember him as an aggressive investigative reporter.

SOURCE: From Esquire, September 1979. Copyright © 1979 by David Shaw. Reprinted by permission.

Allen Neuharth

Neuharth quickly advanced in the Knight (now Knight-Ridder) chain, becoming executive city editor of the Miami *Herald*, then assistant executive editor of the Detroit *Free Press* before leaving the company in 1963 to become general manager of Gannett's hometown papers, in Rochester. Three years later, he used an offer from the New York *Daily News* to persuade Gannett to make him executive vice-president of the entire chain. In 1970, he became president, and in 1979, chairman of the board.

Clearly, Neuharth likes to work—thrives on work. He often runs his empire from a mobile command post in the Gannett corporate jet, and he has a fully equipped office—with wire service ticker tape and thirty computerized direct telephone lines—on the second floor of his home in Cocoa Beach, Florida. When Neuharth's wife tried to persuade him to stay in Europe an extra weekend for pleasure after a business trip, he refused. He laughs at the idea of a vacation longer than a weekend. Two weeks in France? "I'd be bored to death. What would I do?" Visit a few museums? "I spent twenty minutes in a museum in Paris." Chateaux? "You've seen one chateau, you've seen them all."

Hard work, Neuharth says, pays dividends. That's why he and Gannett are so successful.

But Neuharth seems reluctant to commit himself fully to the best quality journalism if there is the slightest chance that the investment community might sense some risk to Gannett's ever upward profit curve. Neuharth still speaks of newspapers in merchandising terms—"We have to improve the products we sell"—and virtually every time he mentions the need to "practice the best of journalism" he couples that with a reminder to "practice the best of business."

The preoccupation with the bottom line communicates itself to everyone in the Gannett empire.

THE FUTURE OF THE FOURTH ESTATE
Anthony Smith
This critique of American newspapers was written by a noted British author, media critic, and broadcast producer. It is extracted from the monthly *Intermedia*, published by the International Institute of Communications, London. Smith evaluated the technological and economic transformation of dailies during the 1970s.

The familiar smells, noises, and vibrations of the traditional newspaper industry have disappeared from a large proportion of the American press. In 1970 the first computers began to operate in pioneer newspapers—experimental ambassadors of the space age to the medium of print. The first electronic editor's terminal was put on the market in 1973 by the Harris Corp., one of the leading group of organizations which have brought about an electronic revolution in American newspaper typesetting.

The advent of the computer in newspapers is part of a total transformation of the industry. By examining the effect of the computer upon the newspaper one may discern something of probable larger shifts in society as more and more of its processes become computer-based.

In 1963 there were twelve newspapers in New York; today there are three. Only 185 towns and cities in America, out of more than 1,544 in which newspapers are published, have more than one

---

SOURCE: From *Intermedia*, August, 1978. Copyright © 1978 by the German Marshall Fund of the U.S. and Anthony Smith. Reprinted with permission.

paper, and of these only forty have papers with competing owners. Yet the total number of papers in the U.S. has not dropped significantly for a generation. What has taken place is a reorganization of newspaper markets.

The sense of crisis around the newspaper's current market system arises from the tremendous population shift in the 1950s and 1960s. The old social and business elites have moved out of the cities, taking their social life and talk of city politics with them. When everyone lived in the city—voters as well as leaders—newspapers had a clear set of duties, each presenting its own perspective. A downtown store could advertise, knowing people would travel into the center to do their shopping. The city's major stores and manufacturers could reach out to the suburbs, a valuable and growing market.

Yet for most publishers the medium in the 1970s became more profitable than it ever had been. They have redefined their markets and learned to envelop their readers with a whole range of special material—supplements on food, recreation, hobbies, sports, business—each with complementary advertising. Many put out zoned supplements of local news, financed with full-page ads from local stores. There has been a tremendous growth in the delivery of preprinted advertisement inside the newspaper (15 per cent of the total retail advertising of the Washington *Post* is now preprints).

The U.S. metropolitan newspaper publisher appears to be sitting on a goldmine; all he has to do is get the paper to his readers and pocket the advertising revenue. To the publisher the picture looks different: He has to thicken his paper to embrace the full range of lifestyles of his widespread audience. He has to truck and bundle his papers to reach the farthest suburbs, which in the case of the Los Angeles *Times* are 400 miles away. Inside the central city area he must cope with street sales from vending machines which are easy to rifle, and with ethnic barriers; a large section of residents may be unable to read English or may feel alien to the society the newspaper addresses.

Since 1950 the average American newspaper has increased from 34 to 60 pages. The average reader looks at only one-tenth of the total material which finally reaches him. Only about one-tenth of the editorial material available gets printed. The newspaper wastes most of the material it prints and delivers.

It is not surprising that forward-looking publishers are beginning to wonder whether, in the very long run, breaking some technological barrier might give the daily newspaper a wholly new form and content. One must look at the technologies now in use before envisaging those which might take the newspaper into a new phase of its history.

In the old system, the copy emerges from reporters (who use traditional typewriters) and advertising personnel and passes to an editor who attaches a heading. The copy then goes to the copy-cutting desk; here it is sliced into sections which are handed out to different typesetters whose work later must be reassembled in the correct order.

The linotype machines, which set the text in type, have keyboards, like typewriters, which assemble rows of matrices or metal molds. The operator creates his text in lines of type (about five per minute, with an error every two minutes), then strikes a key which causes molten lead to be poured into the matrices, which are then automatically lifted and deposited in a metal case. The whole process is characterized as "hot metal" printing.

After proofreading and corrections, the next step is makeup—a skilled and time-consuming activity. Zinc engravings of photographs and display advertisements go into a page form—which of course is a mirror-image of the actual printed page. A "mat" mold of the page is made to fit the rollers of the printing press. The stereotype machine then forces molten lead under pressure into the mold, and makes a heavy cylindrical lead plate. This is fitted onto the rollers of a letterpress machine, which can make up to 70,000 copies per hour.

Under this traditional process editorial copy has to be laid out again and again. The reporter, typesetter, proofreader, editor, etc., are essentially copying the text or type on different keyboards.

The essence of the new newspaper technology is "cold type" and the elimination of hot lead. The new print images are generated photographically. The basic copy flows from reporters and advertising people to a computer by means of Video Display Terminals (VDTs). These units have keyboards similar to the typewriter but there the resemblance ends. The reporter using a VDT sees his copy on a screen instead of on paper and can correct his material before pushing the button which passes the whole "file" into computer storage.

The computer can accept material from outside the newsroom without human intervention. The wire services, for example, can feed their copy straight to the computers of their clients, who may then select and edit with no further copying or keyboarding. Proofreading is unnecessary since reporters and editors make corrections in the computer. The computer automatically hyphenates and justifies. It can also be programmed to choose an appropriate typeface. The simplest machine can turn out two-thirds of a mile of column type in one hour.

The type produced by the computer is laid out and pasted up on boards to look like the printed page, then photographed. The negative is used to expose a photo-sensitive printing plate, a thin sheet of metal. Offset printing is based on the principle that ink (which contains oil) and water are mutually repellent. Those areas of the photosensitive layer which contain type and have been exposed attract the ink, while those areas which do not contain type repel the ink and attract water. The process is called "offset" because the litho plate and the paper never actually touch; a blanket roller takes an impression from the plate and presses it on the paper.

No method has yet been marketed for composing an entire page on a screen, and aficionados of the new technology speak of full pagination as a kind of promised land. When managements do reach the point of being able to set pages (and therefore make plates) directly by computer, the way will be open to printing without plates—a newspaper printed directly by computer.

The new technologies have been a battleground of the most variegated kind. Powerful craft unions grew up in the printing industry in the late nineteenth century. Their traditions harked back to ancient craft-based guilds. The International Typographical Union, founded in Cincinnati in 1852, covered the whole spectrum of skills. As printing and engraving developed, it lost many groups— pressmen, engravers, stereotypers, and electrotypers. By the end of World War II 14 unions were involved in American newspaper publishing.

Then the process started to reverse itself, especially after it became clear that new composing machinery would reduce severely membership of the parent union, the ITU. By the end of the decade, if present negotiations are successful, the ITU will join forces with the Newspaper Guild and even may reunite with the pressmen's union. In a totally computerized newspaper there could be a single industrial union; but that lies far ahead, perhaps after many bloody battles.

The powerful labor organization of the East Coast has been severely dented after disputes at the Washington *Post* and New York *Times*. In many parts of the South the unions have failed to mount any serious offensive against the new technology. Many disputes over the new equipment have led to management simply employing nonunion labor and continuing operations without resolving the original dispute. In some papers union organization has simply died. Everywhere the printing worker has to reckon with the reality that computer-based technology can be operated by unskilled people.

American management often gives the appearance, in its private meetings and conventions, of waging a deliberate war against unions. From the perspective of the unions, many publishers seem to be on a technological ego-trip, determined to override rather than work with labor.

At first many local branches of the ITU tried to keep new equipment out of newspaper plants. When that proved ineffective they gained guarantees of lifetime employment for their members, but some of these have proved fragile. Many ITU typesetters who believed their paper had promised them a new job discovered after taking part in a strike on some other issue that their so-called permanent contracts were declared void.

The ITU has watched its membership shrink from more than 100,000 after the War to about 60,000, and hopes the figure will settle at 50,000 when computerization is "over." But the arrival of full pagination and the elimination of page pasteup will open the way to further reductions.

The modern newspaper is the testing ground of something wholly new in human communication systems. Manufacturers are making their equipment ever more "intelligent." Journalists have brought about a progressive upgrading of the services built into their terminals. With the coming of the portable, remote, feed-in, "stand alone" unit, the newspaper becomes a network of minicomputers with a wide repertory of skills.

The Teleram VDT, developed by the American Newspaper Publishers Association, the New York *Times*, and the Teleram Communication Corp., is a fine example. Although it accommodates 616 characters on its four-by-three-inch screen, it will fit under an airline seat; its display memory has 2,048 characters; it records data on a 300-foot cassette which can hold 1,600 words; and it works on a car battery. The reporter can use a Teleram to collect background research from remote computerized data banks. He can then transmit his completed copy at 300 words per minute through a telephone wire, or at 1,200 words per minute if he has access to a high-speed model.

The Teleram transmits six times as fast as a facsimile system and six times as fast as a person dictating copy to a secretary. Given a distance of fifty miles from the publishing center, the unit cost of transmitting copy is reduced to one-quarter.

Today's intelligent Video Display Terminals consist fundamentally of a cathode ray tube which displays text on a screen. The screens vary in size, depending on whether the unit is to be used simply for verifying material being entered by a reporter into the photocomposition system or whether it is being used for more complicated text-editing. The keyboards, once complex and cumbersome, provide single keys carefully labeled for single functions. The user of a terminal does not need more than a few hours' training.

The Washington *Post* has designed a particularly versatile system, with Raytheon, which it is now marketing to other papers. It enables the reporter to use his machine as a note-taker and to retain his notes for all the stories on which he is working at a given moment. The terminal will also record telephone messages and signal that it is holding them. Over the whole newsroom (which will hold 250 terminals) a production manager will preside, prodding reporters to complete work and reminding editors of the priority of various items.

The old technology is piloting in the new. The newspaper's computer contains what amounts to a mediated and filtered social memory of the affairs of an entire community. If it categorizes the material it has accumulated and then transfers the information into a computer, the newspaper creates a new asset which can be resold and reused. Many newspapers have substantial repositories of constantly updated information.

The New York *Times* Information Bank, in operation since 1973, consists of an index to the whole corpus of work in the newspaper since 1969, as well as information from many other publications and from eight wire services. Through a VDT and keyboard, the user (who may be a paying member of the public) may search the files under key words (persons, organizations, geographical place names, subject areas, etc.). Once material has been identified from the bibliographic references on the VDT screen, it can be retrieved from its micro-fiche storage.

The problems with the system have proved to be as interesting as they are serious. The cost of storage is still so great that the Information Bank is too expensive for the staff of the *Times* to use free. What's more, the problems of deciding on systems of access, categories, keyboards, etc., are so great that the researcher has to be extremely skilled and patient to use the bank effectively.

In the era of the computer, the newspaper's distribution system has its own possibilities of commercial exploitation. There are 1.2 million full- or parttime newspaper carriers in the U.S. They are increasingly difficult to find, expensive to employ, and often unreliable. Managements which have acquired a great deal of computer expertise can now transfer to the computer many of the tasks of distribution, circulation, and sales.

The computer can stack newspapers in amounts which correspond to the different orders for agents and retailers; it can print the destination on each bundle; and it can arrange them in the correct order for delivery. The delivery driver merely has to stick a special key into a slot at the loading bay to tell the computer of his intended route. The machine selects a number of bundles, according to route, and shoots them into trucks.

Many publishers believe the increasing speed and sophistication of their delivery mechanisms enable them to operate as general carriers of other companies' printed matter. By 1980 an estimated 18 billion preprints will be delivered to homes in the U.S. The magazine industry is deeply affected by the rising cost of postage. If methods could be devised to automatically insert, inside the local newspaper, the right magazine or preprint into the right mailbox, both sectors could switch part of their business to the newspaper's computerized operations.

There are specialist audiences which have never been satisfied by the available media. The American business community has an insatiable appetite for detailed information about itself and about all industry. The diplomatic and scientific communities are also eager for highly detailed information. The *Wall Street Journal* is one paper that uses advanced technology to identify and reach that audience. In 1974 the *Journal* and the Communications Satellite Corp. (COM-SAT) devised a system of facsimile printing that has developed into a national system covering almost every population center in the U.S. The *Journal* has become the country's first national paper.

The paper is actually produced on a local basis. Stories, head-lines, and advertisements are collected at centers throughout the country and assembled into pages in each region. The pages are photocomposed and the negatives wrapped around a transmitting drum. This high-speed drum scans each page and transmits digital pulses to a geosynchronous satellite, Comstar, which sends them to receiving plants where they are reconverted to light and reexposed. The pages are then printed from lithographic plates. The entire process takes three minutes.

Satellite costs are not related to distance and can undercut the equivalent terrestrial microwave service (rigidly costed by distance) by nine-tenths. The use of satellite could lead to a thorough reorganization of marketing practices now based on a regional monopoly.

A related development is the plan for a U.S. satellite network to book and transmit national and regional newspaper advertising throughout the country. The newspaper has lost a great deal of national advertising to television. It now looks to the satellite (and its own computers) to provide a cheap, convenient, and instant system for collecting national advertising. It is already possible to send display ads in facsimile directly into the computer storage of several papers.

The service will greatly help media planners of large corpora-tions to run advertising campaigns across selected areas of the country. They will no longer have to go through the complicated business of booking separate advertisements in hundreds or thousands of publications. The implications for the pattern of U.S. marketing and advertising campaigns—and of retail distribution—are very great.

The computer can bring about a kind of Hegelian negation of the newspaper. It could change from being a general hold-all to something custom-designed. The way in which newspapers have gradually extended themselves into the distant suburbs (through zoning and special supplements) has taught them much about how to deal with small groups of readers.

Newspaper audiences are no longer being counted only as accumulations of individuals but the percentages of households within a zone. This new concept is a vital step toward the identification of special audiences for special products—of the kind which the computer can supply with relative ease. Finally, the newspaper has increasingly become a carrier of material produced by syndication agencies and wire services. The "sharp end" of the newspaper is no longer editorial singularity but marketing efficiency.

As fewer and fewer owners control more and more newspapers, the values associated with the image of the Fourth Estate have steadily eroded over the past decades. Today chains range from Gannett's 79 papers and Thomson's 57 (almost all small, powerful, local monopolies) to the Times Mirror Co. in Los Angeles, which owns a small group of papers with the huge circulation of nearly two million.

The larger chains are buying up the smaller chains. The Newhouse group now owns the Booth group and Gannett owns both Speidel and Combined Communications' radio and TV outlets. Many of the larger groups own valuable subsidiary utilities such as publishing houses, timber lands, magazines, radio and TV stations, and cable systems.

What is often not recognized is the extent to which economic pressures have been increasing the pace of conglomerate growth in the past few years. The spread of local monopolies has meant that large sums of cash pile up in the publishers' accounts. If they are not used for fresh acquisition within the financial year these cash reserves are taxed.

Many observers expect most of the American daily and Sunday press to be in the hands of eight to ten large groups by the mid-1980s. The new technology contributes to this development because it facilitates cost-cutting (and profit growth) and requires large sums of capital.

The chains and conglomerates are creating new opportunities for the dissemination of information and entertainment, but they are also creating new divisions. They do this because of their efficiency.

In its traditional patterns of ownership and distribution, the newspaper seemed to guarantee information flows required by Western democracies. The mass electorate supposedly formed the basis of public opinion and therefore of social decisions. The newspaper and attendant information media are now being locked into patterns of advertising and distribution which make large quantities of information available to small elites. The information is much more substantial, and perhaps "better" than ever before. But those sections of the audience which do not demand to be informed (and who, in practice, perhaps never were) are now more completely cut off.

The functions of the press as a Fourth Estate demand that the newspaper be a complete social presence, not just a channel for someone else's information. The new technology and the new perceptions which surround it are preparing mass society for important—and perhaps undesirable—internal partitions which may place great strains upon the self-image of democratic societies. The new technology itself does not change social formation. It merely brings home unpalatable truths about the kind of social dividing lines we already have.

Section 21

INTERNATIONAL MEDIA ROLES

Two of the three articles in this discussion of
changing attitudes toward international news
coverage are written by Americans, while the
third, by a Tunisian, looks at the issue with
vehemence from a Third World point of view.

FOREIGN NEWS FLOW AND THE UNESCO DEBATE[1]

Robert L. Stevenson and Richard R. Cole

The authors point out not only the great dominance of world news distribution by Western organizations, but also the two main reasons for this dominance. Their services are, first of all, acceptable to a wide range of users. And their organizational and technological facilities are without equal.

In 1971, the Associated Press estimated that every day outside of the United States, AP news is read or seen on television or heard on radio by one billion people. The AP claims to be the largest news-gathering organization in the world. In 1975, Visnews, a company owned largely by Reuters and the BBC, which is the leading supplier of television news film, reported that Visnews film appeared on virtually all of the world's television screens.[2]

The dominance of Western—and particularly Anglo-American—organizations in the international flow of news is at the center of the world-wide debate over what has come to be known as the new world information order. The debate, however, is larger than news flow. Three distinct areas of concern can be defined.

Information Order Debate

Cultural Domination One broad area of concern to many Third World countries is the dominance of Western—particularly American—popular culture. It is easy to forget how much other countries are influenced by American popular music, television, books and magazines, fashions and lifestyles. The power of American influence goes beyond pop culture to the very symbol of cultural identity, language itself. A British linguist, George Steiner, has argued that the world language of the future is already here: it is the frenetic patois of American business English which brings with it, it is argued, a whole new and often alien set of cultural and social values.[3] If the post-war era of dominant American influence in politics and military affairs was short lived, it continues to gain

SOURCE: Adapted from the background portion of a paper presented to a meeting of the International Studies Association, Los Angeles, March, 1980. Reprinted with permission.

Third World newspapers (from top to bottom), Quito, Ecuador; Bombay, India; Cairo, Egypt

momentum in the often raucous world of mass media, pop culture and business.

Information Domination If knowledge is power, then the nation which controls information from which knowledge is derived is indeed powerful. A concern for control over the generation and exchange of all sorts of data bases is relatively new but gaining momentum. The dominance of the West in this area is, of course, a function of technology, particularly computers and satellites but also the technical infrastructure that permits the transmission of data from one computer to another, often via satellite, and usually outside the control or even knowledge of governments. For example, several airlines in Eastern Europe book local flight reservations on a computer in Atlanta.[4] With the right password, the data from our study can be accessed from an inexpensive, portable computer terminal attached to any telephone in the world.

Many of the Third World countries complain that data about their nations, much of it acquired by remote-sensing satellites controlled by the United States, belongs exclusively to them as part of their national sovereignty even when it is collected and disseminated with benign intent. And some of the industrialized countries as well are worried; their concern is that they cannot guarantee the privacy of their citizens when information is collected, exchanged and acted on by multinational companies outside the control of any one nation.

News Domination This is part of the information order debate which we are addressing. The complaints by Third World countries are directed toward two areas of imbalance. On one hand, it is asserted—as we will see, our data dispute several of these assertions—that Western media, particularly the international wire services and the major domestic media whose influence extends beyond the borders of the country, largely ignore the Third World, devote the meager coverage of this two-thirds of humanity mostly to "bad" news like natural disasters, coups and social unrest while ignoring the positive accomplishments in political, economic and social development, and most damning of all, see the Third World from the alien perspective of Western values. This distorted view of the Third World, it is argued, is transmitted to audiences in the West and in other Third World countries which must rely on the Western news agencies for their international news.

The second complaint follows from the last point. Some Third World countries argue that Western agencies provide them with too much coverage of the West and too little information about their own regions and other parts of the Third World. They contend further that too much of this information is inappropriate to Third World needs and filtered through the distorting lens of Western cultural, political and social values.

Even if one is not willing to accept the sometimes exaggerated claims about the dominance of Western news media and news values, it is certainly clear that the four Western news services—Associated Press, United Press International, Reuters, and Agence France-Presse—and their broadcast counterparts—particularly Visnews and UPITN, both Anglo-American—and the Western media of world stature like the BBC and the *Times* of London, the New York *Times*, Washington *Post*, the commercial American TV networks and news magazines—all exert a powerful and possibly decisive influence in the world of world news. When the New York *Times* correspondent was expelled from Iran in late 1979, a fellow Western correspondent was asked if the *Times* reporting had been unusually harsh or critical. His reply was no, but the Iranian government was well aware of the influence of the *Times* in the United States and the rest of the world.[5]

Western Dominance

Many explanations have been offered to account for the remarkable influence of Western media and news agencies. From them, three general arguments can be identified.

Cultural Imperialism The cultural imperialism argument is largely identified with Herbert Schiller of the University of California at San Diego although others have worked with him to develop the argument.[6] From a Marxist perspective, Schiller and his colleagues argue that the dominance of mass media, culture and information systems is in fact a new form of colonialism, replacing classical 19th century European imperialism and post-war American political and military hegemony but similar in intent: to maintain exploitive control over the Third World, forcing Third World audiences to accept Western media and Western values, often against their will. Such a radical view usually calls for a radical solution to liberate the media. The Western notion of the free flow of information is replaced with the concept of cultural sovereignty, which calls for the mass media to be placed at the service of the state and asserts that nations are responsible for determining what information comes into the country—including that directed at the country by foreign broadcasters—and for determining what information about the country is disseminated abroad.

Media Characteristics A more moderate view is offered by a British sociologist, Jeremy Tunstall, who argues that three characteristics of modern media systems are largely responsible for the dominance of the West. In a book called *The Media Are American*, he says that modern media are politics, business and technology.[7] He points out that even in Third World countries where Western liberal democracy has not fared well and is now often rejected as inappropriate, the symbiotic relationship between politics and mass media is maintained and that in dealing with the West, Third World countries recognize that coverage on the BBC or in the New York *Times* can be as important as the diplomatic cable traffic flowing to Whitehall or Foggy Bottom.

Because so much of the news as well as the pop culture is a commercial product, it is packaged and marketed with the same skill and zeal as with any other consumer product. And if there is one thing that American business does well, it is selling. When news products or entertainment products, both with a high quotient of audience appeal identified by market research, are developed and marketed by an efficient and skillful business comglomerate, it is not surprising that they show up in all parts of the world.

Finally, as Tunstall points out, to speak of modern media is to speak of high technology electronics and satellites. And in these areas, innovation comes almost entirely from the industrialized West and Japan.

News Definition An argument, not always popular in the Third World, says that the dominance of Western news in the world is at least partly the result of the widely acceptable style and definition of "news" in the West. Donald Shaw traced the rise of Western-style "objectivity" along with the development of the telegraph in the latter part of the 19th century. He showed that the only way the new news agencies could sell to partisan newspapers of widely differing political views was to emphasize speed, presentation of facts without elaborate interpretation and more or less equal attention to different points of view.[8] While such "objective" style often lacks coherence and perspective, it is timely and widely acceptable.

A few years ago, the publisher of the *International Herald Tribune*, the remarkable American newspaper published in Paris, noted that half of the paper's readers were Europeans, not American tourists, students or businessmen. He said that more and more Europeans were attracted to the *Trib*'s news style which emphasized brevity and impartiality and to the paper's contents which were largely gleaned from the columns of two of its current owners, the New York *Times* and the Washington *Post*.[9]

Another example of the widespread acceptability of Western-style news is a recent study of the Yugoslav press done for ICA by Lee Becker at Ohio State.[10] He found that coverage of the United

States came largely from the Western news agencies and further, that the Yugoslav papers printed it pretty much as it came from the wires. In tone and topic, the view of the United States in Yugoslav newspapers was largely that of the Western wire services. These examples show how palatable—and marketable—Western news is to widely differing audiences and media systems, a fact that along with the speed with which it is delivered, can account for a large part of its worldwide prominence.

In fact, alternatives to the Western agencies are widely available but not often used. Third World editors and national news agency staffs (which are the usual customers of the news services) in most cases have access to TASS, an agency of world scope but not much used outside of Eastern Europe and a small number of Third World countries, the new Non-Aligned News Agencies pool and a rapidly increasing number of regional and speciality news services. Although many of the alternative services are new and experimental, their use has been spotty at best. One of the crucial questions in the information order debate is why these alternatives are not used more instead of the four Western agencies.

UNESCO Debate

The international debate on the new world information order has centered on UNESCO where it has been presented as an extension of the 1974 proclamation calling for a new economic order based on a more equitable distribution of the world's economic resources. Four UNESCO General Conferences have discussed the issue, although the 1978 General Conference in Paris was the first to reach a compromise consensus.

The consensus seemed to please no one completely and, like so many diplomatic statements, can be interpreted to support very different positions. On the whole, however, the essential elements of the Western concept of press freedom were affirmed so that the statement was more a "victory" for traditional Western values than many Western media critics recognized.

At the 1980 General Conference in Belgrade, communication was again at center stage, and more resolutions were presented. Behind much of the discussion was a report of a commission appointed in 1977 by the UNESCO director general to review "the totality of the problems of communications in modern society" with a goal of "achieving a freer and more balanced international flow of information." The commission, called the MacBride Commission after its president Sean MacBride, tried to reconcile disparate philosophies of the role of mass media. And like the earlier, the report titled *Many Voices, One World*, was palatable in part but satisfied none of the UNESCO delegates completely.

The Belgrade conference established an institute in UNESCO to coordinate communications development and committed the organization to continue to work toward the goal of free and balanced flow. But the political issue of a redistribution of the world's information resources may have burned itself out in Belgrade. And the dominance of the West in the production, dissemination and control of information shows no signs of diminution.

Notes

1. This article has been updated by the authors to summarize and interpret the outcome of the action taken by UNESCO on the report of its International Commission for the Study of Communication Problems at the UNESCO General Conference in Belgrade, Yugoslavia, in the fall of 1980. The complete paper reports progress on a content analysis study undertaken as part of a worldwide study of the national images presented in the media of various countries which UNESCO in 1978 requested the International Association for Mass Communication Research (IAMCR) to perform. The North Carolina project was supported by the U.S. International Communication Agency.
2. Quoted in Jeremy Tunstall, *The Media Are American* (New York: Columbia University Press, 1977).
3. George Steiner, "The Coming Universal Language," *Atlas World Press Review*, October, 1977.
4. Herbert I Schiller, "Computer Systems: Power for Whom and for What?" *Journal of Communication* 28(4): 185−93 (1978), quoting a Harvard University report.
5. Report on "All Things Considered," National Public Radio.
6. Herbert I. Schiller, *Mass Communications and American Empire* (Boston: Beacon Press, 1971).
7. Op. cit.
8. Donald L. Shaw, "News Bias and the Telegraph: a Study of Historical Change," *Journalism Quarterly* 44: 3−12 (1968).
9. James O. Goldsborough, "An American In Paris: The International Herald Tribune," *Columbia Journalism Review*, July−August, 1974.
10. Lee B. Becker and Paul S. Underwood, "Coverage of the United States in the Yugoslav Press," report to U.S. International Communication Agency, March, 1979.

A NEW WORLD INFORMATION ORDER: THE WHYS AND WHEREFORES[1]

Mustapha Masmoudi

The dominance of Western news coverage is here seen from an opposite point of view that claims to speak for a vast portion of humanity. If the claim is true, it represents an attitude that will undoubtedly be more strongly felt in the future and to which the press and mass communications will respond.

SOURCE: Extracted from document No. 31 in a series published for UNESCO's International Commission for the Study of Communication Problems. Undated.

7. Information in the modern world is characterized by basic imbalances, reflecting the general imbalance that affects the international community. They occur in a wide range of fields, particularly in the political, legal and technico-financial spheres.

A. Political Aspects

8. In the political sphere, that is, in respect [to] the conception of information, these imbalances take many forms:

9. A flagrant quantitative imbalance between North and South. This imbalance is created by the disparity between the volume of news and information emanating from the developed world and intended for the developing countries and the volume of the flow in the opposite direction. Almost 80 percent of the world news flow emanates from the major transnational agencies; however, these devote only 20 to 30 percent of news coverage to the developing countries, despite the fact that the latter account for almost three-quarters of mankind. This results in a veritable de facto monopoly on the part of the developed countries.

10. An inequality in information resources. The five major transnational agencies monopolise between them the essential share of material and human potential, while almost a third of the developing countries have no means of protecting themselves against foreign broadcasts. It is frequently difficult for them to compete, particularly since some of these broadcasts are transmitted from stations located within developing countries. In respect [to] television, not only do 45 percent of the developing countries have no television of their own, but this disparity is aggravated still further by the broadcasting in these countries of a large number of programmes produced in the developing countries.

11. A de facto hegemony and a will to dominate. Such hegemony and domination are evident in the marked indifference of the media in the developed countries, particularly in the West, to the problems, concerns and aspirations of the developing countries. They are founded on financial, industrial, cultural and technological power and result in most of the developing countries being relegated to the status of mere consumers of information sold as a commodity like any other. They are exercised above all through the control of the information flow, wrested and wielded by the transna-

tional agencies operating without let or hindrance in most developing countries and based in turn on the control of technology,
illustrated by the communication systems satellite, which are wholly
dominated by the major international consortia.

12. A lack of information on developing countries.   Current events
in the developing countries are reported to the world via the
transnational media; at the same time, these countries are kept
"informed" of what is happening abroad through the same channels. By transmitting to the developing countries only news pro-
cessed by them, that is, news which they have filtered, cut and
distorted, the transnational media impose their own way of seeing
the world upon the developing countries. As a result, communities
geographically close to each other sometimes learn about each
other only via these transnational systems. Moreover, the latter
often seek to present these communities—when indeed they do
show interest in them—in the most unfavourable light, stressing
crises, strikes, street demonstrations, putsches, etc. or even holding
them up to ridicule. If and when the press in the industrialized
countries does present the Third World's problems, achievements
and aspirations in an objective light, it does so in the form of special
supplements or issues, for which high rates of payment are
charged.

13. Survival of the colonial era.   The present-day information
system enshrines a form of political, economic and cultural colonialism which is reflected in the often tendentious interpretation of
news concerning the developing countries. This consists in highlighting events whose significance in certain cases, is limited or
even non-existent; in collecting isolated facts and presenting them
as a "whole"; in setting out facts in such a way that the conclusion to
be drawn from them is necessarily favourable to the interests of the
transnational system; in amplifying small-scale events so as to
arouse unjustified fears; in keeping silent on situations unfavourable
to the interests of the countries of origin of these media. In this way,
world events are covered only insofar as it suits the interests of
certain societies.

Likewise, information is distorted by reference to moral, cultural
or political values peculiar to certain States, in defiance of the
values and concerns of other nations. The criteria governing selection are consciously or unconsciously based on the political and
economic interests of the transnational system and of the countries
in which this system is established. The use of labels and persuasive
epithets and definitions, chosen with the intention of denigrating,
should also be stressed.

14. An alienating influence in the economic, social and cultural spheres. In addition to dominating and manipulating the international news flow, the developed countries practise other forms of hegemony over the communications institutions of the Third World. First of all, they have possession of the media through direct investment. Then, there is another form of control, one which today is far more decisive, namely, the near-monopoly on advertising throughout the world exercised by the major advertising agencies, which operate like the media transnationals and which earn their income by serving the interests of the transnational industrial and commercial corporations, which themselves dominate the business world. A further form of domination is represented by the influence used to oppose social evolution; this is practised quite openly by the institutions engaging in propaganda. Moreover, advertising, magazines and television programmes are today so many instruments of cultural domination and acculturation, transmitting to the developing countries messages which are harmful to their cultures, contrary to their values and detrimental to their development aims and efforts.

15. Messages ill-suited to the areas in which they are disseminated. Even important news may be deliberately neglected by the major media in favour of other information of interest only to public opinion in the country to which the media in question belong. Such news is transmitted to the client countries and is indeed practically imposed on them, despite the fact that readers and listeners in these countries have no interest therein. The major mass media and those who work for them take no account of the real relevance of their messages. Their news coverage is designed to meet the national needs of their countries of origin. They also disregard the impact of their news beyond their own frontiers. They even ignore the important minorities and foreign communities living on their national territory, whose needs in matters of information are different from their own.

16. The fact cannot therefore be blinked that the present information order, based as it is on a quasi-monopolistic concentration of the power to communicate in the hands of a few developed nations, is incapable of meeting the aspirations of the international community, which stands in great need of a system capable of fostering more satisfactory dialogue, conducted in a spirit of mutual respect and dignity. All such political and conceptual shortcomings are worsened—when they are not actually justified—by inadequate international legal structures.

Notes

1. Chapter I, Part A, of "The New World Information Order," by Mustapha Masmoudi, former Secretary of State for Information in Tunisia. The first paragraph, No. 7, is the continuation of the last of seven paragraphs comprising the Introduction. Chapter I also consists of Part B, "Legal Aspects," and Part C, "Technico-Financial Aspects." In Chapter II Masmoudi, from political, legal, and technical-financial viewpoints, describes the new order and relates how it might be established. In Chapter III, he expresses the view that the establishment of a new information order is an essential corollary of a new international economic order, and he stipulates measures that, in his opinion, should be taken by industrialized and developing countries and by international agencies to bring it about.

2. The top five international agencies together possess more than 500 bureaus, maintain 4319 correspondents or stringers abroad in 116 countries, and each issues a daily average of 1.5 to 17 million words.

TRENCH COATS FOR SALE
Don Cook

Cook, the European correspondent of the Los Angeles *Times*, cites the shrunken numbers and diminished role of the once-glamorous foreign correspondents. Even events in Iran and Afghanistan that occurred after this was written have not significantly altered the trend, although some additional major dailies have posted correspondents abroad.

Early last year [1977], the then-ailing Chicago *Daily News* called home from London, Paris, Nairobi, and Hong Kong the last four of its once famous staff of foreign correspondents. Intent on economies, the paper's owners clearly considered on-scene foreign reportage an expendable luxury. (The move didn't help: The *News* was dead by year's end.) Meanwhile, the Scripps-Howard papers had wound up their overseas operations, bringing back their sole roving European correspondent from his base, in Paris. The Pulitzer committee then announced that because it had found no entry that would justify a Pulitzer Prize for international reporting in 1976, it was skipping the award for the first time since it was established 35 years ago.

In Paris today, the Crillon Bar is all but deserted. There are only a handful of American or British correspondents around the city who might turn up as they used to for a quick drink before lunch—but not very often at $6 for a gin and tonic. The Savoy Hotel,

---

SOURCE: From *Saturday Review*, June 24, 1978, pp. 13–16. Copyright © 1978 by Saturday Review. All rights reserved. Reprinted by permission.

Peter Jennings of ABC in his London trench coat

in London, is a comfortable, unchanging mausoleum of nostalgia. Today's tourists never hear the air raid sirens wailing, nor do they see the bar and lobby crowded with trench coats and uniforms and with the likes of Ed Murrow, Larry Rue, Quent Reynolds, Tex O'Reilly, Cliff Daniel, Bill Shirer, Homer Bigart, Helen Kirkpatrick, Ed Beattie, Bill Stoneman, Charlie Collingwood, Johnny Gunther, Drew Middleton, Jimmy Sheehan, Marguerite Higgins, Geof Parsons, and Eric Sevareid. On the banks of the Rhine, the hard-core lunchtime gathering at the press *Stammtisch* at the American Club, near Bonn, is a far cry, half a century, another world away, from the Adlon Hotel, in Berlin. Glamour has long since gone from foreign reporting, and now it is a fading profession as well.

Only three American newspapers still operate full-fledged overseas staffs, with their own correspondents assigned to major capitals on a global basis: the New York *Times* keeps 31 staff reporters overseas; the Los Angeles *Times* has 17 foreign bureaus; and the Washington *Post* fields 13 correspondents abroad. Of course the news agencies—the Associated Press, with 81 American reporters, and the United Press International, with 67, including editors and photographers—operate on a far more extensive global scale. In the magazine field, both *Time* and *Newsweek* also continue to maintain more or less stable worldwide staff deployment.

Apart from these major newspapers, the Baltimore *Sun*, to its great credit, continues to paddle against the financial tide and maintains staff men in London, Paris, Bonn, Moscow, the Middle East, and Hong Kong. Its correspondents cover Africa and Latin America on periodic roving assignments. The *Christian Science Monitor*, with its rather specialized readership, operates similarly, with six staff correspondents overseas. The *Wall Street Journal* has a sizable foreign staff but prefers for its own editorial reasons to concentrate its people; it has a large London bureau, for example, that sends reporters across the Channel on specific assignments but has no staff men in Paris, Brussels, Bonn, Rome, or Moscow. Of the big newspaper chains, only the Hearst Press has any kind of foreign operation, with correspondents in London, Paris, and Rome.

But after that, things get bleak: The Chicago *Tribune* keeps a bureau in London going with a full-time staff man, presumably in memory of Colonel Robert R. McCormick, and also one in Moscow. Paul Block, of the Toledo *Blade*, is the only small-daily publisher who has insisted on having his own experienced staff man roving in Europe from a London base for more than 20 years, despite the feelings of his auditors. Among the magazines, McGraw-Hill and *U.S. News and World Report* keep small staff operations going abroad. And that, dear readers, is about it.*

It is difficult in this business to be precise about statistics and definitions. Organizations often keep up a front by utilizing staff stringers hired abroad on a fixed retainer, without any of the financial extras of special allowances, much travel, and home leave that would be due a staff correspondent sent overseas from the United States. Stringers can be perfectly competent correspondents,

*Editors' note: Soon after this article was written, the Chicago *Tribune* added bureaus in Bonn, Tel Aviv, and Nairobi to its London and Moscow posts. In 1979 the Knight-Ridder group began sending correspondents abroad and by 1981 their bureaus included London, Rome, Paris, Jerusalem, Bangkok, Beijing, Toronto, and San Jose, Costa Rica. Knight-Ridder, the *Tribune*, and the New York *Daily News* had formed the Knight News Tribune press service, called the KNT News Wire. In May 1981 it had the 12 foreign bureaus listed above and eight U.S. bureaus. It served 120 U.S. newspapers (about half the clients of the Los Angeles *Times*/Washington *Post* Service and the New York *Times* Service). The Gannett group and other papers sent staff reporters on assignments abroad for limited times, a policy that did not meet Cook's "trench coat" experience requirements.

but any editor would agree that there is always a professional element lacking when it comes to dealing with a stringer instead of your own man.

In any case, a survey carried out by the Overseas Press Club of America shows that in 1975 there were 429 full-time American correspondents working abroad (including radio and TV network people as well as the writing press). At that time, American news organizations also hired another 247 non-American staffers abroad. This grand total of 676 American news media employees overseas in 1975 contrasts with the totals of 797 three years earlier, in 1972, and 929 back in 1969, when the Vietnam War was at its height. Whatever the definition of "full-time American correspondents," the pattern is clear: There has been a drop of more than one third in their number in the six years from 1969 to 1975, and the decline is still going on [in terms of experienced trench coat wearers].

The picture is particularly depressing for the written word—for it is the American newspapers that are steadily opting out of overseas reporting, giving up the ghost of foreign correspondence. You can never fit quality, competence, experience, competition, into statistics. But certainly the qualitative loss is greater than the statistical loss. Statistically, a television performer counts the same as a writer, but it is the writers who are disappearing.

In days past, there was always a steady influx of lively, hardworking, talented, well-trained top assignment reporters arriving overseas from a variety of American newspapers. They added great zest, drive, competitiveness, and just plain fun—far more than mere numbers—to foreign reporting. With more correspondents around, there was a lot more teaming up on trips, ferreting out stories. If you worked for a Boston or New York paper and a fellow correspondent was writing for an audience in Chicago or Minneapolis, it was natural and a lot more productive for both of you to get together to work on a story. Today this has all but dried up. Correspondents more often than not are competing with themselves—with inertia, limits on expense money, uncertainty, indifference, or negative treatment from the desks back home.

There has been no head-to-head competition between American correspondents sent abroad by newspapers from the same city since the New York *Herald Tribune*—which once had the best staff in the business—folded, in 1966, and left the city to the recondite editorial wisdom of the New York *Times*. In Chicago, the competitive situation was somewhat different between the morning *Tribune* and the afternoon *Daily News*, but that is also finished now anyway. Along with the disappearance of these quality staffs and with Scripps-Howard folding its last foreign tent, the following have also given up on overseas staffs in recent years: Washington *Star*, New

York *Daily News*, Kansas City *Star*, Boston *Globe*, Chicago *Sun-Times*, Philadelphia *Bulletin*, Minneapolis *Tribune*, the Copley Newspapers, the Knight Newspapers. The list would be much longer if it included papers that staffed the Vietnam War and then bowed out. In the magazine field within memory, the old *Saturday Evening Post*, *Collier's*, *The Reporter*, and *Life* used to keep staff correspondents overseas, and all have folded. An awful lot of experience, quality, and talent have disappeared from the ranks of foreign reporting.

Even the columnists scarcely turn up abroad anymore. Joe and Stewart Alsop, Walter Lippmann, and Marquis Childs used to enliven overseas reportage with regular visits to Europe or Asia at least once and often twice a year or more. Today only Joseph Kraft makes a consistent effort to get overseas regularly and to keep up his own foreign diplomatic and political contacts.

It is all too easy to account for the decline. It begins of course with money. A pretty good ball park figure for maintaining a correspondent overseas these days is around $100,000 a year. This will often run higher if the man is charging around vast distances, such as in Africa. In order to cover the single story of the French hauling down their last colonial flag, in Djibouti, a Los Angeles *Times* man flew from Nairobi to Paris and back to Djibouti—a total distance of about 7,000 miles, when the direct flight between the two points would have been barely 1,000 miles if there had been any available connection. It is an expensive business. But probably not all that much more expensive than keeping a man traveling with the president of the United States (certainly in the Nixon days) or following the nonstop peregrinations of the secretary of state. The difference of course is that covering the White House or the State Department offers editors and publishers a sure investment in instant prestige and the certainty of page one headlines. The usefulness and value of a good foreign correspondent are admittedly somewhat more abstract.

But the reason for the decline in American reporting abroad is by no means entirely a lack of money. If the gallant Baltimore *Sun* can squeeze a foreign staff out of its resources, what about the Miami *Herald*, with the second largest advertising lineage in America? Are the people of Miami less sophisticated than the newspaper readers in Baltimore or Los Angeles?

Certainly the newspaper business in the United States is profitable—witness the astronomical prices that papers command when they are bought and sold. According to *Business Week*, good newspaper properties will average pretax profits of from 25 to 30 percent or higher. Sixty percent of American newspapers are now chain owned: Four giants control 20 percent of all circulation; 12 of them control 40 percent. What are these profitable conglomerates doing? What about the Knight-Ridder chain? The Newhouse papers? The Gannett holdings? For them, it seems sufficient to paste up wire service stories, augmenting the copy with either the New York *Times* news service or the Washington *Post*/Los Angeles *Times* wire. The money is there, but the publishers can sell papers without spending it on foreign news. Chain publishers bring to publishing all of the business acumen and intellectual fervor of the local supermarket manager, displaying and merchandising somebody else's products at a minimum cost with maximum profits. Sitting on monopoly morning or afternoon properties, a publisher doesn't need much imagination, spark, or even good journalism to sell newspapers. The chains make plenty out of American journalism, but what are they putting into it? Nothing, when it comes to sustaining American reporting overseas.

Sadly, there has been an unraveling effect: the decline in the number of jobs has been followed by a decline in quality. It used to be that quality was largely maintained through a reservoir of correspondents who first found their feet abroad as number twos or number threes in big bureaus like those in London or Paris and then moved on up to take over a one-man bureau, with a firm footing in an overseas career. Those days are gone. And the paradox is that with fewer jobs to fill, editors are having more and more trouble finding solidly qualified correspondents to fill them. The old reservoir has dried up.

It is relatively easy to take chances trying out reporters on local or national assignments. Not so in sending a man abroad. At home, there is always plenty of backup, and it is easy for an editor to get on the phone, give quick guidance or do the necessary handholding with a reporter who is feeling his way—even to dictate a reporter's lead. If the man flubs it, well, he can be shifted to another assignment where he might work out fine, and the flub hasn't cost very much.

Sending a man abroad is a much bigger investment, and it takes time to rectify or even to discover a mistake. That is why in the old days it was so important to be able to try out a man in a big bureau—like nurturing a good shortstop in a Class A league. There is no guarantee at all that the most competent, experienced, and steady man on a domestic staff will work out overseas.

News assignments on the domestic front are usually fairly precise and well defined. Foreign assignments are totally diffuse. You are a political writer, an economic writer, a diplomatic correspondent, a science reporter, a sportswriter, a war correspondent, a crime writer, a music critic, a cultural writer, an ecology expert, an obituary writer, a columnist—and of course all editors are transfixed by good feature writers. You can be on patrol with the British Army in Ulster one day and covering a Common Market summit conference the next. You can be dodging bullets in Beirut and soon after be writing about the economic impact of an Arab oil price increase. You are an expert on Eurocommunism, nuclear proliferation and the problems of the plutonium fuel cycle, the impact on relations between Norway and Russia of the 200-mile fishing limit in the Barents Sea and why Jacques Chirac is trying to wreck Valéry Giscard d'Estaing's government. You are a military expert on NATO matters, an economic expert on OECD, a disarmament expert on SALT, and a human rights expert in Helsinki or Belgrade.

None of this means that foreign correspondents are automatically the supermen of journalism. As the old saying goes, they put on their trousers one leg at a time, the same as everybody else does. There are round pegs and round holes, and there are square pegs and square holes. Nevertheless, there is a demand and a standard in foreign reporting that is not easy to fulfill automatically. Both the New York *Times* and *Newsweek* had to go outside their own staffs recently to fill one of their key posts overseas—correspondent in Bonn. *Newsweek* hired a British journalist from *The Times*, of London, and the New York *Times* took on an experienced European staff man from the Associated Press for the job. It was yet another example of the dearth of good new talent, the drying up of the old reservoir of experienced men.

And so we are a fading lot. If this fact is indeed a reflection of a fading American interest in the world scene, as it is sometimes claimed to be, or of a fading American sense of involvement in or commitment to international affairs, then it is not merely sad but tragic. Except I suspect that our "fading lot" derives only from publishers' desires to save money by downgrading foreign news and the expense of foreign staffs. Publishers are always ready to determine the tastes of their readers. But the Los Angeles *Times* prints *more* foreign stories on its page one than either the New York *Times* or the Washington *Post*, and this practice hasn't stopped its growth. The soybean farmers of Iowa are a lot more concerned and sensitive about what happens in the European Common Market than are the editors of the Knight-Ridder chain.

Editors spike all that foreign copy and then suddenly wake up to find that some two-bit oil sheikh in the Persian Gulf is making life difficult for their readers and plunging America into a crisis. Where the hell is this place, anyway? Who is this little jerk? Isn't there some correspondent who knows this place? We can't go with the story without copy, can we? Get somebody there. Who can we get? Never mind—just get *somebody* out there to the Persian Gulf! Yeah, but where in the Persian Gulf? How the hell do I know where in the Persian Gulf—that's what correspondents are for, isn't it?

When the Chicago *Daily News* brought Keyes Beech home from Hong Kong, 30 years of experience in reporting the turbulence and the subtleties of the Asian scene disappeared from American journalism. One less reporter in the statistics but experience that will not be replaced in this century. Foreign reportage constantly needs new blood, new faces, new vision, new ideas, new vigor, new styles—a renewal of talent.

Attrition is working in its usual way on the postwar generation of foreign correspondents, the last romantic age in the business. There are good younger correspondents—not a lot, not nearly enough, because there are not a lot of jobs and the writers come and go and never stay around long enough. Publishers may solemnly swear that they intend to sustain things by regularly dispatching topflight assignment men from home to parachute in on the foreign scene. I wonder. Publishers used to have the conviction that their newspapers had to be on top of the news or ahead of the news, not just catching up with the news. Anyway, if the journalistic firemen do parachute in, they will look first for a tired, beat-up, cynical old hand, brooding lonely in the hotel bar, to get a quick fill-in on what's going on and who to see and how it all happened—if there are any old hands still around.

AFTERWORD

THE EVENING STAR
James Reston

Just as this book was ready for the printer, James Reston, in his fine manner, wrote a tribute to the Washington *Star* in its final days. The tribute is included here as a clear and succinct summation of what the many selections in this book have said, and as a foreview of the days that are coming to this hectic, pestered, resilient, and always lively profession.

WASHINGTON, Aug. 4—Time Inc. has announced the death of The Washington *Star*, but for over 100 years it was called by the most beautiful name in American journalism—*The Evening Star*—and everybody knows you cannot kill an evening star.

It will be there winking over the capital until somebody brings it back to earth. All the obit writers have agreed that after the official burial on Friday, Washington will be left with only one daily newspaper, but this is obviously ridiculous, and nobody knows this better than the Meyers and the Grahams, who preside over the Washington *Post*.

They are a tough and resourceful breed, and they have long memories. They remember when *The Evening Star* dominated this city, as the *Post* does today; and how, by the quirks of fate, the persistence and imagination of Eugene Meyer and Phil Graham (with a little help from Kent Cooper of the Associated Press and Colonel McCormick of the Chicago *Tribune*), they turned things around. The guess here is that the wheel will turn again, not right away, but sooner or later.

For Washington has a fatal attraction for people with money and causes. It is the most powerful platform in the world. Nobody will buy the machinery and the debts of the *Star*, but somebody will undoubtedly buy the name and the dream.

Time Inc., which built an empire by rewriting the established newspapers, made a valiant effort here. It inherited the best afternoon newspaper in the country, improved it, and failed. But it doesn't follow that Washington is going to be a one-newspaper town.

What Time Inc. proved in Washington is what other enterprising publishers in Philadelphia, Chicago, Los Angeles, Boston, and

SOURCE: From The New York *Times*, August 5, 1981, p. A23. Copyright 1981 by The New York Times Company. Reprinted by permission.

Cleveland had feared—London and Paris learned the lesson long before—that despite its money and its genius there may be enough readers and advertisers left in all the great cities of the world to sustain one traditional newspaper, with its multiple sections on national, foreign, and local news; its style sections, food sections, travel sections, and sports sections—but not room in the urban ark for two such monsters a day.

The cost of labor, newsprint, modern color presses and distribution out of the central cities into the suburbs, where most people now live, is too great—with newsprint now running at $500 a ton.

Besides, nobody sits on the front porch these days reading the paper and watching the evening star. They get Roger Mudd, John Chancellor, and Dan Rather on television for free. Unfortunately they are also stunned by the television pictures of disaster. Reading has gone out of style, for watching is easier and it keeps the children quiet.

But it is not necessarily true that the printed word is in decline or that the publication of newspapers is a hopeless proposition. We are in the midst today of the greatest printing revolution since the invention of movable type. With the introduction of computer-controlled photocomposition, and with development of the miraculous offset press, the opportunity for publishing newspapers of limited size and purpose is now greater that at any other time in this century.

The coming second urban papers will probably not be general massive backbreakers like the second papers we have today, but probably smaller, specialized publications aimed at a limited audience. The OPEC countries, for example, which are not short of money, are not likely to ignore the possibilities of the Washington audience. Neither are the New Conservatives and the Moral Majority types, who are riding high these days, and will want to publicize their ideas and sustain their present political momentum.

So the prospect is not for the death of ideas and the print medium. The new technology has followed the people into the suburbs, and produced the most vigorous local and community press in the history of the nation.

Not since the days when the old printers wandered the country with a sack of type on their backs and a gun in their desks, printing their news and convictions, has there been such a time in America when people could afford to defend anything they liked, to publish and be damned.

The second big-city dailies are clearly in trouble, but the weeklies, printing the amiable news of marriages and births, and the reunions of families, are somehow surviving the inflation.

Accordingly, the death of the Washington *Star* does not dim the glow of *The Evening Star*. It endured here for over half the life of the Republic, and broke the hearts of the Noyeses and the Kauffmanns in the process, and there is now a lot of silly talk here before the funeral about who killed Cock Robin.

The people of the Washington community killed it, that's who! It seems to be the rule of this town that everybody is open to the most savage criticism except the people. Yet the people here were given a really fine afternoon paper, and they didn't support it by their subscriptions or their advertising, and the ironic fact is that so many of those who are now mourning its loss never bought or backed it.

But Washington will not be a one-newspaper town, no matter what the obit writers say. Nothing will take the place of *The Evening Star*, but somebody may rescue its lovely name.

Index

82 83 84 9 8 7 6 5 4 3 2 1